1 MONTH OF FREE READING

at

www.ForgottenBooks.com

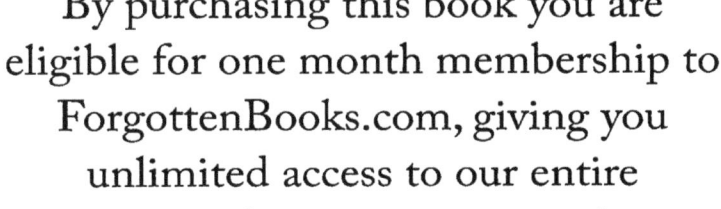

By purchasing this book you are eligible for one month membership to ForgottenBooks.com, giving you unlimited access to our entire collection of over 1,000,000 titles via our web site and mobile apps.

To claim your free month visit:

www.forgottenbooks.com/free977885

* Offer is valid for 45 days from date of purchase. Terms and conditions apply.

ISBN 978-0-260-86393-5
PIBN 10977885

This book is a reproduction of an important historical work. Forgotten Books uses state-of-the-art technology to digitally reconstruct the work, preserving the original format whilst repairing imperfections present in the aged copy. In rare cases, an imperfection in the original, such as a blemish or missing page, may be replicated in our edition. We do, however, repair the vast majority of imperfections successfully; any imperfections that remain are intentionally left to preserve the state of such historical works.

Forgotten Books is a registered trademark of FB &c Ltd.
Copyright © 2018 FB &c Ltd.
FB &c Ltd, Dalton House, 60 Windsor Avenue, London, SW19 2RR.
Company number 08720141. Registered in England and Wales.

For support please visit www.forgottenbooks.com

Black Hills Ponderosa Pine Susceptible to Southwestern Dwarfmistletoe

Frank G. Hawksworth, Plant Pathologist

The reason for the absence of southwestern dwarfmistletoe (Arceuthobium vaginatum (Willd.) Presl f. cryptopodum (Engelm.) Gill) in the ponderosa pine (Pinus ponderosa Laws.) stands in the Black Hills of South Dakota has long been a subject of speculation. One possible explanation was that the ponderosa pine stands in this region might not be susceptible to the southwestern dwarfmistletoe. This possibility was remote, however, since Weir[1] had demonstrated that ponderosa pine from South Dakota was susceptible to the western dwarfmistletoe (A. campylopodum Engelm. f. campylopodum) from California.

A small-scale inoculation test was made in the greenhouse to determine whether ponderosa pine from the Black Hills was susceptible to A. vaginatum. Germinated dwarfmistletoe seeds of the 1960 seed crop were collected from the Roosevelt National Forest near Fort Collins, Colorado in October 1960, and placed on the twigs of five 5-year-old potted pines. Five seeds were planted on each tree. By October 1962, 2 infections on 2 trees had appeared. A severe infestation of aphids, which was later controlled, probably reduced the rate of infection. The number and growth rate of the infections however, were comparable to those on ponderosa pines from several sources within the range of the parasite.

Ponderosa pine from the Black Hills is thus susceptible to A. vaginatum, so other factors are involved in the parasite's absence from this area. Isolation has been considered a factor, but this seems unlikely as the Black Hills pines are not completely dissociated from the main body of ponderosa pine in Colorado. Stands of this tree are scattered throughout eastern Wyoming and western Nebraska, and the species is even more widespread than indicated by the range map published by Curtis and Lynch.[2]

Climatic conditions of the more northern latitude seem to provide the most logical explanation for the absence of A. vaginatum in the Black Hills. Similar conditions must also prevail in Wyoming and Nebraska stands that intervene between the Black Hills and the known northern limit of this dwarfmistletoe in northern Colorado, a few miles south of the Wyoming border.[3] Studies to determine the

Maintained at Fort Collins, Colorado, in cooperation with Colorado State University

exact northern limits of A. vaginatum and the factors affecting it are currently underway.

The lodgepole pine dwarfmistletoe (A. americanum Nutt.) and the limber pine dwarfmistletoe (A. campylopodum Engelm. f. cyanocarpum (A. Nels.) Gill) occasionally attack ponderosa pine in the Medicine Bow National Forest in southeastern Wyoming, but their damage is very minor compared to that caused by A. vaginatum in Colorado and southward.

[1] Weir, J R Experimental investigations on the genus Razoumofskya Bot Gaz. 66: 1-31 1918.

[2] Curtis, J D., and Lynch, D W Silvics of ponderosa pine. U.S. Forest Serv Intermountain Forest and Range Expt Sta. Misc. Pub 12, 37 pp. 1957.

[3] Hawksworth, F G Dwarfmistletoe of ponderosa pine in the Southwest U S Dept Agr Tech Bul 1246, 112 pp. 1961.

July 1963

U.S. FOREST SERVICE
RESEARCH NOTE RM - 2

FOREST SERVICE
U.S. DEPARTMENT OF AGRICULTURE

An Analysis and Simplification of the Blaney-Criddle Method for Estimating Evapotranspiration

John P. Decker, Plant Physiologist[1]

Blaney and Criddle[2] developed a method for estimating evapotranspiration for different vegetation types, and their method has become widely known.[3,4] Their method was studied in preparation for comparative tests of a new method for direct measurement of evapotranspiration.[5] This preliminary study revealed that calculations for the Blaney-Criddle method can be simplified for some applications.

THE BLANEY-CRIDDLE METHOD

Evapotranspiration for a species in a locality is estimated as the measured loss for that species in another locality adjusted for a climatic factor. The underlying assumption is that evapotranspiration from land abundantly supplied with water and occupied by the species is directly proportional to the climatic factor (F) and is otherwise constant. The basic relationship is stated as $U = KF$, where U is consumptive use (evapotranspiration) for the period of estimate, F is the sum of monthly f's for that period (each f is a product of mean monthly temperature and total monthly daylight), and K is an empirical coefficient for that species.

The method for computing K is not entirely clear. On page 15[2] it is indicated that $KF =$ sum of kf's and that $kf = u$. Thus, one could compute K as a sum of monthly k's, each of which was computed as $k = u/f$. This appears to be the only possible direct use of the expression kf. On page 17[2] however, it is stated that K was computed as $K = U/F$. At first glance the two K's appear identical, but they differ numerically because one is based on a sum of products and the other on a product of sums. If the latter procedure is followed, the quantities k and kf need not be introduced. The apparent ambiguity need not be resolved, because direct computation of K is not essential to estimate consumptive use.

SIMPLIFIED METHOD

The simplified method depends on the same assumption and on the same data as the original method. That is, evapotranspiration from land abundantly supplied with water and occupied by a given species is assumed to be di-

Maintained at Fort Collins, Colorado, in cooperation with Colorado State University

rectly proportional to the climatic factor F and is otherwise constant. As before, this relationship can be stated as U = KF. For a known locality let $U_1 = KF_1$. For the locality of estimate let $U_2 = KF_2$. Now, after noting that $U_1/F_1 = K$ and that $U_2/F_2 = K$, a statement $U_1/F_1 = U_2/F_2$ can be made, and the estimating equation becomes

$$U_2 = \frac{F_2 U_1}{F_1}.$$

Use of K is not necessary to transform any data to arrive at this final statement. The remaining question is whether it is convenient. In the original method, one looks up F_2 and K and carries out a one-step computation: $K \times F_2 = U_2$. In the simplified method, one looks up U_1, F_1, and F_2 and carries out a two-step computation:

$$\frac{U_1 F_2}{F_1} = U_2.$$

If one were making many such estimates and had appropriate K's already computed, the original system might save time. If one made such estimates only occasionally, however, the time saved by avoiding one arithmetical step (division) would probably be less than the time required to relearn nomenclature.

COMMON WEAKNESS OF BOTH METHODS

Both methods assume the ratio U_1/F_1 to be constant for a species. Table 15 of Blaney and Criddle[2] show that values range as follows: alfalfa 0.93 - 0.77, corn 0.96 - 0.45, cotton 0.63 - 0.45. The wide ranges for a species indicate that not all variability of evapotranspiration, even for land areas occupied by a cultivated species, can be accounted for by mean monthly temperatures and day lengths. The assumption may be even less valid with natural stands of wild species, because a wider range of stocking density can be expected here, and evapotranspiration has been shown to vary greatly with density of stocking.[5] Although the methods offer promise, more data are required than are currently accessible in the professional literature before the constancy of the ratio--and therefore the reliability of the methods--can be realistically appraised.

---

[1]*Author stationed at Tempe, Arizona, in cooperation with Arizona State University.*

[2]*Blaney, H F., and Criddle, W. D. Determining water requirements in irrigated areas from climatological and irrigation data USDA SCS-TP-96. 48 pp., illus. 1952*

[3]*Penman, H L. Estimating evaporation. Amer. Geophys. Union Trans 37: 43-50 1956.*

[4]*Tanner, C. B., and Pelton, W. L. Potential evapotranspiration estimates by the approximate energy balance method of Penman Jour Geophys. Res. 65: 3391-3413 1960.*

[5]*Decker, J P., Gaylor, W G and Cole, F. D Measuring transpiration of undisturbed tamarisk shrubs. Plant Physiol. 37: 393-397, illus 1962*

FOREST SERVICE
U.S. DEPARTMENT OF AGRICULTURE

Heavy Pruning Reduces Growth of Southwestern Ponderosa Pine

L. J. Heidmann, Research Forester [1]

In 1948, a study to evaluate four intensities of pruning on ponderosa pine was established on the Fort Valley Experimental Forest, Arizona. This study was superimposed on an older thinning study established in 1934 in a 20-year-old stand.

STUDY-PLOT TREATMENTS

The pruning study was installed on four plots that had been given a "crop tree" thinning in 1934; average spacing between crop trees was 8 by 8 feet. Thinning on the four plots was as follows: (A) control, no thinning; (B) no release of dominant trees, other crop trees given light release; (C) all trees within 2 to 3 feet of crop trees were removed; (D) all trees other than crop trees were removed with the exception of very small saplings.

Sixteen trees were pruned to each of four intensity levels on each of the four thinning plots in 1948 as follows: (1) control, only dead branches removed; (2) 20 percent of live crown removed; (3) 40 percent of live crown removed; (4) 60 percent of live crown removed. Tree heights, and diameters at breast height and at 9 feet were measured at the time of pruning (1948), in 1953 and 1958 (table 1).

RESULTS

Removal of 60 percent of the live crown reduced diameter growth at breast height and at 9 feet on all plots. There were no significant differences in diameter growth among the other three pruning intensities (table 2). Diameter growth at breast height was significantly greater on thinned plots than on the unthinned plot.

Pruning intensity did not affect height growth materially. Height growth, however, did vary significantly with thinning; trees on the unthinned plot grew less than those on the thinned plots.

DISCUSSION

Results of this study parallel other findings on the pruning of ponderosa pine. Pearson[2] stated that crown length equal to 30 percent of total tree height is adequate to provide up to 2 inches of diameter growth per decade in young ponderosa pine. Hallin[3] found that one-half the live crown of ponderosa and Jeffrey pines in California can be removed provided four-tenths of the total tree height is left in live crown. In this study, diameter

rectly proportional to the climatic factor F and is otherwise constant. As before, this relationship can be stated as U = KF. For a known locality let $U_1 = KF_1$. For the locality of estimate let $U_2 = KF_2$. Now, after noting that $U_1/F_1 = K$ and that $U_2/F_2 = K$, a statement $U_1/F_1 = U_2/F_2$ can be made, and the estimating equation becomes

$$U_2 = \frac{F_2 U_1}{F_1}.$$

Use of K is not necessary to transform any data to arrive at this final statement. The remaining question is whether it is convenient. In the original method, one looks up F_2 and K and carries out a one-step computation: $K \times F_2 = U_2$. In the simplified method, one looks up U_1, F_1, and F_2 and carries out a two-step computation:

$$\frac{U_1 F_2}{F_1} = U_2.$$

If one were making many such estimates and had appropriate K's already computed, the original system might save time. If one made such estimates only occasionally, however, the time saved by avoiding one arithmetical step (division) would probably be less than the time required to relearn nomenclature.

COMMON WEAKNESS OF BOTH METHODS

Both methods assume the ratio U_1/F_1 to be constant for a species. Table 15 of Blaney and Criddle[2] show tht values range as follows: alfalfa 0.93 - 0.77, corn 0.96 - 0.45, cotton 0.63 - 0.45. The wide ranges for a species indicate that not all variability of evapotranspiration, even for land areas occupied by a cultivated species, can be accounted for by mean monthly temperatures and day lengths. The assumption may be even less valid with natural stands of wild species, because a wider range of stocking density can be expected here, an evapotranspiration has been shown to vary greatly with density of stocking. Although the methods offer promise, more data are required than are currently accessible in the professional literature before the constancy of the ratio--and therefore the reliability of the methods--can be realistically appraised.

DEPARTMENT OF AGRICULTURE

Heavy Pruning Reduces Growth of Southwestern Ponderosa Pine

L. J. Heidmann, Research Forester [1]

In 1948, a study to evaluate four intensities of pruning on ponderosa pine was established on the Fort Valley Experimental Forest, Arizona. This study was superimposed on an older thinning study established in 1934 in a 20-year-old stand.

STUDY-PLOT TREATMENTS

The pruning study was installed on four plots that had been given a "crop tree" thinning in 1934; average spacing between crop trees was 8 by 8 feet. Thinning on the four plots was as follows: (A) control, no thinning; (B) no release of dominant trees, other crop trees given light release; (C) all trees within 2 to 3 feet of crop trees were removed; (D) all trees other than crop trees were removed with the exception of very small saplings.

Sixteen trees were pruned to each of four intensity levels on each of the four thinning plots in 1948 as follows: (1) control, only dead branches removed; (2) 20 percent of live crown removed; (3) 40 percent of live crown removed; (4) 60 percent of live crown removed. Tree heights, and diameters at breast height and at 9 feet were measured at the time of pruning (1948), in 1953 and 1958 (table 1).

RESULTS

Removal of 60 percent of the live crown reduced diameter growth at breast height and at 9 feet on all plots. There were no significant differences in diameter growth among the other three pruning intensities (table 2). Diameter growth at breast height was significantly greater on thinned plots than on the unthinned plot.

Pruning intensity did not affect height growth materially. Height growth, however, did vary significantly with thinning; trees on the unthinned plot grew less than those on the thinned plots.

DISCUSSION

Results of this study parallel other findings on the pruning of ponderosa pine. Pearson[2] stated that crown length equal to 30 percent of total tree height is adequate to provide up to 2 inches of diameter growth per decade in young ponderosa pine. Hallin[3] found that one-half the live crown of ponderosa and Jeffrey pines in California can be removed provided four-tenths of the total tree height is left in live crown. In this study, diameter

Table 1.--Average diameter and height of crop trees prior to pruning in 1948

Plot	Trees per acre, 1958	Percent of live crown removed				Average
		0	20	40	60	
	Number					
		DIAMETER BREAST HEIGHT (INCHES)				
A	5,576	3.3	3.4	3.2	3.5	3.4
B	3,729	4.4	4.8	4.9	4.7	4.7
C	3,851	3.9	3.6	4.3	3.8	3.9
D	1,612	5.4	4.7	4.9	5.0	5.0
Average	3,692	4.2	4.1	4.3	4.2	4.2
		HEIGHT OF CROP TREES (FEET)				
A	5,576	16.2	16.2	15.6	16.1	16.0
B	3,729	19.8	21.0	22.0	20.8	20.9
C	3,851	16.6	16.5	18.5	17.4	17.2
D	1,612	21.9	21.2	19.8	20.9	21.0
Average	3,692	18.6	18.7	19.0	18.8	18.8

growth was not reduced by pruning if 31 percent or more of the tree height was left in live crown.

The pruning study might have been more meaningful if trees had been pruned to leave specified percentages of tree height in live crown. Average percentages of tree height in live crown did vary with intensity of pruning (table 3). For each combination of thinning and pruning, however, there was a wide variation in percentage of residual crown.

SUMMARY

In 1948, 64 crop trees on each of four thinning plots were selected and assigned one of four pruning treatments as follows: control; 20 percent of live crown removed; 40 percent of live crown removed; 60 percent of live crown removed. Diameters at breast height and at 9 feet and tree height were measured in 1948, 1953, and 1958.

The results agree generally with other findings on the pruning of ponderosa pine. Forty percent of the live crown can be removed without significantly affecting diameter growth if at least 31 percent of total tree height is left in live crown. Height growth was not materially reduced by the degrees of pruning tested.

Diameter and height growth were significantly greater on thinned plots than on the unthinned plot.

---

[1] Author stationed at Flagstaff, Arizona, in cooperation with Arizona State College

[2] Pearson, G A Management of ponderosa pine in the Southwest. U S Dept. Agr. Agr Mono 6, 218 pp, illus. 1950

[3] Hallin, William E Pruning ponderosa and Jeffrey pine. U S. Forest Serv Calif Forest and Range Expt Sta. Res. Note 115, 4pp 1956

Table 2.--Average increase in diameter and height by thinning treatment and pruning intensity, 1949-58

Plot	Trees per acre, 1958	Percent of live crown removed				Thinning level averages
		0	20	40	60	
	Number					
		INCREASE IN D.B.H. (INCHES)				
A	5,576	0.59	0.74	0.50	0.37	0.55
B	3,729	.86	.75	.72	.49	.70
C	3,851	.80	.70	.83	.47	.70
D	1,612	1.01	.82	.83	.59	.81
Average	3,692	.82	.75	.72	.48	.69
		INCREASE IN DIAMETER AT 9 FEET (INCHES)				
A	5,576	.86	.99	.80	.62	.82
B	3,729	1.04	.92	.82	.63	.85
C	3,851	1.13	1.05	1.06	.75	1.00
D	1,612	1.27	1.03	1.04	.73	1.02
Average	3,692	1.08	1.00	.93	.68	.92
		INCREASE IN HEIGHT (FEET)				
A	5,576	5.72	5.97	5.72	5.45	5.72
B	3,729	7.77	7.06	7.59	7.70	7.53
C	3,851	7.13	6.62	6.84	6.16	6.69
D	1,612	8.22	7.94	7.47	7.54	7.79
Average	3,692	7.21	6.90	6.90	6.71	6.93

Table 3.--Average percentage of total tree height in live crown immediately after pruning

Plot	Trees per acre, 1958	Percent of live crown removed			
		0	20	40	60
	Number	Percent			
A	5,576	46	39	28	19
B	3,729	46	39	30	21
C	3,851	52	41	31	21
D	1,612	56	40	34	23
Average	3,692	50	40	31	21

July 1963

U.S. FOREST SERVICE
RESEARCH NOTE RM - 4

Extent of Decay Associated With
Fomes Igniarius Sporophores in Colorado Aspen

Thomas E. Hinds, Plant Pathologist[1]

The most destructive decay of aspen (Populus tremuloides Michx.) is caused by Fomes igniarius var. populinus (Neu.) Camb. This fungus accounted for 59 percent of the decay found in a recent study of aspen in Colorado (5).[2] It is almost impossible to find stands of any age that are not damaged to some degree by F. igniarius, and trees with advanced stages of decay usually bear numerous sporophores (2) or conks (Fig. 1).

The abundant fruiting of F. igniarius on aspen and closely related trees has led to a number of attempts to relate decay cull to the number, size, and distribution of conks as an aid to cruising and scaling. In one phase of a general investigation of heartwood decays in poplars on the Petawawa Forest Experiment Station Reserve, Ontario, Riley and Bier (7) found that decay extended a variable distance (1 to 6 feet) above and below F. igniarius conks. Since only 11 trees were studied in this phase, the authors did not attempt to develop rules for culling. In Minnesota aspen, Horton and Hendee found that the length of decay, which ranged from 2 to 5 1/2 feet above and below fruiting bodies, was related to both the size and number of the fruiting bodies (6). In another Minnesota study, Brown concluded that the extent of F. igniarius decay was more closely related to the maximum height than to the number of conks on aspen trunks (3). Christensen et al. (4) state that site index, degree of suppression, rate of growth of the tree, and other factors would make it difficult to establish any general rule for accurately estimating decay cull in aspen from conks or other external indicators.

Despite these conflicting findings, and as a followup of earlier work in Colorado (5), the present study was made to determine the upper and lower limits and volume of decay associated with F. igniarius conks on individual trees. Such information would be useful in appraising the merchantability of aspen stands, and might lead to more complete utilization of partially decayed trees that are now considered total losses.

[1] The author gratefully acknowledges the assistance of Ross W Davidson, formerly with the Beltsville Forest Disease Laboratory, in identifying numerous decay fungi

[2] Numbers in parentheses refer to Literature Cited at the end of this Note

 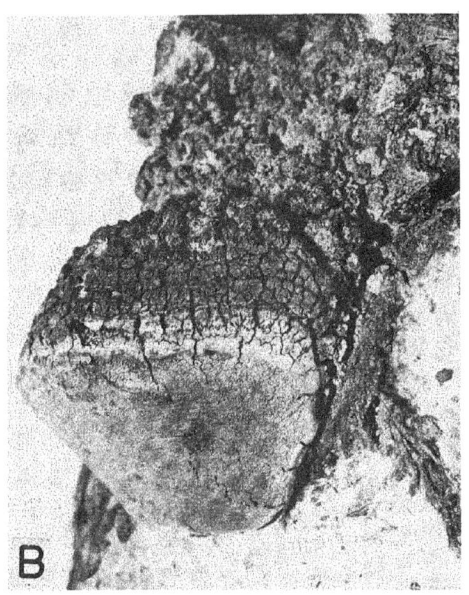

Figure 1 -- A, Fomes igniarius sporophores on a 12-inch d b h. aspen B, Sporophore, actual size.

FIELD METHODS

The study was limited to dominant, codominant, and intermediate trees of merchantable size bearing F. igniarius conks. Groups of 5 to 15 such trees were selected in representative aspen stands of apparently uniform site and age class. The elevation, aspect, and slope were recorded for each group. Site class was determined from the age and height of dominant and codominant trees in accordance with Baker's site classification (1).

Diameter at breast height, crown class, tree vigor, approximate location of sporophores and other external decay indicators were recorded on individual tree forms before trees were felled. After felling, total tree height and actual height and size of all sporophores were recorded.

A total of 113 trees were examined on 11 areas in the Grand Mesa - Uncompahgre, Roosevelt, Routt, San Juan, and White River National Forests in Colorado in 1959 and 1960. The sampled stands occurred on sites 1 to 3 and ranged in age from 85 to 175 years. The study trees varied from 8 to 23 inches in diameter at breast height, and all contained F. igniarius decay.

Each tree was cut into 8-foot bolts to a top diameter of 4 inches inside bark. Diameter inside bark and average diameter of visible decay were recorded for each cut. The upper and lower limits of rot columns were determined by further dissection of bolts. Where the identity of the causal fungus was in doubt, field isolations were made and the resulting cultures submitted to the Beltsville Forest Disease Laboratory for determination.

Board-foot volumes to a 6-inch top and cubic-foot volumes to a 4-inch top were calculated by means of the Scribner Decimal C Log Rule and Smalian's formula, respectively. Board-foot defect volumes were calculated according to standard scaling practice. Cubic-foot rot volumes were calculated by Smalian's formula except that, where rot ended within a bolt, it was treated as a cone.

RESULTS

Total cull amounted to 80 percent of the gross board-foot volume (34 percent of the cubic-foot volume) in this study. F. igniarius accounted for 89 percent of the board-foot cull (91 percent of the cubic-foot cull), and the remaining cull attributed to other decays was omitted from the calculations.

Average length of decay above the highest sporophore was 13.0 ± 0.8 feet. Only 27 trees had decay that did not extend to ground level, and the average length of decay below the lowest sporophore was 10.9 ± 0.9 feet for these trees. The average lengths of decay above and below sporophores were not significantly different, so they were combined to give an average of 12.0 ± 0.7 feet.

A summary of the number of sporophores per tree and percentage of cull is shown below:

Total sporophores (No.)	Trees (No.)	Board-foot cull (Pct.)	Cubic-foot cull (Pct.)
1 - 3	35	61 ± 3.6	19 ± 1.9
4 - 9	46	79 ± 2.8	35 ± 1.9
10 +	32	95 ± 1.5	47 ± 2.3

The height of the highest sporophore by 16-foot height classes and percentage of cull is given in the following tabulation:

Height of highest sporophores (Ft.)	Trees (No.)	Board-foot cull (Pct.)	Cubic-foot cull (Pct.)
0 - 16	41	57 ± 3.3	21 ± 1.7
17 - 32	41	74 ± 3.4	31 ± 2.5
33 +	31	87 ± 2.5	44 ± 2.5

There was no apparent relationship between amount of decay and other factors such as age class, aspect, crown class, elevation, linear distribution of sporophores, rot diameter at breast height, site, sporophore size, and tree diameter.

DISCUSSION

In commercial aspen stands in Colorado, any tree bearing F. igniarius sporophores is usually considered to be a cull (that is, at least two-thirds of the board-foot volume lost due to decay). The above results suggest that this practice results in some waste, particularly in trees that have only a few sporophores or when the sporophores are low on the bole. In the 41 trees with sporophores 0 to 16 feet high, although 44 percent of the 119 logs were complete culls, 56 percent were merchantable and 46 percent were completely free of decay. Of the 112 logs in the 35 trees with 1 to 3 sporophores, 46 percent were complete culls, 54 percent were merchantable, and 41 percent were completely free of decay.

There was no significant difference in amount of cull in trees bearing 1 to 3 sporophores at any height and any number of sporophores 0 to 16 feet on the bole. The two classes were combined to give 59 ± 3.2 percent board-foot cull (20 ± 1.6 percent cubic-foot cull). The 52 trees in these two classes contained 156 logs, of which 49 percent were culls, 51 percent merchantable, and 39 percent free of decay. Measurement of tree volumes would be simplified if the cull of the combined classes were used. On a board-foot basis, a tree with 1 to 3 sporophores located any place on the bole or a tree with any number of sporophores not higher than 16 feet on the bole would be classified as merchantable (59 percent cull). A tree with sporophores not in these two classes would be unmerchantable.

Fire wounds are common in aspen stands over 85 years old in Colorado. Some of the old wounds are still open and, no doubt, provided excellent infection courts for decay. In this study, 43 percent of the sample trees had old basal wounds, the result of fire or fallen trees. Because of these basal wounds and subsequent decay, it is not out of the ordinary to find longer decay columns and greater cull than found in the studies mentioned earlier.

Davidson et al. (5) found that decay averaged 25 percent of the cubic-foot volume in trees infected with F. igniarius. This average included incipient infections in young trees, and suggested that decayed wood volumes in older stands where sporophores were present would be somewhat higher. Total cubic-foot volume of decay in the present study amounted to 31 percent of the gross cubic-foot volume.

SUMMARY

A total of 113 commercial-sized aspen bearing Fomes igniarius sporophores were felled and dissected on 11 areas in 5 National Forests of Colorado. Average length of decay above and below the highest and lowest sporophore was 12.0 ± 0.7 feet. Estimated board-foot cull for an individual tree with 1 to 3 sporophores at any height, or any number of sporophores 0 to 16 feet on the bole, is 59 ± 3.2 percent (20 ± 1.6 percent cubic-foot cull). A tree with sporophores not in these two classes should be considered a total cull.

LITERATURE CITED

1. Baker, F. S
   1925   Aspen in the central Rocky Mountain region. U S Dept. Agr. Bul. 1291, 47 pp illus
2. Basham, J T
   1958   Decay of trembling aspen. Canad. Jour Bot. 36· 491-505, illus.
3. Brown, R M
   1934   Statistical analyses for finding a simple method for estimating the percentage heart rot in Minnesota aspen Jour. Agr. Research 49: 929-942
4. Christensen, C. M, Anderson, R. L., Hodson, A. C., and Rudolf, P. O
   1951   Enemies of Aspen U.S. Forest Serv Lake States Forest Expt. Sta, Aspen Report 22, 16 pp.
5. Davidson, R W., Hinds, T. E., and Hawksworth, F G.
   1959   Decay of aspen in Colorado. U S Forest Serv. Rocky Mountain Forest and Range Expt Sta. Sta. Paper 45, 14 pp. illus.
6. Horton, G S. and Hendee, C.
   1934.   A study of rot in aspen on the Chippewa National Forest. Jour Forestry 32· 493-494.
7. Riley, C G. and Bier, J E
   1936   Extent of decay in poplar as indicated by the presence of sporophores of the fungus Fomes igniarius Linn Forestry Chronicle 12: 249-253

Stand Volume Tables

for

Immature Ponderosa Pine in the Black Hills

Charles E. Boldt, Research Forester [1]

The volume tables presented here give direct estimates of total and merchantable cubic-foot volumes per acre for immature ponderosa pine stands in the Black Hills. The tables provide a timesaving shortcut for determining stand volumes, since they eliminate the need for summing estimates for individual trees or size classes.

Table 1 gives estimates of total cubic-foot volume per acre, including stumps and upper stemwood of all trees. Two values are required to use this table: (1) basal area of the stand, in square feet per acre, and (2) average total height of dominant and codominant trees, in feet.

Table 2 provides estimates of stand merchantable volume, in trees 6.0 inches d.b.h. and larger, exclusive of volume in upper stemwood smaller than 4.0 inches d.i.b. and in stumps 0.5 foot high. Use of this table also requires two values: (1) basal area of trees larger than 5.9 inches d.b.h., in square feet per acre, and (2) average total height of dominants and codominants, in feet.

Basal areas can be obtained from either plots or point samples, well distributed throughout the stand. The height value required by both tables should be an arithmetic average of total heights of five or more dominants and codominants on each plot or near each point where basal area is measured. When volume estimates are made for sapling or pole stands that have an overstory composed of remnants of a parent stand, the overstory trees should be excluded from the basal area and height samples.

These volume tables were derived from data collected by Myers and Van Deusen on 60 sample plots used in a study of periodic growth in immature pine stands in the Black Hills.[2] Graphic analysis of the data revealed a strong linear correlation between total cubic-foot volume per acre and the product of basal area times average total height of dominants

Maintained at Fort Collins, Colorado, in cooperation with Colorado State University

and codominants. A regression line was fitted to the data by the method of least squares:

$$V_T = 0.392\, B_T H$$

where V_T = stand volume in cubic feet per acre, B_T = basal area per acre, all stems in square feet, and H = average total height of dominants and codominants, in feet.

Stand merchantable volume was similarly correlated with basal area of merchantable trees and average total height of dominants and codominants. Another least-squares regression equation was computed for that relationship:

$$V_M = 0.372\, B_M H - 96.3$$

where V_M = stand merchantable volume in cubic feet per acre, B_M = basal area of all trees larger than 5.9 inches d.b.h., in square feet per acre, and H = average total height of dominant and codominant trees.

These two equations were used to compute the volumes shown in the tables. They can also be used to obtain volume estimates for combinations of basal area and average height in between those given in the tables.

Merchantable cubic-foot volumes may be converted to standard cord measure by applying appropriate conversion factors. For an estimate of the number of rough (unpeeled) cords per acre, divide merchantable cubic-foot volume by 77. For an estimate of the number of cords of peeled wood, divide merchantable cubic-foot volume by 98.[3] Cord estimates thus obtained will be sufficiently accurate for most purposes, although probable limits of error cannot be given.

---

[1] Author stationed at Rapid City, South Dakota, in cooperation with the South Dakota School of Mines and Technology.

[2] Myers, Clifford A., and Van Deusen, James L. Growth of immature stands of ponderosa pine in the Black Hills U S Forest Serv Rocky Mountain Forest and Range Expt Sta. Paper 61, 14 pp., 1961

[3] Woodfin, R O., Jr, and Landt, E F Conversion of cubic-foot volumes of Black Hills ponderosa pine to cords. U S. Forest Serv Rocky Mountain Forest and Range Expt Sta Res Note 31(Rev) 2 pp. 1960

Table 1.--Total cubic-foot volume for immature stands of ponderosa pine in the Black Hills of South Dakota and Wyoming

Cubic feet per acre, entire stems, inside bark						Average total height of dominant and codominant trees		
Stand basal area, all stems	Average total height, feet							
	20	30	40	50	60	70	80	90
Sq. ft./acre	Volume per acre, cubic feet							
10	78	118	157	196				
20	157	235	314	392				
30	235	353	470	588				
40	314	470	627	784				
50	392	588	784	980				
60	470	706	941	1176				
70	549	823	1098	1372				
80	627	941	1254	1568	1882			
90	706	1058	1411	1764	2117			
100	784	1176	1568	1960	2352			
110	862	1294	1725	2156	2587			
120	941	1411	1882	2352	2822			
130	1019	1529	2038	2548	3058			
140	1098	1646	2195	2744	3293	3842	4390	
150	1176	1764	2352	2940	3528	4116	4704	5292
160	1254	1882	2509	3136	3763	4390	5018	5645
170	1333	1999	2666	3332	3998	4665	5331	5998
180	1411	2117	2822	3528	4234	4939	5645	6350
190	1490	2234	2979	3724	4469	5214	5958	6703
200	1568	2352	3136	3920	4704	5488	6272	7056
210	1646	2470	3293	4116	4939	5762	6586	7409
220	1725	2587	3450	4312	5174	6037	6899	
230	1803	2705	3606	4508	5410			
240	1882	2822	3763	4704				
250	1960	2940	3920	4900				
260	2038	3058	4077	5096				

Blocks indicate extent of basic data.
Standard error of estimate = 79.7 cubic feet = 3.5 percent at mean volume.

Table 2.--Merchantable cubic-foot volume for immature Stands of ponderosa pine in the Black Hills of South Dakota and Wyoming

Cubic feet per acre, excluding 0.5-foot stumps and stemwood less than 4.0 inches d.i.b.				Average total height of dominant and codominant trees		
Basal area in trees larger than 5.9 inches d.b.h.	Average total height, feet					
	20	30	40	50	60	70
Sq. ft./acre	Volume per acre, cubic feet					
10		15	52			
20	52	127	201			
30	127	238	350			
40	201	350	499	648		
50		462	648	834	1020	
60		573	796	1020	1243	1466
70		685	945	1206	1466	1726
80		796	1094	1392	1689	1987
90		908	1243	1578	1912	2247
100		1020	1392	1764	2136	2508
110		1131	1540	1950	2359	2768
120		1243	1689	2136	2582	3028
130		1354	1838	2322	2805	3289
140			1987	2508	3028	3549
150			2136	2694	3252	3810
160			2284	2880	3475	4070
170			2433	3066	3698	4330
180			2582	3252	3921	4591
190			2731	3438	4144	4851
200			2880	3624	4368	
210			3028	3810	4591	

Blocks indicate extent of basic data.
Standard error of estimate = 80.6 cubic feet = 5.8 percent at mean volume.

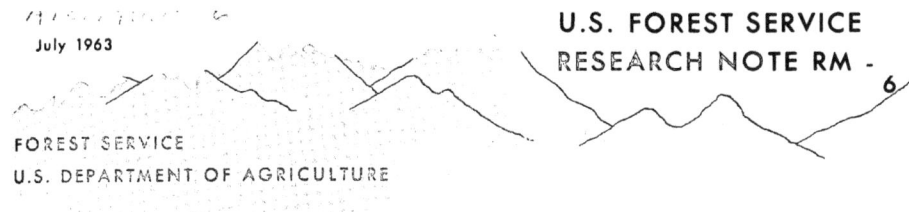

July 1963

U.S. FOREST SERVICE
RESEARCH NOTE RM - 6

FOREST SERVICE
U.S. DEPARTMENT OF AGRICULTURE

A Comparison of 16 Grasses and Forbs for Seeding Chaparral Burns

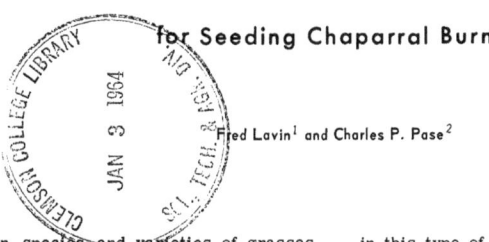

Fred Lavin[1] and Charles P. Pase[2]

Sixteen species and varieties of grasses and forbs were test-planted on the Tonto National Forest after the Boulder Mountain fire of June 1959. This wildfire swept over 21,700 acres of steep, broken chaparral between Roosevelt Reservoir and the south end of the Mazatzal Mountains.

An exploratory species adaptation study was begun on a small portion of the burn in July 1959 and completed November 1961. The study area was located near the Three Bar Experimental Watersheds at an elevation of 3,500 feet. Annual precipitation since the start of the study averaged 22.80 inches (table 1). Dominant vegetation on the site consisted of shrub live oak, birchleaf mountainmahogany, and sugar sumac. Little herbaceous vegetation was present before the fire. The aspect is northerly with approximately a 10 percent slope. The soil is a thin, gravelly, sandy loam derived from granitic parent material.

The main object of the study was to determine whether there are species other than weeping lovegrass adapted for seeding burns in this type of chaparral. Weeping lovegrass was chosen as the standard for comparison because it has been widely seeded throughout the Arizona chaparral type. This species is easy to establish and produces large, vigorous plants valuable for livestock forage. It has a major weakness, however, in that many originally good stands have deteriorated rapidly and been lost within a few years.

PROCEDURE

The 16 species and varieties tested can be divided into warm-weather and cool-weather growers on the basis of growth habit. The warm-weather growers consisted of Caucasian, sand, Turkestan, King Ranch and little bluestem; Lehmann, sand and weeping lovegrass; switchgrass and buffelgrass. The cool-weather growers were composed of Cicer and sicklepod milkvetch, black and Indian mustard, a mixture of cold-hardy alfalfa varieties including Ladak, and Hardinggrass.

Planting was done in the fresh burn before the loose surface ash had been disturbed by

Table 1.--Precipitation in inches at reseeding test plots near Three Bar Experimental Watershed A, Tonto National Forest, Arizona[1]

Year	Jan.	Feb.	Mar.	Apr.	May	June	July	Aug.	Sept.	Oct.	Nov.	Dec.	Total
1959	0.76	4.56	0	0.15	0.16	0.28	0.37	7.30	0.73	7.85	0.61	9.60	32.37
1960	3.62	.93	1.17	0	.66	.10	.83	1.90	1.62	3.12	.41	.44	14.80
1961	2.04	.82	2.52	.03	0	0	1.54	1.67	4.24	.46	.59	7.31	21.22
Average													22.80

[1] Prefire average for 1957 and 1958 was 27.34 inches.

Table 2.--Relative success[1] and vigor[1] of 16 species and varieties test seeded by broadcast on the fresh ashes of a chaparral burn, July 17, 1959

Species	September 1959		June 1960		November 1960		November 1961	
	Relative success	Vigor	Relative success	Vigor	Relative success	Vigor	Relative success	Vigor
Alfalfa (mixture of cold-hardy varieties)	T	G	O	--	O	--	O	--
Bluestem								
Caucasian	F	G	P	P	P	G	VP	G
King Ranch	G	G	F	F	G	E	G	E
Little	T	F	O	--	O	--	O	--
Sand	T	F	O	--	O	--	O	--
Turkestan	T	G	F	G	F	E	F	E
Buffelgrass	E	E	O	D	P	E	T	G
Hardinggrass	T	F	VP	F	O	--	O	--
Lovegrass								
Lehmann	E	E	G	F	E	E	E	E
Sand	T	G	O	--	T	F	O	--
Weeping	F	G	F	E	F	E	F	F
Milkvetch								
Cicer	T	E	VP	G	P	E	P	E
Sicklepod	T	G	VP	G	P	E	P	E
Mustard								
Black	O	--	F	G	F	E	F	E
Indian	O	--	F	G	P	G	F	E
Switchgrass	T	F	O	--	O	--	O	--

[1] Key to ratings:
E = excellent
G = good
F = fair
P = poor
VP = very poor
T = trace
O = failure
D = dead

rain. Each species was broadcast planted with a hand seeder in an unreplicated plot approximately 1/8 acre in size. There is a possibility that some poor seed may have been planted since there was no time for seed-germination tests.

Ocular ratings as shown in table 2, were made on each species and variety tested. The relative success rating is based on density and distribution of plants in the stand, together with their general appearance. The vigor rating is based entirely on the size and appearance of the individual plants.

RESULTS

Lehmann lovegrass (fig. 1) and King Ranch bluestem were the outstanding species throughout the duration of the study with average ratings of excellent and good, respectively. Turkestan bluestem, weeping lovegrass, and black and Indian mustard rated fair. Ratings of all other species and varieties ranged from poor to failure.

Buffelgrass at the start was the most vigorous species and rated excellent the first growing season. This stand died during the first winter, however. A poor stand composed entirely of new seedlings became established the second growing season but was killed during the second winter. The third growing season only a few scattered buffelgrass seedlings could be found.

Weeping lovegrass maintained a fair stand during the three growing seasons of the study. At the last observation, however, numerous dead plants were found. These apparently had been drought killed. Black and Indian mustard did not germinate and become established until the first winter after they were planted, but

Figure 1 --Lehmann lovegrass test planting on chaparral burn at the end of the third growing season.

have maintained fair stands since that time. Poor stands of Caucasian bluestem and Cicer and sicklepod milkvetch are maintaining themselves. Poor initial stands of sand lovegrass, alfalfa, Hardinggrass, switchgrass, and sand and little bluestem died out before the end of the study.

Turkestan and King Ranch bluestem, black and Indian mustard, and Lehmann lovegrass are all reproducing by natural reseeding.

---

[1] Range Conservationist, Crops Research Division, Agricultural Research Service

[2] Research Forester, Rocky Mountain Station. Work reported here was done in cooperation with the University of Arizona and Arizona State College

COMMON AND BOTANICAL NAMES OF SPECIES MENTIONED

Alfalfa	Medicago sativa
Bluestem, Caucasian	Andropogon caucasicus
Bluestem, King Ranch	A. ischaemum hort. var. KING RANCH
Bluestem, little	A. scoparius
Bluestem, sand	A. hallii
Bluestem, Turkestan	A. ischaemum
Buffelgrass	Pennisetum ciliare
Hardinggrass	Phalaris tuberosa var. stenoptera
Lovegrass, Lehmann	Eragrostis lehmanniana
Lovegrass, sand	E. trichodes
Lovegrass, weeping	E. curvula
Milkvetch, Cicer	Astragalus cicer
Milkvetch, sicklepod	A. falcatus
Mountainmahogany, birchleaf	Cercocarpus betuloides
Mustard, black	Brassica nigra
Mustard, Indian	B. juncea
Oak, shrub live	Quercus turbinella
Sumac, sugar	Rhus ovata
Switchgrass	Panicum virgatum

July 1963

U.S. FOREST SERVICE
RESEARCH NOTE RM - 7

DEPARTMENT OF AGRICULTURE

Estimating Past Diameters of Ponderosa Pines

in Arizona and New Mexico

Clifford A. Myers, Research Forester

Past diameters of ponderosa pines in Arizona and New Mexico can be estimated with the tables presented here. Two measurements must be made on each tree, both at breast height: (1) diameter and (2) radial growth of wood for any desired period. Radial growth of wood is measured on increment cores extracted along the best estimate of average radius. Bark thickness is not measured; the tables make allowance for bark growth.

Separate tables are presented for blackjack and old-growth ponderosa pines, because blackjacks have thicker bark than old-growth pines of equal diameter. Rapidly tapering ponderosa pines with dark, furrowed bark are called blackjacks in the Southwest. Old-growth trees are less tapering than blackjacks and have yellowish bark that forms broad, flat plates on the oldest trees.

Past diameters are given in the tables for several combinations of present diameter and periodic radial growth. For example, if the present diameter of a blackjack is 20.0 inches and radial wood growth totaled 0.45 inch for a particular period, the diameter was 19.0 inches at the beginning of the period. Interpolation may be used to obtain past diameters when present diameters and amounts of radial growth differ from those given in the tables. Past diameters of trees with radial growth less than 0.40 inch (blackjacks) or 0.55 inch (old-growth) can be obtained by subtracting twice the amount of radial growth from present diameter. Bark growth of such trees is too small to affect diameter measurements made to the nearest 0.1 inch.

The following relationships apply to blackjack ponderosa pines now 8 to 38 inches in diameter:

Conversion of diameter outside bark to diameter inside bark:
  d.i.b. = 0.9344 (d.o.b.) - 1.1923
Conversion of diameter inside bark to diameter outside bark:
  d.o.b. = 1.0698 (d.i.b.) + 1.2840

For old-growth ponderosa pines now 12 to 38 inches in diameter:

Conversion of diameter outside bark to diameter inside bark:
d.i.b. = 0.9498 (d.o.b.) - 1.1217

Conversion of diameter inside bark to diameter outside bark:
d.o.b. = 1.0524 (d.i.b.) + 1.1918

Correlation coefficient of all four equations is +0.9998.

The standard errors of estimate are 0.0165, 0.0186, 0.0143, and 0.0158, respectively.

Past diameters can be computed with the following equations; they were obtained by combining the two equations of each set given above.

For blackjacks:
Past d.o.b. = present d.o.b. + 0.01 - 2.14 (radial growth)

For old-growth pines:
Past d.o.b. = present d.o.b. + 0.01 - 2.10 (radial growth)

Basic data were obtained from 676 blackjacks and 595 old-growth trees, with samples taken from all major areas of commercial ponderosa pine in Arizona and New Mexico. Diameters to the nearest 0.1 inch were measured with a diameter tape. Bark thickness at breast height was measured to the nearest 0.05 inch at three points on each tree.

Table 1.—Present and past diameters of blackjack ponderosa pines in Arizona and New Mexico

Present d.b.h. outside bark inches	Radial wood growth in inches																				
	0.40	0.45	0.55	0.65	0.75	0.85	0.95	1.05	1.15	1.25	1.35	1.45	1.55	1.65	1.75	1.85	1.95	2.05	2.15	2.25
	Past d.b.h. outside bark in inches[1]																			
8.0	7.0	6.8	6.6	6.3	6.1	5.8	5.6	5.3	5.1	4.8	4.6	4.3	4.0	3.8	3.5	3.3	3.0	2.8	2.5	2.3
9.0	8.1	8.0	7.8	7.5	7.3	7.0	6.8	6.5	6.3	6.0	5.8	5.5	5.2	5.0	4.7	4.5	4.2	4.0	3.7	3.5
10.0	9.1	9.0	8.8	8.6	8.4	8.2	8.0	7.7	7.4	7.2	6.9	6.7	6.4	6.2	5.9	5.7	5.4	5.2	4.9	4.6
11.0	10.1	10.0	9.8	9.6	9.4	9.2	9.0	8.8	8.5	8.3	8.1	7.9	7.6	7.4	7.1	6.9	6.6	6.4	6.1	5.8
12.0	11.1	11.0	10.8	10.6	10.4	10.2	10.0	9.8	9.5	9.3	9.1	8.9	8.7	8.5	8.3	8.0	7.8	7.5	7.3	7.0
13.0	12.1	12.0	11.8	11.6	11.4	11.2	11.0	10.8	10.5	10.3	10.1	9.9	9.7	9.5	9.3	9.0	8.8	8.6	8.4	8.2
14.0	13.1	13.0	12.8	12.6	12.4	12.2	12.0	11.8	11.5	11.3	11.1	10.9	10.7	10.5	10.3	10.0	9.8	9.6	9.4	9.2
15.0	14.1	14.0	13.8	13.6	13.4	13.2	13.0	12.8	12.5	12.3	12.1	11.9	11.7	11.5	11.3	11.0	10.8	10.6	10.4	10.2
16.0	15.1	15.0	14.8	14.6	14.4	14.2	14.0	13.8	13.5	13.3	13.1	12.9	12.7	12.5	12.3	12.0	11.8	11.6	11.4	11.2
17.0	16.1	16.0	15.8	15.6	15.4	15.2	15.0	14.8	14.5	14.3	14.1	13.9	13.7	13.5	13.3	13.0	12.8	12.6	12.4	12.2
18.0	17.1	17.0	16.8	16.6	16.4	16.2	16.0	15.8	15.5	15.3	15.1	14.9	14.7	14.5	14.3	14.0	13.8	13.6	13.4	13.2
19.0	18.1	18.0	17.8	17.6	17.4	17.2	17.0	16.8	16.5	16.3	16.1	15.9	15.7	15.5	15.3	15.0	14.8	14.6	14.4	14.2
20.0	19.1	19.0	18.8	18.6	18.4	18.2	18.0	17.8	17.5	17.3	17.1	16.9	16.7	16.5	16.3	16.0	15.8	15.6	15.4	15.2
21.0	20.1	20.0	19.8	19.6	19.4	19.2	19.0	18.8	18.5	18.3	18.1	17.9	17.7	17.5	17.3	17.0	16.8	16.6	16.4	16.2
22.0	21.1	21.0	20.8	20.6	20.4	20.2	20.0	19.8	19.5	19.3	19.1	18.9	18.7	18.5	18.3	18.0	17.8	17.6	17.4	17.2
23.0	22.1	22.0	21.8	21.6	21.4	21.2	21.0	20.8	20.5	20.3	20.1	19.9	19.7	19.5	19.3	19.0	18.8	18.6	18.4	18.2
24.0	23.1	23.0	22.8	22.6	22.4	22.2	22.0	21.8	21.5	21.3	21.1	20.9	20.7	20.5	20.3	20.0	19.8	19.6	19.4	19.2
25.0	24.1	24.0	23.8	23.6	23.4	23.2	23.0	22.8	22.5	22.3	22.1	21.9	21.7	21.5	21.3	21.0	20.8	20.6	20.4	20.2
26.0	25.1	25.0	24.8	24.6	24.4	24.2	24.0	23.8	23.5	23.3	23.1	22.9	22.7	22.5	22.3	22.0	21.8	21.6	21.4	21.2
27.0	26.1	26.0	25.8	25.6	25.4	25.2	25.0	24.8	24.5	24.3	24.1	23.9	23.7	23.5	23.3	23.0	22.8	22.6	22.4	22.2
28.0	27.1	27.0	26.8	26.6	26.4	26.2	26.0	25.8	25.5	25.3	25.1	24.9	24.7	24.5	24.3	24.0	23.8	23.6	23.4	23.2
29.0	28.1	28.0	27.8	27.6	27.4	27.2	27.0	26.8	26.5	26.3	26.1	25.9	25.7	25.5	25.3	25.0	24.8	24.6	24.4	24.2
30.0	29.1	29.0	28.8	28.6	28.4	28.2	28.0	27.8	27.5	27.3	27.1	26.9	26.7	26.5	26.3	26.0	25.8	25.6	25.4	25.2
31.0	30.1	30.0	29.8	29.6	29.4	29.2	29.0	28.8	28.5	28.3	28.1	27.9	27.7	27.5	27.3	27.0	26.8	26.6	26.4	26.2
32.0	31.1	31.0	30.8	30.6	30.4	30.2	30.0	29.8	29.5	29.3	29.1	28.9	28.7	28.5	28.3	28.0	27.8	27.6	27.4	27.2
33.0	32.1	32.0	31.8	31.6	31.4	31.2	31.0	30.8	30.5	30.3	30.1	29.9	29.7	29.5	29.3	29.0	28.8	28.6	28.4	28.2
34.0	33.1	33.0	32.8	32.6	32.4	32.2	32.0	31.8	31.5	31.3	31.1	30.9	30.7	30.5	30.3	30.0	29.8	29.6	29.4	29.2
35.0	34.1	34.0	33.8	33.6	33.4	33.2	33.0	32.8	32.5	32.3	32.1	31.9	31.7	31.5	31.3	31.0	30.8	30.6	30.4	30.2
36.0	35.1	35.0	34.8	34.6	34.4	34.2	34.0	33.8	33.5	33.3	33.1	32.9	32.7	32.5	32.3	32.0	31.8	31.6	31.4	31.2
37.0	36.1	36.0	35.8	35.6	35.4	35.2	35.0	34.8	34.5	34.3	34.1	33.9	33.7	33.5	33.3	33.0	32.8	32.6	32.4	32.2
38.0	37.1	37.0	36.8	36.6	36.4	36.2	36.0	35.8	35.5	35.3	35.1	34.9	34.7	34.5	34.3	34.0	33.8	33.6	33.4	33.2

[1] Values below the dashed line were computed from the equations. Elsewhere, past d.i.b. was converted to past d.o.b. by extending the computed line to the origin.

Table 2.--Present and past diameters of old-growth ponderosa pines in Arizona and New Mexico

Present d.b.h. outside bark inches	Radial wood growth in inches																		
	0.55	0.65	0.75	0.85	0.95	1.05	1.15	1.25	1.35	1.45	1.55	1.65	1.75	1.85	1.95	2.05	2.15	2.25
	Past d.b.h. outside bark in inches[1]																		
12.0	10.7	10.5	10.2	10.0	9.8	9.5	9.3	9.1	8.8	8.6	8.4	8.1	7.9	7.7	7.4	7.2	7.0	6.7
13.0	11.8	11.6	11.4	11.1	10.9	10.7	10.4	10.2	10.0	9.7	9.5	9.3	9.0	8.8	8.6	8.3	8.1	7.9
14.0	12.8	12.6	12.4	12.2	12.0	11.8	11.5	11.3	11.1	10.8	10.6	10.4	10.1	9.9	9.7	9.4	9.2	9.0
15.0	13.8	13.6	13.4	13.2	13.0	12.8	12.6	12.4	12.2	11.9	11.7	11.5	11.2	11.0	10.8	10.5	10.3	10.1
16.0	14.8	14.6	14.4	14.2	14.0	13.8	13.6	13.4	13.2	13.0	12.7	12.5	12.3	12.1	11.9	11.6	11.4	11.2
17.0	15.8	15.6	15.4	15.2	15.0	14.8	14.6	14.4	14.2	14.0	13.7	13.5	13.3	13.1	12.9	12.7	12.5	12.3
18.0	16.8	16.6	16.4	16.2	16.0	15.8	15.6	15.4	15.2	15.0	14.7	14.5	14.3	14.1	13.9	13.7	13.5	13.3
19.0	17.8	17.6	17.4	17.2	17.0	16.8	16.6	16.4	16.2	16.0	15.7	15.5	15.3	15.1	14.9	14.7	14.5	14.3
20.0	18.8	18.6	18.4	18.2	18.0	17.8	17.6	17.4	17.2	17.0	16.7	16.5	16.3	16.1	15.9	15.7	15.5	15.3
21.0	19.8	19.6	19.4	19.2	19.0	18.8	18.6	18.4	18.2	18.0	17.7	17.5	17.3	17.1	16.9	16.7	16.5	16.3
22.0	20.8	20.6	20.4	20.2	20.0	19.8	19.6	19.4	19.2	19.0	18.7	18.5	18.3	18.1	17.9	17.7	17.5	17.3
23.0	21.8	21.6	21.4	21.2	21.0	20.8	20.6	20.4	20.2	20.0	19.7	19.5	19.3	19.1	18.9	18.7	18.5	18.3
24.0	22.8	22.6	22.4	22.2	22.0	21.8	21.6	21.4	21.2	21.0	20.7	20.5	20.3	20.1	19.9	19.7	19.5	19.3
25.0	23.8	23.6	23.4	23.2	23.0	22.8	22.6	22.4	22.2	22.0	21.7	21.5	21.3	21.1	20.9	20.7	20.5	20.3
26.0	24.8	24.6	24.4	24.2	24.0	23.8	23.6	23.4	23.2	23.0	22.7	22.5	22.3	22.1	21.9	21.7	21.5	21.3
27.0	25.8	25.6	25.4	25.2	25.0	24.8	24.6	24.4	24.2	24.0	23.7	23.5	23.3	23.1	22.9	22.7	22.5	22.3
28.0	26.8	26.6	26.4	26.2	26.0	25.8	25.6	25.4	25.2	25.0	24.7	24.5	24.3	24.1	23.9	23.7	23.5	23.3
29.0	27.8	27.6	27.4	27.2	27.0	26.8	26.6	26.4	26.2	26.0	25.7	25.5	25.3	25.1	24.9	24.7	24.5	24.3
30.0	28.8	28.6	28.4	28.2	28.0	27.8	27.6	27.4	27.2	27.0	26.7	26.5	26.3	26.1	25.9	25.7	25.5	25.3
31.0	29.8	29.6	29.4	29.2	29.0	28.8	28.6	28.4	28.2	28.0	27.7	27.5	27.3	27.1	26.9	26.7	26.5	26.3
32.0	30.8	30.6	30.4	30.2	30.0	29.8	29.6	29.4	29.2	29.0	28.7	28.5	28.3	28.1	27.9	27.7	27.5	27.3
33.0	31.8	31.6	31.4	31.2	31.0	30.8	30.6	30.4	30.2	30.0	29.7	29.5	29.3	29.1	28.9	28.7	28.5	28.3
34.0	32.8	32.6	32.4	32.2	32.0	31.8	31.6	31.4	31.2	31.0	30.7	30.5	30.3	30.1	29.9	29.7	29.5	29.3
35.0	33.8	33.6	33.4	33.2	33.0	32.8	32.6	32.4	32.2	32.0	31.7	31.5	31.3	31.1	30.9	30.7	30.5	30.3
36.0	34.8	34.6	34.4	34.2	34.0	33.8	33.6	33.4	33.2	33.0	32.7	32.5	32.3	32.1	31.9	31.7	31.5	31.3
37.0	35.8	35.6	35.4	35.2	35.0	34.8	34.6	34.4	34.2	34.0	33.7	33.5	33.3	33.1	32.9	32.7	32.5	32.3
38.0	36.8	36.6	36.4	36.2	36.0	35.8	35.6	35.4	35.2	35.0	34.7	34.5	34.3	34.1	33.9	33.7	33.5	33.3

[1] Values below the dashed line were computed from the equations. Elsewhere, past d.i.b. was converted to past d.o.b. by extending the computed line to the origin.

Taper Table for Pole-Size Ponderosa Pines in Arizona and New Mexico

Clifford A. Myers, Research Forester

Forest managers often need estimates of the number of posts or other piece products on a tract of forest land. Such estimates are complicated by the fact that pieces of several sizes may be equally merchantable. For example, posts vary in length and minimum top diameter; the size demanded depends on the end use.

The number of pieces in a tree can be determined from a table of tree diameters at various heights (table 1). Diameters are plotted over the corresponding heights, and the points are connected by smooth lines to form taper curves. The figure thus formed for any tree may then be subdivided into products of different lengths and diameters. Potential products are limited by the lengths and minimum top diameters accepted locally.

Several ways of dividing a tree may be tried to determine the method that will produce the most valuable combination of products. A table, similar to a standard volume table, can be prepared to show the number of pieces of each size in average trees of each diameter and height class. Such a table will show gross contents; a cull factor is needed for each tract to estimate the number of unacceptable pieces that will have to be deducted because of decay, crook, or fork.

Diameters for ponderosa pines in table 1 were computed from measurements of 139 trees obtained by personnel of the Southwestern Region, U. S. Forest Service. Sample trees were measured in all areas of commercial ponderosa pine in Arizona and New Mexico.

Maintained at Fort Collins, Colorado, in cooperation with Colorado State University

Table 1. Diameters at various heights of the average tree in each total height and diameter class, immature ponderosa pine in Arizona and New Mexico

Diameter breast height outside bark (Inches)	Total height (Feet)	Height above ground level in feet																				
		1	4	8	12	16	20	24	28	32	36	40	44	48	52	56	60	64	68	72	76	80
		Diameter inside bark in inches																				
5.5	30	5.4	4.6	4.1	3.7	3.2	2.4	1.6	0.7													
	40	5.4	4.6	4.2	3.9	3.7	3.3	2.9	2.2	1.5	0.8	0										
6.5	30	6.2	5.4	4.8	4.3	3.8	3.0	2.0	0.8													
	40	6.2	5.4	4.8	4.4	4.1	3.8	3.3	2.5	1.8	0.9	0										
	50	6.2	5.4	4.9	4.7	4.5	4.3	4.1	3.7	3.2	2.6	2.1	1.6	0.6								
7.5	30	7.0	6.2	5.6	5.0	4.4	3.6	2.5	1.2													
	40	7.0	6.2	5.6	5.1	4.7	4.3	3.7	3.0	2.3	1.5	0										
	50	7.0	6.2	5.8	5.5	5.2	4.9	4.5	4.0	3.4	2.9	2.2	1.7	0.7								
	60	7.0	6.3	5.9	5.6	5.5	5.4	5.1	4.8	4.5	4.0	3.5	3.0	2.4	1.9	1.1	0					
8.5	30	7.9	7.0	6.4	5.7	5.1	4.3	3.2	1.9													
	40	7.9	7.0	6.4	5.8	5.4	4.9	4.3	3.6	2.9	2.0	0										
	50	7.9	7.1	6.6	6.3	5.9	5.6	5.1	4.6	3.9	3.4	2.6	2.0	0.9								
	60	8.0	7.2	6.7	6.6	6.4	6.2	6.0	5.6	5.4	4.8	4.2	3.6	2.8	2.2	1.4	0					
9.5	30	8.9	7.9	7.2	6.4	5.8	5.1	3.9	2.5													
	40	8.9	7.9	7.2	6.7	6.2	5.5	4.8	4.2	3.5	2.5	0										
	50	8.9	8.0	7.4	7.1	6.6	6.2	5.7	5.1	4.4	3.8	3.0	2.3	1.1								
	60	9.0	8.1	7.7	7.4	7.2	6.9	6.6	6.3	5.9	5.5	4.8	4.1	3.2	2.5	1.7	0					
10.5	30	9.9	8.8	8.0	7.3	6.6	5.9	4.8	3.0													
	40	9.9	8.8	8.2	7.6	7.1	6.3	5.5	4.8	4.0	2.9	0										
	50	9.9	8.9	8.3	7.9	7.3	6.9	6.2	5.5	4.8	4.1	3.2	2.4	1.2								
	60	10.0	8.9	8.4	8.1	7.7	7.3	6.8	6.4	5.9	5.7	5.1	4.3	3.4	2.6	1.8	0					
	70	10.1	9.0	8.6	8.3	8.0	7.8	7.6	7.2	6.8	6.4	6.0	5.5	4.8	4.0	3.3	2.5	1.7	0.6			
11.5	30	10.8	9.8	8.9	8.1	7.4	6.6	5.3	3.2													
	40	10.8	9.8	9.1	8.5	7.9	6.9	6.0	5.2	4.2	3.0	0										
	50	10.8	9.8	9.1	8.7	8.0	7.5	6.8	6.0	5.2	4.4	3.6	2.8	1.3								
	60	10.8	9.8	9.3	8.9	8.5	8.1	7.6	7.1	6.5	6.0	5.3	4.5	3.5	2.7	2.0	0					
	70	10.9	9.9	9.4	9.2	9.0	8.6	8.4	8.0	7.8	7.4	6.9	6.1	5.3	4.5	3.7	2.8	2.0	0.9			
12.5	30	11.8	10.7	9.9	8.9	8.1	7.0	5.6	3.3													
	40	11.8	10.7	10.0	9.3	8.6	7.5	6.4	5.4	4.3	3.1	0										
	50	11.8	10.7	10.0	9.5	8.9	8.3	7.6	6.8	6.0	5.2	4.3	3.3	1.8								
	60	11.9	10.7	10.1	9.6	9.2	8.7	8.2	7.6	6.9	6.2	5.5	4.6	3.7	2.8	2.1	0					
	70	11.9	10.8	10.2	9.8	9.5	9.2	8.8	8.3	7.8	7.2	6.7	6.5	5.6	4.8	3.8	3.0	2.2	1.1			
	80	12.0	10.9	10.3	10.0	9.8	9.6	9.3	9.0	8.6	8.2	7.9	7.6	7.2	6.8	6.2	5.5	4.5	3.6	2.5	1.3	0

Agriculture --- CSU, Ft. Collins

July 1963

U.S. FOREST SERVICE
RESEARCH NOTE RM - 9

FOREST SERVICE
DEPARTMENT OF AGRICULTURE

Estimating Volumes and Diameters at Breast Height from Stump Diameters, Southwestern Ponderosa Pine

Clifford A. Myers, Research Forester

There is a close correlation between stump diameter inside bark and diameter at breast height outside bark (d.b.h.) of southwestern ponderosa pines. Stump diameters may thus be used to estimate the d.b.h. and volume of trees that have been cut and hauled away.

The procedure for determining d.b.h. and volume from stump diameter is as follows:
1. Tally the stumps of the missing trees by average diameters inside bark 1 foot above ground level on the uphill side.
2. Convert stump diameters to d.b.h. by means of table 1.
3. Construct a curve of tree height over d.b.h. from measurements of trees remaining on and adjacent to the area. Read the average height of trees in each d.b.h. class.
4. Obtain the volume of one tree in each d.b.h. class (with the average height of the class) from the appropriate standard volume table.
5. Multiply the volume of one tree in each d.b.h. class by the number of trees tallied in the class, and total the class volumes.

Table 1 summarizes the following linear relationships:
For immature ponderosa pines with stump diameters of 4 to 11 inches:
 D.b.h. = 0.23 + 1.05 (stump diameter)
 Correlation coefficient(r): 0.999. Standard error of estimate: 0.12 inch.
For immature and old-growth ponderosa pines with stump diameters of 12 to 40 inches:
 D.b.h. = 1.32 + 0.96 (stump diameter)
 Correlation coefficient(r): 0.999. Standard error of estimate: 0.21 inch.

The relationships were computed from diameter measurements of 1,483 felled trees. All areas of commercial ponderosa pine in Arizona and New Mexico were represented in the sample.

Table 1.--Diameter outside bark at breast height from diameter inside bark at the top of a stump 1 foot high on the uphill side, southwestern ponderosa pine

(In inches)

Stump diameter, inside bark	Diameter breast high, outside bark	Stump diameter, inside bark	Diameter breast high, outside bark
4.5	5.0	23.5	23.9
5.5	6.0	24.5	24.8
6.5	7.1	25.5	25.8
7.5	8.1	26.5	26.8
8.5	9.2	27.5	27.7
9.5	10.2	28.5	28.7
10.5	11.3	29.5	29.6
11.5	12.3	30.5	30.6
12.5	13.3	31.5	31.6
13.5	14.3	32.5	32.5
14.5	15.2	33.5	33.5
15.5	16.2	34.5	34.4
16.5	17.2	35.5	35.4
17.5	18.1	36.5	36.4
18.5	19.1	37.5	37.3
19.5	20.0	38.5	38.3
20.5	21.0	39.5	39.2
21.5	22.0	40.5	40.2
22.5	22.9		

nd Scalping on Survival

Pine in the Southwest

eidmann[2]

spring. The dry period usually occurs in May and June, but may extend from early May to late July. In many areas, dense stands of perennial grasses take the available soil moisture that might be used by pine seedlings or transplants during the dry period (Pearson, 1942).

This progress report describes some methods used to conserve soil moisture at two recent plantations at Arizona.

THE STUDY

In the early spring of 1960, 1,280 ponderosa pine transplants (2-1) were planted at A-1 Mountain west of Flagstaff, Arizona, and 9,600 were planted at Jones Mountain south of Flagstaff. The Jones Mountain site had been burned by wildfire in the spring of 1959 and immediately seeded with a mixture of grasses. The plantation is on a fairly uniform slope with a southeasterly aspect. The soil is fairly deep but with outcroppings of rock throughout the area. A barbed wire fence was built around the entire plantation to exclude domestic livestock but not wildlife.

The study at Jones Mountain was designed to test four methods of planting. No site preparation was done because vegetation was sparse at planting time. The study consisted of four replications of four randomized treatment plots. In each plot, 600 trees were planted at a spacing of 6 by 6 feet by one of the following planting methods:

1. Standard depth--tree set in ground up to the root collar.
2. Standard depth with three-rock mulch--three nearly flat rocks, approximately 6 to 8 inches in diameter, placed around the tree stem (Rotty, 1958).
3. Deep planting--trees set in ground to the terminal bud.
4. Deep planting with three-rock mulch (fig. 1).

In each plot, 100 trees were randomly selected at the start of the study to be checked for survival. All the trees were sprayed with a 10-percent solution of TMTD (tetramethylthiuramdisulfide) to reduce browsing by deer and elk (Heidmann, 1962).

The plantation at A-1 Mountain was located on a 10-year-old burn. Several attempts to plant the site had failed mainly because of competing vegetation, and browsing and trampling by cattle and deer. The aspect is easterly with a gentle slope. A deer- and cattle-proof fence surrounds the plantation. The ground cover is a mixture of weed species and perennial grasses, mainly mountain muhly (<u>Muhlenbergia</u> <u>montana</u> (Nutt.) Hitchc.) and Arizona fescue (<u>Festuca</u> <u>arizonica</u> Vasey).

The A-1 Mountain study, designed to test four degrees of mechanical site preparation and four planting methods, consisted of eight replications of four plots (15 by 33 feet). Each plot received one of the following four scalping treatments:

1. None--check plot.
2. Scalped spots 16 inches in diameter.
3. Scalped spots 26 inches in diameter.
4. Complete scalping--entire plot scalped.

Forty trees, (10 planted by each of the four planting methods used at Jones Mountain) were planted on each plot.

RESULTS

Survival by the four methods of planting was as follows after two growing seasons:

	Percent
Standard depth - mulched	68
Standard depth - no mulch	64
Deep planting - no mulch	58
Deep planting - mulched	56

Differences in survival were not significant. Over half the mortality during the first 2 years at Jones Mountain was caused by drought; most losses occurred during the first summer (table 1). Approximately 21 percent of total mortality occurred the first winter and was assumed to be winterkill (excessive desiccation of the plant tissues during the winter when tips were exposed to drying winds and the soil was frozen). About 15 percent of the losses were attributed to poor physiological condition of the trees-- inability to produce new roots after field planting. (Stone, 1955). Very little mortality resulted from animals or from frost heaving, which at times may be quite serious. Although deer and elk had browsed 21 to 25 percent of the trees during the 2 years, few were killed directly by browsing.

Table 1.--Causes of mortality at Jones Mountain and A-1 Mountain after two growing seasons

Causes of mortality	Jones Mountain		A-1 Mountain	
	Proportion of trees in sample[1]	Proportion of total mortality	Proportion of trees planted[2]	Proportion of total mortality
Drought	21.8	55.5	8.6	61.8
Physiologically weak[3]	5.8	14.9	2.0	14.6
Winterkill[4]	8.1	20.8	1.6	11.8
Frost heaving	.7	1.8	.08	.6
Missing	1.5	3.9	.16	1.1
Animal	.6	1.6	.55	3.9
Unknown	.6	1.5	.86	6.2
Total	38.8	100.0	13.8	100.0

[1] 1,600 trees.
[2] 1,280 trees.
[3] Trees that did not grow.
[4] Includes all trees that died during the first winter.

Eighty-six percent of the trees were still alive after two growing seasons at A-1 Mountain, with survival ranging from 70 to 96 percent for the various treatments (table 2). Survival was significantly better on scalped than on unscalped plots, but there was no significant difference between scalping treatments. Survival of trees planted to a standard depth with a three-rock mulch was significantly better than that of trees planted by the other three methods, regardless of scalping treatment, except that trees planted in completely scalped plots survived equally well, regardless of planting methods.

Drought was the most important cause of mortality at A-1 Mountain; it accounted for 62 percent of all losses (table 1). About 15 percent of the losses were attributed to poor physiological condition of the stock, and 12 percent to winterkill. Gophers caused about 4 percent of total mortality.

DISCUSSION

Despite one of the driest summers on record, initial survival at A-1 Mountain was excellent. At Jones Mountain, survival was acceptable except for losses caused by competition from grasses.

Precipitation during the summer of 1960 was subnormal especially for the critical months of June and July (table 3). Rainfall for the 2 months at A-1 Mountain was less than one-fourth of the long-term average and less than one-third at Jones Mountain.

Reduced survival at Jones Mountain in comparison with A-1 Mountain is attributed to competition from planted grasses. When trees were planted in April, little herbaceous vegetation was evident at Jones Mountain; by midsummer, however, a luxuriant stand of grass covered the area (fig. 2).

Table 2.--Percent survival by scalping treatment and planting method at A-1 Mountain after two growing seasons

Planting method[1]	Scalping treatment				Average
	Check	16-inch spots	26-inch spots	Complete	
	---------- Percent ----------				
Standard; no mulch	70	84	90	94	84
Standard; mulch	91	96	94	95	94
Deep; no mulch	72	78	84	91	81
Deep; mulch	71	82	94	91	84
Average	76	85	90	93	86

[1] Standard: Root collar at ground line.
  Deep: Terminal bud at ground line.
  Mulch: Three rocks around stem.

Figure 2.--
Stand of orchardgrass (Dacty glomerata L.) at Jones Mou 1961, 1 year after p ponderosa pine.

Table 3.--Comparison of rainfall at Jones Mountain and A-1 Mountain during period April-September 1960, with 50-year average (1909-58) at Fort Valley Experimental Forest

Period compared		Jones Mountain	A-1 Mountain	Fort Valley Experimental Forest
		----- Inches -----		
April	1-15	0.83	0.73	
	16-30	.12	.82	
		.95	1.55	1.47
May	1-15	1.81	.84	
	16-31	.00	.06	
		1.81	.90	.78
June	1-15	.34	.29	
	16-30	.00	.00	
		.34	.29	.67
July	1-15	.08	.27	
	16-31	.59	.28	
		.67	.55	3.04
August	1-15	.87	1.79	
	16-31	2.28	1.55	
September	1-15	1.16	2.44	
	16-30	.13	.00	
		1.29	2.44	1.81

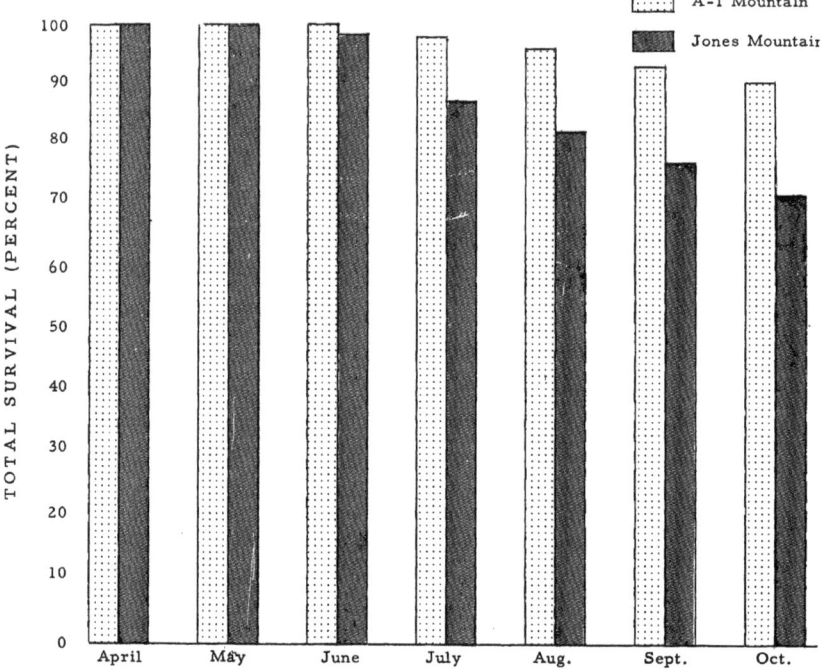

Figure 3.--*Average monthly survival of ponderosa pine transplants at Jones Mountain (October survival estimated) and A-1 Mountain during the first growing season.*

Mortality was negligible until July (fig. 3), when the seeded grasses were growing vigorously and drought conditions had existed for several weeks.

Survival was good on grass-free areas at Jones Mountain. For example, 29 of 31 trees on a fire road were alive and in good condition the second summer. Baron (1962) found in California that, when ponderosa pine is planted a year after grass is seeded, mortality is considerably higher than when the two are introduced at the same time. Mortality is reduced still further when no grass is seeded.

Total mortality was almost three times as high at Jones Mountain as at A-1 Mountain. Although it is not possible to compare the two plantations statistically, some pertinent observations may be made. At Jones Mountain competition was mainly from seeded grasses that grew actively during the spring dry period. At A-1 Mountain the cover was a mixture of brush, grass, and weed species. The grass was mainly mountain muhly, which does not begin active growth until the summer rainy period. Mortality at A-1 Mountain began later in the first summer than at Jones Mountain and was not so severe (fig. 3).

A large percentage of the trees at Jones Mountain were browsed by deer and elk; a few trees were chewed by rabbits at A-1 Mountain. Deer repellents were applied to the transplants at Jones Mountain, but too late to be effective. Although little mortality at Jones Mountain was attributed directly to animals, trees were undoubtedly weakened so that they were much more susceptible to drought and winterkill.

Many small trees died at each plantation. Diameter at the root collar of measured dead transplants at Jones Mountain, A-1 Mountain, and two other plantations in 1961 averaged only 0.17 inch. Very few dead seedlings had diameters greater than 3/16 inch. Clark and Phares (1961) and Klawitter (1961) have emphasized the danger of planting small stock.

A mulch of three rocks helped to increase survival where vegetation was undisturbed, but influenced survival little where vegetation was completely eliminated.

CONCLUSIONS

Adherence to the following practices should improve planting success of ponderosa pine in the Southwest:

1. Use only large planting stock--at least 0.19 inch in diameter at the root collar and a well-developed root system at least 8 inches long.
2. Destroy competing vegetation.
3. Handle planting stock carefully at all stages from the nursery bed to the planting site so only truly live trees will be planted.
4. Protect all plantations from browsing by livestock and game animals.

LITERATURE CITED

Baron, Frank J.
1962. Effects of different grasses on ponderosa pine seedling establishment. U.S. Forest Serv. Pacific Southwest Forest and Range Expt. Sta. Res. Note 199. 8 pp., illus.

Clark, Bryan F., and Phares, Robert E.
1961. Graded stock means greater yields for shortleaf pine. U.S. Forest Serv., Central States Forest Expt. Sta. Tech. Paper 181. 5 pp., illus.

Heidmann, L. J.
1962. Deer repellents are effective on ponderosa pine in the Southwest. Jour. Forestry 61: 53-54, illus.

Klawitter, Ralph A.
1961. Seedling size affects early survival and height growth of planted cypress. U. S. Forest Serv. Southeast Forest Expt. Sta. Res. Note 155. 2 pp., illus.

Pearson, G. A.
1942. Herbaceous vegetation a factor in regeneration of ponderosa pine in the Southwest. Ecol. Monog. 12: 315-338, illus.

Rotty, Roland
1958. Three rocks can contribute to tree planting survival. Florists' Exch. 131 (14):29-39.

Stone, Edward C.
1955. Poor survival and the physiological condition of planting stock. Forest Sci. 1:90-94, illus.

A Seeding Test with Fourwing Saltbush (Chamiza) in Western New Mexico

H. W. Springfield [1]

Fourwing saltbush, generally called chamiza in New Mexico (Atriplex canescens (Pursh) Nutt.) is one of the most important and best known range shrubs in the Southwest. It provides forage the year around and is especially valuable as a source of energy and nutrients for livestock and game during winter and spring.

Seeding of chamiza on rangelands where adapted has been recommended by several investigators (Wilson, 1931; Bridges, 1941 and 1942; Reynolds et al., 1949). Little information is available, however, on how best to prepare the seedbed and plant the seed to obtain satisfactory stands.

This report summarizes results of experiments at one site in western New Mexico to compare the effects of different methods of seeding and seedbed preparation on the establishment, survival, and growth of chamiza.

LITERATURE REVIEW

Studies in New Mexico by Wilson (1931) showed that seed produced near Las Cruces at an elevation of 3,900 feet grew poorly near Galisteo, 220 miles north at an elevation of 6,100 feet. But chamiza grew well from seed collected near Estancia, which is only about 40 miles south of Galisteo. Springfield and

Figure 1.--

Pitting disk in operation.

[1] Range Conservationist, located at the Station's project headquarters at Albuquerque, in cooperation with the University of New Mexico; central headquarters are maintained at Fort Collins in cooperation with Colorado State University.

Housley (1952) found seed collected in northern New Mexico gave better results at sites throughout the State than seed collected in southern New Mexico; also that spring and midsummer seedings were more successful than fall seedings.

Bridges (1941) reported that, of 26 trials with chamiza near Las Cruces, 11 were failures, 15 were partially successful, and 1 produced a good stand. He attributed the failures to poor seedbed preparation and seeding at the wrong time of year, and stated that a seedbed that will help hold the available moisture and also insure proper covering of the seed is apparently necessary.

Anderson and Swanson (1949) described the pitting disk and cultipacker-seeder as efficient companion units that provide for moisture conservation, prepare a firm seedbed, and plant at varying depths in a single operation. Anderson et al. (1957) reported that chamiza is the only shrub that showed any promise for seeding in the desert grassland of the Southwest. They recommended the seed be "de-winged" in a hammermill for easy handling.

In southern Arizona and western Texas, according to Barnes et al. (1958), a pitted seedbed will insure establishment of a grass stand where nonpitted areas result in complete failure, they attributed the difference to increased moisture. Effective life of the pits was found to vary from 4 to 5 years in the Southwest desert to 10 years on the shortgrass plains. Pitting is recommended for native ranges in Wyoming where studies have shown substantially higher forage yields and grazing capacities on pitted range than on unpitted range (Rauzi and Lang, 1956; Lang, 1958; Rauzi et al., 1962).

A number of investigators have reported better grass establishment where some form of packing or soil firming is used. In studies with wheatgrass in Oregon, Hyder et al. (1955) concluded that rolling is a reliable method of covering broadcast seed and firming the seedbed on freshly plowed areas. The operation is limited in efficiency, however, because compaction of the soil above the seed reduces emergence and may restrict germination due to poor aeration. Other studies with wheatgrass in Colorado by McGinnies (1962) showed that cultipacking improved seedling stands. Packing before seeding was better than packing afterwards.

PROCEDURES

The experimental area is located near the Monica Guard Station on the Cibola National Forest, 22 miles southwest of Magdalena, New Mexico. Elevation is 7,500 feet; estimated

Figure 2.--Some methods tested:

A, cultipacker-seeding on unprepared seedbed;

B, cultipacker-seeding on pitted seedbed;

Figure 3.--
Chamiza plants were counted within a milacre and measured in 1962 to determine survival and development.

annual precipitation is 12 inches; and the soil is a shallow, gravelly loam. Native vegetation consists principally of blue grama (Boutelona gracilis (H.B.K.) Lag.), ring muhly (Muhlenbergia torreyi (Kunth) Hitchc.), three-awns (Aristida spp.), wolftail (Lycurus phleoides H.B.K.), broom snakeweed (Gutierrezia sarothrae (Pursh) Britt. & Rusby), and widely scattered juniper (Juniperus spp.) trees. Relative amounts and composition of the native grass cover in 1951 were as follows:

	Ground cover, line intercept (Percent)	Yield, air-dry (Pounds per acre)
Blue grama	6.2	96
Three-awn	.6	12
Wolftail	.1	7
Ring muhly	.6	Not clipped

Two methods of seeding and four kinds of seedbeds were compared. Methods of seeding included: (a) drilling and (b) cultipacker-seeding. Seedbeds were prepared by: (1) plowing, (2) pitting, (3) plowing and pitting, (4) no cultural treatment.

Field plots were arranged in two blocks with a split-plot design. Seedbed-preparation plots were 16 1/2 by 132 feet, or 1/20 acre. Each method-of-seeding plot, which embraced four of these smaller plots, was 66 by 132 feet. A constant seeding rate of 20 pounds or 250,000 viable seeds per acre was used for all comparisons. The chamiza seed obtained from the U.S. Soil Conservation Service

C, cultipacker-seeding on plowed seedbed;

D, drilling on unprepared seedbed and (foreground) pitted seedbed.

Nursery near Albuquerque and dewinged in a hammermill had been collected from shrubs planted June 25-29, 1951.

Plots were plowed with a two-disk plow pulled by a small, wheel-type tractor. The disks were 26 inches in diameter. The soil was plowed to a depth of 5-6 inches, and pitting was done with a "cutaway" disk.[2] About half of each disk had been cut off, and the disks were arranged on the main shaft so that the cut half of adjacent disks faced in opposite directions. Pits prepared with this implement were about 4 to 6 inches deep, 8 to 12 inches wide, 24 to 30 inches long, and 18 inches apart. The soil was very dry and became almost powdery after it was plowed or pitted.

Seed was drilled with a regular 6 1/2-foot grain drill. The drill was equipped with single-disk furrow openers and drag chains, but no depth regulators. Cultipacker-seeding was done with a special seeder.[2] The rear set of rollers was shifted 2 inches so as to run in the same track as the front rollers. Small seed hoppers were so mounted that the seed fell into the grooves made by the first roller and were pressed into the soil and covered by the rear roller. Equipment used in the experiment and types of seedbed prepared are shown in figures 1 and 2.

After the experimental site was seeded, it was fenced to exclude livestock. Rabbits, however, were not excluded.

Results of the experimental seedings were evaluated by various means in 1951, 1952, 1953, and 1962. On August 29, 1951, chamiza seedlings were counted in a 1-foot-square frame located randomly 20 times in each plot.

In October 1952 and 1953, yield of the young chamiza stands was estimated on ten 9.6-square-foot circular plots located at random within each seeded area. Yield in grams per plot was estimated by the weight-estimate method.

[2] *The Nursery Division, U. S. Soil Conservation Service, Albuquerque, New Mexico, furnished the cutaway disk and cultipacker-seeder. The cultipacker-seeder was a special seeder constructed by Joe Downs and Darwin Anderson of SCS.*

In August 1962, survival and development of chamiza plants were determined by plant counts and measurements. A milacre sampling frame, 6.6 feet square, was located at random 15 times within each plot. Height and diameter of every plant in the plot were measured to the nearest inch (fig. 3).

RESULTS

Seedling Emergence and Early Growth

Emergence of chamiza 2 months after seeding varied from 5.2 to 60.1 seedlings per milacre:

Method of seedbed preparation	Grain drill	Cultipacker-seeder
	(Number of seedlings per milacre)	
None	9.6	5.2
Pitted	24.0	30.5
Plowed	29.6	60.1
Plowed-pitted	25.3	48.8

Though the number of seedlings on pitted, plowed, or plowed and pitted seedbeds ranged from 24 to 60 per milacre, average differences were not significant. As might be expected, however, significantly fewer seedlings emerged on unprepared seedbeds. It is of interest that nearly half as many seedlings emerged on an unprepared seedbed as on a pitted seedbed where the seed was drilled into the soil.

In an overall comparison, seedling emergence on plots seeded with a cultipacker-seeder was about the same as that where the seed was drilled. There was a trend, however, toward more seedlings wherever the cultipacker-seeder had been used on loose seedbeds. Drilling on a plowed or plowed-pitted seedbed may have covered some seed too deeply. On unprepared seedbeds, however, drilling apparently resulted in better seed placement and coverage than did the cultipacker-seeder.

Production of the young chamiza stands, determined from estimates in 1952 and 1953, was significantly higher on plowed and plowed-pitted seedbeds than on the other two kinds of

Table 1.--Production of young chamiza stands by method of seedbed preparation and method of seeding

Method of seedbed preparation	Production of chamiza (estimated air-dry weight per acre)			
	Grain drill		Cultipacker-seeder	
	1952	1953	1952	1953
	-------- Pounds --------			
None	20	71		30
Pitted	39	112	21	97
Plowed	102	257	91	222
Plowed-pitted	100	205	87	239

seedbeds (table 1). Apparently, moisture relations on the plowed seedbeds were more favorable for establishment and growth of the young plants. The difference in yield between pitted and unprepared seedbeds was not significant. Neither was the difference between seeding methods.

Yields in 1953, when the chamiza stands were 2 years old, were twice as high on plowed seedbeds as on pitted seedbeds. The yield of native grasses on the untreated check plots that year averaged only 115 pounds per acre, compared with chamiza yields of more than 200 pounds per acre on plowed seedbeds and about 100 pounds on pitted seedbeds.

Condition of 11-Year-Old Stands

Eleven years after the plots were seeded, some differences among chamiza stands were still evident (fig. 4). A significantly greater number of plants was present on prepared than on unprepared seedbeds:

Method of seedbed preparation	Grain drill	Cultipacker-seeder
	(Number of seedlings per milacre)	
None	5.0	5.2
Pitted	11.6	10.4
Plowed	11.2	13.2
Plowed-pitted	9.4	16.4

No differences in number of plants were measured, however, among pitted, plowed, or plowed-pitted seedbeds.

Comparisons of the two seeding methods indicated better stands where cultipacker-seeding was used on plowed seedbeds and where drilling was used on pitted seedbeds. Beneficial effects of cultipacker-seeding were especially noticeable on plowed-pitted seedbeds. This may be explained by the firmer seedbeds and better moisture relations obtained from cultipacker-seeding than those from drilling into the loose soil left by plowing and pitting.

Density of stocking of all stands on the prepared seedbeds was considered fully satisfactory. Standards proposed for chamiza stands, based on limited study, are as follows: Good stand--more than 6,000 mature plants per acre; Fair stand--1,000 to 6,000 plants per acre; Poor stand--less than 1,000 plants per acre. By these standards, the stands on unprepared seedbeds were fair and those on prepared seedbeds were good.

The number of dead chamiza plants present in 1962 was low on all plots--from 0.4 to 1.2 percent of the total number of plants observed. Despite this evidence of low mortality, many seedlings that emerged in 1951 failed to become established or died during the intervening years. Fewer than half the

Unprepared seedbed					Pitted

GRAIN DRILL

Figure 4.--
Appearance of chamiza stands in August 1962, 11 years after they were seeded by different methods.

Plowed					Plowed-pitted

Unprepared seedbed   Pitted

CULTIPACKER-SEEDER

Plowed   Plowed-pitted

seedlings present on prepared seedbeds in 1951 survived as mature plants in 1962, as shown below:

Method of seedbed preparation	Survival (Percent)
Pitted	41.4
Plowed	29.9
Plowed-pitted	35.4

These figures suggest that pitting may have aided plant survival.

Young plants of chamiza--plants that became established several years subsequent to 1951--were relatively numerous. In general, their number in 1962 was proportional to the number of mature chamiza plants present:

Method of seedbed preparation	Mature plants	Young plants
	(Number per milacre)	
None	5.1	0.9
Pitted	11.0	2.6
Plowed	12.2	2.1
Plowed-pitted	12.9	2.8

Native grasses became reestablished in pits and on plowed areas during the 11-year period. Although the extent of this recovery was not evaluated, it may have affected survival and growth of chamiza.

Plant Heights and Diameters

Average heights of chamiza plants in 1962 were about the same, regardless of the method of seedbed preparation or seeding (table 2). None of the apparent differences was significant.

Diameters of individual plant crowns likewise were nearly the same. Crowns of plants on unprepared seedbeds were as large as those on pitted or plowed seedbeds.

Crown Cover of Chamiza Stands

Crown cover of shrub stands is usually a reliable index to the amount of browse available and to the effectiveness of the stands for soil protection. Cover of the seeded stands at Monica was computed by multiplying average crown area of individual plants by the average number of plants per milacre plot. Crowns were assumed to be circular.

Crown-cover measurements in 1962 indicate that chamiza cover on prepared seedbeds was substantially better than on the unprepared seedbed (fig. 5). While figure 5 shows greater crown cover on the plowed and plowed-pitted areas than on the area pitted only, these greater cover measurements were not significant.

Table 2.--Average heights and diameters of chamiza plants in 1962

Method of seedbed preparation	Average height		Average diameter	
	Grain drill	Cultipacker-seeder	Grain drill	Cultipacker-seeder
	------------ Inches ------------			
None	12.3	10.7	11.8	11.2
Pitted	10.9	10.4	10.8	10.5
Plowed	13.0	11.8	12.3	11.7
Plowed-pitted	13.8	10.6	12.8	10.5

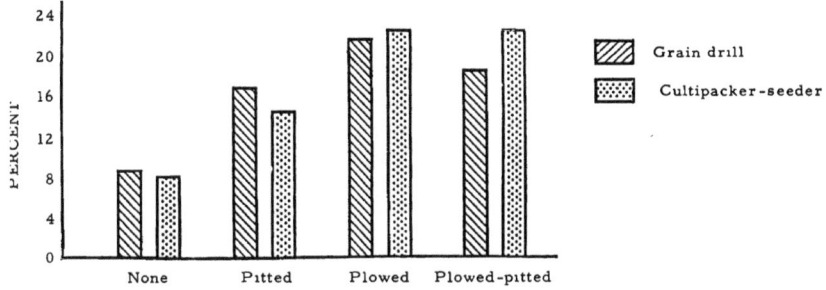

Figure 5.--
Crown cover of chamiza stands in 1962.

Weather conditions no doubt affected the success of the test seedings. Precipitation at the nearest Weather Bureau stations, Magdalena (38 years of record) and Augustine (24 years of record), was below average during the first 6 years:

Year	Magdalena	Augustine
	(Inches of precipitation)	
1951	6.42	7.71
1952	9.13	9.37
1953	8.20	8.35
1954	10.19	10.54
1955	8.31	7.99
1956	7.24	4.22
1957	13.64	13.27
1958	12.60	9.32
1959	15.38	7.72
1960	9.68	12.51
1961	12.49	11.30
Average:		
11-yr.	10.30	9.30
Long-term	12.36	11.02

During the 11-year period, 1951 through 1961, precipitation at Magdalena was less than the long-term average 7 years and at Augustine it was below average 8 years. Growth of the chamiza plants probably was curtailed because of the relatively dry weather that prevailed.

Growth of chamiza may also have been influenced by conditions of the soil and native plant cover. Soils at Monica are underlain by a compact caliche layer at depths of 10 to 16 inches. No chamiza plants are found naturally near the experimental site. The closest native stands are on somewhat deeper soils several miles away. A fairly dense native grass cover at Monica no doubt had some effect on establishment and growth of the chamiza, particularly where the seedbed was not prepared (fig. 6).

CONCLUSIONS

Seedbed preparation probably is necessary to obtain good stands of chamiza in western New Mexico. Although plants were successfully established by drilling or cultipacker-seeding on an unprepared seedbed, the resulting stands were much poorer than those on prepared seedbeds.

Under certain conditions, the seeding of chamiza on unprepared seedbeds could be a worthwhile practice. For example, many ranges in the Southwest support a satisfactory cover of herbaceous plants but no browse. On such ranges, particularly those reserved for winter grazing, drilling chamiza into the undisturbed herbaceous cover might result in a fair stand of browse needed to supplement the animal diet.

Figure 6.-- Native ground cover o this untreated chec plot in 1962, as i 1961, was mainly blu grama with a few pla of ring muhly, three awn, and wolftail (Chamiza stand at lef was established b cultipacker-seeding o a pitted seedbed).

Of the methods of seedbed preparation tested, none proved definitely superior. Where the native cover is composed mainly of undesirable plants, plowing probably would be preferable. But where there is a remnant stand of desirable species, pitting is perhaps better than plowing. Although in this study pitting gave no advantage over plowing, the method deserves consideration because it damages only about a third of the native cover and is cheaper than plowing.

Neither of the two methods of seeding tested was found generally superior. The results suggest that drilling is a better method for seeding unprepared or pitted seedbeds, however, while cultipacker-seeding is better for seeding loose seedbeds.

LITERATURE CITED

Anderson, Darwin, and Swanson, A. R.
    1949. Machinery for seedbed preparation and seeding on Southwestern ranges. Jour. Range Mangt. 2: 64-66, illus.

_____, Hamilton, Louis P., Reynolds, Hudson G., and Humphrey, Robert R.
    1957. Reseeding desert grassland ranges in southern Arizona. Ariz. Agr. Expt. Sta. Bul. 249, 32 pp., illus.

Barnes, Oscar K., Anderson, Darwin, an Heerwagen, Arnold.
    1958. Pitting for range improvement i the Great Plains and the Southwest Desert Regions. U. S. Dept. Agr. Prod. Res. Rpt. 23, 17 pp., illus.

Bridges, J. O.
    1941. Reseeding trials on arid range land. N. Mex. Agr. Expt. Sta. Bul. 278, 48 pp., illus.

_____
    1942. Reseeding practices for New Mexico ranges. N. Mex. Agr. Expt. Sta. Bul. 291, 48 pp., illus.

Hyder, Donald H., Sneva, Forrest A., and Sawyer, W. A.
    1955. Soil firming may improve range seeding operations. Jour. Range Mangt. 8: 159-163, illus.

Lang, Robert L.
    1958. Range-pitting trials in the Big Horn Mountains of Wyoming. Wyo. Agr. Expt. Sta. Bul. 357, 7 pp., illus.

McGinnies, William J.
    1962. Effect of seedbed firming on the establishment of crested wheatgrass seedlings. Jour. Range Mangt. 15: 230-234.

Rauzi, Frank, and Lang, R. L.
    1956. Improving shortgrass range by pitting. Wyo. Agr. Expt. Sta. Bul. 344, 11 pp., illus.

_____, Lang, R. L., and Becker, C. F.
    1962. Mechanical treatments on shortgrass rangeland. Wyo. Agr. Expt. Sta. Bul. 396, 16 pp., illus.

Reynolds, H. G., Lavin, F., and Springfield, H. W.
    1949. Preliminary guide for range reseeding in Arizona and New Mexico. U.S. Forest Serv. Southwest Forest and Range Expt. Sta. Res. Rpt. 7, 14 pp., illus.

Springfield, H. W., and Housley, R. M., Jr.
    1952. Chamiza for reseeding New Mexico rangelands. U. S. Forest Serv. Southwest Forest and Range Expt. Sta. Res. Note 122, 3 pp., illus.

Wilson, C. P.
    1931. The artificial reseeding of New Mexico ranges. N. Mex. Agr. Expt. Sta. Bul. 189, 37 pp., illus.

sive Runoff Plot[1]

Hickey, Jr.,[2] and E. J. Dortignac[3]

SIZE AND SHAPE OF PLOTS

The ideal plot for measuring surface runoff and erosion is a miniature natural watershed. Unfortunately, watersheds of similar size and shape with homogeneous soil, geology, plant cover, and microclimate are seldom available. Each watershed is a distinct entity and behaves in a separate manner in regard to runoff and erosion. This is also true of surface runoff plots with artificial boundaries or borders. Yet, plots do provide an opportunity for testing or evaluating different plant treatments and conditions on areas with reasonably similar soil, geology, and microclimate.

Size of plot has a marked effect on the measured runoff and erosion. But the actual amount of surface runoff and erosion from plots is less important than measured differences between plots or treatments.

Runoff plots have been built in a square or rectangular shape. Square plots have the advantage that the ratio of plot border to plot area is less than for rectangular plots. The main advantage of a rectangular plot is that a longer slope is provided for a given area.

In this study, it was decided that each plot (fig. 1) should be at least 10 feet wide to reduce border disturbance and border effects on microclimate. Also, a wider plot would make it difficult to measure and evaluate changes in vegetation and surface soil conditions without walking or standing inside the plot. The plot length used was 30 to 32 feet (angled lower edge, fig. 1). This provided 310 square feet of runoff area.

PLOT CONSTRUCTION

Several kinds of construction were tried, but a runoff plot with the following features proved most efficient and economical.

Borders

Rough lumber treated with a wood preservative provided the cheapest and most

32 ft.

Plot borders
(1- by 8-in boards)

Figure 4.--
Calking compound
seals corners and
knotholes.

Collection trough
(4-in. sewer pipe,
12 ft. long)

Runoff pipe to
catchment basin
(2-in. plastic hose,
8 ft. long)

Water and sediment
storage tank
(55-gal. steel drum)

Figure 5.--
Soil is sifted
into the crack
between board and
plot.

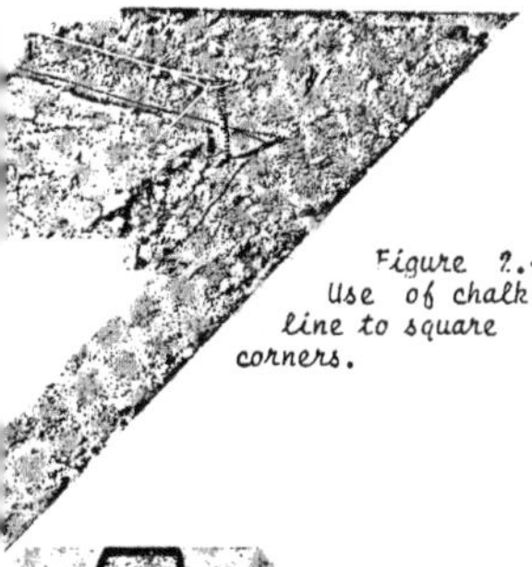

Figure 2.--
Use of chalk
line to square
corners.

Figure 6.--
Soil is sloped and compacted on outside edge of plot.

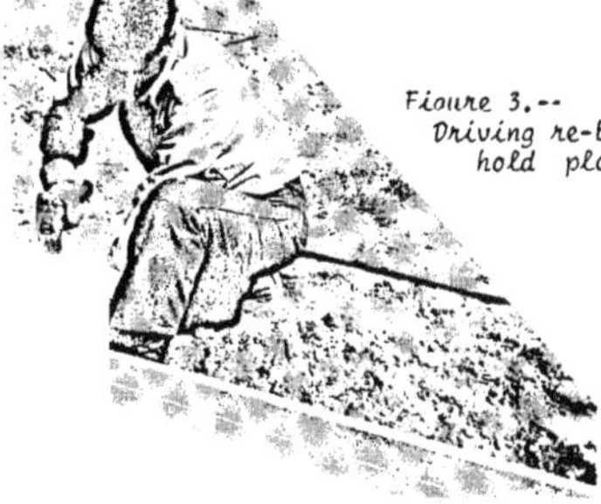

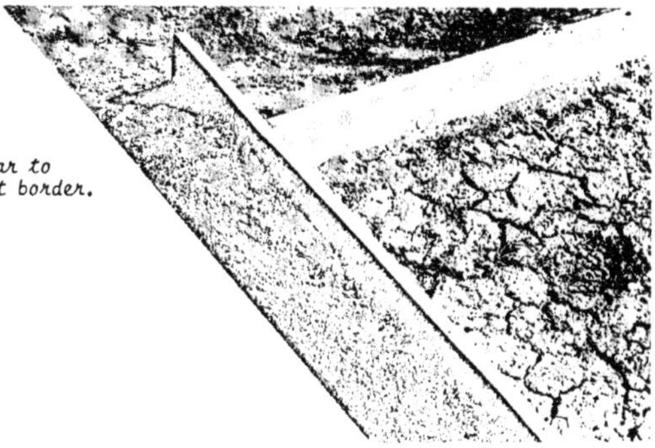

Figure 3.--
Driving re-bar to
hold plot border.

Figure 7.--
Sealing the hose connector to the collection trough.

Collection Trough

Runoff water and sediment were collected by a slotted trough made from 4-inch sewer pipe, made of paper impregnated with asphalt. This pipe permitted muddy water to flow naturally over the trough-soil interface, enter, and flow freely down the pipe into the storage tanks or drums.

The installation of the collection trough required one 12-foot length of sewer pipe, two sealed couplings, one plastic hose connector, one radiator hose clamp, two re-bars, some plastic cement, and the following hand tools:

1. A pruning saw for use in cutting a 2-inch strip from the sealed couplings.

2. Brace and expansion bit to drill a hole for the plastic hose connector.

3. Two types of hammers -- a claw hammer for general use and a 4-pound hammer for driving re-bars into the ground.

4. A 2-foot level for obtaining a slope on the sewer pipe to insure proper drainage.

The collection trough was constructed by sawing a 2-inch slot along the length of a 12-foot section of pipe. The pipe ends were sealed with caps constructed from sewer-pipe couplings that had one end nailed closed with a wood disk. The caps were sealed both inside and out with plastic cement. A 2-inch strip was cut from each cap to coincide with the slot in the pipe.

A 3-inch-diameter expansion bit was used to drill a hole in the pipe for inserting the hose connector. The hose connector was sealed in the hole, flush with the inside of the pipe, with plastic cement (fig. 7).

A shallow trench was dug angling toward the lower edge of the plot. The pipe was placed in this trench, with the hose connector at the lower end, and held there by iron re-bars driven into the ground on the downhill side. The lower edge of the 2-inch slot was placed flush with the soil surface (fig. 8). The soil at the lip of the collection trough was tamped and sealed to the pipe with polyester resin. This prevented runoff water from undercutting the collection trough. A 2-inch plastic hose was clamped to the connector in the pipe with a radiator hose clamp (fig. 9). This hose, which led to the catchment basin, was placed in a 12-inch trench to prevent livestock damage by trampling.

Figure 8.--
Making the collection trough flush with the soil surface.

COST OF RUNOFF PLOTS

Surface runoff plots as described are relatively inexpensive. Cost of plot materials approximates $26. Materials needed with specifications and prices [5] are tabulated below.

Item	Cost
4 steel drums (55 gallon)	([6])
12 ft. impregnated-fiber sewer pipe w/couplings @ 38¢	$4.56
4 steel 6 ft. posts (for drum anchorage) @ 93¢	3.72
Plastic cement	.03
8 radiator hose clamps @ 17¢	1.36
9 hose connections (2 in.) @ 52¢	4.68
74 ft. lumber @ $44/M bd.-ft.	3.26
Cutting and welding (Lids and couplings) @ $3.50/hr.	2.00
8 ft. plastic hose (2 in.) @ 38¢	3.04
22 iron re-bars @ 17¢	3.74
Wood preservative	.15
Total	$26.54

The construction and installation of each surface runoff plot required 1 man-day of labor, based on the construction of 84 plots by a 2-man team.

OTHER MATERIALS TESTED

Other less expensive materials were tested to determine which functioned most efficiently. Methods of construction and types of materials were tested throughout the fall and winter of 1958-59.

[5] *Costs are for April 1962 at Albuquerque, New Mexico.*

[6] *Barrels were acquired free of charge from Government surplus stocks.*

Figure 11.--
Soil mound border was unsatisfactory.

Plot Borders

A soil ridge or mound was first tried as a plot border (fig. 11). Soil was mounded to a chalk line at a height of 8 inches. Although this method was the most economical, the borders were disturbed by the trampling of livestock. Also, wind and rain eroded the borders, which increased the sediment load of surface runoff. This method was discarded.

In the second method, 1-by-8-inch rough lumber was used for plot borders. The boards were placed in a 3-inch trench along the plot boundaries and secured in place with 2-foot iron re-bars. Loose soil was tamped in the fissures along the soil-board interface. Soil was tamped outside the wood borders to the original ground level (fig. 12). This method was rejected because the boards alone were not sufficiently rigid to withstand the disturbances by grazing livestock and the action of wind and rain.

The third method was similar to the second, but provided additional support to the wood borders by banking soil against the boards outside the plots (fig. 13). This method proved quite satisfactory, as it gave the additional support and protection needed against wind action and trampling livestock.

Collection Troughs

Three methods of collecting runoff and sediment were tried.

Diversion toward the middle at the lower end of the runoff plot by the use of a V-shaped border (fig. 12) was discarded for two reasons: (1) runoff concentration at the apex of the V necessitated too large a trough and hose, and (2) a great deal of trouble was encountered with litter clogging the V.

In the second method, a collection trough the width of the plot was placed perpendicular to the long axis of the plot. Since the terrain even on small plots usually slopes one way or the other, an excessive amount of soil disturbance was necessary within the confines of the plot itself. This method was also discarded.

The third method was essentially the same as the second except that the trough was placed at an angle across the lower end of the plot. Direction of the angle conformed to the slope of the terrain. This method functioned well and required a minimum of soil disturbance.

Figure 12.--
Wood border alone was unsatisfactory.

Figure 13.--
Wood border banked with soil on outside proved the most effective. Note the V-shaped collection trough.

A, *polyethylene sheeting;*

B, *roofing ridge;*

D, *wooden frame;*

F, *impregnated-fiber sewer pipe.*

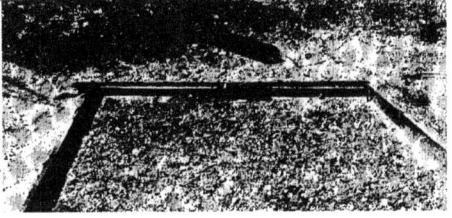

SUMMARY

Construction and installation of a simple, inexpensive runoff plot for measuring surface runoff and erosion are described. One-by-eight-inch boards are used for the frame, supported by dirt mounded against the outside. A slotted, impregnated-fiber sewer pipe 4 inches in diameter forms the collection trough at an angle across the bottom of the 10-by-30-foot plot. Runoff flows by gravity through a hose into collection barrels in a trench.

The materials considered best cost roughly $26 per plot. One man-day was required to build one of these plots. Several other materials and shapes of collection troughs tested were discarded as impractical.

Eighty-four of these surface runoff plots have been in constant operation for 4 years. To date, no repairs have been necessary (fig. 15). Maintenance consists simply of removing Russianthistle plants that collect in the trenches, and an occasional mouse nest in the collection troughs.

Figure 15.--Corner of plot border and collection trough 4 years after installation. No maintenance was needed.

Height-age Curves for Austrian Pine in Windbreaks on Loess Soils of Nebraska

D. H. Sander[1]

Austrian pine (Pinus nigra austriaca, Schneid) is an important component of many Nebraska windbreaks. This species is relatively fast growing, provides good windbreak density in both summer and winter, and is relatively free of insects and diseases.

This note reports the heights that Austrian pines have attained at different ages on a range of sites, and a means of rating site capability or site quality.

Study methods were similar to those previously used for ponderosa pine.[2] Tree heights at 2-year intervals were obtained by measuring internodes along the entire stem of each tree. Only dominant trees that were free to grow and represent maximum site potential were measured. No suppressed or otherwise damaged trees were used. Heights were plotted against ages for each tree, and the resulting family of growth curves was smoothed by regression methods. Site capability was expressed as height at 20 years of age (fig. 1).

Five trees were sampled on each site, except for one site with low site capability and one site in the 54-year age class. Trees sampled by age classes were:

Age class (Years)	Trees (Number)	Sites (Number)
6 to 20	99	21
22	59	13
26 to 30	16	4
34 to 54	11	3

Sampling sites were well distributed throughout the Loess Plains region of Nebraska. Trees that had been planted 22 years or less were sampled in field windbreaks. Older pines (26 to 54 years) were sampled from farmstead windbreaks.

Figure 1 shows the smoothed curves up to age 54. The data indicate Austrian pine grows relatively rapidly during the first 20 years after planting--approximately 1 foot per year on the average site. The growth rate decreased 0.025 foot per year on the average site, which results in a growth rate of only 0.2 to 0.3 foot per year 50 years after planting.

The height growth of Austrian pine in the Loess Plains of Nebraska compares favorably with height growth in Europe up to age 50 years. According to Petri,[3] total height of

Austrian pine growing in the Rheinland-Pfalz is quite similar at 50 years of age to that attained in Nebraska. Height growth in Europe was slower, however, during the early years, and faster after 40 to 50 years. Petri's data were based on 21 Austrian pine provenances sampled on a variety of sites.

The curves are fairly accurate for predicting site capability and future height of windbreak trees. Statistical errors are of two kinds: (1) the error inherent in smoothing height-age curves or the failure of all trees to conform to a uniform curve, and (2) the error involved in measuring trees in the field due to variability in tree heights. The error in predicting site capability or total height reduces from ±5.4 feet at 6 years to ±0.9 foot at 18 years with a five-tree sample. The small sample size for ages 30 through 54 prevented accurate evaluation of the error in that age range. Sample data, however, fit the curves well.

[1] *Soil Scientist,* located at the Station's project headquarters at Lincoln in cooperation with the University of Nebraska; central headquarters are maintained at Fort Collins in cooperation with Colorado State University.

[2] Sander, D. H. *Growth curves for ponderosa pine in Nebraska windbreaks.* U. S. Forest Serv Rocky Mountain Forest and Range Expt. Sta. Res Note 82, 3 pp., illus. 1962.

[3] Petri, H. *Wachstumsverhältnisse der Schwarzkiefer im nördlichen Rheinland-Pfalz* Forstarchiv 32 (10), (201-6). 16 refs. 1961.

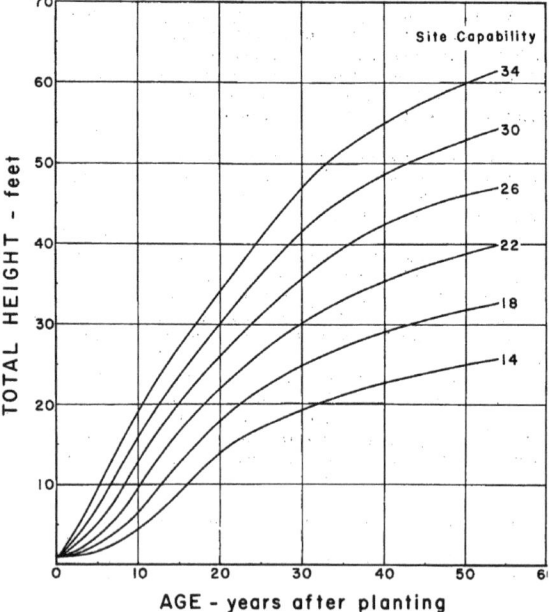

Figure 1.--
Height-age curves for Austrian pines in Nebraska windbreaks. Site capability is expressed as height in feet at 20 years after planting.

of Rain Gages

Jr., and George Garcia[1]

a measuring stick must be used, or the gage must be unbolted and its contents poured into a graduate or other container for weighing. If snowfall is not likely to be a problem, the length and corresponding weight can be reduced considerably, depending on (1) amount of precipitation likely to be encountered, and (2) frequency with which the gages are to be emptied.

An alternative design to make weighing easier consists basically of an open standard rain gage locked inside a steel pipe or oil-well casing embedded in concrete (fig. 2). Thus the gage can be removed from its bullet-proof case and weighed, but it has two disadvantages compared to the previous design: (1) an early freeze can rupture the gage, and (2) a determined vandal could knock the bottom out of the gage or batter in the projecting collar.

Hiding or camouflaging a rain gage seems to invite trouble. A well-kept gage, painted a pleasing color, posted with a prominent sign in a conspicuous place creates the impression that it is serving a useful purpose. The gage should be painted with a good rust preventative. Red lead paint has been recommended as the best. Aluminum paint may be used, but requires more frequent maintenance.

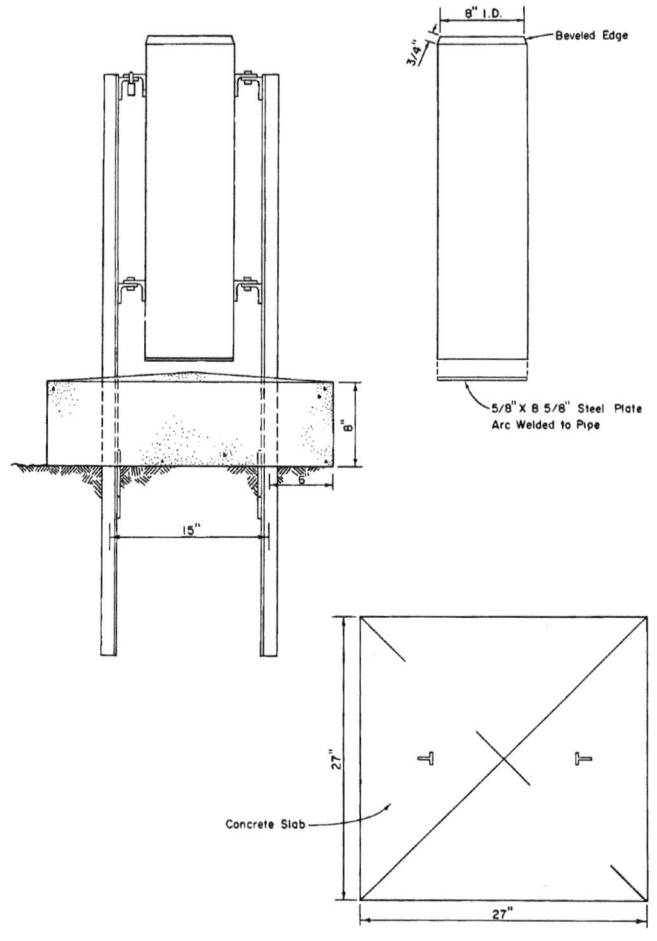

Figure 1.--Tamper-proof case made of steel pipe.

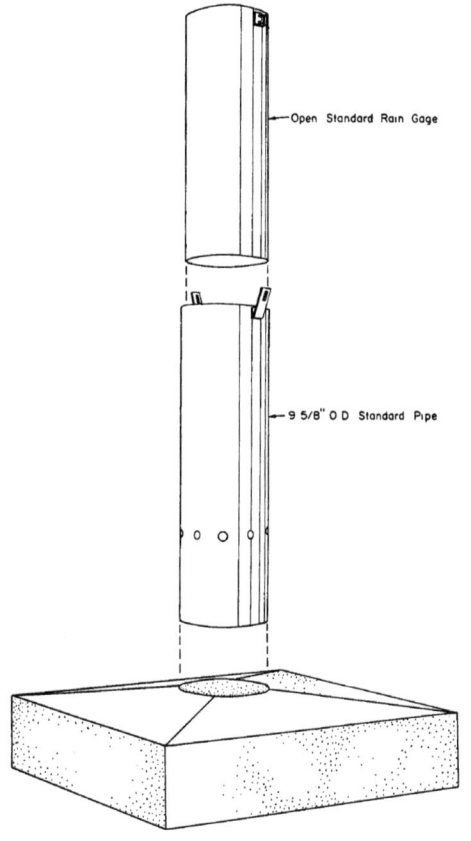

Figure 2.--Standard gage inside a steel casing.

Construction Details

The following materials are required for the steel-pipe gage described first:

Quantity	Item	Size
1	8-inch inside diameter standard steel pipe	30 inches long
1	Circular steel plate	5/8 inch thick × 7 5/8 inches in diameter
2	Steel fenceposts	5 feet long
8	"L" brackets	1/4 inch × 2 inches
3	Bolts	3/8 inch × 1 inch
3	Padlock	
1	Concrete slab	27 × 27 × 8 inches

The circular steel plate is arc welded to one end of the steel pipe. A 3/4-inch bevel is ground on the other end of the pipe. With a little care, a knife edge superior to that usually found on most commercial gages may be obtained.

Four of the "L" brackets are then welded to the steel fenceposts. One should be welded flush with the top of each post and another 20 inches below. The remaining four brackets are then welded to the rain gage on opposite sides and 20 inches apart so they will coincide with those on the fenceposts.

The two steel posts are then driven 20 inches into the ground 15 inches apart. This distance may vary slightly, since the distribution of holes in the 1/4-inch "L" brackets may vary with the manufacturer.

A 27- by 27- by 8-inch concrete slab is then poured around the steel fenceposts. The slab should be sloped four ways from the center to reduce splash and allow for runoff. This size slab is probably the minimum if only poor concrete sand is available. Extreme pressure on the steel posts causes smaller slabs to crack. The size can be reduced, however, if better quality sand and gravel are available.

The rain gage is then bolted and padlocked to the brackets on the fenceposts.

For the standard gage locked within the steel case, the following materials are required:

Quantity	Item	Size
1	Open standard rain gage	30 inches
1	Standard pipe or oil well casing (9 5/8 inches, outside diameter)	34 inches
2	Hasps (hinged straps and staples)	6 inches
1	Padlock	
1	Bolt	1/2 inch × 1 inch
1	Concrete slab	27 × 27 × 8 inches

A series of 1/2-inch holes are bored around the steel casing 9 inches above the bottom edge. The two hinged straps are then welded on opposite sides to the upper edge of the casing. The two staples are welded on opposite sides of the rain gage to the lower edge of the 4-inch collar.

The steel casing is placed on the ground at the desired location and leveled with a hand level. A 27- by 27-inch concrete slab is then poured around the casing. The concrete should be sloped four ways from the bottom edge of the holes in the casing to a height of 8 inches at the outer edges. The rain gage is placed inside the steel casing and bolted and padlocked by the two hasps, which hold the gage in a vertical position and prevent its removal.

[1] *Research Foresters, located at the Station's project headquarters in Albuquerque, in cooperation with the University of New Mexico; central headquarters are maintained at Fort Collins, in cooperation with Colorado State University.*

. DEPARTMENT OF AGRICULTURE

Controlling Cane Cactus with 2,4-DP

by

George Garcia and Wayne C. Hickey, Jr.[1]

Cane cactus, Opuntia spinosior (Engelm. & Bigel.) Tourney, is an aggressive cholla cactus in the Southwest, particularly at lower elevations. Terminal joints that fall to the ground take root readily when surface moisture conditions are adequate. Impenetrable thickets often encroach on valuable grazing land and compete for moisture and nutrients with more useful vegetative types.

Mechanical control of the cane cactus is difficult because of its unusual sprouting characteristic. As late as 1959 no herbicides were available to control cholla cacti economically on extensive areas.[2]

In 1961 an area was sprayed with 2,4,5-T acetic acid in a 25-percent solution; it showed only a 50-percent kill 1 year after treatment.[3]

When a new herbicide, 2,4-DP (R-H Brush Rhap LV-4-DP),[4] was applied on cane cactus in 1961 and 1962, a 95- to 100-percent kill resulted. Within 2 days after spraying, plants showed discoloration; by the fourth day, they wilted and drooped; at the end of 2 weeks, no signs of life could be detected. Reexamination in November 1963 of the areas sprayed in 1961 and in 1962 revealed that no resprouting had occurred (fig. 1).

Figure 1.--Cane cactus plant sprayed with 2,4-DP. Six days after spraying, some of the smaller terminal joints had fallen to the ground.

Research reported here was conducted in cooperation with the Bureau of Land Management, U. S. Department of the Interior.

Methods of Application

Three types of sprayers were used, all of which gave satisfactory results. Varying the droplet size from a fine mist to large drops apparently had no effect on the percent kill; the important factor was to cover the plant completely with the herbicide solution.

In the first trial in 1961, a garden-type hand sprayer with a 1 1/2-gallon tank capacity was used. This low-pressure, compressed-air sprayer with built-in pump produced fairly large droplets.

A power mist blower, which blows out a large volume of air at high speed, was also used. Atomizing nozzles inject a small amount of liquid solution into the airstream; the spray was easily adjusted from a fog or mist to large droplets. This lightweight, rugged sprayer with a 2.77-gallon tank capacity, was easily backpacked.

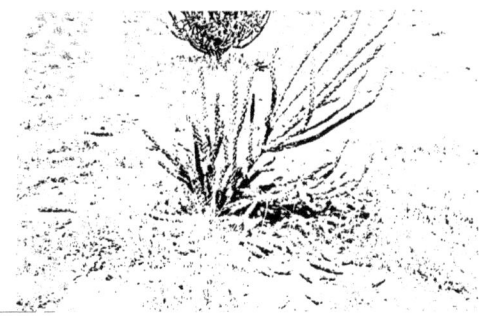

In 1962, 400 acres were sprayed by a power sprayer on a two-wheeled trailer pulled with a pickup truck. A one-cylinder air-cooled engine powered the air compressor and an agitator inside the spray tank. Attached to the compressor were two high-pressure hoses with spray guns on which the spray was easily adjusted from a mist to large droplets. Areas inaccessible by truck were sprayed with a portable mist blower.

Date of Application

In 1961, a spraying was done at two different times: one in May as soon as new growth began, another 30 days later. The 1962 spraying was done when new growth first became visible (May).

Percentage kill was the same, but the plants sprayed when the cacti were just beginning new growth responded faster than those sprayed 30 days later.

Rate of Application

Several mixtures were used, including the following combinations, by part:

2,4-DP	Diesel Oil	Water
1	8	16
1	1	22
1	0	23
1/3	1	22-2/3
1	3	20

In the 1961 trials, a mixture of 1 part 2,4-DP, 8 parts diesel oil, and 16 parts water was used. Most of the 400-acre spraying job in 1962 was done with 1 part herbicide, 3 parts diesel oil, and 20 parts water.

The number of gallons per acre varied with the density and size of the cacti, but 1 gallon was usually sufficient to cover 14 to 20 plants.

Variations in the percentage of water used did not affect the results. Reductions in the amount of diesel oil produced no change in plant reaction or percent kill, but eliminating it completely doubled the time of plant reac-

U.S. FOREST SERVICE

Notes on the Introduction of

Deciduous Tamarisk[1]

Jerome S. Horton[2]

Several species of deciduous tamarisk were introduced into the United States during the last century. One of these species, <u>Tamarix pentandra</u> Pallas, has become aggressively naturalized and now occupies extensive areas of flood-plain lands (Robinson, 1958). Another species, <u>Tamarix gallica</u> L. has become naturalized in coastal lands along the Gulf of Mexico. A third species, <u>Tamarix tetrandra</u> Pallas, is still widely used as an ornamental shrub. Taxonomy of the deciduous species has been greatly confused in the past and is still subject to considerable research.

Nurserymen in the early 1800's were apparently the first to introduce tamarisk into the United States. In 1823, tamarisk was offered for sale in New York City by the Old American Nursery operated by Lawrence & Mills. Bartram's in Philadelphia was selling tamarisk by 1828. During the 1830's several nurseries along the eastern seaboard included tamarisk among their ornamental shrubs.

The National Agricultural Library (formerly U. S. Department of Agriculture Library) in Washington, D. C., has a Nursery and Seed Trade Catalog Collection with price lists back to 1792. The following list, compiled from the early catalogs that have been preserved, includes those nurseries selling tamarisk before 1840, a period when the shrub seemed to be offered more widely as an ornamental.

1823 (November) -- Lawrence & Mills, "Treatise and catalog of fruit and ornamental trees, shrubs etc., cultivated at the Old American Nursery, Flushing-Landing, near New-York." On page 29 under "hardy shrubs, ornamental for their fruit or foliage" is listed "French tamarisk, an ornamental shrub" 37 1/2 cents.

---

[1] The author is indebted to Dr. Elbert L. Little, Jr., Dendrologist, U. S. Forest Service, Washington, D. C., for his help in obtaining historical information.

[2] Research Forester, located at the Station's project headquarters at Tempe, in cooperation with Arizona State University; central headquarters is maintained at Fort Collins, in cooperation with Colorado State University.

1824--Stephen F. Mills & Company, "Catalog of Fruit and Ornamental Trees, shrubs, etc., cultivated at the Old American Nursery, Flushing-Landing, near New-York" lists on page 31, "French tamarisk, much admired".

1826--Stephen F. Mills & Company, "Catalogue of Fruit and Forest Trees, Flowering Shrubs and Plants, for sale by Stephen F. Mills & Company at Flushing-Landing, on Long-Island, near New-York", not only listed on page 39 "French tamarisk, much admired, (Tamarix gallica)," but also included German tamarisk (Tamarix germanica) for 37 cents.

1828--Bartram's Botanical Garden, Philadelphia, listed on page 28 both French "much admired" and German tamarisk for 37 cents.

1831--William Prince & Sons, Linnaean Botanical Garden and Nursery, Flushing, Long-Island, near New-York, listed on page 55 "French tamarisk, much admired (Tamarix gallica)" and German tamarisk (Tamarix germanica) for 37 to 50 cents.

1832-39--William Prince and Sons continued to list the two species of tamarisk in available catalogs of 1832, 1835, 1837, and 1839.

1832--William Kenrick's Nursery, Boston, on page 24 lists French and German tamarisk for 50 cents.

1832--Michael Floy, Harlam Nursery, New York. Both French and German are listed, and their beauty as ornamental shrubs thoroughly extolled.

1833--Brighton Nurseries, Boston, on page 17 offered French and German tamarisk for 50 cents.

1833-34--Nursery of William Kenrick in Newton, near Boston, listed on page 27 only French tamarisk (Tamarix gallica) for 50 cents.

1836-37--Sinclair Nursery in Baltimore on page 25 offered French tamarisk for 50 cents.

The earliest authentic records of tamarisk in the Southwest were also in nursery catalogs. Tamarisk was listed in 1856 by A. P. Smith in the catalog of the Pomological Garden and Nursery in Sacramento, California. In the same year, the Suscol Nursery, Suscol, California, listed African and German tamarisk.[3]

Tamarisk apparently was not naturalized to any extent in the Southwest by the 1850's because none of the U. S. Government explorers of that decade reported the genus. It is doubtful, therefore, whether the Spanish or Mexican occupation had brought tamarisk into the area. The statement of Standley (1923, p. 828) that tamarisk was "cultivated for ornament especially in the arid portions of northern Mexico, sometimes escaping" would indicate only local distribution in Mexico even as late as 1923.

Escalante reported "taray" growing at Fort Pierce Wash near the Utah-Arizona border in 1776 (Auerbach, 1943; Christensen, 1962). The Spanish word "taray" was translated to mean tamarisk, but Martinez (1937) states that, in Mexico, Salix, Eysenhardtia and Caesalpinia are often called "taray" but that tamarisk is not. Since Salix is common along the streams and washes of southern Utah, it is logical that Escalante could have been referring to Salix.

Later the U. S. Department of Agriculture began growing tamarisk and perhaps introduced some new species into the United States. The 1868 Annual Report of the Department (U.S. Dept. Agr., 1869, p. 123) indicates that six species of tamarisk were established in the Department Arboretum. The 1870 report of the Commissioner of Agriculture (U. S. Dept. Agr., 1871) gives a map of the Arbore-

[3] Robinson, T. W. Introduction, spread, and areal extent of saltcedar (Tamarix) in western conterminous United States (In preparation for publication, U. S. Geological Survey, Menlo Park, Calif.)

Thus the widespread use of tamarisk in the West provided an excellent seed source for the rapid aggressive spread in the next several decades.

It is difficult to distinguish which species were utilized in the early plantings. This confusion was recognized by such early botanists as Thornber (1916) who states, for instance, that T. parviflora (now known as T. tetrandra) was often sold as T. gallica. He is the earliest authority to use the common name saltcedar synonomously with tamarisk.

Early herbarium specimens give some clues as to the species actually present in the United States. All tamarisk specimens in four herbaria have been examined; only three species of deciduous tamarisk were deposited prior to 1920. The four herbaria[4] were: National Herbarium, U. S. National Museum, Smithsonian Institution (US); Pomona College (POM); University of Arizona (ARIZ); and Colorado State University (CS). Many of these specimens were incorrectly labeled due to the confusion in taxonomy.

Identification of the specimens has been tentatively changed by the author (table 1) following the species separation used by McClintock (1951) and revised by Horton (1957): the herbarium labels, without change, are shown in table 1. All specimens with 4-merous flowers are listed under Tamarix tetrandra. The 5-merous specimens are divided into T. pentandra, and T. gallica.

T. pentandra has a lobed disk with the filaments inserted below and at the notches of the disk. The petals are persistent and the anthers usually obtuse. Showy flowers occur on the old wood in the spring, and on much-branched panicles developed on new wood from late spring throughout the summer. A more complete description of this species as growing in Arizona is included in Horton and Flood (1962).

[4] *Herbarium abbreviations are according to Lanjouw and Stafleu (1959).*

Table 1 --Herbarium specimens of tamarisk species collected prior to 1920, grouped to follow species separation used by McClintoc (1951) and revised by Horton (1957) Information copied from labels in the herbaria[1]

Date		Collector and number	Collector's identification	Locality	Notes	Herbarium number
			TAMARIX TETRANDRA PALLAS			
	1871	Dr. Parry	T. parviflora	Ag. Grounds[2]		US 1092
	1871	Dr. Parry	T. africana	Ag. Grounds[2]		US 1092
	1876	Vasey	T. africana	Agricultural Grounds[2]	--	US 1092
May 11,	1879	Lester F. Ward	T. gallica	Ct. Ave.	Garden	US 13244
	1880	Vasey	T. tetranda Pall.	Ag. Grounds[2]	Cult., nearest the walk	US 1092
Apr 14,	1880	Marcus E. Jones	Tamarix	St. George, Utah	Cultivated	POM 8685
	1885	A. L. Schott	T. africana	District of Columbia	--	US 22686
May 13,	1885	A. L. Schott	T. germanica	Washington, D. C.		US 24800
May 1,	1886	A. L S.	T. germanica	U. S Bot Garden, D. C.	--	US 13245
May 3,	1886	A. L. S.	Tamarix	Bot. Garden, D C		US 13246
	1888	Mrs M. L Nash	T. gallica L.	Texas	--	US 1089
May 5,	1891	Geo. B. Sudworth	T. gallica	Agricultural Grounds, Washington, D.C.	Herb. of Forestry Div.	US 47835
May 15,	1892	J. W Toumey 101	T. gallica	Catalina Mts, Ariz.	--	US 21250
Mar 30,	1894	Marcus E. Jones 5002a	T. gallica	Harrisburg, Utah	2800 ft.	US 7209
Apr 5,	1894	Marcus E. Jones 5014	T. gallica	Beaverdam, Ariz.	1800 ft. Same sheet as abov	
May 5,	1894	Marcus E. Jones 5014	T. gallica	Silver Reef, Utah	Gravel, Alt 4500 ft.	POM 8685
May 16,	1895	Charles L. Pollard 210	T. gallica	Washington, D C Grounds U S Dept. Agric	--	US 23753
May 3,	1896	Juliet King	T. gallica L	Ia. Circle, Wash., D C	From coll of Forestry Div. USDA	US 47937
Apr 29,	1897	Biltmore Herbarium 5711	T. parviflora DC	From plants in cultivation at Biltmore, North Carolina	--	US 33180
Apr	1898	Mrs J.M. Milligan	T. gallica L	Bonham, Texas	--	US 50428
Apr 11,	1899	W F Wight	T. gallica	Stanford Arboretum, Santa Clara Co., Calif.	Cultivated	US 46779
	1911	Elmer Stearns 133	T. gallica	El Paso, Texas	Cultivated	US 50287
Apr 11,	1917	I. Johnston	T. gallica	Wilmington, Calif.	Scraggly shrub, sand dunes	POM 291
May 30,	1917	I Johnston	T. gallica L [3]	South of Ontario, Calif	Large shrub, damp ground along road	POM 291
			TAMARIX PENTANDRA PALLAS			
	1875	Vasey	Tamariscus	Ag. Grounds[1]		US 1089
	1875	Vasey	Tamariscus	Ag. Grounds[1]		US 1092
	1875	Vasey	Tamarix	Ag. Grounds[1]	--	US 1092
	1880	Vasey	T. gallica	Ag. Grounds[1]	Cult	US 1089
July 7,	1883	W. P Conant	Tamarix	Agri. Grounds, D. C.	--	US 1092
	1885	A L. Schott	T. indica	Dist. of Columbia	--	US 22686
June 10,	1893	J. J. Thornber	T. gallica	Brookings, S. Dakota	Col Grounds	ARIZ 7506
May	1897	Dr. Vinson	T. gallica	Columbus, Ohio	--	ARIZ 7506
Aug 17,	1897	Biltmore Herbarium 4730	T. gallica	Biltmore, North Carolina	In cultivation	US 33180
Aug 18,	1901	T H. Kearney	T. gallica [4]	Tempe, Ariz.	Common in river bottoms	US 41090
Apr 15,	1902	S M. Tracy and F. S Earle 55	T. gallica L.	Barstow, Texas	--	US 44178
July 6,	1909	Ivar Tidestrom 2402	T. gallica	Kanab, Utah	In cultivation Alt. 1480 meters	US 50810

Table 1.--(continued)

Date		Collector and number	Collector's identification	Locality	Notes	Herbarium number
y 12,	1909	E. W. Nelson 4	T. gallica	Winslow, Ariz.	Introduced	US 564498
y 21,	1911	Geo. L. Fisher 116	T. gallica	Nara Visa, N Mex.	Cultivated	US 660074
y 23,	1910	J. J. Thornber	T. hispida var. aestivales	Campus, Univ. of Ariz Tucson	--	ARIZ 75074
ril 9,	1913	J. J. Thornber	T. juniperina	Plant introduction Garden 10012 and 10043. Campus, Univ of Ariz	A handsome erect tree or shrub with flowers in lateral racemes	ARIZ 75077 ARIZ 75078
ril	1913	J. J. Thornber 8135	T. odesseyana	Plant intro Garden, Univ of Ariz Tucson	--	ARIZ 75080
y 22,	1913	J. J. Thornber 7370	T. hispida aestivales	Plant Intro Garden, Univ. of Ariz.		ARIZ 75073
y 22,	1913	J J. Thornber	T. hispida var.	Plant Introduction Garden, Campus, Univ. of Arizona	One of our most handsome shrubs with rose-red flowers and silvery foliage	ARIZ 75076
y 22,	1913	J. J. Thornber	T. odesseyana	Plant intro Garden, Univ. of Ariz. Tucson	Flowers light pink or nearly white	ARIZ 75079
） 12,	1913	S. B. Parish 8612	T. africana	Borders of Salton Sea at Travertine	A single shrub	ARIZ 75056
t 13,	1913	J.N. Rose & Wm. R. Fitch 17899	T. gallica L.	Vicinity of Pecos City, Texas	--	US 760963
1y	1916	J. J. Thornber 9152	T. hispida v. aestivales	Plant Introduction Garden, Campus, Univ. of Ariz.	--	ARIZ 75075
r 5,	1920	P. A. Munz & R.D. Harwood 3558	T. pallasii	Salton Sea, Calif.	Alkali sand. Alt. -150 ft.	POM 8215
			TAMARIX GALLICA L.			
r	1877	J. F. Joor	T. gallica L	Galveston I , Texas	On the beach. Completely naturalized. Collected again July 1884	US 724423
p 16,	1877	Lester F. Ward	T. gallica	Galveston, Texas	--	US 132460
p	1885	A. L. Schott	T. germanica	Agr Dept Pk., D.C.		US 132448
1y	1894	Dr. H. Hapeman	T. gallica	Galveston, Texas		ARIZ 75065 US 504285
）r 9, ）r 12,	1894	A. Arthur Heller 1528	T. gallica	Corpus Christi, Neueces Co., Texas		US 213939 ARIZ 75070 ARIZ 75077
）r 17,	1896	A.A. & E. Gertrude Heller 2925	T. gallica	Near the Cliff House, San Francisco, Calif.	--	US 277759
p 22,	1901	S. M. Tracy 7525	T. gallica	Galveston Id., Tex	--	US 442182
p 8,	1912	Geo. L. Fisher	T. gallica	Galveston, Texas	Tree 20 ft. high	US 503210
）r 17,	1913	J. J. Thornber	T. gallica	Botanical Plant Intro. Garden, Univ. of Ariz. Tucson, Ariz.	--	ARIZ 75061
ay	1913	Alice Tamson[5]	T. gallica	Tucson, Ariz.	--	ARIZ 75062
ay 21,	1913	J. J. Thornber	T. gallica	Plant Intro. Garden,	A large shrub with diffuse spreading branches Scarcely a desirable plant	ARIZ 75060

[1] Herbarium abbreviations: US = National Herbarium, POM = Pomona College Herbarium, ARIZ = University of Arizona.
[2] U. S. Department of Agriculture, Washington, D. C.
[3] No flowers, foliage resembles T. tetrandra.
[4] No flowers, foliage resembles T. pentandra.
[5] Name illegible.

T. gallica has a definite angled disk with the filaments inserted on the points of the disk. Petals are deciduous and the anthers usually mucronate. The racemes are usually borne on open, scarcely branched panicles. The inflorescences are not particularly showy.

The earliest specimen of T. tetrandra was collected in 1871 from the U. S. Department of Agriculture Arboretum in Washington, D. C. The many specimens collected before 1900 show that this species was widely spread in the United States as an ornamental shrub; it often may have been the French tamarisk offered in the catalogs in the 1820's and 1830's.

T. pentandra was not mentioned in the United States in early references, but many early specimens can be identified as this species. This species, widely cultivated and often praised as a handsome shrub, may have been one of those introduced by nurserymen in the first half of the 19th century; perhaps, the one so persistently labeled: "Much admired".

The first United States collection of T. gallica was made in Texas where it was naturalized on Galveston Island in 1877. The species was not collected from the Department of Agriculture grounds until 1885. Inasmuch as the shrub is not nearly so attractive as the other two species -- flowers are scattered and relatively inconspicuous -- it is doubtful if this species was one of the two introduced and highly praised by the early nurserymen.

Only three specimens of deciduous tamarisk examined could not be readily identified as one of these three species. Two were similar to T. tetrandra, except that each anther was tipped with a very long, dark-red mucro about as long as the anther: C. S. Crandall 1153, June 11, 1889, Lawn, Lansing Mich. (CS 14083), and unknown collector in 1890, Agricultural College, Mich. (POM 135659). These are perhaps from the same shrub.

Another specimen, J. J. Thornber 8087, April 1915, campus of University of Arizona, Tucson (ARIZ 75059), was labeled T. gallica. Miss Elizabeth McClintock,[5] in her study of tamarisk taxonomy, identified it as T. africana Poiret. This identification is logical because the specimen has characters similar to the descriptions of that species: short spring racemes only about 1 inch long, large flowers, and capsules twice the size of the average T. pentandra.

[5] *Associate Curator of Botany, California Academy of Science, San Francisco.*

Literature Cited

Auerbach, Herbert S.
    1943. Father Escalante's journal with related documents and maps. Utah Hist. Quart. 11: 1-142.

Christensen, Earl M.
    1962. The rate of naturalization of Tamarix in Utah. Amer. Midland Nat. 68: 51-57.

Gray, Asa.
    1895-97. Flora of North America. v. 1, pt. 1. Edited by R. L. Robinson, 506 pp. New York: American Book Co.

Horton, J. S.
    1957. Inflorescence development in Tamarix pentandra Pallas (Tamaricaceae). Southwest. Nat. 2: 135-139, illus.

    _____ and Flood, John E.
    1962. Taxonomic notes on Tamarix pentandra in Arizona. Southwest. Nat. 7: 23-28, illus.

Lanjouw, J., and Stafleu, F. A.
    1959. Index herbariorum. pt. 1. The herbaria of the world. Ed. 4, 249 pp.

Martinez, Maximo.
    1937. Catalogo de Nombres Vulgares y Cientificos de Plantas Mexicanas. 551 pp.

McClintock, Elizabeth.
    1951. Studies of California plants. 3. The tamarisks. Calif. Hort. Soc. Jour. 12: 76-83.

Thornber, J. J.
    1916. Tamarisks for southwestern planting. Ariz. Agr. Expt. Sta. Timely Hints for Farmers 121, 8 pp., illus.

U. S. Department of Agriculture.
    1869. Report of the Commissioner of Agriculture, 1868. 671 pp.

―――― 1871. Report of the Commissioner of Agriculture, 1870. 688 pp.

April 1964

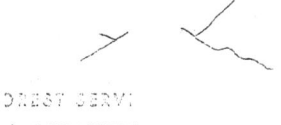

Estimating Number of Visitors to National Forest Campgrounds

Larry W. Tombaugh[1] and L. D Love[2]

Foresters are concerned with accurate statistics on the amount and kinds of use made of various recreation areas.[3] Since count of every visitor to all areas is not possible, a reliable method of estimating use is needed.

Visitor-use figures are used to:

1. establish schedules for visitor information programs, road maintenance, and trash disposal,
2. predict depreciation rates of facilities,
3. determine the need for enlarging campgrounds, and
4. identify trends and patterns of use.

Estimates of visitor use are difficult to obtain because recreation is not a static entity, but a dynamic interplay of people, areas, and activities.

In this study, three methods currently used to estimate the number of visitors to National Forest campgrounds were evaluated:

1. sporadic counts by recreation guards,
2. automatic traffic-counter readings converted to visitor numbers, and
3. estimates by field personnel (ranger estimates).

In addition, improvements in the first two methods are proposed.

PROCEDURES

Comparisons of the three methods were limited to 12 selected campgrounds in National Forests of Arizona, New Mexico, Colorado, Wyoming, and South Dakota. At each campground, visitors and vehicles were counted for two 4-day periods covering a Friday-through-Monday sequence. For the same 4-day periods, estimates of visitor numbers were obtained from personnel of the National Forests.

At all campgrounds, a daily-use record was made for each unit (table, fire grate, and trash container in a localized spot within a forest campground). All units were observed from 8:00 a.m. until 7:00 p.m. on Friday through Sunday, and from 8:00 a.m. until 5:00 p.m. on Monday. A record was also kept of the off-unit users--those who entered a campground but did not use a designated unit. Visitors were counted only once for as long as they remained and used the campground.

The estimates of visitor numbers by the three methods were compared with the actual numbers of visitors (including off-unit users) to the campgrounds. Because the estimating methods and the actual counts were both measuring the same population--numbers of visitors--they were statistically treated as paired data. (All statistical procedures are based on Snedecor.[4]) Standard deviations of mean differences and coefficients of variation were computed for each of the three methods. Table 1 shows these comparisons along with the variation in the accuracy of the estimating methods.

Table 1.--Comparison of actual count with three methods used to estimate numbers of visitors

Method vs. count	Mean differ-ence	Standard devia-tion	Coeffici-ent of variation
			Percent
Recreation guard (on two camp-grounds for one 4-day period, and one campground for two 4-day periods)	128.00	460.10	359.5
Traffic counter (on four camp-grounds for two 4-day periods)	666.38	605.77	90.9
Ranger estimates (on two camp-grounds for two 4-day periods and two campgrounds for three 4-day periods)	1,255.60	1,988.44	158.4

PROPOSED METHODS

The size of the coefficients of variation indicates that the present techniques for estimating visitors are not producing consistent and reliable results, and require modifications. For the purposes of this study, little can be done to improve the ranger-estimate method of determining visitor numbers; thus, the remainder of the discussion will deal with recreation-guard counts and traffic-counter estimates.

Simulated Recreation-Guard Count

From the daily-use records, which show the number of visitors occupying each unit of the various campgrounds on an hourly basis, a recreation-guard count was simulated by choosing a specific time of day and totaling the number of people at each unit at that time. Four times of day were chosen so as to represent a morning count, a noon count, and an early-and late-afternoon count. Arbitrarily, 10:00 a.m., 12:00 noon, 3:00 p.m., and 5:00 p.m. were chosen.

In a highly controlled study, visitors from day to day are recognized by close and nearly continuous observation. Under actual field conditions, however, it is difficult for a recreation guard who only visits a campground once a day to remember the individual people occupying each unit. Therefore, in simulating a recreation-guard count, the visitor who camped from Saturday through Monday was counted three times to simplify the procedure and to eliminate one source of error. No off-unit users were considered.

The simulated recreation-guard counts for the 96 observation days were compared with the actual total counts from the daily use records for the corresponding days. To determine which time of day yields the most reliable recreation-guard counts, correlation coefficients were computed for each of the four selected times:

Time of day	Correlation coefficient (r)
10:00 a.m.	0.732**
12:00 noon	.780**
3:00 p.m.	.759**
5:00 p.m.	.681**

**Significant at the 1 percent level.

These coefficients indicate that the counts made between 10:00 a.m. and 3:00 p.m. are most closely related to the actual numbers of people on the campground for the entire day.

level). Traffic-counter estimates accounted for 65.1 percent of the variation in the total number of visitors counted per day. Compared with 60.8 percent for the simulated 12:00 noon recreation-guard count, the traffic-counter estimate was more precise.

Regression Analyses

The simulated 12:00 noon recreation-guard count did not identify those visitors who stayed more than 1 day. Each day's count was independent of the next. A regression analysis gives the following prediction equation:

$$Y = 43.68 + 0.846\ X_1 \qquad (1)$$

where Y is the total number of visitors at units for any 1 day, and X_1 is the number of people counted at 12:00 noon of that day by the recreation guard. The regression coefficient (0.846) is significant at the 1 percent level. The standard error of estimate is ±72.85 visitors.

The simulated traffic-counter estimates measure total daily (5:00 p.m.) axle crossings. A regression analysis gives the following prediction equation:

$$Y = 18.44 + 0.494\ X_2 \qquad (2)$$

where Y is the total number of visitors at units for any 1 day and X_2 is the traffic counter reading in total axle crossings for that day read at 5:00 p.m. The regression coefficient (0.494) is significant at the 1 percent level. The standard error of estimate is ±68.73 visitors.

The two prediction equations are averages of 12 campgrounds and may not apply specifically to any one campground.

APPLICATION OF METHODS

Estimates of total number of visitors to a recreation site by recreation guards or by means of traffic counters vary considerably. Errors often exceed the mean values. By means of regression equations, these estimates can be improved and the errors reduced.

In applying the recreation-guard count method, the people at each unit of a campground should be systematically and carefully counted at 12:00 noon every day, regardless of whether they had been counted the previous day. The regression equation corrects for recounts and thus eliminates the necessity of remembering individual parties and their length of stay. Equation (1) estimates the total number of visitors to a campground for the day the noon count is made. The equation should be checked periodically by actually counting the total number of visitors to a campground as well as just those at 12:00 noon.

Equation (2) for the traffic-counter method tends to average a number of variables. Some of these include the amount of off-unit use, the number of times campers leave and enter the campground during their stay, the ratio of trailers to motorized vehicles, and the average number of people per vehicle. The effect of these variables on estimates varies considerably among campgrounds and seasons. For this reason, a traffic counter should be calibrated upon installation and periodically thereafter. Major changes in the character of

April 1964

RESEARCH NOTE RM - 18

FOREST SERVICE

Vegetation Changes Following the Mingus Mountain Burn[1]

by

Charles P. Pase and Floyd W. Pond[2]

Wildfires are common in Arizona's 5 1/2 million acres of chaparral type. Precipitous topography and remoteness from roads make fire control difficult and uncertain. Moreover, the structure of the mature shrub community, consisting largely of sprouting shrubs or those whose germination is greatly improved by heat treatment, indicates a high level of adaptability to repeated fires.

Secondary vegetation which characteristically becomes established immediately after fire, contains a large variety of herbaceous species that are important sources of forage for both wildlife and domestic livestock. This temporary cover diminishes quickly, however, as the shrub cover rapidly resumes its prefire stature.[3][4]

The vegetation changes following fire in Arizona chaparral are little known at present. The purpose of this paper is to report successional changes in chaparral vegetation after the Mingus Mountain fire.

STUDY AREA

In June 1956, a wildfire burned over approximately 18,000 acres of rough mountain land between Jerome and Dewey in central Arizona. The fire began in a relatively open shrub live oak[5] and skunkbush sumac area at 5,000 feet elevation, and stopped within the ponderosa pine type at 6,500 feet near the top of Mingus Mountain. The lower area was aerially seeded with weeping lovegrass; the higher area, above 6,000 feet, to both weeping lovegrass and crested wheatgrass.

At Jerome, 8 miles north of the burn at an elevation of 5,245 feet, longtime average precipitation is 17.08 inches, 51 percent of which falls from November 1 through May 1. From 1956 to 1961, the years of the study, precipitation averaged 17.77 inches, with a range of 6.11 to 25.87 inches.

Topography of the burned area consists of steep, hilly country at the lower end interspersed with numerous shallow, narrow valleys. Deep canyons, long, steep slopes with occasional benches, and mesas occur at the higher elevations.

---

[1] Personnel of the Watershed Management Department of the University of Arizona, the Arizona Game and Fish Department, and the Prescott National Forest assisted in the vegetation measurements.
[2] Research Forester and Range Conservationist, respectively, located at the Station's project headquarters at Tempe, in cooperation with Arizona State University; central headquarters maintained at Fort Collins, in cooperation with Colorado State University.
[3] Horton, J. S., and Kraebel, C. J. Development of vegetation after fire in the chamise chaparral of southern California. Ecology 36: 244-262. 1955.
[4] Pond, Floyd W., and Cable, Dwight R. Recovery of vegetation following wildfire on a chaparral area in Arizona. U. S. Forest Service, Rocky Mountain Forest and Range Expt. Sta. Res. Note 72, 4 pp., illus. 1962.
[5] Common and botanical names of plants are listed on p. 8.

On the lower area, the coarse soils are poorly developed, shallow, and are derived from granitic parent material. The finer textured, better developed soils, at higher elevations, are derived from shales, sandstones, and limestones, and contain considerably more organic matter.

METHODS

Vegetation was measured on 30 permanent sample plots in the lower area and 20 in the upper area, all within the shrub type. No permanent sample plots were located in the pine type.

Each sample plot consisted of two 50-foot line intercept transects. Vegetation was measured each fall by the procedure outlined by Canfield.[6]

Each transect was paralleled by 10 permanently marked 9.6-square-foot circular plots spaced 5 feet apart. Production of herbaceous material and total weight of shrubs on the ground was determined on five selected permanent plots by the weight-estimate method.[7] Of the five remaining plots, one was selected, estimated, and clipped each year for use in the double-sampling technique to correct weight estimates.[8]

Production in the pine type was determined at one site in 1961 by the same method, based on sixty-six 9.6-square-foot circular plots.

Part of the lower burned and seeded area was treated with 2,4,5-T and silvex in 1957, 1958, and 1959. This application was part of a general evaluation of chemical shrub control by the Arizona Agricultural Experiment Station. The affected plots were discarded until 1961 when they were again measured to compare grass and shrub production on both treated and untreated areas. Air-dry grass production averaged over 1,000 pounds per acre on the treated area in 1959.[9]

RESULTS AND DISCUSSION

Production And Distribution Of Shrubs

Both crown canopy and accumulated weight of shrubs, reduced to zero in June 1956, were still increasing six growing seasons after the fire (fig. 1). The 41.7 percent canopy cover probably represents three-fourths of the original estimated cover of 50 to 60 percent. Air-dry weight of shrubs on the entire area averaged 4,180 pounds per acre, and was still increasing slowly at the end of study (fig. 2).

Shrub composition was largely shrub live oak, although its relative importance de-

[6] Canfield, R. H. Sampling ranges by the line-interception method. U. S. Forest Serv. Southwest Forest and Range Expt. Sta. Res. Rpt. 4, 28 pp., illus. 1942. (Reprinted 1957)
[7] Pechanec, J. F., and Pickford, G. D. A weight-estimate method for determination of range or pasture production. Amer. Soc. Agron. Jour. 29: 894-904. 1937.
[8] Wilm, H. G., Costello, David F., and Klipple, G. E. Estimating forage yield by the double-sampling method. Amer. Soc. Agron. Jour. 36: 194-203. 1944.
[9] Schmutz, Ervin M., and Whitman, David W. Shrub control studies in the oak-chaparral of Arizona. Jour. Range Manat. 15: 61-67. 1962.

Figure 1.--Typical shrub live oak chaparral on Mingus Mountain, elevation 5,000 feet:

A, August 1956, after wildfire;

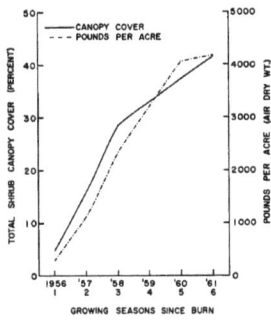

Figure 2.--Crown cover and total weight of all shrubs following June 1956 wildfire.

creased as seedling shrubs and halfshrubs regained prominence in the stand (table 1). At the end of the sixth growing season, composition was shrub live oak 68.0 percent, broom snakeweed 11.8 percent, and skunkbush sumac 9.0 percent. Manzanitas made up .4 percent. The more desirable species for game and livestock use--hairy cercocarpus, desert ceanothus, Wright silktassel--made up about 5.0 percent of the cover.

Fire greatly reduced desert ceanothus, and pointleaf and Pringle manzanitas. These shrubs reproduce primarily by seeds, although both manzanitas may extend themselves by ground layering in the absence of fire. Desert ceanothus may rarely sprout from the root crown when the top is destroyed. Seeds of all three species germinated in the spring after

Table 1. --Percent composition of shrubs based on line intercepts
(average of upper and lower areas[1])

Species	1956	1957	1958	1960	1961
	- - - - - Percent - - - - -				
Broom snakeweed	0	[2]T	7.20	11.49	11.80
Catclaw mimosa	5.74	2.74	3.19	2.16	2.37
Desert ceanothus	.04	T	.35	1.45	1.78
Hairy cercocarpus	.40	1.38	2.08	1.64	2.26
Pointleaf manzanita	0	.08	.15	.21	.38
Pringle manzanita	0	0	.39	1.56	2.02
Shrub live oak	81.02	80.36	69.45	70.48	68.00
Skunkbush sumac	11.32	12.88	14.76	9.19	9.04
Others	1.48	2.56	2.43	1.82	2.35
Total	100.00	100.00	100.00	100.00	100.00

[1] Upper area = 6,500 ft. elevation, 8 miles south of Jerome.
Lower area = 5,000 ft. elevation, 8 miles northeast of Dewey.

[2] T = trace.

the fire, and in lesser amounts for several following springs. By 1961, there were 335 pointleaf manzanita and 4,063 desert ceanothus seedlings per acre on the lower area. On the upper area, pointleaf manzanita was absent, but there were 3,677 Pringle manzanita and 340 desert ceanothus seedlings per acre (table 2).

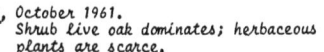

October 1961. Shrub live oak dominates; herbaceous plants are scarce.

Table 2. --Density of shrub seedlings at two elevations following wildfire on Mingus Mountain. Fire burned in June 1956; observations made each autumn

Species	Lower area					Upper area				
	1956	1957	1958	1960	1961	1956	1957	1958	1960	1961
					Plants per acre					
Desert ceanothus	0	2,748	2,581	4,565	4,063	0	0	340	272	340
Pointleaf manzanita	0	486	287	239	335	0	0	0	0	0
Pringle manzanita	0	0	0	0	0	0	2,860	3,541	3,155	3,677

Table 3. --Vegetation recovery on the Mingus Mountain Burn, expressed as percent of 9.6-square foot plots in which species occurs (shrubs were considered present when any part of the canopy extended into the plot)

Species	Lower area					Upper area				
	1956	1957	1958	1960	1961	1956	1957	1958	1960	1961
					Percent					
Shrubs and halfshrubs:										
Broom snakeweed	0	16.3	21.0	31.6	42.6	0	6.0	12.0	22.0	25.5
Catclaw mimosa	10.5	11.0	8.9	14.7	12.1	0	0	0	0	0
Desert ceanothus	0	23.7	27.3	28.9	31.0	0	0	4.5	7.0	6.5
Hairy cercocarpus	.5	1.0	3.2	5.3	4.7	11.5	21.0	19.5	22.5	19.5
Pointleaf manzanita	0	8.9	2.6	3.7	4.2	0	0	0	0	0
Pringle manzanita	0	0	0	0	0	0	16.5	17.0	17.5	16.5
Shrub live oak	37.9	44.2	40.0	49.4	51.0	48.0	57.5	56.5	62.5	61.5
Skunkbush sumac	7.9	15.2	16.3	18.4	19.5	1.5	4.5	5.5	7.5	6.0
Grasses:										
Bottlebrush squirreltail	0	.5	.5	0	.5	0	2.5	4.0	10.5	21.5
Crested wheatgrass	--	--	--	--	--	0	14.0	20.5	17.5	13.0
Longtongue mutton bluegrass	0	0	0	.5	.5	1.0	2.0	2.5	4.0	3.0
Side-oats grama	9.5	7.9	6.8	10.0	15.2	10.5	15.0	23.0	32.5	33.5
Weeping lovegrass	3.7	5.3	9.5	12.6	12.1	.5	2.0	1.5	4.0	6.0
Forbs:										
Arizona rockcress	0	0	0	1.6	0	0	1.0	3.0	2.0	0
Hoarhound	0	0	0	0	0	0	0	0	3.0	2.5
Eaton penstemon	0	1.0	0	0	0	0	4.5	7.0	6.5	4.0
Few flowered goldenrod	0	0	0	0	0	0	5.0	15.5	23.0	22.5
Wrights verbena	0	28.9	5.8	1.6	2.6	0	9.0	11.5	0	2.5
Palmer penstemon	0	2.1	5.3	2.6	.5	0	25.0	26.5	25.5	2.5
Toadflax penstemon	0	0	1.0	1.0	0	0	0	13.5	13.0	8.5
White dalea	0	.5	1.6	0	0	0	2.0	2.5	0	0

Shrub live oak and broom snakeweed occurred most frequently on the circular 9.6-square-foot plots on both upper and lower areas (table 3). On the lower area, the low occurrence of pointleaf manzanita (4.2) was primarily due to its restriction to the vicinity of older colonies. This was also true, but to a lesser extent, for Pringle manzanita (frequency 16.5) and desert ceanothus (frequency 6.5) in the upper area. Catclaw mimosa was absent from the upper area, and the frequency of desert ceanothus and skunkbush sumac was much reduced (table 3).

Production And Distribution Of Herbaceous Plants

Within the chaparral type, weeping lovegrass was considerably more successful in the lower than in the upper area. Although native grasses recovered about 1 year later at the upper elevation, they contributed greatly to that area's superiority in grass production. Grass production during the best year was just under 200 pounds per acre on the upper area, and just under 100 pounds on the lower area (table 4). Production on all sites

Table 4. --Total herbaceous production at two elevations following wildfire on Mingus Mountain

Species	Lower area					Upper area				
	1956	1957	1958	1960	1961	1956	1957	1958	1960	1961
					Air-dry pounds per acre					
Grasses:										
Bottlebrush squirreltail	0	0	1	0	0	0	1	5	12	13
Crested wheatgrass	--	--	--	--	--	0	0	39	31	21
Longtongue mutton bluegrass	0	0	0	[1]T	1	T	T	8	8	8
Side-oats grama	T	8	9	15	13	4	14	65	111	89
Weeping lovegrass	T	27	29	28	60	0	T	14	8	12
Others	T	5	18	13	23	T	1	10	26	14
Total grasses	T	40	57	56	97	4	16	141	196	157
Forbs:										
Arizona rockcress	0	0	0	0	0	0	T	1	0	0
Hoarhound	0	0	0	0	0	0	0	0	8	6
Eaton penstemon	0	T	0	0	0	0	T	5	8	2
Few flowered goldenrod	0	0	0	0	0	0	1	19	14	5
Wrights verbena	0	10	1	T	T	0	3	14	0	T
Palmer penstemon	0	2	18	21	2	0	12	197	79	1
Toadflax penstemon	0	T	T	0	0	0	0	5	5	2
White dalea	0	T	1	0	0	T	T	4	0	0
Others	0	3	8	10	6	0	6	14	13	6
Total forbs	0	15	28	31	8	T	22	259	127	22
Total herbaceous	T	55	85	87	105	4	38	400	323	179

[1]Trace

averaged 100 pounds per acre by 1958 and was slowly increasing at the end of the study (fig. 3). Basal area reached a peak in 1960 and declined slightly in 1961.

Weeping lovegrass, seeded on both upper and lower areas, occurred on 12.6 percent of the circular plots in 1960 in the lower area, but never exceeded a frequency of 6.0 percent in the higher area. Crested wheatgrass, seeded only in the higher area, reached a peak frequency of 20.5 percent in 1958, and dropped to 13.0 percent by 1961. Side-oats grama was most widespread of all grasses, native or seeded; it occurred on a maximum of 15.2 percent of the lower plots and 33.5 percent of the upper plots. Bottlebrush squirreltail was also much more frequent on the upper area (table 3).

Forbs, unlike grasses, reached a peak in both production and frequency of occurrence during the second and third growing seasons after the fire, and then declined rapidly. In the upper area, however, several forbs, notably hoarhound and few flowered goldenrod, became prominent a year or more after peak production had been reached by Palmer penstemon and Wrights verbena.

Only three forbs produced more than 10 pounds per acre in any year--Palmer penstemon, few flowered goldenrod, and Wrights verbena (table 4). Palmer penstemon, at its peak three growing seasons after the fire, produced about 50 percent of the total herbaceous production in the upper area. By 1961, Palmer penstemon contributed less than 1 percent of total herbaceous production in the upper area. During the peak year of forb production, three growing seasons after the fire, forbs in the lower area produced approximately one-half as much as grasses; in the upper area, forb production was approximately twice that of grasses.

The first forb to become prominent in the postfire vegetation in the lower area was Wrights verbena, which reached a peak frequency of 28.9 percent by the second growing season, then declined rapidly to 2.6 in 1961. In the upper area, Palmer penstemon had a frequency of 25.0 percent in the second growing season, remained high for 3 years, then rapidly declined to a frequency of 2.5 percent (table 3).

By 1961, six growing seasons after the fire, few flowered goldenrod was the most common forb in the higher elevations (frequency 22.5 percent), while no single forb was common in the lower area.

Grass Production On Sprayed Plots

Sprayed vegetation plots were used only to compare production on treated and untreated areas in 1961. On the untreated area, native grasses produced 37 pounds per acre, while weeping lovegrass produced 60 pounds. On areas where shrubs had been sprayed (mostly

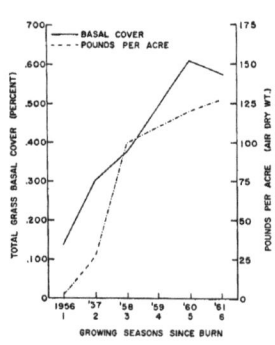

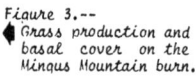

Figure 3.--
Grass production and basal cover on the Mingus Mountain burn.

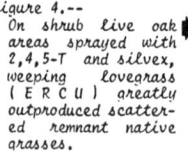

Figure 4.--
On shrub live oak areas sprayed with 2,4,5-T and silvex, weeping lovegrass (ERCU) greatly outproduced scattered remnant native grasses.

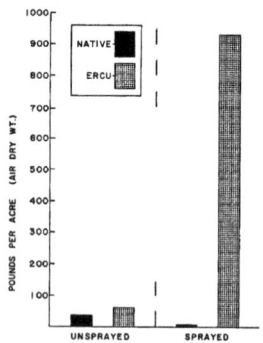

- 6 -

Deer used hairy cercocarpus, Wright silktassel, and desert ceanothus moderately the winter of 1957-58. Little grass was used-- only 2 percent use of side-oats grama and of weeping lovegrass. None of the more abundant forbs were taken in quantity. During the winter of 1958-59, with grazing by both deer and cattle, use of grasses increased significantly. Eaton penstemon was the most heavily grazed forb, with purple nightshade second.

Percent use of shrubs was based on total weight rather than annual growth, and would ordinarily be expected to decrease as the sprouts grew older and larger. Annual growth increments on many shrubs, especially hollyleaf buckthorn, were difficult to detect.

Production And Use In The Fringe Pine

Herbaceous production in the pine type in 1961 was considerably higher than that in the upper chaparral. Grass production alone amounted to 426 pounds per acre. Twenty grass species were found in the plots, but only nine of these produced over 5 pounds per acre. The highest producer was weeping lovegrass, with almost three-fourths of the total grass herbage. The other seeded species, crested wheatgrass, produced less than 1 pound per acre.

Species	Production (Lbs/Acre)	Use (Percent)
Grasses:		
Blue grama	14	T
Dryland sedge	7	4
Hairy grama	12	13
Longtongue muhly	36	4
Plains lovegrass	5	26
Red three-awn	6	4
Side-oats grama	22	31
Single three-awn	15	2
Weeping lovegrass	294	16
Other grasses	15	T
	426	
Forbs:		
Flannel mullein	23	T
Other forbs	5	T

Use in the vicinity of the study plots was considered light to moderate. Three grasses were used in excess of 15 percent, the highest use being on side-oats grama (31 percent). Weeping lovegrass, the major producer, was utilized only 16 percent.

SUMMARY

Chaparral crown canopy and total shrub weights were still increasing six growing seasons after a wildfire on Mingus Mountain. Shrub live oak was the main component of the shrub community (68.0 percent) at this time.

Pointleaf and Pringle manzanitas and desert ceanothus plants were greatly reduced by the fire, but seedlings of these species were numerous within 5 years. Desert ceanothus seedlings outnumbered manzanita seedlings at the lower elevations (5,000 feet), but the reverse was true at higher elevations (6,500 feet).

Production of herbaceous species tended to be small except in one small area where shrub canopy was kept low by repeated chemical applications. On unsprayed plots, seeded and native grasses reached peak production in 1960, with about 200 pounds per acre at the higher elevations and 60 pounds per acre a lower elevations. On the sprayed area, production of weeping lovegrass alone exceeded 900 pounds per acre in 1961. Production o forbs reached a peak during the second and third growing season after the burn, and ther rapidly declined.

Grazing, by deer only in 1957-58 and by cattle and deer in 1958-59, was not excessive

COMMON AND BOTANICAL NAMES OF PLANTS MENTIONED

GRASSES AND GRASSLIKE:

Agropyron desertorum (Fisch.) Schult.
   Crested wheatgrass
Aristida orcuttiana Vasey
   Single three-awn
A. longiseta Steud.
   Red three-awn
Bouteloua curtipendula (Michx.) Torr.
   Side-oats grama
B. gracilis (H.B.K.) Lag.
   Blue grama
B. hirsuta Lag.
   Hairy grama
Carex geophila Mackenz.
   Dryland sedge
Eragrostis curvula (Schrad.) Nees
   Weeping lovegrass
E. intermedia Hitchc.
   Plains lovegrass
Muhlenbergia longiligula Hitchc.
   Longtongue muhly
Poa longiligula Scribn. & Williams
   Longtongue mutton bluegrass
Sitanion hystrix (Nutt.) J. G. Smith
   Bottlebrush squirreltail

FORBS:

Arabis perennans S. Wats.
   Arizona rockcress
Dalea albiflora A. Gray
   White dalea
Marrubium vulgare L.
   Hoarhound
Penstemon eatoni A. Gray
   Eaton penstemon
P. linarioides A. Gray
   Toadflax penstemon
P. palmeri A. Gray
   Palmer penstemon
Solanum xantii A. Gray
   Purple nightshade
Solidago sparsiflora A. Gray
   Few flowered goldenrod
Verbascum thapsus L.
   Flannel mullein
Verbena wrightii A. Gray
   Wrights verbena

SHRUBS:

Arctostaphylos pringlei Parry
   Pringle manzanita
A. pungens H.B.K.
   Pointleaf manzanita
Ceanothus greggii A. Gray
   Desert ceanothus
Cercocarpus breviflorus A. Gray
   Hairy cercocarpus
Garrya wrightii Torr.
   Wright silktassel
Gutierrezia sarothrae (Pursh) Britt. & Rusby
   Broom snakeweed
Mimosa biuncifera Benth.
   Catclaw mimosa
Pinus ponderosa Lawson
   Ponderosa pine
Quercus turbinella Greene
   Shrub live oak
Rhamnus crocea Nutt.
   Hollyleaf buckthorn
Rhus trilobata Nutt.
   Skunkbush sumac

Arizona Gambel Oak

and Peter F. Ffolliott[1]

Well-prepared charcoal contains about one-third the weight and one-half the volume of the wood from which it is made.[5] If average solid wood content of 80 cubic feet per cord is assumed, charcoal recovery of approximately 1,000 pounds per cord could be expected. The charcoal would have a specific gravity of approximately 0.42, and a density of 26 pounds per cubic foot. If manufactured to acceptable quality standards, it would be suitable for marketing in either lump or briquet form.

---

[1] *Technologist and Research Forester, respectively, located at Flagstaff, in cooperation with Arizona State College; central headquarters are maintained at Fort Collins, in cooperation with Colorado State University.*

[2] *Little, Elbert L., Jr. Southwestern trees. A guide to the native species of New Mexico and Arizona. U. S. Dept. Agr. Handb. 9, 109 pp., illus. 1950.*

[3] *One Gambel oak tree on the study area measured 36.9 inches in diameter, breast high, and 76 feet in height. The first fork in the stem was 24 feet above the ground.*

[4] *U. S. Forest Products Laboratory. Methods of determining the specific gravity of wood. U. S. Forest Serv., Forest Prod. Lab. Tech. Note B-14, 6 pp., illus. 1956.*

[5] *U. S. Forest Products Laboratory. Charcoal production, marketing, and use. U. S. Forest Serv., Forest Prod. Lab. Rpt. 2213, 137 pp., illus. 1961.*

Table 1.--Specific gravity of Gambel oak at breast height by the increment core method

Size class	Trees	Specific gravity[1]				Density[1]	
		Maximum	Minimum	Mean	95 percent confidence interval	Mean	95 percent confidence interval
	No.					Lbs. per cu. ft.	
Saplings and small poles (2.0 - 6.9 inches)	15	0.706	0.596	0.653	±0.022	40.7	±1.37
Large poles (7.0 - 10.9 inches)	20	.693	.569	.624	± .015	38.9	± .94
Sawtimber (11.0 inches and over)	13	.696	.572	.625	± .024	39.0	±1.50
All classes	48	.706	.569	.634	± .010	39.6	± .62

[1] Based on ovendry weight and green volume.

Root Development of Ponderosa Pine Transplants at Lincoln, Nebraska[1]

Charles E. Boldt and Teja Singh[2]

Rapid, vigorous root development is a key factor in survival and establishment of nursery-grown trees after they are transplanted. In most environments occupied by ponderosa pine (Pinus ponderosa Laws.), drought, intensified by vegetative competition, restricts initial growth.

Young forest trees have numerous enemies: soil-inhabiting insects, burrowing rodents, foliage and stem insects, and browsing animals. If either top or root growth is slow, the feeding by enemies either above or below ground can be fatal. If root growth is rapid, however, accompanying top growth can be rapid and the impact of insect and mammal feeding will be minimized.

Recent root excavations at Lincoln, Nebraska, revealed that pine roots can grow rapidly after transplanting, if environmental conditions are favorable. Root systems of three young ponderosa pines were excavated and diagramed in August 1959. All three trees had been transplanted as bareroot, 2-1 stock from the Bessey Nursery (U. S. Forest Service) to a field test area on the campus of the College of Agriculture at Lincoln.

Transplanting had been done in April of 1956, 1958, and 1959. The trees are hereafter referred to as 4-season, 2-season, and 1-season trees, even though 1959 growth was probably not complete at the time of excavation.

The soil was Wabash silt loam, fairly typical of the best medium- to heavy-textured, alluvial soils of southeastern Nebraska. The site was on the margin of a flat bottom that borders a small drainage. Free water was encountered at a depth of 6.3 feet during excavation.

After they were transplanted by the dug-hole method, the trees received no special care except two or three diskings per season

---

[1] Research reported here was done in cooperation with the University of Nebraska at Lincoln. Central headquarters for the Rocky Mountain Station is maintained at Fort Collins in cooperation with Colorado State University. The advice and assistance of Dr. J. E. Weaver, botanist, University of Nebraska, are gratefully acknowledged.

[2] The authors are currently Research Forester for the Rocky Mountain Station at Rapid City, South Dakota, and Research Assistant, Utah State University, Logan.

to keep weeds down. The trees were given no supplemental water.

The root system of the 4-season tree was excavated by digging a straight access trench with one face tangent to the root collar. The vertical roots and some of the laterals were uncovered by digging away the wall of the trench with a trowel and ice pick. Other laterals were exposed by digging radial trenches outward from the root collar.

The less extensive root systems of the two younger trees were excavated by first removing the soil from around the lateral roots and then digging away the central column of earth containing the vertical roots.

The roots of each tree were diagramed to scale on coordinate paper as they were excavated. Vertical projections (figs. 1, 2, 3) show all roots as though oriented along a single vertical plane.

All three root systems contained two distinct kinds of roots. One group of roots penetrated almost vertically beneath the tree and apparently functioned as tap roots. A second group radiated out in all directions to form a strong set of laterals that generally remained within 2 feet of the soil surface.

Root development in the 1-season tree (fig. 1) was confined almost entirely to simple extension, with little branching. There was little difference between total elongation of vertical and lateral roots. In response to some unknown stimulus, two primary laterals turned downward rather abruptly and became "sinkers."

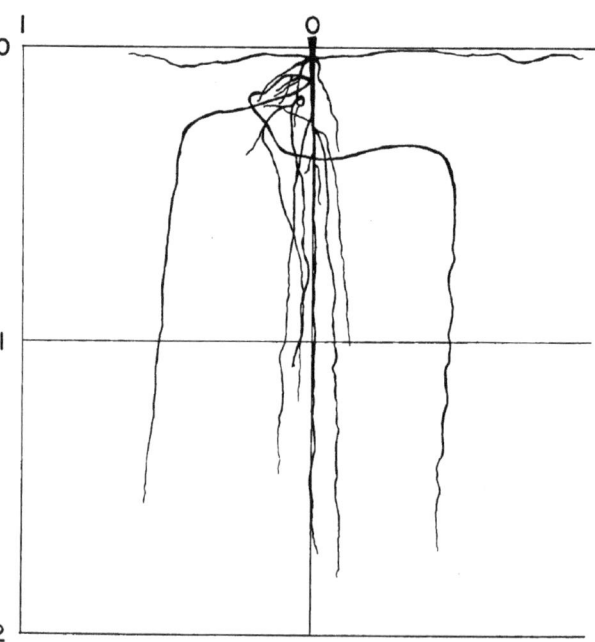

Figure 1.--
Vertical projection of root system of 1-season ponderosa pine. Grid units are feet.

The extensive root system of the 2-season tree (fig. 2) showed clearly that growth was rapid in the second year after transplanting. Numerous roots had emerged from near the root crown, 3 to 4 inches below the soil surface. Most of these grew downward to form a compact column of fine primary roots with many secondary branches. The remainder developed into laterals that were generally longer and somewhat thicker than the verticals, but had fewer branches. Two vertical roots that penetrated to within about a foot of the water table had many fine branches near their tips.

The root system of the 4-season tree (fig. 3) was similar in form to that of the 2-season tree. The strong central column of vertical roots had penetrated to the free water level and produced numerous branches to tap this water supply. One of the lateral roots was more than 13 feet long. At time of excavation this 4-season tree was about 30 inches tall.

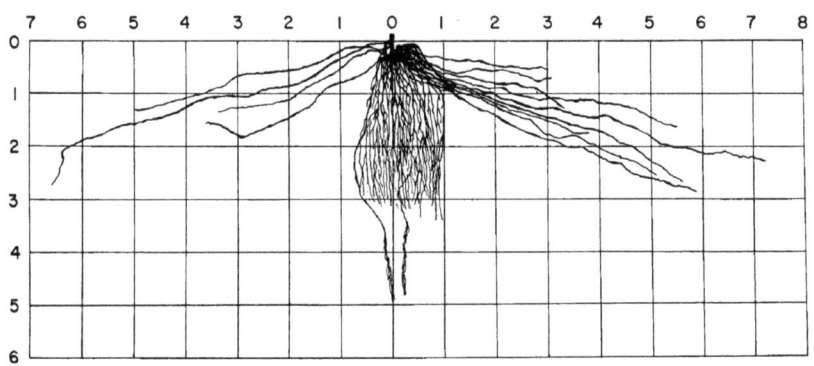

Figure 2.--Vertical projection of root system of 2-season ponderosa pine. Grid units are feet.

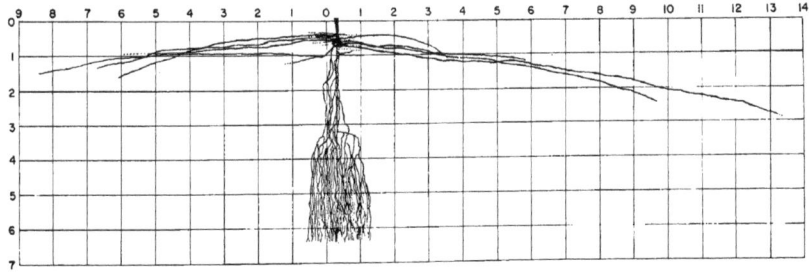

Figure 3.--Vertical projection of root system of 4-season ponderosa pine. Grid units are feet.

Perhaps the impressive root growth made by these trees on a cultivated soil cannot be duplicated on many forest soils. But one thing is strikingly clear: ponderosa pines can extend their roots very rapidly in good soils that are free of competing vegetation.

Experience and research have demonstrated repeatedly that site preparation is necessary to permit successful forestation of heavily vegetated sites. Site preparation has frequently consisted of merely scalping the vegetation from planting spots 1 to 2 feet in

July 1964

U.S. FOREST SERVICE

RESEARCH NOTE RM - 21

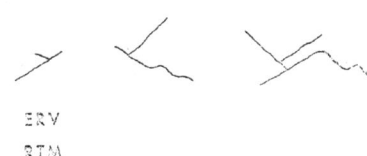

ERV
RTM

Range Utilization Patterns as Affected by Fencing and Class of Livestock[1]

Wayne C. Hickey, Jr. and George Garcia[2]

How to obtain uniform use of the range by livestock is an important and difficult problem in the Southwest. Stoddard and Smith[3] pointed out that "no western mountain range and few level ranges can be uniformly utilized." Utilization may reach 100 percent around water, but declines as distance from water increases.[4]

Many suggestions for obtaining uniform utilization have been advanced: cross fencing, salting away from water, fertilizing outlying areas, reseeding outlying areas to more preferred species, and using minerals or supplemental feeding in ungrazed areas. None of the past studies have indicated, however, how utilization patterns in fenced pastures may change when the pastures are grazed by different classes of livestock. Also, there is little information on changes in grazing patterns caused by fencing.

The objective of this note is to give an example of how fencing small watersheds and stocking them with different classes of cattle affected the grazing patterns at one location in the Rio Grande Basin.

STUDY SITE

The San Luis experimental site, 58 miles northwest of Albuquerque, New Mexico, consists of three adjacent watersheds (529, 525, and 364 acres), with southerly drainage, in the transition zone between woodland and semi-desert grassland. Principal forage species are alkali sacaton (Sporobolus airoides Torr.) and galleta (Hilaria jamesii (Torr.) Benth.). Average annual precipitation is 13 inches.[5]

Three distinct topographic types exist on the watersheds--"uplands," "breaks," and "alluvium" (figs. 1 and 2). The high, rocky hills of the "uplands," or headwaters, terminate in rocky "breaks," from which steep

---

[1] Research reported here was conducted in cooperation with the Bureau of Land Management, U. S. Department of the Interior.
[2] The authors are Range Conservationist (Research) and Forestry Research Technician; Rocky Mountain Forest and Range Experiment Station, Albuquerque, New Mexico.
[3] Stoddart, Laurence A., and Smith, A. D. Range Management. 547 pp., McGraw-Hill Book Co., New York, New York. 1955.
[4] Holscher, Clark E., and Woolfolk, E. J. Forage utilization by cattle on northern Great Plains ranges. U. S. Dept. Agr. Cir. 918, 27 pp. 1953.

[5] U. S. Soil Conservation Service. Isohyetal Map, 1951.

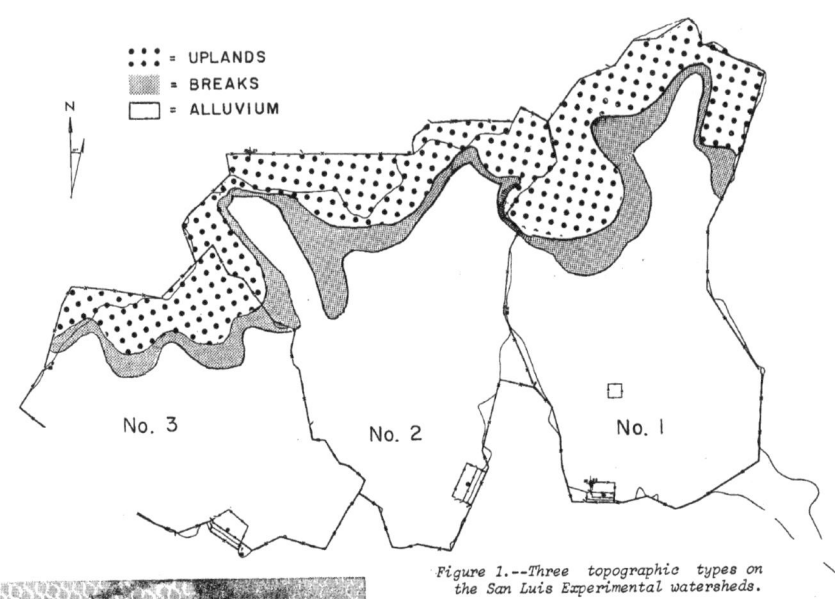

Figure 1.--Three topographic types on the San Luis Experimental watersheds.

Figure 2.--On the San Luis watersheds, the three distinct topographic types are:

Uplands

Breaks   Alluvium

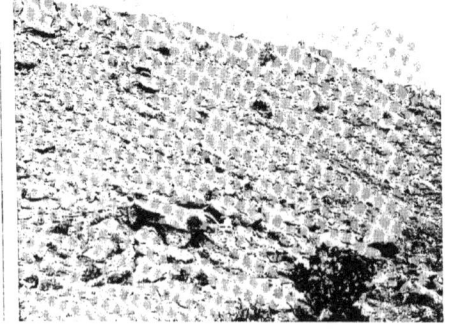

Figure 3.--A stock watering tank is located at the southern end of each watershed.

hillsides extend down to the gently sloping "alluvial" grassland. A stock watering tank is located in this grassland at the southern end of each watershed (fig. 3).

METHODS

The three watersheds were grazed from October to May each year (winter grazing) by various classes of Hereford cattle (table 1).

Prior to 1954, the watersheds were grazed by mixed classes of cattle and horses. Although the area had been broken down into individual grazing allotments, there were few fences, and grazing was more or less on a community-allotment basis. Grazing use was excessive but fairly uniform.

During the first two winters of study (1954-55 and 1955-56) the watersheds were unfenced and were grazed as part of the open range. The next year (1956-57) the lower half of the exterior boundary was fenced. Fencing was completed June 30, 1957, and thereafter animals were confined to individual watersheds during the winter grazing seasons. Fences were constructed along the hogbacks or dividing lines between the in-

Table 1.--Average utilization and average variation of utilization from the mean on the San Luis watersheds, New Mexico, 1954-62

Years	Classes of cattle grazed	Galleta		Alkali sacaton	
		Utilization	Variation	Utilization	Variation
		- - - - Percent - - - -			
1954-55, 1955-56	Yearling steers	32	10.0	39	15.7
1956-57	Mixed herd (cows of all ages, calves, bulls, yearling steers, yearling heifers)	79	12.7	80	19.9
1957-58	Yearling heifers	24	6.3	31	7.6
1958-59	Old cows and calves	21	14.6	46	27.7

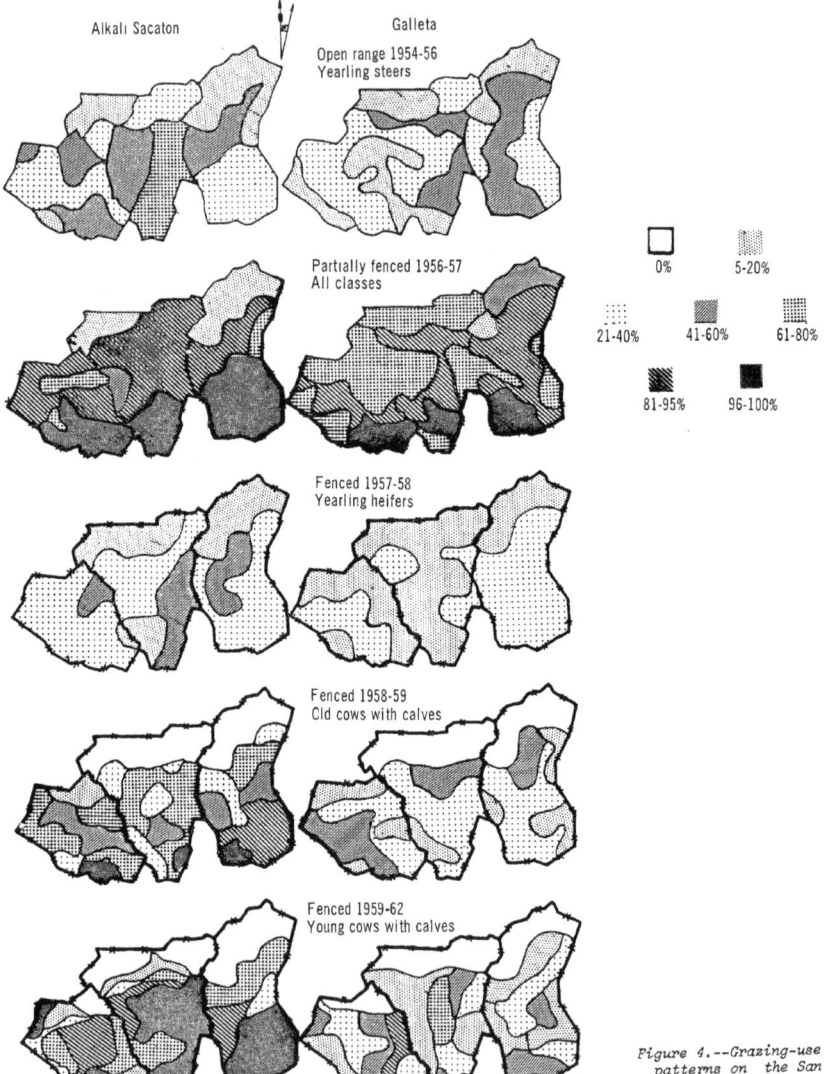

Figure 4.--*Grazing-use patterns on the San Luis watersheds.*

these 2 years was predominantly by yearling steers. During the period, grazing was fairly uniform (fig. 4, table 1). The uplands to the north were used only slightly less than the flat or gently sloping alluvium closer to water. The rocky breaks appeared to present a challenge to yearling steers. At any rate, they tended to graze outlying areas, walk to water, drink and rest, then walk back to distant localities before grazing again. Consequently, use around watering tanks was no heavier than it was in some of the more distant areas.

1956-57.--The east, west, and south boundary fences served as a funnel to the only water in the immediate area, which was located at the extreme southern end of each watershed. Lack of complete control prior to fencing resulted in nearly doubling the anticipated stocking of the three watersheds. Although utilization on all three watersheds was heavy, it was fairly uniform except on areas immediately surrounding the stock tanks. Here utilization of the principal forage species averaged 98 percent. Cows and calves tended to use the juniper areas or areas sheltered by the breaks (fig. 5). Cows also spent a great deal of time around water. Bulls spent most of their time around water and seldom moved as far north as the other classes of cattle, except when following a cow in heat. Yearlings continued to use the uplands.

Figure 5.--Sheltered areas, such as this, received extremely heavy use from cows and calves.

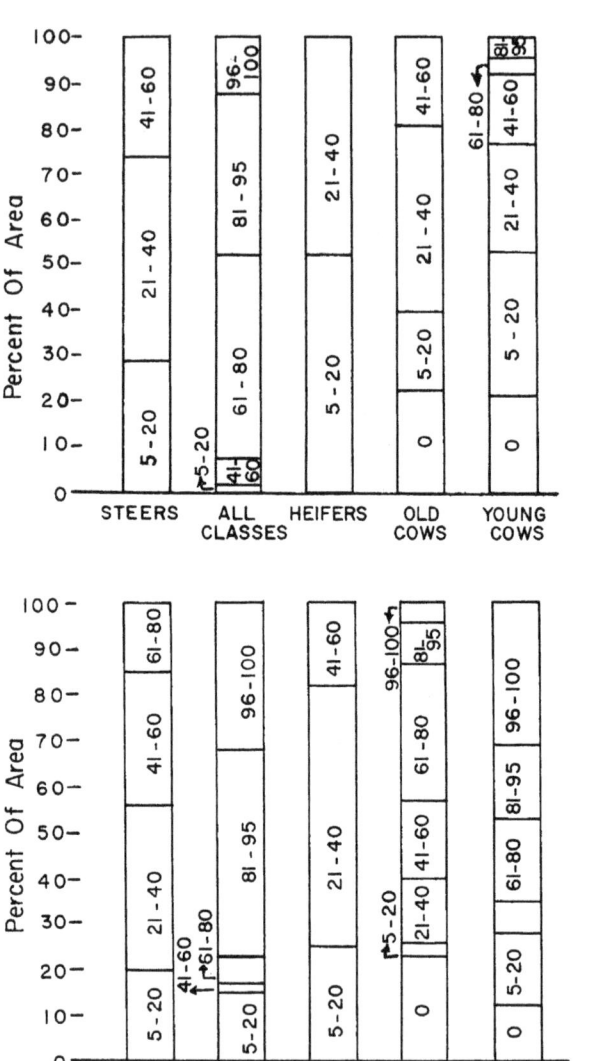

weather. As forage in the lower, alluvial grasslands declined, the young cows used the outer edges of the more difficult terrain, uplands, and breaks. When grazing in steeper terrain, the cows left their calves hidden in the sheltered areas or in the sagebrush flats surrounding the water. Utilization in the vicinity of water was heavier than at any other time except in 1956-57 when cows, as well as other classes of cattle, were present.

CONCLUSIONS

1. Utilization patterns on small watersheds grazed by yearling cattle were about the same before and after fencing.

2. Yearling cattle utilize grasses more uniformly over variable terrain than do either cows with calves or mixed classes of cattle.

3. Yearling heifers are more active than yearling steers on steep, rocky terrain.

4. Cows and calves tend to utilize alkali sacaton and galleta immediately surrounding water much more heavily than do yearlings.

5. Old cows with calves tend to utilize the sheltered areas predominantly, and enter open terrain only when forced out due to lack of forage.

6. Young cows with calves use the open grasslands more than old cows, and enter the edges of the more inaccessible terrain only when faced with a lack of forage.

7. On rough terrain more uniform utilization may be attained by grazing with yearling heifers. When grazed as open range, mixed classes give most uniform use.

July 1964

U.S. FOREST SERVICE
RESEARCH NOTE RM - 22

Use of the Grazed-Plant Method for Estimating Utilization of Some Range Grasses in New Mexico

H. W. Springfield[1] and Geraldine Peterson[2]

The grazed-plant method of estimating utilization has stimulated much interest among range managers. Because the method is rapid and easy to use, it could be a valuable tool in managing large range areas. Several investigators have found the grazed-plant method gives reasonably reliable estimates of utilization. The method has been used successfully for estimating the utilization of Idaho fescue (Festuca idahoensis),[3] bearded bluebunch wheatgrass (Agropyron spicatum),[4] and crested wheatgrass (A. desertorum).[5]

Grazed-plant guides for estimating the utilization of blue grama (Bouteloua gracilis), Kentucky bluegrass (Poa pratensis), mountain muhly (Muhlenbergia montana), and Arizona fescue (Festuca arizonica) were developed in New Mexico from studies conducted on National Forest ranges grazed by cattle in 1961 and 1962. The guides give reasonably precise estimates of utilization up to about 40 to 45 percent utilization by weight.

METHODS OF STUDY

Data for the grazed-plant studies were obtained on National Forest grazing allotments representative of a variety of vegetation types and range conditions (table 1). The data were taken on 100-plant paced transects. Number of transects for each species, together with the number of allotments sampled, was as follows:

	Number of 100-plant transects	Number of allotments sampled
Blue grama	168	24
Kentucky bluegrass	174	25
Mountain muhly	126	20
Arizona fescue	108	18

[1] *Range Conservationist, located at the Station's project headquarters at Albuquerque, in cooperation with the University of New Mexico; central headquarters are maintained at Fort Collins in cooperation with Colorado State University.*
[2] *Statistician, located at central headquarters, Fort Collins, in cooperation with Colorado State University.*
[3] *Hurd, Richard M., and Kissinger, Neland A., Jr. Estimating utilization of Idaho fescue (Festuca idahoensis) on cattle range by percent of plants grazed. U. S. Forest Serv. Rocky Mountain Forest and Range Expt. Sta. Paper 12, 5 pp. 1953.*
[4] *Mattox, James E. A study of percent of plants grazed method of utilization determination and its application. Mont. Agr. Expt. Sta. Mimeo. Cir. 88, 140 pp. 1955.*
[5] *Springfield, H. W. Estimating the utilization of crested wheatgrass from counts of grazed plants. U. S. Forest Serv. Rocky Mountain Forest and Range Expt. Sta. Res. Note 38, 6 pp., illus. 1959.*

Table 1.--Distribution of 100-plant transects by National Forest, vegetation type, and range-condition class, 1961-62

Distribution	Blue grama	Kentucky bluegrass	Mountain muhly	Arizona fescue
	- - -	Number of transects		- - -
National Forest:				
Carson	12	42	30	42
Cibola	78	12	48	36
Lincoln	36	54	12	12
Santa Fe	42	66	36	18
Vegetation type:				
Mixed conifer	12	102	36	30
Ponderosa pine	48	72	78	78
Pinyon-juniper	108	0	12	0
Range-condition class:				
Good	12	18	6	12
Fair	96	90	72	42
Poor	60	66	48	54

Selection of study areas was based on information in allotment analyses, discussions with grazing specialists, and field examination. For each study area, the vegetation type, range-condition class, and grazing season were recorded. On most allotments only one area was studied, but on a few allotments two areas were studied. Transects were taken in the summer of 1961, and repeated on the same study areas in the summer of 1962.

Individual plants observed on paced transects were used for the grazed-plant counts and utilization estimates. A transect consisted of 100 individual plants of one species. Utilization was estimated for each plant on every transect. If less than 5 percent of the herbage was missing, the plant was classed as ungrazed. All transects, six on each study area, had random starting points and directions of travel. Study areas, generally 20 to 100 acres in size, were relatively uniform as to vegetation and topography.

The ocular-estimate-by-average-of-plants method[6] was the standard measure of utilization. The estimate of utilization for each transect was the average of the utilization percentages for the 100 plants observed. Before estimates were made for a species on any area, the technician was trained to estimate varying degrees of utilization by clipping and weighing different amounts of herbage from individual plants.

The method was modified wherever blue grama or Kentucky bluegrass formed a sod. Instead of an individual plant, a 3-inch-diameter circle of sod was used as an observation. Supplemental studies conducted in June 1961, showed that 3-, 4-, or 5-inch loops were better than 2- or 6-inch loops for delimiting plant units. Field experience indicated the grazed-plant data could be taken more readily with a 3-inch loop than with the 4- or 5-inch loops. The loop and 30-inch handle were made of 1/4-inch welding rod.

The data were analyzed by regression with the model: $Y = b_1 X_1 + b_2 X_2$, where Y = percent utilization, X_1 = percent number of plants grazed, and $X_2 = X_1^2$. Separate regression analyses were computed by year, vegetation type, and range-condition class for each species. The resulting regression lines were compared by analysis of covariance.

[6] Pechanec, J. F., and Pickford, G. D. . comparison of some methods used in determining percentage utilization of range grasses. Jour Agr. Res. 54: 753-765. 1937.

RESULTS

Comparatively strong relationships were found between number of plants grazed and estimated utilization by weight for the four grasses studied. Statistical analyses reduced the relationships to three curves--one each for blue grama and Kentucky bluegrass, and a combined curve for mountain muhly and Arizona fescue (fig. 1). Multiple regression equations for the three curves are as follows:

	Regression equation	Correlation coefficient
Blue grama	$Y = 0.11X + 0.0024X^2$	0.99
Kentucky bluegrass	$Y = .08X + .0036X^2$	.98
Mountain muhly-Ariz. fescue	$Y = .11X + .0029X^2$	.98

Statistical analyses showed no differences of practical importance between years, vegetation types, or range-condition classes. Though some statistical differences were found, the differences often amounted to less than 3 percent in utilization.

The curves in figure 1 may be used as guides for estimating utilization of any one of the four grasses on a range area, provided certain procedures are followed. The first step is to select a random starting point and direction of travel. Next, pace off a transect, observe 100 plants of one species, and record the number grazed. Then, using the curve, convert this number of plants grazed to percent utilization. This procedure is repeated for each transect. The final step is to average the utilization percentages for all transects to obtain an estimate of utilization for the area.

Using the curves to convert number of plants grazed to percent utilization for each transect may prove tedious and could introduce personal errors. For these reasons, table 2 was devised to make conversion more convenient, more rapid, and less subject to personal errors.

An example of how to use table 2 follows: Assume 50 random paced transects are taken on a Kentucky bluegrass area. The number of grazed plants and corresponding utilization estimates would be tabulated and averaged as shown below:

Transect number	Grazed plants (Number)	Estimated utilization (Percent)
1	64	19.8
2	46	11.3
3	72	24.3
4	30	5.6
5	80	29.3
6	44	10.5
:	:	:
:	.	.
:	:	:
50	56	15.7
	Total	765.0
	Average	15.3

This average, 15.3 percent, would be the estimate of utilization of bluegrass for the area sampled.

A large number of grazed-plant transects must be taken to arrive at a reliable estimate of utilization for any range area, regardless of whether the area is a small pasture, a site within a pasture, or a fairly large range unit with uniform topography and vegetation. The number of transects needed will depend on the degree of confidence desired in the utilization estimate, and on uniformity of grazing on the area. In the example given above for Kentucky bluegrass, the confidence intervals for different numbers of transects would be as follows:

	Confidence interval	
	0.95	0.99
12 transects	15.3 ± 5.82	15.3 ± 8.73
24 transects	15.3 ± 4.10	15.3 ± 6.15
48 transects	15.3 ± 2.90	15.3 ± 4.35
60 transects	15.3 ± 2.58	15.3 ± 3.87

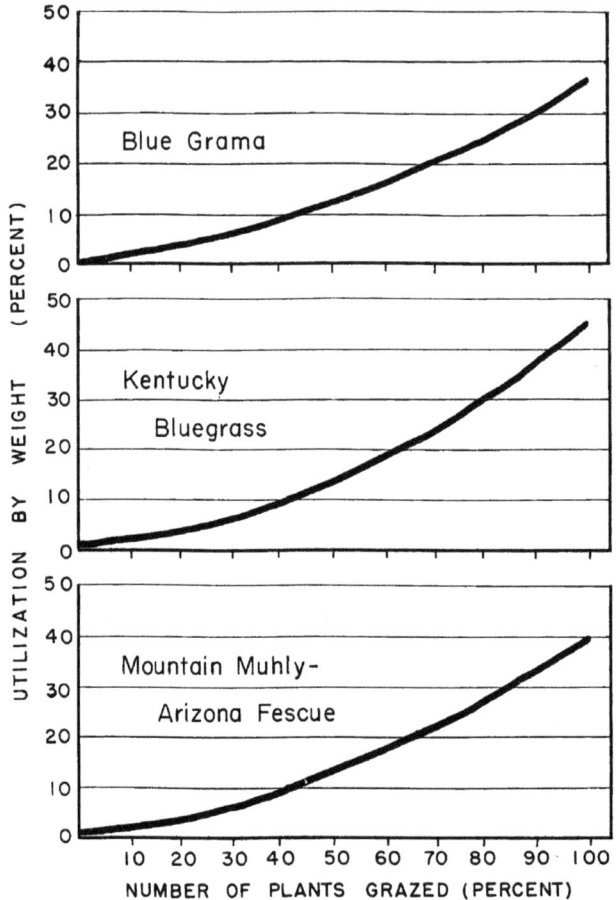

Figure 1.—Grazed-plant utilization curves.

Table 2.--Conversion from number of plants grazed to percent utilization by weight

Number of plants grazed	Blue grama	Kentucky bluegrass	Mountain muhly or Arizona fescue	Number of plants grazed	Blue grama	Kentucky bluegrass	Mountain muhly or Arizona fescue
	------ Percent ------				------ Percent ------		
2	0.2	0.2	0.2	52	12.5	13.8	13.8
4	.5	.4	.5	54	13.2	14.8	14.6
6	.8	.6	.8	56	14.0	15.7	15.5
8	1.1	.9	1.1	58	14.8	16.7	16.4
10	1.4	1.2	1.4	60	15.6	17.7	17.3
12	1.7	1.5	1.8	62	16.4	18.7	18.2
14	2.1	1.8	2.2	64	17.2	19.8	19.2
16	2.4	2.2	2.6	66	18.1	20.9	20.2
18	2.8	2.6	3.0	68	19.0	22.0	21.2
20	3.2	3.0	3.4	70	19.9	23.1	22.2
22	3.7	3.5	3.9	72	20.8	24.3	23.2
24	4.1	4.0	4.4	74	21.7	25.5	24.3
26	4.6	4.5	4.9	76	22.6	26.8	25.4
28	5.1	5.0	5.4	78	23.6	28.0	26.5
30	5.6	5.6	6.0	80	24.6	29.3	27.7
32	6.1	6.2	6.6	82	25.7	30.6	28.8
34	6.7	6.8	7.2	84	26.7	32.0	30.0
36	7.2	7.5	7.8	86	27.8	33.4	31.3
38	7.8	8.2	8.5	88	28.8	34.8	32.5
40	8.4	8.9	9.2	90	29.9	36.2	33.8
42	9.0	9.7	9.9	92	31.0	37.6	35.1
44	9.7	10.5	10.6	94	32.2	39.1	36.4
46	10.4	11.3	11.4	96	33.3	40.7	37.7
48	11.0	12.1	12.2	98	34.5	42.2	39.0
50	11.7	12.9	13.0	100	35.7	43.8	40.4

These figures clearly show the need for a large number of transects if a high degree of confidence is desired in the utilization estimate. In this example, if 48 transects were used to obtain the average, the true value of percent utilization should lie between 12.4 and 18.2 at the 0.95 confidence level, or between 11.0 and 19.6 at the 0.99 level.

The large number of transects is required because the number of plants grazed per transect on an area may vary from 0 to 100. Fewer transects would be needed if the number of plants grazed per transect varied only from 40 to 60, or 70 to 90. Based on the 1961-62 studies, a variation of from 15 to 95 in number of plants grazed per transect can be expected. With this much variation, 50 transects are needed to give a reasonably reliable estimate of utilization for a range area.

Time records kept for grazed-plant studies on crested wheatgrass indicate that only about 5 minutes are required to observe 100 plants along a paced transect and record the data. At 5 minutes per transect, one man could sample an area with 50 grazed-plant transects in about 4 hours if distances between the transects were not too great.

[7] See footnote 5, p. 1.

DISCUSSION AND CONCLUSIONS

The grazed-plant guides may be used for estimating the utilization of blue grama, Kentucky bluegrass, mountain muhly, and Arizona fescue, provided certain limitations of the method are recognized. A number of precautions also must be heeded to avoid biased estimates.

Random sampling of the paced transects is essential for an unbiased estimate. A systematic sample on a grid over the whole area would be satisfactory, but a selected sample based on judgment or chosen for accessibility could lead to very biased results.

Also, a large number of transects should be taken over the range area. Results of these studies suggest 50 transects are needed to give reliable estimate of utilization. If experience with the method shows less variation in the number of grazed plants per transect than found in the 1961-62 studies, fewer transects will be necessary. Degree of confidence desired in the utilization estimate likewise affects the number of transects required. At the 0.99 confidence level, 50 transects are needed for a reasonably precise estimate of utilization. On the other hand, 25 transects give a reasonably good estimate at the lower 0.95 confidence level.

The curves shown in figure 1 may be used for estimating utilization, but table 2 probably will prove more satisfactory. In using either the curves or the table, the main precaution is to convert from number of plants grazed to percent utilization for <u>each transect</u>. Then, average the utilization percentages for all transects to obtain an estimate for the entire area.

A notable limitation of the grazed-plant guides is that they cannot be used on heavily grazed areas. None of the relationships extends beyond 45 percent utilization. For blue grama, the maximum is 36 percent utilization because at this point all plants are grazed. The upper limit is 44 percent for Kentucky bluegrass, and 40 percent for mountain muhly and Arizona fescue. In practice, only range areas with utilization averages substantially less than these upper limits can be sampled satisfactorily. The reason is that, when all plants on a transect are grazed, the utilization could be anywhere from 40 to 100 percent. Therefore, when 100 grazed plants are recorded for one or more transects on an area, the estimated utilization for that area will be in doubt. Consequently, the method can be applied only to areas where all transects have at least one ungrazed plant. As a rule of thumb, the method should not be used where fewer than 5 percent of the plants in the stand are ungrazed.

One further precaution concerns sampling areas where the grass has made considerable regrowth after grazing. During the 1961-62 studies, data were not collected on several areas because the individual grass plants had regrown enough after grazing to obscure the stubble. This problem was encountered with all four species, but especially with Kentucky bluegrass. The method apparently works best on areas where grazing use is current or where very little if any regrowth has taken place since the grass was grazed.

The grazed-plant guides appear to have special value for mid-season utilization checks. Grazing begins in early June on many allotments in New Mexico. A check on utilization often is needed in August to decide when the grazing season should end. The grazed-plant method provides a convenient and practical way of making this mid-season utilization check. When the method is used in August, its shortcomings may be less troublesome than when it is used at the end of the summer season. First, all transects are likely to have at least a few ungrazed plants, and, second, the grazing is more apt to be current, thus avoiding the problem of regrowth obscuring the stubble.

Despite its limitations and the necessary precautions, the grazed-plant method has merit as a relatively rapid way of estimating utilization. The method may be difficult to apply on yearlong ranges, but should work well on summer ranges.

July 1964

U.S. FOREST SERVICE
RESEARCH NOTE RM - 23

SERVICE
EPARTMENT OF AGRICULTURE

Sawmill and Logging Residues from Ponderosa Pine Trees in the Black Hills

E. F. Landt and R. O. Woodfin, Jr.[1]

Sawmill and logging residues are an important source of raw material in the Black Hills. The material has been of little value locally in the past, however, because of lack of markets. The increasing use of sawmill residue for pulpwood has brought the Black Hills supply into the focus of the Lake States pulp and paper industry. This increase in interest brought with it the need for an accurate determination of the amounts and kinds of residues available for use, from both logging and milling. A previous study provided information on the proportion of a log that ends up as residues, but it did not provide information on the entire tree.[2] Therefore, the study reported here was undertaken to include the logging aspects, and in general arrive at the portion of the tree that ends up as lumber, and that which becomes residue.

This investigation required that both logging and milling residues be measured so that

[1] *Technologists, located at Rapid City, in cooperation with South Dakota School of Mines and Technology; central headquarters are maintained at Fort Collins, in cooperation with Colorado State University.*
[2] *Kotok, E. S. An estimate of residues at a small sawmill in the Black Hills. U. S. Forest Serv. Rocky Mountain Forest and Range Expt. Sta. Res. Note 17, 6 pp., illus. 1955.*

a complete accounting of what happens to a tree could be made. The entire stem of the sawtimber trees from stump to a 4-inch top, excluding the limbs, was measured. Residue conversion factors were computed for "putting the tree back together again," and for determining the volumes of the various kinds of residues that resulted during processing, from the woods to finished lumber.

METHODS

Logging residues were measured on 300 trees; 50 trees were selected at random on each of six different logging operations. The 300 trees were selected along a line from the stream bottom to the ridgetop to include variation in tree form due to site. Each tree was measured and scaled after it had been felled and bucked, but before the logs were skidded. Log bucking was not controlled but taken as normal practice. Total tree height to 8-inch (sawtimber minimum top, d.i.b.) and 4-inch (pulpwood minimum top, d.i.b) tops, and measurements of logs, tops, and cull logs were identified by individual tree (fig. 1). Diameter and length were measured on each log of the tree for cubic foot content determinations by Smalian's formula. Logs were scaled by the Scribner Decimal C Log Rule. Separate measurements were made to determine the volume of the tops included in the portion of the tree from the 8-inch point to the 4-inch point.

The ovendry weight of each log, tree top to a 4-inch d.i.b., and cull log, was computed by multiplying cubic foot content by 24.1 pounds per cubic foot, the average ovendry density of Black Hills ponderosa pine.[3] The weight of the bark on logging residues was computed with a factor of 11 percent bark weight per rough green cord.[4]

These weights and the net log scale of trees were used to determine logging residue conversion factors in terms of ovendry tons per M b.m. net log scale.

Sawmill residues were measured at six sawmills with circular headrigs. Two of the mills did not have resaws, two had cant sash gang resaws, and two had horizontal band resaws. A total of 277 logs were sampled from logs available at the six mills. At each mill the logs were selected by diameter and length classes from both sound and defective logs (logs with scalable defect):

---

[3] Drow, J. T., Dohr, A. W., and Bellosillo, S. *Mechanical properties of ponderosa pine from the Black Hills.* U. S. Forest Serv. Forest Prod. Lab. Rpt. 2090, 18 pp., illus. 1957.

[4] Landt, E. F., and Woodfin, R. O., Jr. *Pulpwood characteristics of Black Hills ponderosa pine.* Tappi, 42 (10): 809-812, illus. 1959.

Figure 1.--Measuring top of a ponderosa pine sawtimber tree for cubic foot determinations.

mills. Twenty-five 16-foot boards were selected from each 4-, 6-, 8-, and 10-inch width class. Each board was weighed before and after surfacing, but before trimming, to isolate the weight of shavings. Next the dry trim was collected and weighed. Moisture contents of the boards, determined by a moisture meter, were used to convert the weight of shavings and trim to an ovendry weight. Conversion factors for shavings and surfaced trim were expressed in ovendry tons per M b.m. rough lumber.

RESULTS

Logging residues.--Conversion factors for tops left in the woods, cull logs, and bark averaged 0.3215, 0.3918, and 0.0678 ton per M b.m. net Scribner log scale, or 0.2776, 0.3383, and 0.0585 ton per M b.m. rough lumber tally, respectively.

Actual volume of tops left in the woods averaged 4.65 cubic feet per tree, and by logging area ranged from an average of 2.92 to

9.08 cubic feet per tree (table 1). The volume of tops between the 8-inch point and the 4-inch point averaged 3.08 cubic feet per tree, and by logging area ranged from an average of 2.60 to 3.53 cubic feet per tree (table 1).

Table 2 shows the average cubic foot volume of tops for trees by d.b.h. For example, a 9-inch tree averaged 5.65 cubic feet of tops (8-inch d.i.b. to 4-inch d.i.b.) whereas a 20-inch tree averaged 1.90 cubic feet of tops.

Sawmill residues.--The original intention was to obtain a regression of each yield residue per M b.m. on log diameter at each mill type from the sample log data for sound and defective logs separately. The frequency distribution of log diameters in the population,

Table 1.--Volume of tops in Black Hills ponderosa pine sawtimber trees on six logging areas (50 trees from each area)

Logging area	Average d.b.h.	Scribner log scale per tree		Scalable defect	Average volume of tops per tree			
		Gross	Net		8- to 4-inch d.i.b.		Left in woods	
	Inches	Bd. ft.		Percent	Cu. ft.	Cords[1]	Cu. ft.	Cords[1]
Benchmark	15.7	202	174	13.9	3.53	0.0465	4.45	0.0586
Redbird	16.4	250	102	59.2	2.60	.0343	9.08	.1196
Bobcat	17.1	293	264	9.9	2.95	.0389	3.78	.0498
Iron Creek	14.4	201	160	20.4	3.31	.0436	3.91	.0515
Lost Gulch	14.5	155	116	25.2	3.18	.0419	2.92	.0385
Norris Peak	17.9	281	230	18.2	2.92	.0385	3.75	.0494
Average	16.0	230	175	23.9	3.08	.0406	4.65	.0612

[1] 75.9 cubic feet in a standard rough cord (see text footnote 4).

Table 2.--Volume of tops in Black Hills ponderosa pine trees between 8 inches d.i.b. and 4 inches d.i.b. (Basis: 300 trees)

D.b.h.[1] (inches)	No. of trees	Volume of tops per tree		
		Raw data	Curved data[2]	
		Cu.ft.	Cu.ft.	Rough cords[3]
9	1	5.65	5.46	0.0719
10	12	4.75	4.95	.0652
11	21	4.59	4.46	.0588
12	35	3.98	3.98	.0524
13	32	3.58	3.58	.0472
14	36	2.98	3.16	.0416
15	28	2.79	2.90	.0382
16	31	2.39	2.65	.0349
17	19	3.00	2.43	.0320
18	25	2.38	2.25	.0296
19	17	2.21	2.10	.0277
20	8	1.90	2.00	.0264
21	12	3.28	1.89	.0249
22	7	2.31	1.78	.0235
23	7	1.87	1.70	.0224
24	2	1.33	1.64	.0216
25	2	1.03	1.57	.0207
26	3	2.10	1.50	.0198
27	1	1.27	1.44	.0190
28	0	--	1.39	.0183
29	1	1.40	1.34	.0177

[1] Inch classes; i.e., 10-inch class = 10.0-10.9.
[2] Curve fitted by hand.
[3] 75.9 cubic feet in a standard rough cord (see text footnote 4).

as obtained from a previous study,[5] would then be used with the regression to obtain a weighted residue estimate for the population. The analysis showed nonsignificant regressions for all residue items except slabs, which indicates that residue amounts could be considered independent of log diameter. The slab regressions showed significantly greater amounts of slabs from small logs at all mills, but were not particularly good for prediction purposes due to the large unaccountable error ($r^2 < 0.35$). The conversion factors were therefore obtained separately for sound and defective logs as a simple average of the individual logs for each mill type (table 3).

[5] *Landt, E. F., and Woodfin, R. O., Jr. Amounts and grades of lumber from Black Hills ponderosa pine logs. U. S. Forest Serv. Rocky Mountain Forest and Range Expt. Sta. Sta. Paper 42, 24 pp., illus. 1959.*

Table 3.--Conversion factors for residues at three types of circular-headrig sawmills cutting 4/4 rough lumber from ponderosa pine in the Black Hills

Type of mill, condition of logs, and weighted averages	Chippable residues				Fine residues			Total all residues
	Slabs	Edgings	Rough trim	Cull lumber	Sawdust	Bark		
	Ovendry tons per M b.m. rough lumber tally[1]							
NO RESAW:								
Sound logs	0.3157 ± 0.0536	0.1470 ± 0.0318	0.0675 ± 0.0568	0	0.6425 ± 0.0660	0.2589 ± 0.0424		1.4316 ± 0.1144
Defective logs	0.4764 ± 0.1396	0.1730 ± 0.0288	0.1542 ± 0.0330	0.1144 ± 0.1260	0.9047 ± 0.2098	0.2937 ± 0.0444		2.1164 ± 0.4246
Weighted average[2]	0.3880 ± 0.0695	0.1587 ± 0.0217	0.1065 ± 0.0341	0.0515 ± 0.0567	0.7604 ± 0.1012	0.2745 ± 0.0307		1.7398 ± 0.2012
CANT SASH GANG MILLS:								
Sound logs	0.2467 ± 0.0428	0.1104 ± 0.0152	0.0862 ± 0.0266	0	0.4834 ± 0.0612	0.1909 ± 0.0216		1.1176 ± 0.0940
Defective logs	0.3461 ± 0.0572	0.1473 ± 0.0240	0.1831 ± 0.0394	0.0667 ± 0.0546	0.6677 ± 0.0826	0.2456 ± 0.0306		1.6565 ± 0.1890
Weighted average[2]	0.2914 ± 0.0349	0.1270 ± 0.0136	0.1298 ± 0.0230	0.0300 ± 0.0245	0.5663 ± 0.0501	0.2155 ± 0.0181		1.3601 ± 0.0995
HORIZONTAL BAND MILLS:								
Sound logs	0.2594 ± 0.0436	0.2531 ± 0.0416	0.1090 ± 0.0330	0	0.3992 ± 0.0596	0.2786 ± 0.0338		1.2993 ± 0.1414
Defective logs	0.3891 ± 0.0776	0.2881 ± 0.0426	0.1863 ± 0.0496	0.2136 ± 0.1550	0.6285 ± 0.1180	0.3125 ± 0.0470		2.0181 ± 0.3488
Weighted average[2]	0.3178 ± 0.0424	0.2688 ± 0.0298	0.1438 ± 0.0288	0.0961 ± 0.0704	0.5024 ± 0.0624	0.2939 ± 0.0282		1.6228 ± 0.1751

[1] 95 percent confidence limit.

[2] Weighted average obtained by averaging sound and defective conversion factors with weights of 0.55 and 0.45, respectively, the relative rough lumber recovery volumes of sound and defective logs obtained from a previous study (see text footnote 5).

Planing mill residues.--The remaining residue category consists of shavings and dry trim. The conversion factor for shavings was found to average 0.3442 ton per M b.m., while that for dry trim averaged 0.0458 ton. No significant difference was found in amount of shavings and trim produced at the five different planing mills.

Relation of lumber recovery to residue.-- With reference to all mill types, from 56 to 60 percent of the tree ends up as sawing and planing residues, while 21 to 23 percent ends up as lumber (fig. 4). The remaining 19 to 21 percent ends up as logging residues. The mills without resaws converted more of the tree into sawmill residues (60 percent) and less into lumber than the mills with resaws. However, even sawmills with resaws yielded only 21 to 23 percent of the tree as lumber.

DISCUSSION

Results of residue measurements of Black Hills ponderosa pine sawtimber trees to a 4-inch top diameter showed that from 77 to 79 percent of the tree ends up as residues. Logging residues totaled 19 to 21 percent, while sawmill and planing mill residues totaled from 56 to 60 percent. Sawmills with conventional circular headrigs and without resaws produced from 1 to 4 percent more residues than did mills with resaws. This was due primarily to the greater amounts of sawdust at the mills without resaws. As can be seen in figure 4, most residues are produced at the sawmill.

Chippable residues make up from 18 to 24 percent of the tree. The total in form of slabs, edgings, rough trim, and cull lumber ranged from 0.5782 to 0.8265 ton per M b.m. rough lumber tally, whereas chippable logging residue in the form of tops and cull logs added an additional 0.6159 ton per M b.m. Sawmills would therefore have access to a total of from 1.1941 to 1.4424 tons of chippable material per thousand board feet rough lumber tally if all the residues could be debarked and assembled economically for chipping. Generally, chippable sawmill residues have a cost advantage because most of the cost of transportation and production has been paid for by the lumber. Results of this study showed that sawmills can expect to recover from one-half to two-thirds of a unit of chips (one unit = 2,400 pounds ovendry) for every 1,000 board feet of 4/4 lumber cut. These amounts are based on current utilization standards where the minimum top diameter saw log is 8 inches.

With the exception of slabs, log diameter did not affect the amount of residues per M b.m. produced at the three types of mills. Because the relation was weak, even for slabs, the means were used as conversion factors.

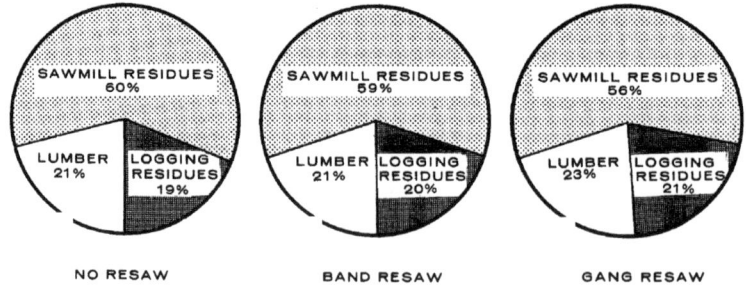

Figure 4.--Proportion of the tree (to a 4-inch top) in logging residues, sawmill residues, and lumber at three types of circular headrig sawmills.

Scalable defect in logs, however, did have a strong influence on residue yields. Generally, the amount of chippable residue produced from cutting 1,000 board feet of lumber from defective logs was double that from sound logs. Also, mill type influenced residue yields, especially sawdust. For example, the circular headrig mills without resaws produced the highest proportion of sawdust. Mills with resaws, where more of the lumber from a log was cut on thinner saws than the circular headrig, produced about 1,000 pounds of sawdust per M b.m. of lumber produced. In contrast, the mills without resaws, where all the log was cut into lumber on the circular headrig, produced about 1,500 pounds of sawdust per M b.m. of lumber.

To illustrate the magnitude of the amounts of residue produced in a normal lumbering operation, logging and sawmill residue weights were computed for a gang resaw mill cutting 30,000 board feet of rough green 4/4 lumber per day (table 4). This example shows that the gang resaw mill would produce 17.3 tons of ovendry chippable residues a day (30×0.5782= 17.3 tons) plus 18.4 tons of chippable material in the form of tops and cull logs in the woods (30 × 0.2776 + 30 × 0.3383). In addition, 35.2 tons of ovendry sawmill and planing residues would be produced in the form of sawdust, bark, shavings, and trim. Similar calculations can be made for mills without resaws or with a band resaw by using the residue conversion factors listed in table 3.

Table 4. --Estimated weight of ovendry logging and sawmilling residues from the production of 30 M b.m. of 4/4 ponderosa pine lumber by circular headrig sawmill with cant gang resaw

Product	Residue conversion factor	Total weight	
	Tons per M b.m. rough lumber tally	- - - - Tons - - - -	Percent
RESIDUES:			
Logging --			
Tops left in woods	0.2776	8.3	
Cull logs	.3383	10.1	
Bark	.0585	1.8	
Total		20.2	21
Sawmill--			
Chippable	.5782	17.3	
Sawdust	.5663	17.0	
Bark	.2155	6.5	
Total		40.8	43
Planing--			
Shavings	.3442	10.3	
Trim	.0458	1.4	
Total		11.7	13
All residues		72.7	77
LUMBER:			
Surface dry		21.6	23
Total		94.3	100

SUMMARY AND CONCLUSIONS

Results of measurements on 300 trees and 277 saw logs revealed that Black Hills ponderosa pine trees yield from 77 to 79 percent of the tree weight to a 4-inch top diameter in residues of various kinds. Only 21 to 23 percent ends up as lumber (fig. 4). These proportions of residues and lumber were determined by use of conversion factors developed for logging residues, sawmill residues, and planing residues for three kinds of circular headrig sawmills, and for both sound logs and logs with scalable defect.

The defective logs without exception showed larger conversion factors than the sound logs. Significant differences were also found between the conversion factors for the various kinds of sawmill residues produced at three types of circular headrig sawmills. For example, the largest amount of total residue was produced at sawmills with no resaws, but the largest amount of chippable residue was produced at the band resaw mills. Chippable residue yields ranged from one-half a unit at the gang resaw mills to two-thirds a unit at the band resaw mills.

July 1964

U.S. FOREST SERVICE
RESEARCH NOTE RM - 24

U.S. DEPARTMENT OF AGRICULTURE

Soil Water Storage Under Natural and Cleared Stands of Alligator and Utah Juniper in Northern Arizona

C. M. Skau[1]

Will clearing juniper appreciably affect soil water storage? This question was investigated on Beaver Creek Watershed on Arizona's Mogollon Rim. Here, clearing operations have been underway since 1957 for purposes of improving forage and water yields.

This area experiences two distinct "wet" periods--a summer period from about July to September, and a winter period from about December to April. Emphasis was given to sampling at the beginning and ending of "wet" periods, or over the widest range of soil water storage. Emphasis was also given to warmer months or "growing season" when soil water differences between cleared and natural areas presumably would be more pronounced.

Soil water measurements were restricted to percent water by weight in the upper 2 feet of soil, a Springerville clay to clay loam. For quantitative comparisons, a difference of 1 percent by weight over the upper 2 feet of soil is approximately equal to a layer of water three-tenths of an inch deep.[2]

Ten pairs of 50-foot-square plots were located at 1/2- to 3-mile intervals along and 100 yards away from boundaries of areas recently cleared of juniper. Five pairs were in the Utah juniper (Juniperus osteosperma (Torr.) Little) type and five pairs in the alligator juniper (J. deppeana Steud.) type. A pair consisted of plots located 50 to 100 yards on either side of a clearing boundary (aspect, slope, and slope position being similar). Plots of a pair were then matched for number and height of trees, soil depth, and soil type (table 1). In the clearing operation, trees are left on the ground; this makes it possible to determine tree number and height for cleared plots.

A Veihmeyer tube was used to obtain four randomly located samples from each plot on each of nine dates. Cores were weighed, ovendried at $104°$ C. for 48 hours, and reweighed. Percent moisture was calculated by dividing weight lost by ovendried weight.

To better interpret results, measurements of ground cover (table 1) and precipitation (table 2) were also obtained.

---

[1] *Research Forester, Rocky Mountain Forest and Range Experiment Station with central headquarters maintained at Fort Collins, in cooperation with Colorado State University.*
[2] *Skau, C. M. Some hydrologic characteristics in the Utah juniper type of northern Arizona. 1960. Unpublished Ph.D. thesis on file at Mich. State Univ., East Lansing.*

RESULTS AND DISCUSSION

Table 2 summarizes results of 90 comparisons: 9 dates times 10 plot pairs. More water was stored on cleared plots for 75 of the 90 comparisons. Differences were small, however, ranging from -6.6 to +8.7 percent, with only 15 exceeding ± 4.0 percent. The overall average difference between cleared and natural plots was 1.1 percent for alligator juniper and 2.5 percent for Utah juniper--less, in either case, than a layer of water 1.0 inch deep.

Interestingly, the differences between cleared and natural plots were not particularly related to the level of soil water; twice in late June, for example, near the end of droughtlike weather, there was an average difference of about 2 percent. Similarly, on April 4, 1960, following considerably above-average winter precipitation, the average difference was well within the sampling error.

Differences in stored water were not pronounced in the "growing season" or warmer months. One explanation is provided in table 1: in September, cleared plots supported one to nine times as much ground cover as natural plots. Perhaps these volunteer species keep soil water at the same level found in natural areas.

From a practical point of view, the investigations indicate that: (1) clearing may considerably increase water available for forage production, and (2) clearing will have little effect on water yields insofar as they are influenced by soil water storage in the upper 24 inches. Not only is there little difference in stored water between cleared and natural areas, but much storage capacity remains unused year-round. These soils have a water storage capacity of about 3 to 3-1/2 inches of water per foot of soil in the range between near wilting point and saturation.[2] The corresponding range in percent water by weight is from about 17 at the wilting point to 37 percent at saturation. The highest value measured from one plot was about 29 percent on April 4, 1960, following considerably above-average winter precipitation. Unused storage capacity would be about 2.70 inches.

Finally, it should be emphasized that the conclusions are conditioned by: (1) the limited number of sites and dates used, (2) the fact that all soils were at least 2 feet deep, and (3) the assumption of matching paired plots.

Table 1.--Comparison of data from paired plots in cleared (C) and natural (N) stands of two juniper species on two types of soil, Springerville clay (C) and Springerville clay loam (CL)

Species and plot pairs		Number of trees		Average height		Average ground cover[1]		Average soil depth[2]		Soil type	
		C	N	C	N	C	N	C	N	C	N
				Ft.		Lbs./acre		Ft.			
Alligator juniper:	1	5	4	9	11	82	48	2.3	2.9	C	C
	2	4	8	10	10	87	37	2.0	2.0	C	C
	3	11	8	11	10	55	44	2.8	3.0	C	C
	4	9	7	12	13	99	16	3.5	4.0	CL	CL
	5	10	9	12	10	72	39	2.7	3.2	CL	CL
Utah juniper:	1	6	4	9	10	90	48	2.3	2.3	C	C
	2	1	1	14	14	118	13	2.0	2.1	C	C
	3	5	9	17	15	37	6	2.8	3.1	C	C
	4	1	5	15	10	62	44	2.8	3.5	C	C
	5	5	6	10	12	24	24	3.2	3.0	C	C

[1] As of September 1959, based on 5 milacre subplots; vegetation clipped and dried at 67°F.
[2] Based on 5 random samples per plot.

Table 2.--Comparisons of average soil moisture in the upper 2 feet for five cleared[1] and five natural[1] plots in each of two juniper types on nine sampling dates, 1959-60

Date		Average soil moisture			Average precipitation between sampling dates
		Cleared	Natural	Difference	
		- - - - Percent - - - -			Inches
		ALLIGATOR JUNIPER			
1959:	June 30	19.0	17.0	2.0	--
	July 25	21.0	19.4	1.6	0.98
	August 3	19.0	18.1	.9	1.64
	September 4	20.5	19.6	.9	3.12
1960:	April 4	27.8	29.2	-1.4	15.04
	May 12	27.0	25.1	1.9	1.64
	June 29	19.3	17.4	1.9	.35
	September 14	25.5	24.7	.8	6.84
	December 1	24.2	22.6	1.6	2.90
	Average			1.1	
		UTAH JUNIPER			
1959:	June 30	18.6	16.3	2.3	--
	July 25	23.0	18.9	4.1	1.23
	August 3	19.2	17.7	1.5	1.11
	September 4	21.6	19.8	1.8	3.42
1960:	April 4	27.7	26.1	1.6	12.72
	May 12	26.6	22.1	4.5	1.52
	June 29	18.0	16.2	1.8	0
	September 14	21.3	19.2	2.1	4.16
	December 1	21.7	18.9	2.8	2.75
	Average			2.5	

[1] Average of twenty 2-foot-deep samples; i.e., four random samples per plot for five plots.

August 1964

U.S. FOREST SERVICE
RESEARCH NOTE RM -25

FOREST SERVICE
U.S. DEPARTMENT OF AGRICULTURE

Some Factors Affecting Germination of Fourwing Saltbush

by

H. W. Springfield[1]

Because of many desirable characteristics, fourwing saltbush (Atriplex canescens) is one of the most valuable browse plants on Southwestern ranges. Studies of native stands indicate this species grows under a wide variety of environmental conditions, withstands drought, heat, and cold, and provides palatable, nutritious forage the year round for both game and livestock. More than 40 years ago, animal husbandmen recognized the importance of fourwing saltbush as forage for range cattle, and advocated increasing it on New Mexico range. But they admitted their attempts to establish stands artificially were largely unsuccessful (Foster, et al. 1921).

Through the years, fourwing saltbush has been seeded numerous times by ranchers and public agencies; some succeeded, but most of them failed. We cannot explain the failures until more is learned about the factors governing successful establishment. More information is needed on how germination and establishment are affected by source of seed, age of seed, conditions of seed storage, depth and time of seeding, soil moisture and temperature, insects, diseases, rodents, rabbits, and other factors.

This report presents preliminary information on the effects of differences in source of seed, treatment of seed, and temperatures on germination of fourwing saltbush seed in the laboratory. Several of the findings appear to have application value for range seedings.

LITERATURE REVIEW

A number of exploratory studies were conducted from 1924 to 1928 near Las Cruces, New Mexico, with fourwing saltbush seed collected locally (Wilson 1928). Germination tested at 68° to 86°F. ranged from 0 to 36 percent for 11 lots of seed; percentage germination decreased little if any until the seed was at least 6 or 7 years old. Based on other studies conducted from 1936 to 1941 on the College Ranch north of Las Cruces, N. M., Bridges (1941) concluded that, in spite of numerous failures, reseeding with fourwing saltbush will eventually be successful. Of 26 seeding trials, the seed failed to germinate in 11, and while some germination took place in 15 trials, only 1 gave a good stand. He attributed the failures to rabbit depredation, poor seedbed preparation, and seeding at the wrong time of year.

[1] *Range Conservationist, located at Albuquerque, in cooperation with the University of New Mexico; central headquarters are maintained at Fort Collins, in cooperation with Colorado State University.*

The Woody Plant Seed Manual (U. S. Forest Serv., 1948) reports fourwing saltbush seed exhibit variable dormancy. Some lots germinate promptly without any pretreatment; others germinate over a period of 1 or 2 years after sowing in nursery beds. In one series of tests, stratification at 41°F. did not improve germination. The Manual lists the following information:

	Seeds per pound (Number)	Germination (Percent)
Low	10,500	4
Average	22,500	18
High	40,000	47

Recommendations were to conduct germination tests in sand flats at 50°F. (night) to 77°F. (day) for 20 to 30 days.

Detailed studies by Hervey [2] with fourwing saltbush seed collected near Delta, Colorado, showed removal of the wings by hammer-milling improved the ease of handling, but did not affect germination. Fewer seeds stored in sealed containers at 37° to 41°F. germinated than seeds stored open or in sealed containers at room temperatures for 3 years (19 percent, compared with 21 and 24 percent). Vermiculite proved a good medium for germination tests in petri dishes because results were close to those obtained in the nursery. Treating seed with fungicides did not affect germination percentages. Temperature had no influence on germination until it dropped below 59°F. Germination was 47 percent at 68°F., 45 percent at 59°F., and 7 percent at 39°F.

Inhibitors in the seed coat and bracts may be responsible for the generally low germination percentages. Germination of other species of Atriplex in Australia was found to be inhibited by substances diffusing from the fruit bracts, and the inhibitor was classed as a chloride (Beadle 1952). Koller's studies with an annual Atriplex in Israel (1957) indicated the presence

---

[2] *Hervey, Donald F. Factors which influence the reseeding of certain browse species in Colorado. 1955. (Unpublished doctoral dissertation on file at School of Forestry, Agricultural and Mechanical College of Texas, College Station, Texas.)*

Table 1.--Description of eight sites in Arizona and New Mexico where fourwing saltbush seeds were collected in 1961, and the number of seeds per pound

Seed source	Identification No.	Characteristics of collection site			Date seed collected	Seeds per pound	
		Geographic location	Elevation	Annual precipitation		Winged	De-winged
			Feet	Inches		Number	
NEW MEXICO:							
Isleta	A-27	1 mi. E. of Isleta	5,000	9	Oct.	18,000	29,200
Mountainair	A-43	5 mi. S. of Mountainair	6,700	14	Oct.	19,100	38,100
Corona	A-48	6 mi. W. of Corona	6,300	15	Oct.	25,300	38,800
Ionica	A-79	20 mi. W. of Magdalena	6,600	13	Nov.	14,800	27,900
Glenwood	A-94	3 mi. S. of Glenwood	4,500	14	Oct.	28,900	51,300
ARIZONA:							
Flagstaff	A-85	18 mi. NW. of San Francisco Peaks	6,500	17	Dec.	34,000	58,100
Beaver Creek	A-86	3 mi. SE. of Camp Verde	3,500	14	Dec.	26,600	53,800
Chevelon	A-78	30 mi. S. of Winslow	6,200	15	Nov.	17,500	31,100

stored dry at 55° or 39°F. had germinated, but more than 50 percent of the seed stored wet at 53°F. germinated and could not be used for further tests.

The germination tests of Isleta, Mountainair, and Corona seed were begun January 11 in petri dishes with wet vermiculite as the substrate. Twenty-five seeds were put in each dish. Three germination temperatures were compared: 73°F., 54°F., and 39°F. The dishes were arranged in a factorial design which provided four replicates of every treatment applied to each seed source. Germinated seeds were counted at 2-day intervals for 28 days.

All eight sources of seed listed in table 1 were included in the second test. Procedures were the same as in the first test except that one of the seed was soaked. Half of the seeds in each lot were de-winged before the germination test was begun February 8. Three temperatures were compared: 77°F., 58°F., and 2°F. Germinated seeds were counted every day for 36 days.

RESULTS

First Test--Three Seed Sources

Seed collected near Isleta and Mountainair germinated better than seed from Corona:

	Germination after 28 days (Percent)
Isleta	49.9
Mountainair	44.0
Corona	16.5

Soaking the seed for 8 hours to remove chlorides or other inhibitors had no effect on germination (table 2). Isleta seed tended to germinate better when not soaked, but the average responses of all three sources showed no significant difference in germination between soaked and unsoaked seed.

Germination was significantly higher at an average temperature of 54°F. than at 73°F.

Table 2.--Comparison of fourwing saltbush seeds soaked in water for 8 hours and those not soaked as shown by percentage germination; seeds from three collection sites in New Mexico

Storage temperature	Average germination temperature	Seed treatment	Seed sources			
			Isleta	Mountainair	Corona	Average
			- - - - Percent germination - - - -			
55° F.	73.3° F.	Soaked	24	43	9	25.3
		Not soaked	52	38	8	32.7
	54.5° F.	Soaked	66	58	42	55.3
		Not soaked	70	60	18	49.3
39° F.	73.3° F.	Soaked	33	40	11	28.0
		Not soaked	54	27	11	30.7
	38.9° F.	Soaked	0	0	0	0
		Not soaked	0	0	0	0

All three sources of seed germinated better at the lower temperature. No seeds germinated at 39°F.

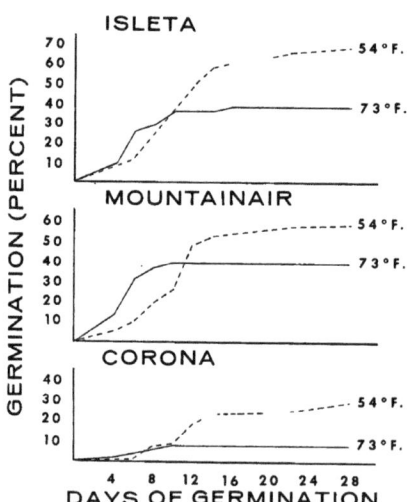

Figure 1.--Germination rates of fourwing saltbush seed at 54° F. and 73° F. during a 28-day test period.

Germination began faster at 73°F. than at 54°F. (fig. 1). On the sixth day, for example, about twice as many seeds had germinated at the higher temperature. By the tenth day, however, germination had stopped at 73°F., but was rapid at 54°F. Rate of germination continued to be rapid at 54°F. until the fourteenth day.

None of the seeds stored dry at 39°F. for 52 days, then put in petri dishes with wet vermiculite for 28 days at 39°F., germinated. Apparently the seed remained dormant for the entire 80 days at this relatively low temperature.

De-winging the seed did not affect the final germination percentages (table 3). Winged and de-winged seed germinated about the same regardless of seed source or germination temperature, although the de-winged seed germinated more quickly than the winged seed (fig. 2). This was most pronounced for seed germinated at 54°F., where germination of de-winged seeds remained higher than winged seeds for 26 days. In contrast, at 73°F. the winged seed equaled the de-winged seed in germination by about the tenth day.

Second Test--Eight Seed Sources

Germination varied considerably according to source of seed and germination temperature. Isleta seed germinated better than seed from

Table 3.--Comparison of winged and de-winged fourwing saltbush seeds as shown by percentage germination at end of 28 days; seeds from three collection sites in New Mexico

Storage temperature	Average germination temperature	Seed treatment	Seed sources			
			Isleta	Mountainair	Corona	Average
			---- Percent germination ----			
55° F.	73.3° F.	Winged	33	49	10	30.7
		De-winged	43	32	7	27.3
	54.5° F.	Winged	60	64	34	52.7
		De-winged	76	54	26	52.0
39° F.	73.3° F.	Winged	53	32	5	30.0
		De-winged	34	36	17	29.0
	38.9° F.	Winged	0	0	0	0
		De-winged	0	0	0	0

any of the other seven sources. Based on average germination for all treatments included in the 36-day test, the different sources could be grouped as follows:

	Percent
High germination:	
Isleta	74.3
Medium germination:	
Mountainair	45.7
Flagstaff	42.3
Corona	36.7
Low germination:	
Chevelon	29.3
Glenwood	27.3
Monica	26.3
Beaver Creek	26.3

The germination percentages showed no apparent relationship with elevation, annual precipitation, or latitude of the collection site, or with size of seed (number of seeds per pound).

Germination was significantly higher at average temperatures of 58°F. or 42°F. than at 77°F. (fig. 3). For all sources of seed tested, germination was substantially less at the highest temperature. Improvement in percent germination at 58°F. compared with 77°F. was especially pronounced for the Corona, Glenwood, Flagstaff, and Beaver Creek seed. Though there was a trend toward higher germi-

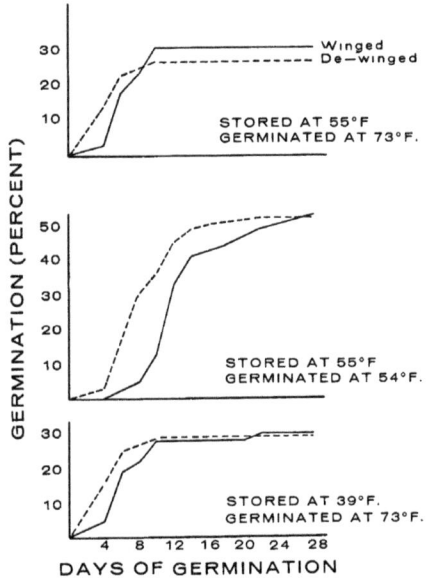

Figure 2.--Germination rates for winged and de-winged fourwing saltbush seed during a 28-day test period.

nation at 58°F. than at 42°F., the difference between average percent germination under these two temperatures was not significant statistically.

Rate of germination varied with temperature (fig. 4). At 77°F., germination was rapid from the fourth to the tenth day, then practically stopped. At 58°F., germination was slow until the tenth day, then became extremely rapid. This rapid rate continued for 4 days, after which germination took place more gradually for 14 days, then stopped. At 42°F., no germination was observed until the sixteenth day; the rate was moderately fast from the eighteenth to the thirty-fourth day, and appeared to have stopped by the thirty-sixth day. A final check showed no germination on the thirty-eighth day.

De-winging the seed did not affect final germination in the second test. Average germination percentages indicate a slight benefit from de-winging, but the differences are not significant (table 4). Of eight sources of seed, only the Monica seed showed consistently higher germination for de-winged seed under all three temperature conditions.

The de-winged seed germinated more quickly (fig. 5); under temperatures of 77°F. and 58°F., more than twice as many de-winged as winged seed had germinated by the sixth day. But by the tenth day at 77°F. and by the twenty-fourth day at 58°F., germination of the winged seed practically equaled that of the de-winged seed.

Results of the second test generally were in accord with those of the first test. Germination percentages of the three sources of seed used in both tests, however, showed large variability (tables 3 and 4). Results of the two tests for winged seed germinated at the middle temperature illustrate this variability:

Seed source	First test: 54°F.	Second test: 58°F.
	(Percent germination)	
Isleta	60	92
Mountainair	64	48
Corona	34	40

The reasons for these rather large differences in germination between the two tests are not

Table 4.--Comparison of winged and de-winged fourwing saltbush seeds at three germination temperatures as shown by percentage germination at end of 36 days; seeds from eight collection sites in New Mexico and Arizona

Germi-nation temper-ature	Seed treatment	New Mexico					Arizona			Average
		Isleta	Moun-tainair	Corona	Monica	Glen-wood	Flag-staff	Beaver Creek	Chevelon	
		Percent germination								
6.6° F.	Winged	60	36	14	12	10	26	6	22	23.3
	De-winged	50	42	26	26	2	20	12	30	26.0
7.6° F.	Winged	92	48	40	12	40	48	48	44	46.5
	De-winged	88	56	40	48	44	64	40	16	49.5
1.8° F.	Winged	76	60	44	24	32	44	28	32	42.5
	De-winged	80	32	56	36	36	52	24	32	43.5

readily explained. Large variability among seeds in the different sample lots probably was a factor, but induced dormancy of the embryos caused by inadvertent exposure to high or low temperatures, or other conditions, may also have been a factor.

Cutting tests.--In an attempt to explain some of the germination results, cutting tests were conducted on small samples of seed. From 50 to 200 individual seeds of each source were checked to see if they were filled.

Individual seeds were cut in half and examined with a hand lens to determine the presence of an embryo and endosperm. Results of this examination were as follows:

Seed source	Number of seeds filled (Percent)	All seed	Filled seeds only
		(Percent germination)	
Isleta	93	74	80
Mountainair	63	46	73
Corona	68	37	54
Monica	49	26	54
Glenwood	80	27	34
Flagstaff	65	42	64
Beaver Creek	61	26	43
Chevelon	60	29	48

The differences in number of seeds filled partially explain some of the germination results. For example, only about half of the Monica seed was filled, which accounts in part for the relatively low average 26 percent germination of this source. By contrast, the seed from Flagstaff which was 65 percent filled gave 42 percent germination, and the Isleta seed, 93 percent filled, gave 74 percent germination.

The percentage of seed filled does not fully explain the germination results, however. Embryo dormancy or other characteristics of the seed apparently influenced their germination. Examples are the Beaver Creek seed which was 61 percent filled yet only 43 percent of the filled seed germinated, and the Glenwood seed which was 80 percent filled but only 34 percent of these filled seed germinated.

DISCUSSION

These tests showed germination of fourwing saltbush varied with source of seed. In a comparison of eight sources, seed collected at Isleta, New Mexico, showed significantly higher germination than seed from other sources. Three sources of seed were intermediate, while the remaining four sources were low in germination. Part of the variation in germination among sources can be explained by differences in the number of seeds that were filled, or contained embryos. The number of seed with embryos probably was determined by some environmental factors during pollination and seed maturation, such as temperature, moisture, or wind. The embryos in seeds from some sources exhibited a greater dormancy than seed from others, also. It is obvious, therefore, that when collecting wild seed of fourwinged saltbush, seed source is an important consideration. Further research is needed, however, to determine whether geographical source or environmental conditions should be the main consideration in deciding where and when to collect seed.

Removing the wings from the seed did not improve the total germination of fourwing saltbush. The de-winged seed, however, germinated more quickly than the winged seed. This faster germination is desirable because the right combination of temperature and soil moisture is of short duration in many range areas. Other advantages of de-winging the seed are: (1) ease of handling, especially when the seed is to be drilled, (2) reduction in bulk, and (3) easier coverage with soil. Soaking fourwing saltbush seed to remove chlorides or other suspected inhibitors does not seem necessary.

Temperature strongly influenced germination of fourwing saltbush. Germination of seed from all eight sources was higher at temperatures from $42°$ to $58°F$. than at temperatures of $73°$ to $77°F$. Rates of germination were lower at the lower temperatures, but these lower rates could be a benefit. The developing seedling might undergo a hardening process that would make it less susceptible to frost damage. Additional studies are needed to define more clearly the optimum temperatures for germination, but indications from this study were that the optimum temperatures may vary with source of the seed.

Until additional information is obtained concerning temperature effects on germination of fourwing saltbush seed, the findings from these tests might be used as preliminary guides. They indicate that germination is better within the range of $40°$ to $60°F$. than at temperatures of $70°F$. or higher. For most range areas in the Southwest, temperatures of $40°$ to $60°F$. correspond with the spring and fall seasons, whereas temperatures above $70°F$. correspond with the summer season. This suggests fourwing saltbush should be seeded in the spring or fall, as temperatures probably would be too high during the summer, especially at the lower elevations. Although the summer months appear unfavorable from the standpoint of temperatures, these months are best when considering dependability and amount of precipitation in the Southwest. Because of the apparent conflict between temperature and moisture

U.S. FOREST SERVICE
RESEARCH NOTE RM - 26

gust 1964

REST SERVICE
. DEPARTMEN F AG ICULTURE

Preventing Metal Corrosion from Emulsifiable Ethylene Dibromide Packaged for Bark Beetle Control[1]

R. H. Nagel[2]

Experiments with emulsified insecticides to kill bark beetles in pine and spruce indicated ethylene dibromide to be the most effective of five fumigants.[3][4] Use of an emulsion reduced handling and transportation because only the emulsifiable concentrate -- 20 percent of the emulsion volume -- had to be shipped to the infested Forest, where water is readily obtained from streams and beaver ponds.

For spruce beetle control, a field-size batch of emulsion was formed by mixing 4 gallons of water with 1 gallon of an emulsifiable concentrate containing, percent by weight, 34 ethylene dibromide, 5.6 emulsifier, and 60.4 solvent (No. 2 fuel oil). When this formula was released to control agencies in 1952, the storage life of the concentrate had not been evaluated. It was hoped that supplies would be prepared and applied while fresh; that is, soon after mixing, or, at most, before the end of the control season. For one reason or another, however, stocks are often carried over for several seasons. Deterioration of the emulsifiers, phase separation during subzero temperatures, and corrosion of storage containers occur when this product has to be stored for use the following season.

Of several suggested methods advanced for dispensing the concentrate to treating crews by the gallon, refillable gallon cans proved to be both popular and practical during the 1952 field trials. For crewmen, the gallon can provided a simple, handy, time-saving, and nonhazardous way to transfer a measured gallon of concentrate into "jeep" cans when forming 5-gallon batches of emulsion. Whether loaded or empty, the gallon cans handled easily and, in cartons of 6, were readily loaded and moved by truck or pack animal. Unfortunately, their tin lining corroded rapidly.

---

[1] Assistance of R. D. Chisholm who suggested additives and helped design storage tests in 1952 is gratefully acknowledged. Dr. Chisholm, who retired December 31, 1962, was chemist, Entomology Research Division, Agricultural Research Service, U. S. Department of Agriculture, Moorestown, New Jersey.
[2] Entomologist, Rocky Mountain Forest and Range Experiment Station, with central headquarters maintained at Fort Collins, in cooperation with Colorado State University.
[3] Massey, C. L., Chisholm, R. D., and Wygant, N. D. Ethylene dibromide for control of Black Hills beetle. Jour. Econ. Ent. 46: 601-604. 1953.
[4] Massey, C. L., Chisholm, R.D., and Wygant, N. D. Chemical control of the Engelmann spruce beetle in Colorado. Jour. Econ. Ent. 46: 951-955. 1953.

While they still used the cans and appreciated their usefulness, several control operators expressed the hope that corrosion could be inhibited. With that objective, storage-life evaluations were started on October 30, 1952. The evaluations produced an effective and relatively economical means for preventing corrosion in metal containers. The purpose of this paper is to present a brief account of the work and the improved formulation.

Materials and Methods

Because corrosion inside steel and tin storage containers was believed to be caused by bromine and hydrobromic acid -- hydrolytic products of the ethylene dibromide molecule -- experimental lots of concentrate were treated with acid acceptors, and their effects on corrosion and emulsifiability studied. Two acceptors were used, epichlorohydrin and glycidyl phenyl ether, each at exploratory rates of 0.6 (0.05 lb./gal.), 1.2, and 2.4 grams per 100 milliliters of formulation. In three replicates, screw-top pint cans, manufactured of light, medium, or heavy tinplate, were then partially filled (400 ml.) with experimental concentrates. One group of these cans was stored on shelves at room temperatures, another at a constant oven temperature of 54° C. At the same time, a series of epichlorohydrin mixtures in Erlenmeyer flasks was also stored in the oven, each flask with strips of drum steel and tinplate.

Results and Conclusions

In the cans stored at room temperature, both acceptors, even at the lowest concentra-

September 1964

U.S. FOREST SERVICE
RESEARCH NOTE RM - 27

FOREST SERVICE
U.S. DEPARTMENT OF AGRICULTURE

Overwintering Habits of *Ips lecontei* Sw. and *Ips confusus* (Lec.) in Arizona and New Mexico

John F. Chansler[1]

Ips lecontei Sw., the Arizona five-spined engraver, is a bark beetle pest of ponderosa pine in central and southern Arizona. Out-

[1] *Entomologist, located at Albuquerque, New Mexico; central headquarters are maintained at Fort Collins, in cooperation with Colorado State University.*

breaks, frequent on the Prescott National Forest, have caused severe tree mortality in the pole stands (fig. 1). Ips confusus (Lec.), the California five-spined engraver, is a common pest of pinyon pine in Arizona and New Mexico. Outbreaks of this bark beetle have been widespread, causing extensive tree mortality in relatively short periods (fig. 2). Outbreaks of these two bark beetles are especial-

Figure 1.--*Ponderosa pine killed by Ips lecontei, Prescott Ranger District, Prescott National Forest, Arizona.*

Figure 2.--*Pinyon pine killed by Ips confusus, Bandelier National Monument, New Mexico.*

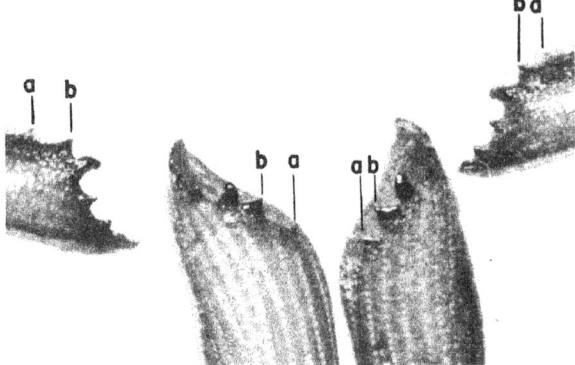

Figure 3.--Elytral declivity from Ips lecontei on left and I. confusus on right. Note that the distance between the first tooth (a) and second tooth (b) is 1.5 to 2 times greater on I. lecontei.

ly serious when they occur around homesites, and in National Parks, Monuments, and other areas of high recreational use.

The two species are similar in size, and have five teeth on each side of the elytral declivity. The species can be separated by the arrangement of the first and second teeth in reference to the declivital suture. I. confusus has the first declivital tooth nearly equidistant from the declivital suture and the second tooth. The first declivital tooth of I. lecontei is closer to the declivital suture, which results in a relatively large space between the first and second tooth (fig. 3).

Development from the egg to the adult stage is rapid between April and October. Usually three and sometimes four generations are produced by each species during this period, which leaves little time between attack periods to evaluate or control infestations. November through March (when the insects hibernate) is therefore the most favorable time to evaluate and control outbreaks. The overwintering habits of these beetles were studied to aid development of evaluation and control procedures.

The overwintering adults of both species commonly feed in colonies in portions of the inner bark not eaten by the larvae or associated insects (fig. 4). In many pinyon trees, colonies of Ips confusus were so numerous and large that the feeding chambers coalesced and lost their individual identity. In ponderosa pine, each colony of Ips lecontei was served by one entrance hole and usually contained 25 to 150 members. The colonies are apparently established during the fall, when adults emerge from pupal cells in other portions of the same tree or other trees.

OVERWINTERING STAGE OF DEVELOPMENT

Data were collected during the winter months of 1960-61 and 1961-62. During these years both I. lecontei and I. confusus overwintered as adults in standing trees. Most of the individuals in the last generation reached the adult stage by November. However, some were adults by October in 1961; all by December of that year (table 1).

BROOD DENSITIES AND DISTRIBUTION IN THE HOST

Three to seven infested trees of each species were felled each month, and the infested portion of the bole was cut into 12-inch lengths. The infested portion of the felled tree was determined by spot checks along the bole. Bolts were cut between ground level and 25 feet. Seven ponderosa pines were sampled between 15 and 40 feet. The 12-inch bolts were marked as to tree and height above the ground, and then transported to the laboratory for

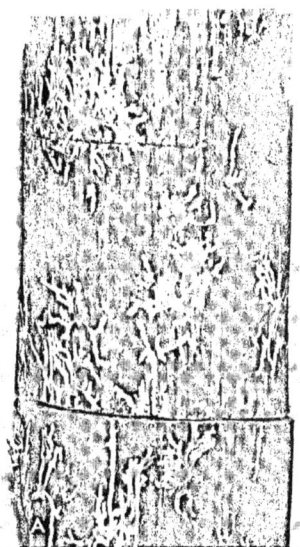

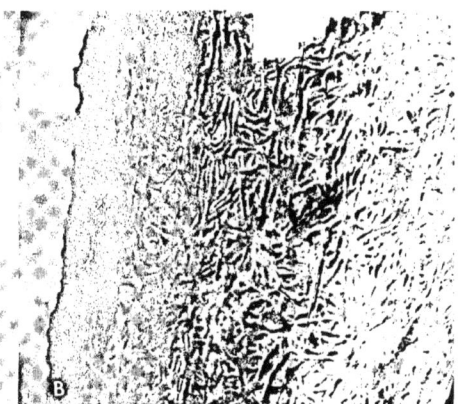

Figure 4.--Hibernating adults feeding on the inner bark make rather deep etchings in the xylem: (A) by Ips lecontei in ponderosa pine, (B) by I. confusus in pinyon.

examination. In the laboratory, the bark was removed from each bolt, and the brood density was determined. A total of 43 ponderosa and 29 pinyon pines were examined.

Mean density of Ips lecontei in the 12-inch sections taken at 1 and 2 feet, 4 and 5 feet, and 9 and 10 feet above the ground (table 2) reveal that brood densities vary considerably at any given height above the ground, even in trees in the same diameter class. In the smallest trees examined, density was greatest at ground level and decreased with height.

Table 1.--Percentage of living insects in the larval, pupal, and adult stages of Ips lecontei and Ips confusus in standing trees, 1960-61 and 1961-62

Sample date	Ips lecontei						Ips confusus					
	1960-61			1961-62			1960-61			1961-62		
	Larvae	Pupae	Adults	Larvae	Pupae	Adults	Larvae	Pupae	Adults	Larvae	Pupae	Adults
						Percent						
October	--	--	--	0.2	0.7	99.1	--	--	--	5.4	4.0	90.6
November	8.9	8.1	83.0	0.0	.6	99.4	0.0	0.1	99.9	.1	.5	99.4
December	1.4	.6	98.0	0.0	0.0	100.0	0.0	.1	99.9	0.0	0.0	100.0
January	0.0	.6	99.4	--	--	--	0.0	0.0	100.0	--	--	--
February	0.0	0.0	100.0	0.0	0.0	100.0	--	--	--	--	--	--

Table 2.--Mean density of overwintering adults in standing pines as determined from 12-inch sections at three heights on the main stem

Sample height above ground (feet)	Ips lecontei in standing ponderosa pine									Ips confusus in standing pinyon pine								
	1-5 inches d.b.h.			6-8 inches d.b.h.			9+ inches d.b.h.			1-5 inches d.b.h.			6-8 inches d.b.h.			9+ inches d.b.h.		
	Average per sq.ft. of bark	$S_{\bar{y}}$	Percent of samples infested	Average per sq.ft. of bark	$S_{\bar{y}}$	Percent of samples infested	Average per sq.ft. of bark	$S_{\bar{y}}$	Percent of samples infested	Average per sq.ft. of bark	$S_{\bar{y}}$	Percent of samples infested	Average per sq.ft. of bark	$S_{\bar{y}}$	Percent of samples infested	Average per sq.ft. of bark	$S_{\bar{y}}$	Percent of samples infested
Ground 2	74	±23	89	109	±19	70	9	±3	25	178	±34	100	314	±47	100	419	±66	100
Ground 5	75	±11	100	129	±14	93	30	±26	54	149	±14	100	222	±30	100	270	±19	100
Ground 10	28	±6	100	101	±14	100	47	±14	60	105	±27	100	143	±42	100	226	±39	100

In the average-size trees (fig. 5), density was relatively low at the base of the tree, increased at varying rates to a maximum density between 5 and 10 feet above ground level, and then gradually decreased with height. The height of maximum densities varied extremely in large trees, but usually occurred between 10 and 30 feet above ground level.

The distribution pattern of Ips lecontei (table 2) shows the percent of samples infested increases with a decrease in diameter of the host. These data indicate that the distribution of the hibernating adults is a function of diameter rather than height. Ostmark[2] found this same relationship in the brood density of the spring and summer generations.

Mean density of Ips confusus at three heights in three size classes of pinyon pine (table 2) shows densities vary greatly at the three heights, even in the same diameter class, and brood density decreases with diameter within trees and apparently between trees. Generally, density dropped gradually from a maximum at or near ground level to a relatively low number at the top of the main stem (fig. 5). The greatest density per 12-inch section was found within the first 5 feet on 86 percent of the 29 pinyons examined, and within the first foot on 55 percent.

SUMMARY AND CONCLUSIONS

Ips lecontei is a serious pest of ponderosa pine in Arizona, while Ips confusus is a seri-

[2] *Ostmark, H. E. Life history and habits of the Arizona five-spined engraver, Ips lecontei. A progress report of studies in 1959-1960. Rocky Mountain Forest and Range Expt. Sta., Fort Collins, Colorado, 21 pp. (Typewritten)*

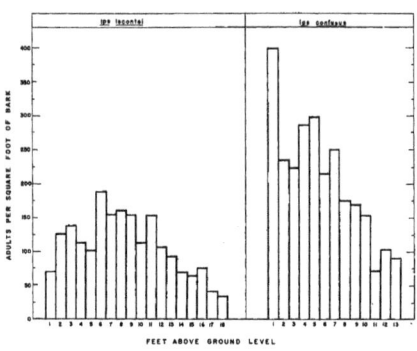

Figure 5.--Brood density per square foot of bark, as determined by complete examination of an infested stem at 1-foot intervals, illustrates the typical distribution pattern of I. lecontei in ponderosa pine and I. confusus in pinyon pine. The trees are 7 inches in diameter at 5 feet above the ground.

ous pest of pinyon pine in New Mexico and Arizona. The two species closely resemble each other morphologically, but they can be readily separated by the spatial arrangement of the first and second declivital teeth. Most of the hibernating beetles of the two species reach adulthood by October, congregate in colonies, and construct feeding galleries in which they pass the winter. The large number and distribution of these colonies result in high brood densities with large variances per unit of bark surface. Hibernating adults of Ips lecontei were found more frequently in stems under 9 inches in diameter than in stems over 9 inches in diameter; densities varied with diameters. Hibernating adults of Ips confusus were consistently present in the largest portions of the infested tree; densities were generally highest at or near ground level and decreased with tree height.

rage Loosen Bark on

ne Pulp Chips

Landt [1]

effective of the conditions studied loosened about a quarter of the remaining bark.

PROCEDURES

As chips from unbarked residues were not available in the area, it was necessary to produce some especially for the study at a chip plant in Custer, South Dakota. Unbarked slabs, edgings, and precommercial thinnings were chipped during August 1962 with a 16-knife Norman chipper. Chips were fractioned into various sizes with a standard laboratory chip screen for physical analysis (table 1).

The chips were then separated into three groups of samples of four each of equal weight for storage at different moisture contents. Samples were adjusted to moisture contents of 17, 38, and 54 percent,[5] and then stored in polyethylene bags at 80°F.

Bark loosening was measured after storage periods of 2, 4, 6, and 8 weeks. After each

---

[5] *Moisture content based on green weight to conform with standard practice in the pulp and paper industry. When based on ovendry weight, moisture contents were 20, 60, and 120 percent respectively.*

Table 1.--Physical analysis of pulp chips from unbarked ponderosa pine slabs, edgings, and precommercial thinnings

Screen size (Inches)	Loose bark	Tight bark	Total bark	Total wood	Bark and wood
			Percent[1]		
SLABS AND EDGINGS					
	1.14	0.52	1.66	7.35	9.01
3/4	3.46	.97	4.43	9.86	14.29
1/2	4.32	.18	4.50	24.59	29.09
3/8	2.81	.03	2.84	18.01	20.85
3/16	6.19	.02	6.21	13.57	19.78
Through 3/16	5.32	--	5.32	1.66	6.98
Total	23.24	1.72	24.96	75.04	100.00
PRECOMMERCIAL THINNINGS					
		.06	.06	.39	.45
3/4	.51	1.27	1.78	15.96	17.74
1/2	2.83	.31	3.14	27.03	30.17
3/8	2.85	.13	2.98	19.16	22.14
3/16	6.43	.03	6.46	14.07	20.53
Through 3/16	7.81	--	7.81	1.16	8.97
Total	20.43	1.80	22.23	77.77	100.00

[1] Based on ovendry weight of wood and bark.

storage period, chips were shaken 10 times in a 1-gallon can to simulate the handling they are normally subjected to in conveyors and blower systems, so as to free any bark that might have loosened during storage.

The loose bark was then removed, and tight bark remaining on the chips was separated from the wood by hand. These three fractions (two bark, one wood) were weighed immediately and again after they were ovendried. Amounts of loose and tight bark were expressed as percentages of the total ovendry weight of bark (table 2). Specific gravity of the chips in each sample was also determined for each moisture content and storage period.

RESULTS AND DISCUSSION

The most significant finding of the study was that almost all of the bark was loosened in the chipping process. Results showed that 93 percent of the bark on slabs and edgings

Table 2.--Percentage of tight bark loosened from chips after 2 to 8 weeks' storage at various moisture contents

Moisture content[1] (Percent)	Slabs and edgings		Precommercial thinnings	
	Length of storage	Tight bark loosened	Length of storage	Tight bark loosened
	Weeks	Percent[2]	Weeks	Percent[2]
17	2	2.64	2	1.97
	4	4.13	4	4.44
	6	4.39	6	2.54
	8	2.72	8	1.25
38	2	.43	2	1.65
	4	4.06	4	4.37
	6	2.30	6	4.33
	8	2.10	8	4.81
54	2	7.44	2	6.16
	4	20.81	4	9.68
	6	23.39	6	11.87
	8	20.90	8	17.82

[1] Moisture content based on green weight.
[2] Based on ovendry weight of total bark in sample, 100 percent loose bark would mean that all chips are bark-free.

and 92 percent in the case of precommercial thinnings was loosened by the mechanical action of the chipper knives.

None of the storage conditions investigated proved very effective. The best of these--storage at 54-percent moisture content for a minimum of 4 weeks in the case of chips from slabs and edgings, and 8 weeks for chips from precommercial thinning--accounted for the loosening of about one-fifth of the remaining bark (table 2). This would be equivalent to about 2 percent of the total bark content.

Analysis of variance showed that both storage time and moisture content affected bark loosening. However, any appreciable effects required a minimum of at least 4 weeks at 54-percent moisture content (table 2). Storage for periods longer than 4 weeks did not appear to cause any further bark loosening in chips from slabs and edgings.

All the chips showed extensive blue stain after 4 weeks' storage, but analysis of variance of average specific gravity showed no significant change even after 8 weeks of storage.

Total bark content, about the same for both types of chips, made up about 25 percent of the total volume in slabs and edgings and about 22 percent in precommercial thinnings. The total tight bark content, or that remaining after chipping and storage, was also very similar, and accounted for almost 1.7 and 1.8

percent of the total volume, respectively. Most of the tight bark was on the chips retained in the 3/4-inch screen (table 1).

CONCLUSION

In view of the high percentage of the total bark content that is loosened in the chipping of ponderosa pine sawmill residue and precommercial thinnings, the problem of bark removal may not be so important as first thought. It is likely that an even higher percentage of the bark would be loosened if the material were chipped during the active growing season. Elimination of the need for complete debarking would greatly enhance the utilization of precommercial thinnings because of the high costs involved in handling the material. The acceptable levels of bark content, however, must be determined by the pulp and paper processing industry.

zona and New Mexico, 1960

by
t L. Miller[1]

TREND

Lumber production in Arizona and New Mexico has generally increased in recent years (fig. 1). Production in 1960 was 9 percent greater in Arizona but slightly less in New Mexico than respective estimates of the 1958 Census of Manufactures.[2]

Comparison of production in 1952 and 1960 shows considerable difference in proportion by species (table 1). A shift to more production of Douglas-fir and other softwoods and less ponderosa pine is apparently due to more access roads into Douglas-fir and fir-spruce timber.

ARIZONA PRODUCTION

Species.--Almost nine-tenths of the 1960 lumber output was ponderosa pine (table 2). Douglas-fir, the true firs, and Engelmann spruce followed in production, in that order. Ponderosa pine was the principal species produced in all but Graham County where Douglas-fir led.

Counties.--Although lumber was produced in 10 of the 14 counties in Arizona (fig. 2), output was concentrated in Apache, Coconino, and Navajo Counties (table 2). Together they contained more than one-half of the active

[2] U. S. Bureau of the Census. Lumber production and mill stocks, 1959 and 1958. Series M24T(59)-1. June 19, 1961.

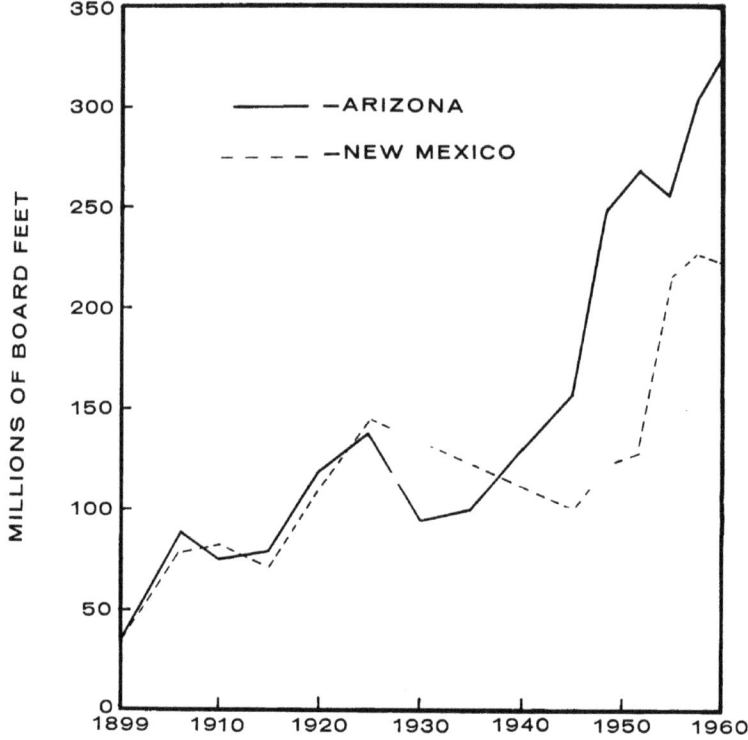

Figure 1.--Lumber production in Arizona and New Mexico, 1899-1960. The annual production figures for years previous to 1960 were obtained from the following sources:

1899-1945 -- Steer, Henry B. Lumber Production in the United States, 1799-1946. U. S. Dept. Agr. Misc. Pub. 669, 233 pp., 1948.

1948 -- U. S. Forest Service. Lumber production in the Western States and Alaska, 1948. 3 pp.. 1950. Washington, D. C.

1952 -- U. S. Forest Service. Timber Resource Review. (Unpublished data not presented in term of lumber production in the published report of the TRR.)

1954 -- U. S. Bureau of the Census. Census of Manufacturers. Lumber and timber basic products Bul. MC24-A. 1957.

1958 -- U. S. Bureau of the Census. Census of Manufacturers. Lumber production and mill stocks 1959 and 1958. Series M24T(59)-1. June 19, 1961.

Table 1.--Arizona and New Mexico lumber production by species, 1952 and 1960

Year[1]	Ponderosa pine		Douglas-fir		Other softwoods		Hardwoods		Total	
	M b.m.	Pct.	M b.m.	Pct.	M b.m.	Pct.	M b.m.	Pct.	M b.m.	Pct.
1952	324,364	81.5	33,070	8.3	40,516	10.2	1	([2])	397,951	100.0
1960	390,658	70.1	80,947	14.5	85,250	15.3	777	0.1	557,632	100.0

[1] 1952 figures from unpublished data obtained as part of the Timber Resource Review.
[2] Less than 0.1 percent.

Table 2.--Arizona lumber production by counties and species, in thousands of board feet, lumber tally, 1960

County	Active sawmills	Douglas-fir	Ponderosa pine	True firs and others[1]	Engelmann spruce	Total	Proportion
	Number	- - - - - - - M board feet - - - - - - -					Percent
Apache	10	14,949	108,882	3,042	2,200	129,073	39.1
Coconino	5	2,768	105,899	3,675	1,250	113,592	34.4
Gila, Graham, Greenlee, Pima, and Pinal	6	593	8,528	271	200	9,592	2.9
Mojave, Yavapai	6	--	12,075	--	--	12,075	3.7
Navajo	11	4,822	56,968	3,680	57	65,527	19.9
Total	38	23,132	292,352	10,668	3,707	329,859	100.0
		- - - - - - - - - Percent - - - - - - - - -					
Proportion		7.0	88.7	3.2	1.1	100.0	

[1] All true firs, except for 71 M b.m. white bark and limber pines from Graham County.

sawmills, and produced more than nine-tenths of the State's total output. Production per mill was particularly high in Coconino County, where average mill output was 22.7 million board feet.

Mill classes.--Twelve of the 38 active mills produced more than 5 million board feet, and turned out 87 percent of the State's total (table 3). Small mills (those producing less than 1 million board feet) were few and sawed less than 1 percent of the State's output.

Trend.--Number of existing mills and distribution by production class did not change significantly between 1958 and 1960. Four mills were idle in 1960, as compared with only one in 1958. Ownership turnover was frequent. Eighteen percent of the mills active in 1960 had come under new ownership since 1958, with changes occurring in most production classes. Three mills went out of existence in the same period, including one that burned in 1960.

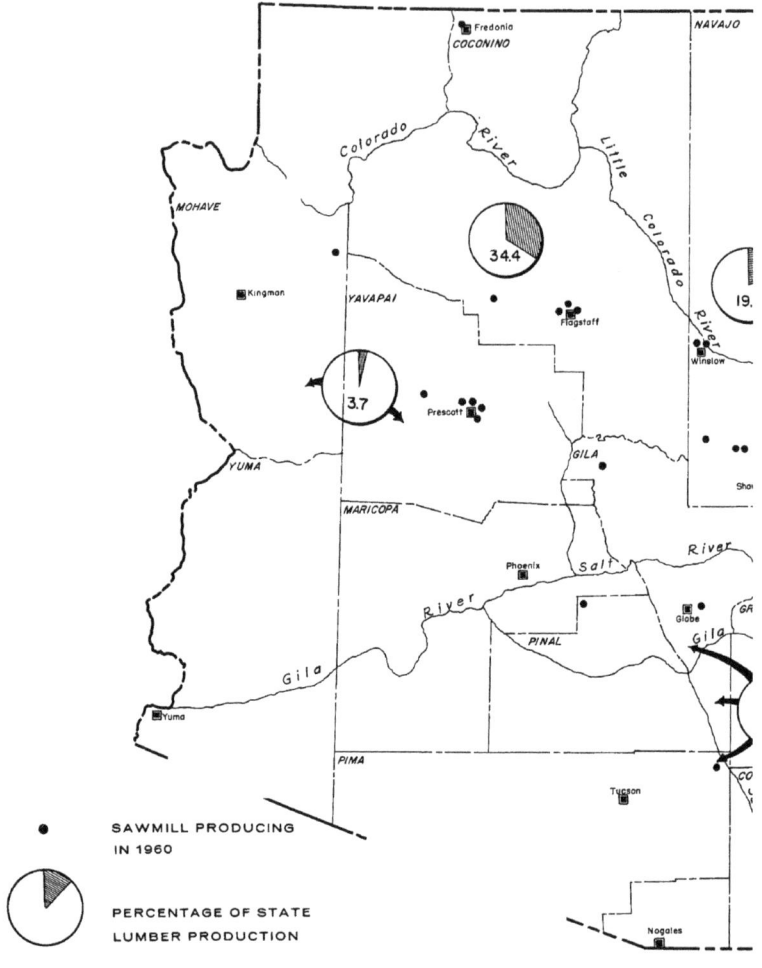

Figure 2.--Sawmills active in Arizona in 1960, with percentage of lumber produc

Table 3.--Arizona lumber production by mill production classes, 1960

Production class (M b.m. per yr.)	Active mills	M b.m.	Percent
	Number		
1 - 49	1	35	([1])
50 - 199		880	0.3
200 - 499		489	.1
500 - 999	2	1,221	.4
1,000 - 4,999	15	41,474	12.6
5,000 and more	12	285,760	86.6
Total	38	329,859	100.0

[1] Less than 0.1 percent.

NEW MEXICO PRODUCTION

Species.--Ponderosa pine, Douglas-fir, and Engelmann spruce, the principal species produced (table 4), accounted for 89 percent of the State's production. Ponderosa pine was the leading species in 14 counties and made up 43 percent of New Mexico's total output.

Counties.--Sawmills operated in 19 of the 32 counties in 1960. Production and number of mills were concentrated in the north-central part of the State (fig. 3). Colfax, Sandoval, Rio Arriba, and Taos Counties in northern New Mexico and Catron County on the western border contained about one-half of the sawmills and produced almost three-fourths of the State's total output (table 4). Sandoval County ranked highest in production per mill, with an average mill output of more than 4 million board feet.

Mill classes.--More than four-fifths of the State's total output was produced by mills that sawed at least 1 million board feet each (table 5). Thirteen of the 37 mills in this group produced at least 5 million board feet.

New Mexico has a large number of small mills, but they contribute relatively little to total output. About two-thirds of the active mills sawed less than 1 million board feet, and turned out only 15 percent of the State's production.

Thirty mills were inactive in 1960.

Trend.--No appreciable changes in number of mills or distribution by production class occurred between 1958 and 1960. However, 20 percent of existing mills were inactive in 1960, as compared to only 11 percent in 1958.

Turnover in ownership was fairly frequent. Fifteen percent of the mills active in 1960 had come under new ownership since 1958, with changes taking place in all except the largest production class. At least six mills went out of business completely in the same period, and five others burned in 1960.

SURVEY METHOD

The surveys in both States were done cooperatively by the U.S. Forest Service and the U.S. Bureau of the Census. Production data were obtained principally by mailing inquiries to all known sawmill operators. A complete list of mills was prepared with the help of the National Forests, and the Bureau of Land Management and the Bureau of Indian Affairs, U.S. Department of the Interior.

Reports were obtained from all mills that produced 5 million board feet or more. Production for mills that did not reply was estimated by sampling within each State.

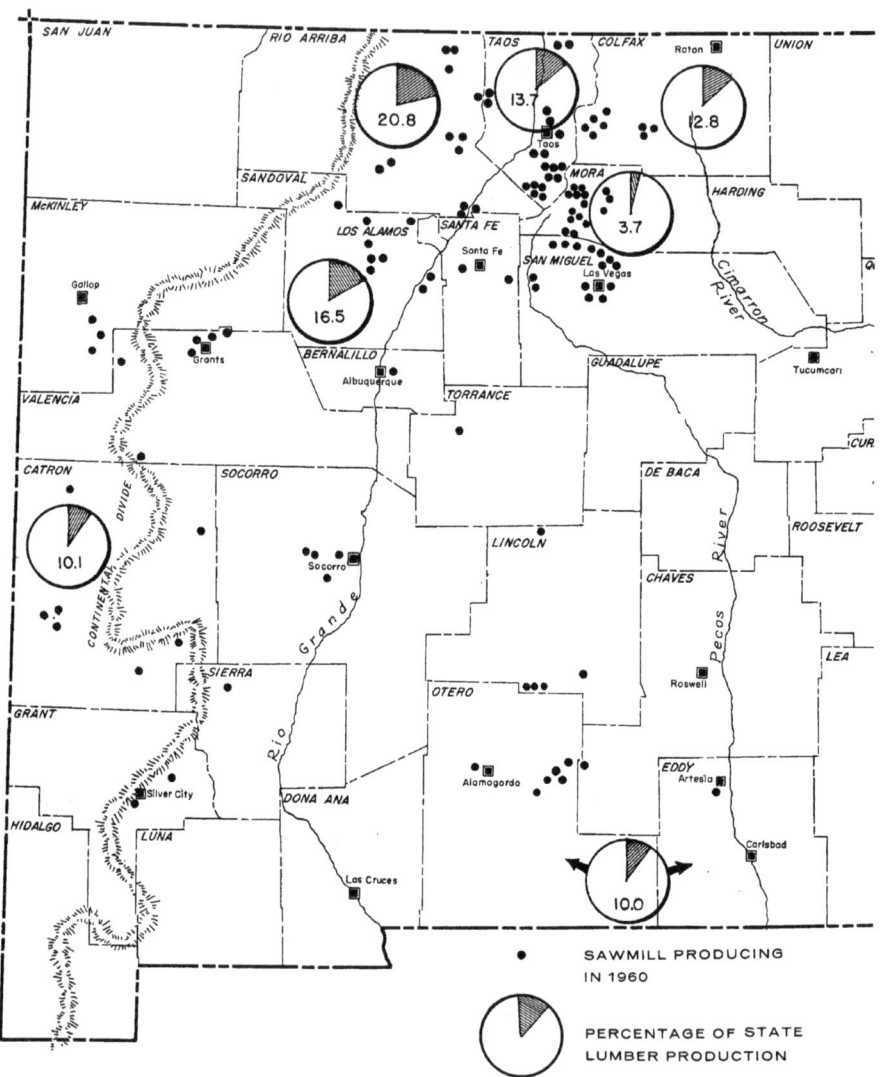

Figure 3.--Sawmills active in New Mexico in 1960, with percentage of lumber production by county (not shown for counties or groups of counties with less than 3.0 percent).

Table 4.--New Mexico lumber production by counties and species, in thousands of board feet, lumber tally, 1960

County	Active saw-mills	Douglas-fir	Ponderosa pine	True firs	Engelmann spruce	Other[1]	Total	Proportion
	Number	---------	---------	M board feet	---------	---------	---------	Percent
Catron	7	5,046	17,229	439	72	250	23,036	10.1
Colfax	8	12,025	4,992	0	11,592	577	29,186	12.8
Lincoln, Chavez	6	820	4,030	2,218	235	13	7,316	3.2
Mora	15	5,348	2,127	513	419	84	8,491	3.7
Otero, Eddy	7	6,441	5,145	8,590	951	1,525	22,652	10.0
Rio Arriba	12	5,007	18,849	1,403	22,018	0	47,277	20.8
Sandoval	9	8,938	21,174	2,888	4,521	0	37,521	16.5
San Miguel	14	1,639	1,707	327	141	0	3,814	1.7
Santa Fe, Bernalillo, Torrance	4	2,117	3,357	533	2	0	6,009	2.6
Socorro, Grant, Sierra	7	1,891	4,153	0	0	50	6,094	2.7
Taos	19	8,343	12,487	3,366	6,895	180	31,271	13.7
Valencia, McKinley	9	200	3,056	200	350	1,300	5,106	2.2
Total	117	57,815	98,306	20,477	47,196	3,979	227,773	100.0
		----------	----------	Percent	----------	----------		
Proportion		25.4	43.2	9.0	20.7	1.7	100.0	

[1] Four-fifths of this volume was made up of white bark, limber, and pinyon pines, and one-fifth was aspen and cottonwood.

Table 5.--New Mexico lumber production by mill production classes, 1960

Production class (M b.m. per yr.)	Active mills	M b.m.	Percent
	Number		
1 - 49	27	1,466	0.6
50 - 199	21	9,390	4.1
200 - 499	17	4,704	2.1
500 - 999	15	18,684	8.2
1,000 - 4,999	24	62,162	27.3
5,000 and more	13	131,367	57.7
Total	117	227,773	100.0

Personal contacts on a random sample basis were made with selected nonresponding mills as follows:

Production class (Mb.m./yr.)	Mills sampled[3] (Percent)
1,000 - 4,999	25
500 - 999	10
200 - 499	5
50 - 199	5
1 - 99	5

The estimated production of the nonrespondents was added to the total production of respondents to obtain the total estimated production for each State.

[3] *At least two mills were selected in each class, and as a result these sampling rates were actually exceeded in most cases.*

ACCURACY OF THE SURVEYS

Production reports were received from 26 active respondent mills in Arizona. These mills turned out 309,844,000 board feet, or 94 percent of State's total output. For the 12 nonrespondent mills, an additional 20,015,000 board feet was estimated by sampling. Sampling error was 36.9 percent of the estimated part of Arizona's production, and 2.2 percent of the State's total output.

In New Mexico, the production of 178,649,000 board feet reported by 74 active respondent mills constituted 78.4 percent of the State's production. For the nonrespondent mills, an additional 49,124,000 board feet was estimated by sampling. Sampling error was 37.5 percent of the estimated part of New Mexico's production, and 8.2 percent of the State's total output.

Forage Production and Stocking Rates on Southern Arizona Ranges Can be Improved[1]

Dwight R. Cable and S. Clark Martin[2]

Most semidesert cattle ranges in southern Arizona can grow more grass and beef than they do. Early plot studies in the Southwest showed that mesquite control increased grass production (Parker and Martin 1952),[3] and indicated that maximum benefits could be expected only with good grazing management. These findings have not been verified experimentally on a practical scale. This paper discusses increases in forage production and carrying capacity within 5 years after changing the grazing management on two range units recently cleared of mesquite and two mesquite-infested units on the Santa Rita Experimental Range.

---

[1] Ranchers participating in the study are Keith S. Brown, H. H. Robinson, and Felix Ruelas, cooperators on the Santa Rita Experimental Range.
[2] Range Conservationists, located at Tucson, Arizona in cooperation with the University of Arizona; central headquarters maintained in cooperation with Colorado State University at Fort Collins.
[3] Names and dates in parentheses refer to Literature Cited, p. 11.

DESCRIPTION OF THE STUDY RANGES

Four units of the Santa Rita Experimental Range near Tucson, Arizona, are being used in this study. They contain from 659 to 996 acres each, and lie at elevations of from 3,700 to 4,800 feet (fig. 1). The soils on the flatter slopes, primarily coarse sandy loams of the Whitehouse and Tumacacori series, grade into shallow stony phases of Coronado coarse sandy loam on the steeper slopes. Subsoils of the Tumacacori series are loose and open, while those of the Whitehouse and Coronado series are clay loam.

Average annual precipitation varies from about 14.5 inches at the lowest elevation to 19 inches at the highest elevation. The precipitation falls in two distinct rainy seasons: about 56 percent of the total annual precipitation falls during the summer growing season, early July till late September, and 33 percent falls from December through April; the remaining 11 percent falls in the relatively dry periods separating these precipitation periods. Usually all available soil moisture is

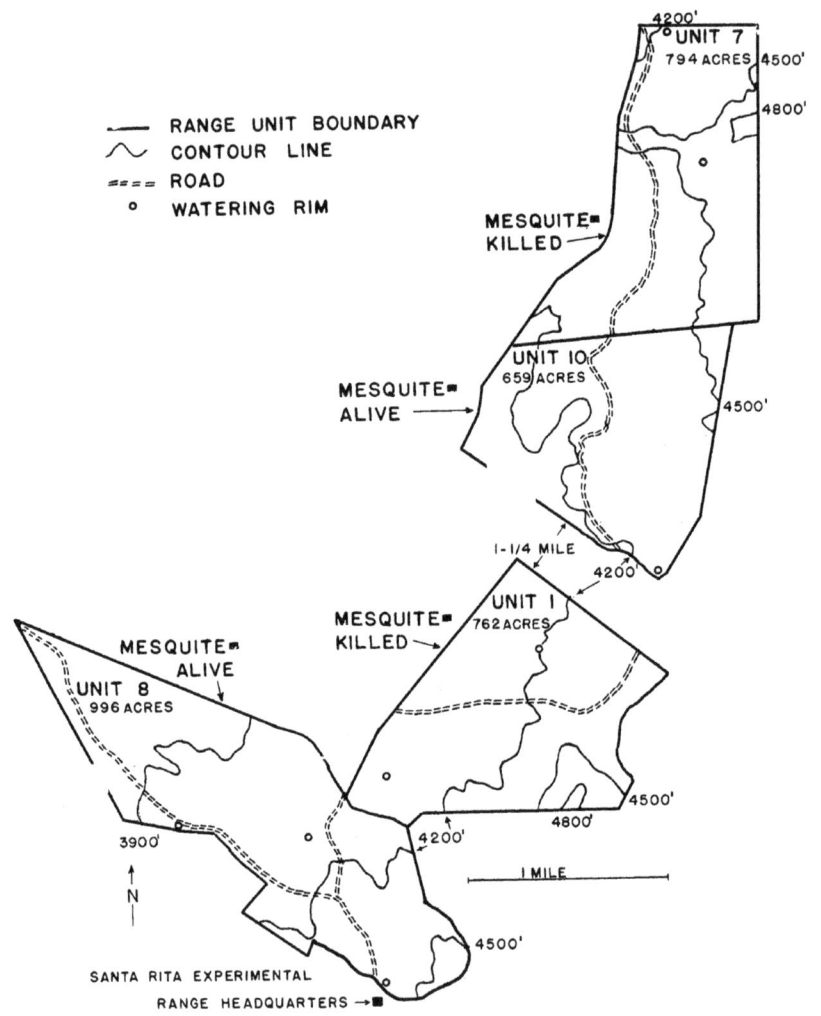

Figure 1.--Range units used in the study.

removed by evaporation and transpiration during the dry periods preceding each rainy season. Summer rainfall, which produces about 90 percent of the perennial grass herbage (Culley 1943), varied greatly during the study period:

	Precipitation	
	Mesquite-killed	Mesquite-alive
	(Inches)	
Lowest year	4.60	5.58
Highest year	15.41	19.32
Average year	10.14	11.64
Longtime average	9.62	10.02

Maximum daytime temperatures in summer are usually in the high eighties or low nineties, although the temperature may rise above $100°$ F. on 1 or 2 days during the summer. Winter minimums generally are in the upper thirties although freezing temperatures, seldom lower than $20°$ F., have been recorded at the range headquarters, 4,300 feet, an average of 27 nights each winter.

Vegetation cover.--Vegetation on the range units in 1957 consisted of a relatively good stand of native perennial grasses overtopped on two of the units by an invasion stand of velvet mesquite (Prosopis juliflora var. velutina (Woot.) Sarg.). Invading mesquite had been killed on the other two units. Perennial grass basal intercept averaged 0.82 and 1.09 percent on the mesquite-killed and mesquite-alive units, respectively, and perennial grass herbage production averaged 218 and 299 pounds per acre air-dry.

Grama grasses, principally sprucetop (Bouteloua chondrosioides (H.B.K.) Benth.), side-oats (B. curtipendula (Michx.) Torr.), black (B. eriopoda Torr.), and slender (B. filiformis (Fourn.) Griffiths), comprised from one-half to three-fourths of the perennial grass stand. Arizona cottontop (Trichachne californica (Benth.) Chase) and Aristida hamulosa Henr. made up most of the remainder. Predominant annual grasses were sixweeks three-awn (Aristida adscensionis L.) and needle grama (B. aristidoides (H.B.K.) Griseb.).

Total shrub crown intercept averaged 9.58 and 12.16 percent, of which mesquite comprised 2 percent on the mesquite-killed units and 31 percent on the mesquite-alive units. Other common shrubs were velvetpod mimosa (Mimosa dysocarpa Benth.), false mesquite (Calliandra eriophylla Benth.), catclaw acacia (Acacia greggii A. Gray), and Engelmann pricklypear (Opuntia engelmannii Salm-Dyck).

The mesquite stands before treatment averaged from about 80 to 180 plants per acre on the four range units. Although some small areas with very dense stands (up to 775 trees per acre on 0.5-acre plot) had essentially no perennial grass understory, most of the area on the range units still had fair to good stands of perennial grasses. Mesquite control was essentially complete by 1957. Vegetation characteristics of study ranges in 1957 are summarized as follows:

	Mesquite-killed	Mesquite-alive
Perennial grass basal intercept (Percent)	0.82	1.09
Perennial grass herbage production (Lbs/A)	218	299
Annual grass herbage production (Lbs/A)	179	38
Shrub crown intercept (Percent)	9.58	12.16
Mesquite crown intercept (Percent)	0.19	3.76
Mesquite density (Trees/A)	9	128

Grazing history.--The four range units had been grazed yearlong by cattle since 1915. From 1915 to 1925 the stocking rate averaged from 32 to 34 head per section. Declining productivity soon showed, however, that such rates of stocking were too high, and numbers were reduced more or less progressively until around 1940. During the 16-year period 1941-56 immediately before the change in grazing management, the stocking rate averaged 16, 13, 14, and 15 head per section on units 1, 7, 8, and 10, respectively. Utilization of perennial grasses during this period averaged 60, 58, 59, and 47 percent on the four units.

Recent rainfall history.--Summer rainfall during the period 1946-53 was generally deficient: 1947, 1948, 1952, and 1953 were markedly below the longtime mean, and there were moderate summer rainfall shortages in some of the range units in 1949 and 1951. Precipitation for the summers of 1952 and 1953 was 65 percent of the longtime average in units 1 and 8, and 57 percent of the mean in units 7 and 10. This 8-year period of generally low rainfall, climaxed by two successive summers of severe drought, had reduced the perennial grass stand to a rather low state of productivity by the time the mesquite-control program began in 1954 (fig. 2a).

METHODS

Mesquite control.--Mesquites were killed in range units 1 and 7 by spraying diesel oil on the stem bases as described by Reynolds and Tschirley (1957). Oiling was started in 1954 and completed in 1957. New plants and the few small plants that were missed in the original treatment were sprayed during the summer of 1960. Spraying the original stand cost about 5 cents per tree, half for oil (1-1/2 pints per tree average) and half for labor. The 1960 spraying also cost about 5 cents per tree, 80 percent for labor and 20 percent for oil (3/4 pint per tree average).

The basal oiling treatment killed most trees within a few weeks. The few trees that survived were usually located in sandy washes where stream-deposited sand buried the

Figure 2.--Grass stand before and after mesquite

A. September 1953, after many years of close grazing, and two consecutive dry summers, 1952 and 1953.

This equation differs from those reported by Reid, et al. (1963) in two important respects. First, the independent variables are the yields of annual and perennial grass (pounds per acre) rather than the reciprocals of these values. Second, the dependent variable is the estimated number of animals needed to obtain 40 percent use on perennial grasses, rather than the reciprocal of "actual percent use." Each range unit has its own equation, which is recomputed each year to include data from the year immediately past.

Vegetation measurements.--Several kinds of vegetation data are being obtained yearly on or immediately adjacent to 20 randomly located permanent 100-foot line transects in each range unit.

1. Herbage yields of annual and perennial grasses are expressed as pounds per acre air-dry. Since 1954, estimates have been obtained by a double-sampling method similar to that described by Wilm et al. (1944).

2. Line intercept measurements of perennial grasses (basal intercept) and shrubs (crown intercept) began in 1953 in units 1 and 8, 1954 in unit 7, and 1955 in unit 10. Intercept is measured by Canfield's (1942) method.

3. Utilization of perennial grasses is measured by the ungrazed-plant-count method of Roach (1950). Prior to establishment of permanent transects, utilization was measured each year on 10 paced transects per range unit.

4. Numbers and crown diameters of living mesquites on plots 100 by 200 feet overlying each of the line transects were recorded in 1957. Most of the mesquites in units 1 and 7 had been killed at the time this count was made.

It should be noted that the mesquite-control program began in 1954, the permanent transects were established from 1953 to 1956, and the grazing treatment change was made in 1957. Consequently, data taken before 1957 show the response of vegetation to current rainfall, unmeasured influences, and to mesquite control. Responses measured after 1957 include the influence of better grazing management.

RESULTS AND DISCUSSION

The grass cover improved substantially on all four range units during the study period. Grass production, especially of annual grasses, increased most conspicuously on the mesquite-killed units (fig. 2). Mesquite-alive units produced almost no annual grass in dry summers, and only moderate amounts in summers of average or above-average rainfall.

Changes in Perennial Grass Herbage Production

Perennial grass production varied greatly during the 1954-61 study period (fig. 3):

	Herbage Production	
	Mesquite-killed	Mesquite-alive
	(pounds per acre)	
Lowest year	133	142
Highest year	660	638
8-year average	331	347

Highest production in 1958 was from 4.5 to 5 times as much as in 1956, the year of lowest production. Yields in these 2 years, 1956 and 1958, were near the all-time extremes for the study area. Summer rainfall, grazing management, and mesquite density appear to be the major factors that affected perennial grass production during this period.

Although the individual influences of these variables on perennial grass production cannot be completely isolated at this time, some indication of their separate effects can be obtained by (1) correlating total perennial grass production per acre with total summer rainfall to estimate the direct effect of rainfall, (2) determining production per acre per inch of summer rainfall by years to evaluate trends in production with time, and (3) comparing total production per acre and production per acre per inch of summer rainfall on mesquite-alive units with those on mesquite-killed units.

Correlation with summer rainfall.--Low grass production was associated with low

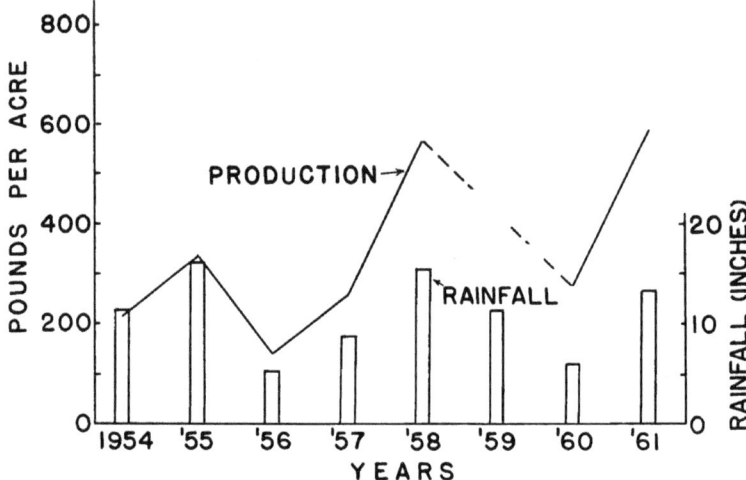

Figure 3.--*Perennial grass herbage production and June-September rainfall--average for four range units.*

summer rainfall, and high grass production with high summer rainfall, as would be expected (fig. 3). The correlation between total summer rainfall and perennial grass production accounts for only 39 percent (r = 0.622) of the variation in production, but is highly significant. Other rainfall variables such as the size and spacing of individual storms undoubtedly influence rainfall effectiveness, but no adequate evaluation of these variables is available.

Trends with time.--The trend in summer rainfall during this period was slightly downward, but not significantly so. Perennial grass production, on the other hand, exhibited a generally upward trend on both the mesquite-killed and mesquite-alive units (fig. 3). This upward trend in production, without a comparable increase in summer rainfall, implies improved productivity independent of rainfall. The extent of this improvement can be seen by expressing production in terms of pounds per acre per inch of summer rainfall.

Perennial grass production on the mesquite-killed and the mesquite-alive range units increased an average of 4.63 and 3.71 pounds per acre per inch of summer rainfall, respectively, for each year during the study period (fig. 4). Average production per acre per inch of rainfall on the four units increased from 19 pounds in 1954 to 45 pounds in 1961.

Several factors contributed to this increase in productivity, but the specific causes cannot be pinpointed. The rising trend in productivity was initiated by above-average summer rainfall in 1954 and 1955 following the 1947-53 period of generally unfavorable rainfall. Improvement subsequent to 1957 has been attributed to improved management: a reduction in utilization objective to 40 percent (actual use averaged 35 percent), coupled with alternate-summer deferment, which started in the 1957-58 grazing year. Productivity of adjacent range units, managed differently, did not improve during this period. Range unit 9, which lies between units 1 and 10, has been managed

- 6 -

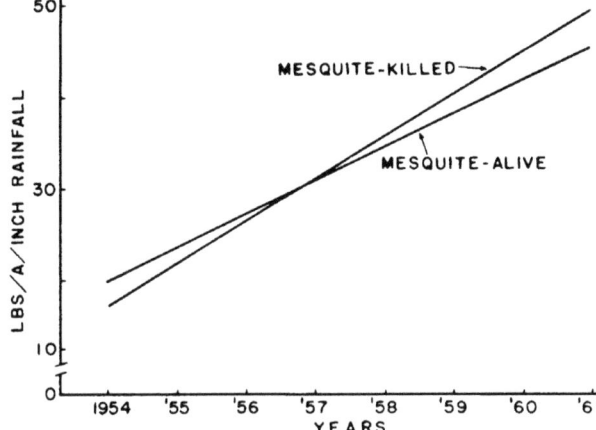

Figure 4.--
Change in perennial grass production per inch of June-September rainfall on mesquite-killed and mesquite-alive range units.

in the same way as the four study units except that since 1958 this unit has been grazed yearlong and has carried extra cattle in alternate summers. Productivity in unit 9 increased from 1954 to 1957, but has decreased since 1958. Also, on three larger adjacent units, where grazing has been yearlong and utilization has averaged somewhat higher (about 45 percent), there has been a slight but not significant downward trend in productivity.

Total summer rainfall and the improving trend with time together account for 76 percent of the variation in perennial grass productivity during the 1954-61 period, with rainfall being slightly more influential. The multiple correlation coefficient for this relation is R = 0.87.

Influence of mesquite control.--Between 1957 and 1961, perennial grass herbage production on the mesquite-killed range units increased relative to production on the mesquite-alive units. Production on the mesquite-killed range units increased over twice as much (443 pounds per acre) as did that on the mesquite-alive range units (220 pounds per acre). This difference between the two pairs of range units is significant at p = 0.01.

	Perennial grass production	
	Mesquite-killed	Mesquite-alive
	(Pounds per acre)	
1957	217	299
1961	660	519
Increase	443	220

This improvement due to resquite control, while substantial and important, was slower and much less dramatic than had been reported previously from studies in which moderate to dense stands of mesquite were removed from small plots with very sparse stands of perennial grasses (Parker and Martin 1952). The smaller response in this study was not unexpected, and was probably due to a lower potential for improvement because of the relatively light stand of mesquite and the relatively good stand of perennial grass present at the start of the study.

The somewhat divergent trends in production per inch of rainfall (fig. 4) also show the influence of mesquite control, although with the limited amount of data available, these trends are not significantly different.

Changes In Perennial Grass Basal Intercept

The period 1957-59 has been established as a base for studying the trends in perennial grass cover in this study. On this basis, by 1961 perennial grass basal intercept had increased significantly more (p = 0.01) on the mesquite-killed units, 61.6 percent average increase, than on the mesquite-alive units, 19.4 percent average increase.

	Basal intercept	
	Mesquite-killed	Mesquite-alive
	(Percent)	
1957-59 average	1.38	1.75
1961	2.23	2.09
Change	+61.6	+19.4

Since the basal area of perennial grass plants is relatively insensitive to year-to-year changes in rainfall, this trend indicates long-term cumulative effects of weather and management (in contrast, production of herbage i. highly sensitive to year-to-year changes i rainfall and is therefore more indicative o the short-term effects of weather and man agement).

Changes In Annual Grass Production

Annual grass production varied mor widely from year to year than did perenni; grass production.

	Annual grass production	
	Mesquite-killed	Mesquite-alive
	(Pounds per acre)	
Lowest year	53	22
Highest year	424	163
8-year average	227	74

In the year of highest production annua grasses yielded from 7.5 to 8 times as muc herbage as in the year of lowest productior These differences apparently were response mostly to variations in summer rainfall an in mesquite density.

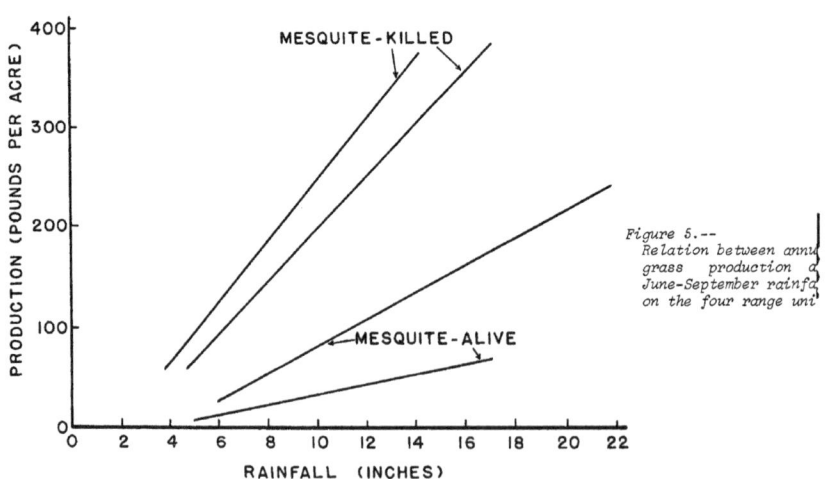

Figure 5.-- Relation between annu grass production a June-September rainfa on the four range uni

Influence of rainfall.--Because the annual grasses complete their life cycle from seed to seed within 6 to 12 weeks during the summer rainy season, they are obviously dependent on summer rain for their growth. Correation coefficients of 0.73 and 0.76 between June-September rainfall and annual grass production on the mesquite-alive and mesquite-killed range units indicate that a little over half of the variation in annual grass production during the 1954-61 period is explained by variations in total summer rainfall. A large part of the remaining variation is probably due to variation in size and spacing of individual storms.

Range-unit regressions of annual grass production and rainfall for the 8-year period show the separate effects of rainfall and mesquite density. Each additional inch of June-September rainfall produced on the average 27 and 31 pounds per acre of annual grass herbage on the two mesquite-killed units, but only 5 and 14 pounds per acre on the mesquite-alive units (fig. 5).

Influence of mesquite density.--As noted above, annual grasses produced more herbage on the mesquite-killed than on the mesquite-alive units; the two mesquite-killed units averaged 227 pounds per acre from 1954 to 1961, while the two mesquite-alive units averaged only 74 pounds per acre.

Relating the rates of change in annual grass production per acre per inch of summer rainfall to mesquite crown intercept for the four range units indicates that annual grass production per inch of summer rainfall decreased markedly, but nonlinearly, as mesquite intercept increased (fig. 6). Thus, with a mesquite crown intercept of 0.25 percent, annual grass production was about 20 pounds per acre per inch of summer rainfall; production dropped to 10 pounds per acre per inch with 2 percent crown intercept, and 5 pounds per acre per inch with 7 percent crown intercept.

Changes In Stocking Rates

Because the stocking rates are based on yearly production of grass herbage, the pattern of change in stocking rates should resemble the pattern of change in grass produc-

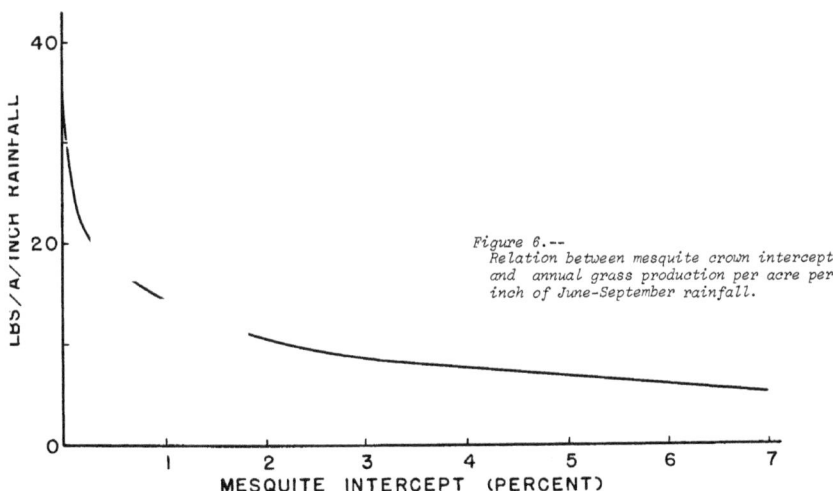

Figure 6.--
Relation between mesquite crown intercept and annual grass production per acre per inch of June-September rainfall.

tion. Also, if the type of management has improved grass productivity, stocking rates during the study period should show improvement over those of prior years.

Direct comparison of stocking rates between the study period and prior years is not valid because utilization averaged much higher during the earlier period. When stocking rates are adjusted to a utilization of 40 percent of the available grass forage, direct comparison is valid.

During the 1954-61 period, the stocking rate for 40 percent use increased an average of 2.5 head per section per year on the mesquite-killed units--from 10.2 head per section in 1954 to 27.4 head per section in 1961 (fig. 7). The rate of increase on the mesquite-alive units was 1.1 head per section per year--from 13.0 head per section in 1954 to 21.0 head per section in 1961. These trends resemble in direction and magnitude those for perennial grass production discussed previously. Thus, the increase in grass production, due both to better management and mesquite control, has made it possible to increase the stocking rates appreciably.

SUMMARY AND CONCLUSIONS

Herbage production of annual and perennial grasses, basal intercept of perennial grasses, and stocking rates have been measured since 1954 on four range units of the Santa Rita Experimental Range, primarily to determine the reaction to mesquite control. Mesquites were killed on two of the units between 1954 and 1957 by spraying diesel oil on the lower trunk of each tree.

The changes in vegetation measured during the 8-year period were caused by three main factors: year-to-year variation in precipitation, management practices, and mesquite control.

The native annual and perennial grasses on these range units are primarily summer growers, and thus depend for their growth primarily on summer rainfall. The correlation between June-September rainfall and perennial grass herbage production is significant, but explains only about 39 percent of the year-to-year variation in production. Annual grass production, on the other hand, is more closely correlated with rainfall: over half of

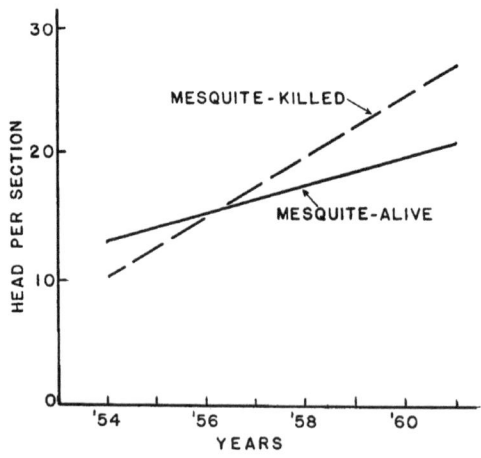

Figure 7.--
Changes in stocking rates for 40 percent use, 1954-61.

- 10 -

LITERATURE CITED

Canfield, R. H.
 1942. Sampling ranges by the line interception method. U. S. Forest Serv., Southwest. Forest and Range Expt. Sta. Rpt. 4, 28 pp., illus.

Culley, Matt
 1943. Grass grows in summer or not at all. Amer. Hereford Jour. 34: 9-10, illus.

Parker, Kenneth W., and Martin, S. Clark.
 1952. The mesquite problem on southern Arizona ranges. U. S. Dept. Agr. Cir. 908, 70 pp., illus.

Reid, E. H., Kovner, J. L., and Martin, S. Clark.
 1963. A proposed method of determining cattle numbers in range experiments. Jour. Range Mangt. 16: 184-187, illus.

Reynolds, Hudson G., and Tschirley, Fred H.
 1957. Mesquite control on southwestern rangeland. U. S. Dept. Agr. Leaflet 421, 8 pp., illus.

Roach, M. E.
 1950. Estimating perennial grass utilization on semidesert cattle ranges by percentage of ungrazed plants. Jour. Range Mangt. 3: 182-185, illus.

Wilm, H. G., Costello, David F., and Klipple, G. E.
 1944. Estimating forage yield by the double sampling method. Amer. Soc. Agron. Jour. 36: 194-203.

ss, and Diameter Relationships

n Colorado and Wyoming

rd A. Myers[1]

6- or 8-inch top (tables 1, 2). Diameters are given to the nearest 0.1 inch when tree heights are in feet (table 3). Diameters at stump height and at breast height (4.5 feet above ground level) are also reported when tree heights are in feet.

Merchantable height is the maximum number of logs and half-logs between the stump and the specified top diameter. Portions of the bole above the height of minimum top saw log diameter were included in the uppermost log or half-log if the standard length (8.15 or 16.3 feet) ended within 4.0 feet above this height. This is the reason for occasional entries of 5 inches in table 1 and of 7 inches in table 2.

Bark Thickness

Differences between diameters inside and outside bark at breast height (table 3) are measures of double bark thicknesses. Bark thickness may be computed from the following linear relationship:

$$T = 0.038 \,(d.b.h.) + 0.115$$
$$[r = 0.992 \quad Syx = 0.018]$$

where T is double bark thickness at breast height and d.b.h. is diameter outside bark 4.5 feet above ground level.

Table 1.--Scaling diameters of logs of the average tree in each merchantable height and diameter class. Utilization to a 6-inch top.

Merchantable logs	Diameter breast height outside bark (inches)	\multicolumn{8}{c}{Position of log in the tree}
		1.0	1.5	2.0	2.5	3.0	3.5	4.0	4.5
		\multicolumn{8}{c}{Diameter inside bark in inches}
1.0	6.5	6							
	7.5	6							
	8.5	6							
	9.5	6							
1.5	7.5	6	6						
	8.5	7	6						
	9.5	8	6						
	10.5	9	6						
	11.5	9	7						
	12.5	10	7						
2.0	7.5	7		6					
	8.5	7		6					
	9.5	8		6					
	10.5	9		6					
	11.5	9		7					
	12.5	10		7					
	13.5	10		7					
	14.5	11		7					
	15.5	11		7					
2.5	8.5	8		7	6				
	9.5	8		7	6				
	10.5	9		7	6				
	11.5	10		8	6				
	12.5	10		8	6				
	13.5	11		9	6				
	14.5	11		9	7				
	15.5	12		10	7				
	16.5	13		10	7				
3.0	9.5	8		7	6	6			
	10.5	9		8	6	6			
	11.5	10		8	6	6			
	12.5	11		9	6	6			
	13.5	11		9	6	6			
	14.5	12		10	6	6			
	15.5	13		10	7	7			
	16.5	13		11	7	7			
	17.5	14		11	7	7			
	18.5	15		12	7	7			
	19.5	16		12	7	7			
3.5	10.5	9		8	7	7	6		
	11.5	10		9	8	7	6		
	12.5	11		9	8	8	6		
	13.5	12		10	8	8	6		
	14.5	13		11	9	8	6		
	15.5	14		11	9	9	6		
	16.5	15		12	10	10	7		
	17.5	15		13	10	10	7		
	18.5	16		13	11	11	7		
	19.5	17		14	11	11	7		
	20.5	18		15	12	12	7		
	21.5	18		15	12	12	7		
	22.5	19		16	13	13	8		
4.0	11.5	10		9	8	8	6	6	
	12.5	11		10	8	8	6	6	
	13.5	12		11	9	9	6	6	
	14.5	13		11	9	9	6	6	
	15.5	13		12	10	10	6	6	
	16.5	14		12	10	10	6	6	
	17.5	15		13	11	11	7	7	
	18.5	16		14	11	11	7	7	
	19.5	17		14	12	12	7	7	
	20.5	18		15	12	12	7	7	
	21.5	18		15	13	13	7	7	
	22.5	19		16	13	13	7	7	
	23.5	19		17	13	13	7	7	
4.5	12.5	11		10	9	9	7	7	5
	13.5	12		11	10	10	7	7	5
	14.5	13		12	10	10	8	8	6
	15.5	14		12	11	11	8	8	6
	16.5	14		13	11	11	8	8	6
	17.5	15		13	12	12	8	8	6
	18.5	16		14	12	12	9	9	6
	19.5	17		15	13	13	9	9	7
	20.5	18		15	13	13	9	9	7
	21.5	19		16	14	14	9	9	7
	22.5	19		16	14	14	9	9	7
	23.5	20		17	14	14	10	10	7
	24.5	20		18	14	14	10	10	7

Merchant-able height logs	Diameter breast height outside bark Inches	Position of log in the tree — Diameter inside bark in inches								Merchant-able height logs	Diameter breast height outside bark Inches	Position of log in the tree — Diameter inside bark in inches							
		1.0	1.5	2.0	2.5	3.0	3.5	4.0	4.5			1.0	1.5	2.0	2.5	3.0	3.5	4.0	4.5
1.0	9.5	8								3.5	12.5	11		10		8	8		
	10.5	8									13.5	12		10		8	8		
	11.5	9									14.5	13		11		9	8		
1.5	9.5	8	7								15.5	14		12		10	8		
	10.5	9	8								16.5	15		13		10	8		
	11.5	10	8								17.5	16		14		10	8		
	12.5	10	8								18.5	17		14		11	8		
	13.5	11	9								19.5	17		15		11	8		
	14.5	11	9								20.5	18		15		12	8		
	15.5	12	9								21.5	18		16		12	8		
	16.5	13	9								22.5	19		16		12	8		
2.0	9.5	8		7							23.5	19		17		13	8		
	10.5	9		8						4.0	12.5	11		10		8		7	
	11.5	10		8							13.5	12		11		8		7	
	12.5	10		8							14.5	13		11		9		7	
	13.5	11		8							15.5	14		12		10		7	
	14.5	12		8							16.5	15		13		11		8	
	15.5	13		8							17.5	16		14		11		8	
	16.5	13		8							18.5	16		15		12		8	
	17.5	14		8							19.5	17		15		13		8	
	18.5	15		8							20.5	18		16		13		8	
	19.5	16		8							21.5	19		16		14		8	
2.5	10.5	9		8	7						22.5	19		17		14		9	
	11.5	10		8	8						23.5	20		18		14		9	
	12.5	10		9	8						24.5	20		18		15		9	
	13.5	11		9	8						25.5	21		18		15		9	
	14.5	12		10	8					4.5	15.5	13		12		11		8	8
	15.5	13		10	8						16.5	14		13		11		9	8
	16.5	14		11	8						17.5	15		14		12		9	8
	17.5	14		11	8						18.5	16		15		13		9	8
	18.5	15		12	8						19.5	16		15		13		9	8
	19.5	16		12	8						20.5	17		16		14		9	8
	20.5	17		13	8						21.5	18		17		14		10	8
	21.5	18		14	8						22.5	18		17		15		10	8
3.0	10.5	9		8		7					23.5	19		18		15		10	8
	11.5	10		9		7					24.5	20		18		15		10	8
	12.5	11		9		8					25.5	21		19		15		10	9
	13.5	12		10		8													
	14.5	12		10		8													
	15.5	13		11		8													
	16.5	14		11		8													
	17.5	15		12		8													
	18.5	15		12		8													
	19.5	16		13		9													
	20.5	17		14		9													
	21.5	18		14		9													
	22.5	18		15		9													

Table 3.--Diameters at various heights of the average tree in each total height and diameter class.

Total height (feet)	Diameter breast height outside bark (inches)	Height above ground level in feet										
		1.0	4.5	9.2	17.3	25.4	33.6	41.8	49.9	58.0	66.2	74.4	82.5
		Diameter inside bark in inches										
30.0	3.5	3.5	3.2	3.1	2.4	1.1							
	4.5	4.6	4.2	3.9	3.1	1.2							
	5.5	5.7	5.2	4.6	3.8	1.3							
	6.5	6.8	6.1	5.4	4.5	1.4							
	7.5	7.9	7.1	6.2	5.2	1.5							
40.0	3.5	3.5	3.3	3.1	2.7	2.3	1.3						
	4.5	4.6	4.2	4.0	3.5	2.7	1.5						
	5.5	5.7	5.2	4.9	4.2	3.5	1.7						
	6.5	6.8	6.1	5.8	5.0	4.2	2.0						
	7.5	7.9	7.1	6.7	5.8	4.8	2.2						
	8.5	9.0	8.1	7.5	6.6	5.4	2.4						
	9.5	10.1	9.0	8.4	7.4	6.0	2.6						
	10.5	11.2	10.0	9.3	8.1	6.6	2.9						
	11.5	12.3	11.0	10.2	8.9	7.2	3.1						
	12.5	13.3	11.9	11.1	9.7	7.8	3.3						

70.0	8.5	9.0	8.1	7.8	7.3	6.9	6.4	5.8	4.6	3.0	1.7		
	9.5	10.1	9.0	8.7	8.2	7.8	7.2	6.8	5.1	3.6	1.8		
	10.5	11.2	10.0	9.6	9.1	8.6	7.9	7.4	5.7	4.0	1.9		
	11.5	12.3	11.0	10.5	9.8	9.2	8.5	7.9	6.2	4.4	2.0		
	12.5	13.3	11.9	11.4	10.5	9.8	9.1	8.4	6.7	4.7	2.1		
	13.5	14.5	12.9	12.2	11.2	10.4	9.7	8.8	7.1	5.0	2.2		
	14.5	15.7	13.8	13.1	12.1	11.1	10.3	9.2	7.5	5.3	2.3		
	15.5	16.8	14.8	14.0	13.0	11.9	10.9	9.6	7.9	5.5	2.4		
	16.5	18.0	15.8	14.9	13.9	12.6	11.5	10.0	8.2	5.7	2.5		
	17.5	19.1	16.7	15.8	14.7	13.3	12.0	10.5	8.4	5.9	2.6		
	18.5	20.3	17.7	16.7	15.6	14.1	12.5	10.9	8.7	6.1	2.6		
	19.5	21.4	18.7	17.6	16.5	14.9	13.0	11.3	9.0	6.3	2.7		
	20.5	22.6	19.6	18.5	17.4	15.7	13.5	11.6	9.3	6.4	2.8		
	21.5	23.7	20.6	19.4	18.3	16.5	14.0	11.9	9.6	6.5	2.9		
	22.5	24.9	21.5	20.4	19.1	17.3	14.5	11.9	9.9	6.6	3.0		
	23.5	26.0	22.5	21.4	20.0	18.1	15.0	12.1	10.1	6.7	3.1		
80.0	9.5	10.1	9.0	8.8	8.4	8.1	7.5	6.6	5.9	4.6	3.0	2.4	
	10.5	11.2	10.0	9.7	9.2	8.8	8.1	7.2	6.4	5.1	3.4	2.5	
	11.5	12.3	11.0	10.6	10.0	9.5	8.8	7.9	6.9	5.5	3.8	2.6	
	12.5	13.3	11.9	11.5	10.8	10.2	9.5	8.5	7.4	6.0	4.2	2.7	
	13.5	14.5	12.9	12.4	11.6	11.0	10.2	9.2	7.9	6.4	4.6	2.8	
	14.5	15.7	13.8	13.3	12.4	11.7	10.9	9.8	8.4	6.9	5.0	2.9	
	15.5	16.8	14.8	14.2	13.2	12.4	11.5	10.4	8.9	7.3	5.4	3.0	
	16.5	18.0	15.8	15.0	14.1	13.2	12.2	11.0	9.5	7.7	5.8	3.1	
	17.5	19.1	16.7	16.0	15.0	14.0	12.7	11.5	10.0	8.1	6.2	3.2	
	18.5	20.3	17.7	16.9	15.9	14.8	13.2	11.9	10.4	8.4	6.5	3.3	
	19.5	21.4	18.7	17.9	16.7	15.5	13.7	12.3	10.8	8.7	6.8	3.4	
	20.5	22.6	19.6	18.8	17.5	16.2	14.2	12.7	11.2	9.0	7.1	3.5	
	21.5	23.7	20.6	19.7	18.4	17.0	14.8	13.2	11.6	9.4	7.4	3.6	
	22.5	24.9	21.5	20.6	19.3	17.8	15.4	13.6	12.0	9.8	7.7	3.7	
	23.5	26.0	22.5	21.5	20.2	18.6	15.9	14.0	12.4	10.1	7.9	3.8	
	24.5	27.1	23.5	22.5	21.1	19.4	16.4	14.5	12.9	10.4	8.1	3.9	
90.0	10.5	11.2	10.0	9.7	9.2	8.9	8.4	7.8	7.3	6.5	4.8	3.7	1.9
	11.5	12.3	11.0	10.6	10.0	9.6	9.1	8.5	7.9	7.0	5.5	4.0	2.1
	12.5	13.3	11.9	11.5	10.8	10.3	9.9	9.3	8.6	7.5	6.1	4.3	2.3
	13.5	14.5	12.9	12.4	11.6	11.1	10.6	10.0	9.1	7.9	6.6	4.5	2.4
	14.5	15.7	13.8	13.3	12.4	11.8	11.3	10.6	9.6	8.3	7.1	4.7	2.6
	15.5	16.8	14.8	14.2	13.2	12.5	12.0	11.2	10.1	8.7	7.6	4.9	2.8
	16.5	18.0	15.8	15.0	14.1	13.3	12.7	11.8	10.6	9.1	8.0	5.0	2.9
	17.5	19.1	16.7	16.0	15.0	14.2	13.4	12.4	11.1	9.5	8.4	5.2	3.1
	18.5	20.3	17.7	16.9	15.9	15.0	14.0	13.0	11.6	9.9	8.8	5.3	3.2
	19.5	21.4	18.7	17.9	16.8	15.8	14.7	13.6	12.1	10.2	9.2	5.5	3.4
	20.5	22.6	19.6	18.9	17.7	16.6	15.3	14.2	12.6	10.6	9.6	5.5	3.6
	21.5	23.7	20.6	19.9	18.6	17.4	15.9	14.7	13.0	10.9	9.9	5.7	3.7
	22.5	24.9	21.5	20.7	19.5	18.2	16.6	15.3	13.4	11.2	10.2	5.9	3.9
	23.5	26.0	22.5	21.6	20.4	19.0	17.2	15.8	13.8	11.5	10.5	6.1	4.1
	24.5	27.1	23.5	22.6	21.3	19.8	17.8	16.3	14.2	11.8	10.8	6.2	4.3
	25.5	28.3	24.4	23.6	22.1	20.5	18.4	16.8	14.6	12.0	11.1	6.3	4.5

Estimation Of Past Diameter

Diameters inside and outside bark at breast height are related linearly, as follows:

$$D.i.b. = 0.9625 (d.o.b.) - 0.1141$$
$$[r = 0.999 \quad Syx = 0.077]$$

$$D.o.b. = 1.0377 (d.i.b.) + 0.1323$$
$$[r = 0.999 \quad Syx = 0.159]$$

where d.i.b. is diameter inside bark and d.o.b. is diameter outside bark.

These relationships may be used to determine past diameter outside bark. The steps are: (1) convert present d.o.b. to present d.i.b. with the first formula, (2) subtract twice the radial growth from present d.i.b. to obtain past d.i.b., and (3) convert past d.i.b. to past d.o.b. with the second formula. This accounts for the growth of both wood and bark.

The equations and a term for radial growth may be combined to produce this equation for direct estimation of past diameter:

Past d.o.b. = Present d.o.b. - 2.08 r + 0.01 (where r is radial wood growth at breast height for any desired period).

As indicated by the relationship between bark thickness and diameter, there is little change in bark thickness as diameter increases 1 inch. If periodic radial growth of the wood is 0.65 inch or less, past diameter outside bark equals present diameter outside bark minus twice radial wood growth. If radial wood growth is 0.70 to 2.00 inches, past diameter outside bark is 0.1 inch less than the difference between present diameter and twice radial wood growth.

Diameter Breast Height From Stump Diameter

Diameters outside bark at breast height may be estimated from diameters inside bark at the tops of stumps 1.0 foot high. The relationships are as follows:

If stump diameter inside bark is 3.0 to 13.9 inches:

$$D.b.h. = 0.9158 (d.i.b.) + 0.2781$$
$$[r = 0.998 \quad Syx = 0.135]$$

If stump diameter inside bark is 14.0 to 30.9 inches:

$$D.b.h. = 0.8735 (d.i.b.) + 0.7914$$
$$[r = 0.988 \quad Syx = 0.408]$$

Breast heights and corresponding stump diameter are shown in columns 2 and 3 of table 3. Sufficiently precise estimates of d.b.h. for other stump diameters than those given usually may be obtained by interpolation.

Estimates of d.b.h. from stump diameters may be used to compute the volumes of trees that have been cut and removed.

Black Hills Beetles from Central Rocky Mountains

cCambridge[1]

imately 5 percent of the beetles emerge. Then emergence is rapid, hitting a peak about August 20 when almost 50 percent of the beetles have emerged. By the end of August, approximately 90 percent of the beetles have emerged, and it is unlikely that further attacks will be made on uninfested trees. Random chance reveals that 1 year in every 5 the beetles will emerge up to 2 weeks earlier than average.

Temperature Records

The time of emergence appears to be related to temperatures during the periods of beetle development--August, September, and October, and the following May, June, and July. The early emergence that occurred in 1939 probably was due to exceptionally warm weather which prevailed during the development period. Conversely, emergence in 1937 and 1962 would be expected to be later than normal. In that regard, emergence in 1962 appears out of line. Perhaps the temperature records, which were taken at the District Ranger's weather station in Bailey, are not

---

[1]*Entomologist, Rocky Mountain Forest and Range Experiment Station, with central headquarters maintained at Fort Collins in cooperation with Colorado State University.*

Table 1.--Data on emergence of Black Hills beetles from ponderosa pine at four locations in Colorado, 1937-39,[1] 1962-63[2]

Year	Colorado location	Elevation	Date cages installed	Cages	Bark area caged	Average beetle emergence	Sum of average temperature departures from normal	
							6-month period[3]	3-month period[4]
				Number	Sq. ft.	Per sq. ft.	Degrees F.	
1937	Evergreen	7,300	July 19	40	80	28.0	-8.8	-2.9
1938	Estes Park	8,000	Before July 11	20	40	21.5	+3.4	+9.0
1939	Estes Park	8,000	Before June 26	15	66	27.3	+10.3	+8.7
1962	Bailey	8,400	July 14	6	42	45.6	-6.9	-5.9
1963	Allens Park	8,500	July 10	10	60	21.6	+4.2	+.3

[1] From unpublished reports filed at Rocky Mountain Forest and Range Experiment Station, Fort Colorado:
    Beal, J. A., and DeLeon, Donald. A study of the Black Hills beetle in southeastern Wyoming and central Colorado, summer of 1937. May 16, 1938.
    DeLeon, Donald. The biology and control of the Black Hills beetle, summary of studies in Colorado and Wyoming, 1935-1938. May 13, 1939.
    DeLeon, Donald. Summary of 1939 Black Hills beetle studies, Colorado and southern Wyoming. February 26, 1940.
[2] From information collected by McCambridge.
[3] August, September, October of year of beetle attack, plus May, June, July of following year (year of emergence).
[4] August, September, October of year of beetle attack.

well related to the temperatures on the emergence plot which is 400-500 feet higher, and on a warm, south-facing slope.

If higher than normal fall and spring temperatures were responsible for the early emergence in 1939, weather records[2] show that early emergence would also have occurred an additional eight times between 1924 and 1963 in the Estes Park area, and three times within that period in the vicinity of Bailey. Excess temperatures during the fall only occurred four times near Estes Park and once near Bailey.

Emergence Cages

Until reliable clues such as temperature are available for predicting the emergence

[2] Average monthly maximum and minimum temperatures taken from: U. S. Weather Bureau. Climatological Data, Colorado. Jan. 1, 1924 - Dec. 31, 1963.

period more precisely, screen cages (figs. 2, 3) can be used for determining whether to extend the control season in the normal years. Cages should be installed early in June for two reasons: to detect start of emergence, and to prevent a false emergence which might occur if the beetles are disturbed when the cages are attached to the trees or when the bolts are cut from the infested trees.

Since beetles emerge from individual trees at different times, enough cages should be installed to accurately determine the start of emergence. Analysis of emergence data from the Bailey Ranger District, Pike National Forest, showed that the start of emergence could be determined 9 times out of 10 if 20 cages were installed throughout the District (approximately 100,000 acres).

Cages should be installed on trees (fig. 2 or on bolts (fig. 3) of densely infested portions of trees of average diameter growing under typical conditions of elevation and exposure. Even though emergence from the

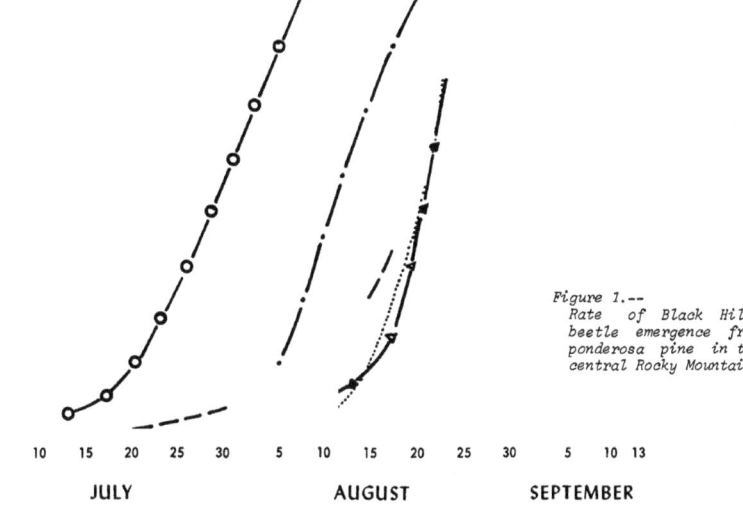

Figure 1.--
Rate of Black Hills beetle emergence from ponderosa pine in the central Rocky Mountains.

north and south sides of the trees takes place contemporaneously, cages installed on trees should be placed on the north side where beetle survival and emergence are significantly greater.

To determine whether a tree is adequately infested, a bark sample about 4 by 6 inches should be taken from each side of the area to be caged or from each end of the section from which a bolt is to be cut to observe density of beetle populations. The fact that a tree is a fader or sorrel-top is not sufficient evidence that the tree is heavily infested. If each sample section has three or more Black Hills beetle pupae or adults, the tree is adequately infested to serve as a cage tree.

The bolt cages may prove to be the more efficient. This will be true if bolt cages assembled at one place will yield reliable emergence data. Care should be used to locate the cages under conditions comparable to the area from which the bolts were cut.

Control Plans

Control projects should always be planned for completion by July 15. Most years, the control season can be extended to August 1, but the only way to be sure whether the beetles have started to emerge is careful observation of the emergence cages. If emergence is average, the control project can continue to August 1, with operational surveys to start after Labor Day. These surveys are to appraise the success of the control project and determine the need for mopup control.

Beetle Development

A brief description of beetle development prior to emergence may be helpful in appraising the advent of emergence.

Figure 2.--
Tree emergence cage, approximately 18 inches wide by 48 inches long, tacked to wood after bark has been shaved smooth around the edges. With the cage folded backward inside edge A is attached first, then edges B, B^1 (not shown), and C. Pint Mason jar is adequate for beetle recovery; regular window screening is used.

Changes in Perennial Grass Cover Following Conversion from Yearlong to Summer-Deferred Grazing in West Central New Mexico[1]

Wayne C. Hickey, Jr. and George Garcia[2]

The Rio Puerco drainage in west central New Mexico has been heavily used by livestock since the days of the early Spanish settlers.[3] Under close, yearlong grazing the vegetation deteriorated.

To determine whether improved management might help to rehabilitate those lands, livestock were excluded from three experimental watersheds during summer months over a 6-year period. Changes in the ground cover index during that time are compared with those during a 6-year period under yearlong grazing. The watersheds were used to test recovery as a cooperative project with the Bureau of Land Management.

[1] *Research reported here was conducted in cooperation with the Bureau of Land Management, U. S. Department of Interior.*
[2] *Range Conservationist and Forestry Research Technician, respectively, located at Albuquerque, in cooperation with the University of New Mexico; central headquarters maintained at Fort Collins, in cooperation with Colorado State University. Mr. Hickey is now Range Conservationist with Region 3, U. S. Forest Service, Albuquerque.*
[3] *Dortignac, E. J. Watershed resources and problems of the Upper Rio Grande Basin. 107 pp., illus. Rocky Mountain Forest and Range Expt. Sta., Ft. Collins, Colo. 1956.*

Study Site

The San Luis experimental site lies in the north central portion of the Rio Puerco drainage, 58 miles northwest of Albuquerque, New Mexico, in the transition zone between semi-desert grassland and woodland. The three watersheds are: WS I, 555 acres, WS II, 471 acres, and WS III, 338 acres. Annual precipitation for the area averages around 10 inches. The soils, which are alluvial, were derived principally from Mancos shale and cretaceous sandstone and are now severely gullied.

Principal forage species are alkali sacaton (Sporobolus airoides Torr.), galleta (Hilaria jamesii (Torr.) Benth.), and blue grama (Bouteloua gracilis (H. B. K.) Lag.). Fourwing saltbush (Atriplex canescens (Pursh) Nutt.) and big sagebrush (Artemisia tridentata Nutt.) are the principal shrubs.

Methods of Study

During the 6-year period ending May 1, 1957, the three watersheds were grazed by cattle yearlong; during the next 6 years they were grazed during winter months only (November through April).

Herbage production of each of the principal forage species was determined each fall after the first frost by a weight-estimate [4] and double-sampling technique.[5] Weight of each species, in grams, was estimated on nine permanent 9.6-square-foot plots at each of 25 sampling spots randomly located on each of the three watersheds. At the sampling spot, weight of herbage on a tenth 9.6-square-foot plot was estimated; then the herbage was clipped and weighed. The relationship between estimated and actual weights was used to adjust the estimate of the herbage weight on permanent plots.

Stocking rates were adjusted annually on the basis of herbage production. The objective was to utilize 55 percent of alkali sacaton.

Utilization was estimated about May 1 each year by the ocular estimate-by-plot method.[6] Mesh wire utilization cages, 9.6 square feet in size, were located at each sampling spot. They were relocated each spring on previously grazed spots to insure that new summer growth was measured. The cages provided examples of ungrazed forage at each site to help the examiner judge utilization.

Ground cover index was taken on 24 clusters of three 100-foot transects randomly distributed over each of the three watersheds. Records from them provided an index to changes in the three principal grass species. Measurements were taken in 1952, 1955, 1958, 1961, and 1963.

A network of nine open standard and four recording rain gages distributed over the three watersheds provided precipitation records. Precipitation was measured weekly from May 1 to November 1. The overwinter meas-

[4]*Pechanec, J. F. and Pickford, G. D. A weight estimate method for the determination of range or pasture production. Amer. Soc. Agron. Jour. 29(1): 894-904. 1937.*

[5]*Wilm, H. G., Costello, D. F., and Klipple, G. E. Estimating forage yield by the double-sampling method. Amer. Soc. Agron. Jour. 36: 194-203. 1944.*

[6]*Pechanec, J. F. and Pickford, G. D. A comparison of some methods used in determining percentage utilization of range grasses. Jour. Agr. Res. 54: 753-765. 1937.*

	Average precipitation	
	Annual (inches)	Growing season (inches)
Yearlong grazing:		
1953-54	12.12	8.24
1954-55	6.86	5.95
1955-56	5.92	2.21
1956-57	12.23	8.35
1957-58	12.00	6.53
Summer-deferred grazing:		
1958-59	10.66	6.81
1959-60	10.28	5.33
1960-61	10.32	9.31
1961-62	6.47	2.70
1962-63	9.19	4.15

Ground Cover Changes Under Yearlong Grazing

During the yearlong grazing, ground cover index declined. Reductions for individual species ranged from 15 to 56 percent (table 2).

Table 2. --Ground cover index of the three principal grasses on the San Luis watersheds

Species and year	WS I	WS II	WS III	Average
	- - - - Percent - - - -			
Alkali sacaton:				
1952	1.00	1.51	2.47	1.66
1955	.74	1.28	2.24	1.42
1958	.56	1.06	1.67	1.10
1961	2.21	3.45	3.17	2.94*
1963	3.11	6.41	5.67	5.06*
Galleta:				
1952	2.92	2.13	1.75	2.27
1955	3.51	2.21	1.53	2.42
1958	3.22	1.42	1.17	1.94
1961	6.60	3.49	2.18	4.09*
1963	12.55	8.43	4.61	8.53*
Blue grama:				
1952	3.28	1.26	.36	1.63
1955	2.10	.61	.44	1.05
1958	1.47	.48	.19	.71
1961	3.15	.96	.53	1.55*
1963	4.25	1.43	.63	2.10*

*Increases were significant at .01 level.

Measurements taken in 1958 showed a greater decline in blue grama than in the other two species. Blue grama was reduced by 56 percent from the 1952 value, while galleta averaged a 15 percent decline and alkali sacaton a 34 percent decline during this period.

Ground Cover Changes Under Deferred Grazing

Under summer deferment, the ground cover index showed a marked change (table 2). Alkali sacaton increased 400 percent, with individual gains of 455, 505, and 240 percent for the respective watersheds. Galleta increased by 290 percent in WS I, 494 percent in WS II, and 294 percent in WS III. For the entire study area galleta increased an average of 359 percent. Average increase for blue grama was 206 percent, a percentage representing gains of 189 percent for WS I, 198 percent for WS II, and 232 percent for WS III.

Tests of summer-deferred grazing resulted in significant increases in cover index compared with yearlong grazing. Although these tests lacked control of utilization and weather elements, the change from a declining ground cover index to an increasing one suggests conversion from yearlong to summer-deferred grazing was beneficial. This change in grazing was mainly responsible for the ground cover increases in alkali sacaton, galleta, and blue grama.

Summary and Conclusions

1. Ground cover changes, production, and utilization of alkali sacaton, galleta, and blue grama were measured during 6 years of yearlong grazing and then during 6 years of summer-deferred grazing.
2. Under yearlong grazing, these perennial grasses declined; under summer-deferred grazing, they increased.
3. The evidence indicates that summer deferment of grazing may be a means of improving the condition of similar rangelands in New Mexico.

Ground-Cover Changes in Relation to Runoff and Erosion in West-Central New Mexico[1]

Earl F. Aldon[2]

Much has been written of the high sediment content of flows in the Rio Puerco Drainage of New Mexico.[3] This drainage contributes almost half of the measured sediment of the Upper Rio Grande Basin, but less than 8 percent of the water yield.[4]

In 1952 a cooperative study was begun on three watersheds in the Rio Puerco Drainage to (1) determine the feasibility of restoring, through grazing management and land treatments, the more deteriorated portions of this region, and (2) obtain information about the effect of soil and vegetation conservation treatments on water and sediment yields.

Preliminary information on vegetation changes under various seasons of grazing in the semidesert type has been reported.[5,6] The objective of this paper is to show the effect of these vegetation changes on sediment yields.

Study Area

The San Luis Experimental Site on the Rio Puerco Drainage consists of three contiguous watersheds: WS I, 555 acres; WS II, 471 acres; and WS III, 338 acres. They are located about 58 miles northwest of Albuquerque, in the transition zone between woodland and semidesert grassland. Principal forage species are alkali sacaton (Sporobolus airoides Torr.), galleta (Hilaria jamesii Torr. Benth.), and blue grama (Bouteloua gracilis (H. B. K.) Lag.). Shadscale saltbush (Atriplex confertifolia Torr. & Frem.), other saltbushes (Atriplex spp.), and big sagebrush (Artemisia tridentata Nutt.) comprise the most common shrubs. Some pinyon pine (Pinus edulis Engelm.) and juniper (Juniperus spp.) trees and cholla cactus (Opuntia spp.) are scattered over the area.

---

[1]*Research reported here was conducted in cooperation with the Bureau of Land Management and the Geological Survey, U. S. Department of the Interior.*

[2]*Research Forester, located at Albuquerque, in cooperation with the University of New Mexico; central headquarters maintained at Fort Collins, in cooperation with Colorado State University.*

[3]*Dortignac, E. J. The Rio Puerco--past, present, and future. N. Mex. Water Conf. Proc. 1: 45-51, illus. 1960.*

[4]*Dortignac, E. J. Watershed resources and problems of the Upper Rio Grande Basin. U. S. Forest Serv., Rocky Mountain Forest and Range Expt. Sta., 107 pp., illus. 1956.*

[5]*Hickey, Wayne C., Jr., and Garcia, George. Range utilization patterns as affected by fencing and class of livestock. U. S. Forest Serv. Res. Note RM-21, 7 pp., illus. 1964.*

[6]*Hickey, Wayne C., Jr., and Garcia, George. Changes in perennial grass cover following conversion from yearlong to summer-deferred grazing in West Central New Mexico. U. S. Forest Serv. Res. Note RM-33, 3 pp. 1964.*

Average annual precipitation is close to 10 inches.[6] The headwaters of the watersheds originate on mesas that break off into steep rocky slopes. These breaks give way to rolling foothills that merge with the alluvial bottoms. A layer of Mesa Verde sandstone overlies Mancos shale. The sandstone breaks and underlying shales form the parent soil material, the texture of which varies from sandy loams to silty clays. The area, which ranges in elevation from 6,500 to 7,000 feet, is typical of the large semiarid area in northwestern New Mexico.

Methods

Runoff and sediment[7] were measured by methods similar to those described by Peterson.[8] Reservoirs constructed to catch runoff and sediment from the watersheds were equipped with a water-stage recorder. Sediment was determined from periodic surveys of the reservoirs to determine area, and from these data capacity curves were developed. The difference in capacity between surveys represents sediment changes. No adjustment was made for sediment that might have passed through an outlet pipe on WS II or through the spillway (at time of overflow). These amounts are considered to be only a small percentage of the total. Moreover, no adjustment was made for compaction of sediment in the reservoirs. Trap efficiency of the reservoirs is not known.

Precipitation and ground-cover measurements are fully described elsewhere.[6] Essentially, the ground-cover measurements consisted of 24 randomly distributed clusters of three 100-foot transects on each of the three watersheds.[9] Both recording and open standard rain gages were used to measure precipitation.

[7]*All runoff and sediment figures used in this paper were prepared by U. S. Geological Survey.*
[8]*Peterson, H. V. Hydrology of small watersheds in the western states. U. S. Geol. Survey Water-Supply Paper 1475-I. 356 pp., illus. 1962.*
[9]*Parker, K. W. A method for measuring trend in range condition on National Forest ranges. U. S. Forest Serv., Washington, D. C. 26 pp., illus. 1951.*

lected, the observed differences in mean value for the two periods cannot be tested for statistical significance.

Ground-cover measurements for the three principal grass species, rock, litter, and bare soil show a loss of ground cover on all watersheds between the years 1952 and 1958 (table 2). During this period litter on WS I and WS II decreased. Bare soil increased on WS I and II, but remained about the same on WS III. The effect of rock, measured on transects, on the hydrology of the area is unknown.

Ground cover and litter increased markedly after 1958, while bare soil decreased. All of the differences are significant at the 1 percent level. Rock occurrence showed a slight increase during this period.

Neither total annual precipitation nor precipitation measured during the growing season, May 1 to November 1, were significantly different between the two periods (table 3).

Covariance analysis with precipitation as covariate showed no difference in seasonal runoff between periods (table 3).

Summary

In 1952 a cooperative study on three San Luis Experimental watersheds in New Mexico was begun to determine the feasibility of restoring the more deteriorated portions of this region. Grazing management was started, but full control of the livestock through overwinter use only was not achieved until 1958. The periods 1952-58 and 1959-62 have been examined to determine the effect this different grazing use had on sediment yield, surface runoff, and ground cover.

Before the uniform grazing treatment, average ground cover, measured by three key grass species, ranged from 3 to 5 percent on the watersheds. Three years later the percentages had doubled: they ranged between 6 and 12 percent; bare ground decreased. Runoff during periods was similar, although the precision of the measurements was such that small changes could not be detected. Sediment production decreased between 0.2 and 0.7 acre-foot per year on the watersheds. The changes may be attributable to the change in grazing use between periods. Ground cover improved under summer-deferred grazing and fencing. Precipitation averages during the two periods were similar.

Table 2.--Ground cover index[1] of principal perennial grass species, rock, litter, and bare soil in each of the years measured

Substance	WS I			WS II			WS III		
	1952	1958	1961	1952	1958	1961	1952	1958	1961
	- - - - - - - - - - - - - - - - - Percent - - - - - - - - - - - - - - - - -								
Galleta	2.92	3.22	6.60	2.13	1.42	3.49	1.75	1.17	2.18
Alkali sacaton	1.00	.56	2.21	1.51	1.06	3.45	2.47	1.67	3.17
Blue grama	3.28	1.47	3.15	1.26	.48	.96	.36	.19	.53
Total grass	7.20	5.25	11.96	4.90	2.96	7.90	4.58	3.03	5.88
Rock	4.44	2.26	4.33	6.83	6.02	8.50	2.42	3.47	5.65
Litter	6.14	2.94	12.31	5.94	5.33	14.65	3.83	4.40	11.32
Bare soil	70.17	82.04	68.05	65.52	77.93	63.72	79.67	80.96	74.20

[1] Occurrence of a basal portion of a plant, litter, bare soil or rock within 3/4-inch loops placed at 1-foot intervals along a 100-foot transect. Litter, bare soil, or rock must occupy half or more of the loop area to be counted (from Parker [9]).

Table 3.--Precipitation, annual and growing season, and seasonal runoff on San Luis watersheds, 1954-62

Year	WS I			WS II			WS III		
	Precipitation		Seasonal runoff[3]	Precipitation		Seasonal runoff[3]	Precipitation		Seasonal runoff[3]
	Annual[1]	Growing season[2]		Annual[1]	Growing season[2]		Annual[1]	Growing season[2]	
	Inches		Acre-feet	Inches		Acre-feet	Inches		Acre-feet
1954	11.16	7.20	19.90	13.10	9.30	19.80	12.10	8.22	33.89
1955	6.70	5.79	34.88	7.19	6.35	24.77	6.69	5.72	15.28
1956	6.12	2.28	6.86	6.21	2.20	10.04	5.44	2.16	4.15
1957	13.29	9.30	89.19	12.05	8.16	88.62	11.34	7.58	58.67
1958	11.68	5.66	7.57	12.72	6.44	17.20	11.61	7.49	35.74
Average	9.79	6.05	31.68	10.25	6.49	32.09	9.44	6.23	29.55
1959	10.53	6.71	18.64	10.72	6.84	24.28	10.72	6.87	21.82
1960	11.74	5.53	13.10	8.48	5.42	14.19	10.62	5.04	10.03
1961	10.40	9.39	31.81	10.60	9.59	44.83	9.95	8.94	37.87
1962	6.78	3.16	11.17	6.25	2.32	2.92	6.38	2.62	2.24
Average	9.86	6.20	18.68	9.01	6.04	21.56	9.42	5.87	17.99

[1] Water year is November 1 - October 31; e.g., 1954 is November 1, 1953 - October 31, 1954.
[2] May 1 - November 1.
[3] April 1 - November 1. Storms outside these dates are usually winter-type storms. Since most winter storms producing runoff were not measured during the study, the few recorded ones were omitted from the table.

Picloram: A Promising Brush Control Chemical[1]

Edwin A. Davis[2]

Picloram (4-amino-3,5,6-trichloropicolinic acid) was recently reported as a plant growth regulator that is more toxic to broad-leaved plants than to grasses.[3] The structural formula of picloram is as follows:

$$\text{Cl} \underset{\text{Cl}}{\overset{\text{NH}_2}{\underset{\text{N}}{\bigcirc}}} \text{Cl} \atop \text{COOH}$$

The solubility of picloram in water at 25°C. is 430 p.p.m.; the potassium salt is highly soluble in water.

The potassium salt of picloram[4] in liquid formulation was evaluated in greenhouse studies for the control of shrub live oak (Quercus turbinella Greene). This shrub, which composes 60 to 80 percent of the chaparral type in Arizona, is one of the most difficult species to control. Interest in its control arises from a desire to increase water yield and forage production.

Picloram was applied on April 9, 1963, to the soil around 2-year-old shrub live oak plants in gallon cans. The soil was a sandy loam. The chemical, applied at rates of 1, 2, 4, 8, and 16 pounds per acre, was compared with 3-phenyl-1, 1-dimethylurea (fenuron)[5] at the same rates. The chemicals were applied as drenches to the soil, in 1/4 inch of water. Each treatment was replicated 4 times, so that 20 plants were treated with each chemical. The soil was subsequently kept moist by uniform irrigations with measured amounts of water, usually applied in 1/4-inch increments.

When the data for all rates of each chemical were pooled, picloram killed 80 percent of the plants and fenuron killed 70 percent. The two chemicals were comparable at the higher rates, but at the lower rates picloram was superior. The pooled toxicity index for all rates was 90 for picloram and 78 for fenuron. The toxicity index is the average of percent dead plants and percent growth reduction.

To evaluate the effect of picloram on grass and its persistence in soil, oats were planted 4 days after treatment and again after 6, 15, and 20 weeks. Picloram was less toxic to oats than was fenuron, but the persistence of the two chemicals was comparable. After 15 weeks, yields of oats were normal in the soil initially treated with 1, 2, and 4 pounds per acre of either picloram or fenuron. After 20 weeks, the mean percent inhibition of oats for all rates (1 to 16 pounds per acre) was 17.8 percent for picloram and 19.0 percent for fenuron.

In another test, conducted with 4-year-old shrub live oak plants, picloram and fenuron were applied as drenches to the soil in 1/4 inch of water, at rates of 2 and 4 pounds per acre. There were two plants per treatment. The chemicals were applied on April 3, 1963, and the soil was then watered regularly as before. The effects of the chemicals were complete after 3-1/2 months. When the data for both rates were pooled, picloram and fenuron killed 75 and 25 percent of the plants, respectively. The mean percentages of stem dieback, original-leaf injury, and growth reduction were considerably higher for picloram than for fenuron. The pooled toxicity indexes were 82 for picloram and 32 for fenuron.

Picloram did not inhibit oats planted in the soil 10 days after treatment, but the 2 and 4 pounds per acre treatments of fenuron caused 27 and 91 percent inhibition, respectively. A summary of overall results for soil-applied treatments comparing 2,3,6-trichloropicolinic acid (picloram) and fenuron for the control of potted shrub live oak plants is as follows:

	Picloram (Percent)	Fenuron (Percent)
2-year-old plants: (Pooled data for treatments of 1, 2, 4, 8, and 16 pounds per acre)		
Dead plants	80	70
Growth reduction	99	86
Toxicity index (average of percent dead plants and percent growth reduction)	90	78
Inhibition of oats after 20 weeks	18	19
4-year-old plants: (Pooled data for treatments of 2 and 4 pounds per acre)		
Dead plants	75	25
Growth reduction	88	40
Toxicity index	82	32
Inhibition of oats after 10 days	0	59

Low-volume foliage sprays of picloram were compared with the butoxy ethanol ester of 2,4,5-trichlorophenoxyacetic acid (2,4,5-T)[6] in which the soil as well as the plants received spray. The chemicals were applied to 2-year-old plants on April 4, 1963, at rates of 1/16 to 2 pounds per acre in 10 gallons per acre in a 2x geometric progression. Neither picloram nor 2,4,5-T at rates up to 2 pounds per acre effectively controlled shrub live oak. The effects of the two chemicals were very different. The 2,4,5-T caused stem dieback and severe leaf injury, whereas picloram did not. However, picloram at 1/2 to 2 pounds per acre inhibited regrowth to a greater extent than 2,4,5-T at the same rates. The morphological characteristics of the regrowth of picloram-treated plants were similar to those which are produced by another herbicide, 2,3,6-trichlorobenzoic acid.

To determine the extent of the foliage activity of picloram the tops of 2-year-old shrub live oak plants were sprayed to the point of

December 1964

U.S. FOREST SERVICE
RESEARCH NOTE RM - 36

FOREST SERVICE
. DEPARTMENT OF AGRICULTURE

WATERSHED MANAGEMENT IN THE ROCKY MOUNTAIN ALPINE

AND SUBALPINE ZONES

M. Martinelli, Jr.[1]

In the semiarid portions of the Western United States, water has been an important-- if not the controlling--factor in the economy since the first permanent settlement. Water diversion and reservoir systems were among the first engineering improvements in many western communities, and are still an important function of many local and Federal agencies. Such diversion and storage operations are based on the idea of gathering and storing the water during the annual peak flow and the occasional heavy snow year so it can be released when needed. In spite of the success of this system, there is still need for land-management practices that can increase total annual water yields or improve summer streamflow.

Very early work was done at Wagon Wheel Gap, Colorado (Bates and Henry 1928).[2] About 20 years ago watershed management research was started in the high-elevation coniferous forests of Colorado. These studies were concentrated in the headwaters of the Fraser River where about three-fourths of the precipitation falls as snow and is held in the snowpack until late spring or early summer when it is released as snowmelt. Forests in this area are composed of lodgepole pine (Pinus contorta Dougl.), Engelmann spruce (Picea engelmannii Parry), and subalpine fir (Abies lasiocarpa (Hook.) Nutt.). The high ridges and summits are covered by alpine tundra vegetation or rock.

In the early 1940's studies were carried out to determine: (1) the relationship between vegetative types and the water equivalent of the snowpack, and (2) the influence of the size of forest openings on the water equivalent of the pack under natural stands of trees. The snowpack was found to be least under the dense pine forests, 14 percent greater in the grasslands, and 30 percent greater in the stands of deciduous aspen (Love and Goodell 1960). The study of forest openings was carried out in mature lodgepole pine where trees averaged 80 feet tall and openings as large as 60 feet in diameter could be found. Under such conditions the water equivalent of the pack was least in the dense forest and greatest in the center of the largest opening. There was a linear increase in water content from the edge of the forest toward the center of the openings (Wilm and Dunford 1948).

---

[1] Research Forester, Rocky Mountain Forest and Range Experiment Station with central headquarters maintained at Fort Collins, in cooperation with Colorado State University.

[2] Names and dates in parentheses refer to Literature Cited, page 6.

The next series of studies was to determine the effect of forest management practices on the snowpack. Three variables were evaluated: Intensity of cut was studied in a mature lodgepole pine forest, pattern or type of cut in mature spruce-fir, and intensity of thinning in young lodgepole pine. The basic findings from these plot studies were:

1. For 5-acre plots surrounded by mature forests, the water equivalent of the snowpack increased with the intensity of cutting. This was also true for a thinning operation on smaller plots in a young forest. In mature lodgepole pine, clear cutting increased the water equivalent of the snowpack by 31 percent; however, the snow disappeared in both the cut and the uncut areas at about the same time. This indicates a faster melt rate in the open areas than in those shaded by trees (Wilm and Dunford 1948).

2. The pattern of timber cutting on small plots within a forest does not affect the water equivalent of the snowpack so long as each pattern removes the same proportion of the original stand. When 60 percent of the mature spruce-fir forest was removed by any of three different cutting patterns--single-tree selection, group selection, and strip clear cut--the increase in snowpack was the same for all patterns. In other words, the snowpack responded to the number of trees cut but not the pattern or arrangement of the cut. Melt rate was found to be slower in the group-selection cuts since the snow was better shaded here than in the other cut areas.

These early plot studies were interpreted to mean that interception was an important phenomenon where timber in snowy regions is managed for increased water yields. The snow held in the crowns of the coniferous trees often melted and the melt water evaporated from the twigs and needles, or at lower temperatures the snow sublimated into the atmosphere directly. In either case, the water held as snow on the trees never became part of the snowpack and was lost to streamflow. Although these plot studies showed rather

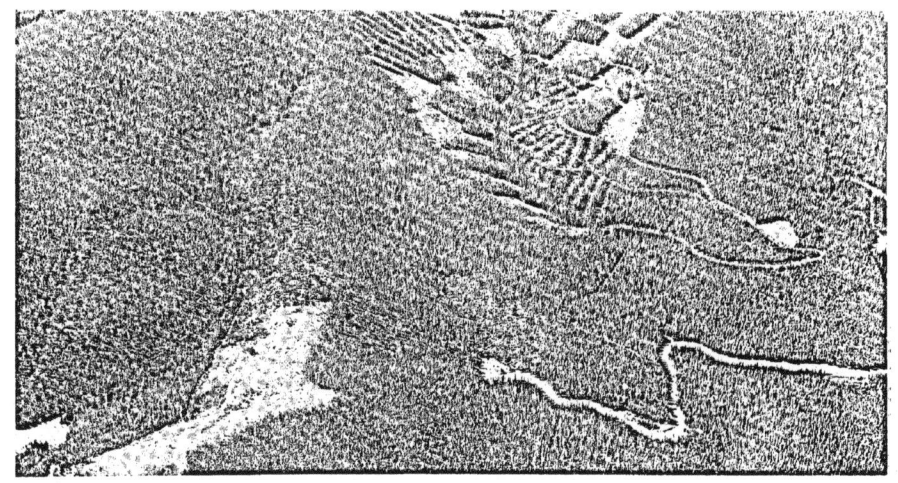

Figure 1.--Fool Creek watershed (center) has been treated to improve water yields. The untreated watershed (right) is the control. Fraser Experimental Forest, Fraser, Colorado. June 25, 1964.

	Yield in area inches		
	Predicted[3]	Actual	Increase
1957	19.6	23.0	3.4
1958	11.4	13.5	2.1
1959	10.5	13.6	3.1
1960	11.1	14.9	3.8
1961	8.8	10.9	2.1

[3]*Yield that might have resulted, according to calibration data, if the area had not been treated.*

Removing the timber from 39 percent of this watershed increased the water yield by 23.5 percent. Most of the increase was due to an enlarged spring runoff. Snowmelt started earlier and produced a higher peak on the cut watershed. There was very little increase in streamflow during the late summer or early fall months. In spite of the increase in runoff, the instantaneous flow from Fool Creek has been less than 22 cubic feet per second per square mile (c.s.m.) and the sediment load has been less than 1.5 cubic feet (wet volume) per acre per year (U. S. Forest Serv. 1961).

Earlier evidence of the change in streamflow following the removal of timber was furnished by the disastrous beetle outbreak in the spruce forests of western Colorado in the early 1940's. A regression analysis was made to compare the streamflow from one area on the White River drainage where 60 percent of the trees had been killed by beetles with that from a nearby area where there had been no beetle damage (Love 1955). Eight years of record showed a 25 percent increase in streamflow from the area where trees had been beetle-killed. Again the increase was the result of higher peak flows during the spring snowmelt (U. S. Forest Serv. 1961).

In both the Fool Creek and the White River studies, the increase in streamflow was the result of happenings on only part of the watershed: on Fool Creek, timber was cut on only 40 percent of the area; on the White River, insects killed the trees on 60 percent of the watershed. If the increases in streamflow that followed these events are attributed to the "treated" areas alone, they are about twice as large as would be expected from the early plot studies on interception. Hence, the watershed data indicate that the increase in streamflow after the harvesting or killing of trees is due as much to the reduction of evapotranspiration as it is to the reduction in interception.

Current watershed studies in the spruce-fir zone are concentrated on learning more about the different kinds of evapotranspiration losses. To determine whether coniferous trees transpire during the winter, and if so when and when such losses take place, an instrument has been developed that will detect the movement of sap in a tree (Swanson 1962). In its present state of development, this instrument also gives a comparative measure or an index to the amount of sap movement taking place. Such information will help determine the seasonal course of transpiration in coniferous trees. Measurements are made on individual trees so the influence of site factors as well as size and species of trees can be studied.

The discussion to this point can be summarized by saying research in watershed management in the subalpine zone is concerned with the effect of vegetation on water yield. In contrast, watershed management in the alpine zone is concerned primarily with the aerodynamics of the wind transport and deposition of snow. Its goal is to increase late summer streamflow--improve the timing.

The decision to study the possibility for increased summer streamflow from alpine areas was based on two observations: that snowfields yield much melt water during the summer, and that summer streamflow is higher for streams draining areas where large amounts of snow persist until late summer than it is for adjacent streams with few summer snowbanks (fig. 2,3).

The amount of water released by snowfields during summer months was studied in the Colorado mountains during the summers

Figure 2.--A typical alpine snowfield in the Front Range of Colorado during the summer. Most years, at the beginning of the summer, snow completely fills the upper bowl and extends below camera point; very little, if any, snow is left by mid-September. Niwot Ridge, Colorado. August 24, 1957.

Figure 3.--Water yield from alpine snowfields was estimated from ablation and water equivalent of the snow. Ablation was measured on stakes; water equivalent was measured with a snow sampler. Precipitation, temperature, and humidity were recorded adjacent to the snowfields. Rollins Pass, Colorado. August 22, 1955.

of 1955 through 1958. Four sites along the eastern side of the Front Range in central Colorado were visited weekly. Ablation and snow density were measured and weather factors were recorded. Average ablation of snow was found to be 1.9 feet per week during July and August for the first 2 years and slightly higher the next 2 summers (Martinelli 1959). Density increased during the summers but averaged between 0.55 and 0.65 gm/cm³.

Short-term studies of the moisture exchange between the snow surface and the atmosphere showed both condensation and evaporation at the snow surface. A diurnal pattern of moisture exchange was found with condensation at nights, evaporation in mornings, and either evaporation or condensation in the afternoons, depending on weather conditions. The net exchange during one 2-week period in August 1957 was a gain of moisture at the snow surface from condensation. During an 11-day period in July 1958, however, there was a net loss of moisture from the snow due to evaporation. In all cases the moisture exchange between the snow and the air averaged 2 to 3 percent of the daily melt and never exceeded 4.5 percent of the daily melt Martinelli 1960).

By combining the above data, we see that on the average 22.5 inches of snow disappear from alpine snowfields each week in July and August. This snow has a density of about 0.60, and even with dry, windy conditions only 2 percent of the water equivalent released by ablation is lost through evaporation. Hence, the summer snowfields yield about 13.2 inches of water (22.5 × 0.6 × 0.98 = 13.2) per week per unit area during July and August.

To this point the alpine snow studies had been concerned with data from individual snowfields. To see just how extensive such snowfields were and to get an idea of their potential contribution to streamflow, aerial photographs were taken of a selected portion of the Front Range in central Colorado twice during the summer of 1956. In an area of 277,000 acres (above 6,000 feet), 8,000 acres of alpine snow disappeared between June 23 and September 16. This snow produced a potential streamflow of 41,300 acre-feet of water; 32,000 acre-feet of this was produced in July and August.[4]

The term potential streamflow is used because no measure was made of evaporation losses from the wet soil surrounding the

[4]Martinelli, M. Jr. An estimate of runoff from alpine snow fields during the summer of 1956. 1965. (In preparation for publication, Rocky Mountain Forest and Range Expt. Sta., U. S. Forest Serv., Ft. Collins, Colo.)

snowfields nor from the water surfaces between the snowfields and the gaging stations. Nor were data available on the ground-water recharge and storage. Streamflow measurements were available for only three small drainages within the larger study area. When just these three streams are considered, the water-yield potential from alpine snowfields amounted to between 60 and 95 percent of the total measured streamflow during July and August 1956.

Once it had been established that summer snowbanks were an important source of summer streamflow, the next step was to try to develop management techniques to capitalize on these finds. Winter observations had indicated that the deep snowbanks formed in the lee of terrain features, small clumps of vegetation, or anything else that provided protection from the wind. These observations also showed that the depth of snow was controlled, at least to a certain extent, by the upwind edge of the terrain feature, and further that many of the natural catchments tended to fill with snow relatively early in the winter.

Tests were started in 1958-59 to see if common slat-and-wire snow fencing placed at the upwind edge of the natural catchments would increase the depth of snow trapped in these areas. There are now 4 years of record from 5 areas and 3 years of record from another[5] (fig. 4).

At three of the test sites, the fences made an appreciable increase in snow depth. At two of the sites the increase in snow depth due to the fence was not significant; at another site two different patterns of fence have failed to improve the natural catch. Best results so far have been when fences were located on the crest of the main ridge, with windswept tundra to the windward and a steep natural catchment immediately to the leeward. Good results were also obtained at places in the lee of the main ridge where the terrain was relatively

[5]*Martinelli, M. Jr. Accumulations of snow in alpine areas, and means of influencing it. 1965. (In preparation for publication, Rocky Mountain Forest and Range Expt. Sta., U. S. Forest Serv., Ft. Collins, Colo.)*

level upwind of natural depressions 20 to 30 feet deep. Poorest results came from an area where the windward approach was down a rather steep slope. In this case, the catchment was 50 to 60 feet deep and rather large. At this spot none of the artificial barriers tried so far have given accumulation patterns as favorable as the natural pattern.

Weather data for the past several winters have shown that a relatively few storms account for most of the snow that accumulates under both natural and fenced conditions. Between 50 and 65 percent of the annual accumulation took place in the five biggest storm periods, and between 25 and 40 percent during the two biggest storm periods each year for the past 4 years. These periods of heavy accumulation are thought to be during or immediately after storms; however, more field data are needed for confirmation.

Additional watershed management research in the alpine area is being undertaken to determine the synoptic situation that produces maximum deposition in the catchments. These studies will also provide detailed information on the wind structure and the concentration of blowing snow in the lower layers of the air during periods of heavy snow drifting. Such information should be of help in the design of more effective snow fences and in the selection of optimum sites of such barriers.

Literature Cited

Bates, Carlos G., and Henry, A. J.
    1928. Forest and stream flow experiment at Wagon Wheel Gap, Colorado. U.S. Monthly Weather Rev., Sup. 30, 79 pp., illus.

Goodell, Bertram C.
    1958. A preliminary report on the first year's effects on timber harvesting on water yield from a Colorado watershed. U.S. Forest Serv. Rocky Mountain Forest and Range Expt. Sta. Sta. Paper 36, 12 pp., illus.

*Address requests for copies to the originating office.

Figure 4.--Slat and wire snow fencing effectively increase snow depths when properly located. Most effective sites are along ridge crests just to the windward of deep natural snowfields. Straight Creek Pass, Colorado. February 24, 1963.

Love, L. D.
1955. The effect on stream flow of the killing of spruce and pine by the Engelmann spruce beetle. Amer. Geophys. Union Trans. 36: 113-118, illus.

─────── and Goodell, B. C.
1960. Watershed research on the Fraser Experimental Forest. Jour. Forestry 58: 272-275, illus.

Martinelli, M., Jr.
1959. Alpine snowfields--their characteristics and management possibilities. Symposium of Hannoversch-Munden. Internatl. Sci. Hydrology Assoc. Pub. 48(1): 120-127, illus.

───────
1960. Moisture exchange between the atmosphere and alpine snow surfaces under summer conditions (preliminary results). Jour. Met. 17: 227-231, illus.

Swanson, Robert H.
1962. An instrument for detecting sap movement in woody plants. U.S.. Forest Serv. Rocky Mountain Forest and Range Expt. Sta. Sta. Paper 68, 16 pp., illus.

U. S. Forest Service.
1961. Increased streamflow continues from the White River of Colorado. In Annual Report, 1960, Rocky Mountain Forest and Range Expt. Sta. 1960: 77.

───────
1962. Timber harvest in Colorado increases streamflow. In Annual Report, 1961. Rocky Mountain Forest and Range Expt. Sta. 1961: 41-43.

Wilm, H. G., and Dunford, E. G.
1948. Effect of timber cutting on water available for stream flow from a lodgepole pine forest. U. S. Dept. Agr. Tech. Bul. 968, 43 pp., illus.

December 1964

U.S. FOREST SERVICE
RESEARCH NOTE RM - 37

OREST SERVICE
.S. DEPARTMENT OF AGRICULTURE

Site-Index Curves for Young-Growth Ponderosa Pine in Northern Arizona

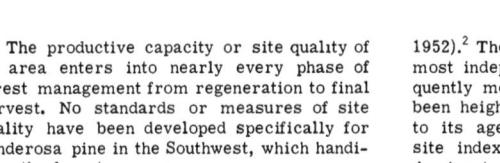

Charles O. Minor[1]

The productive capacity or site quality of an area enters into nearly every phase of forest management from regeneration to final harvest. No standards or measures of site quality have been developed specifically for ponderosa pine in the Southwest, which handicaps the forest manager.

The major objective of the present study was to develop the basic site-index curves for young-growth ponderosa pine by means of which a relative growth capacity may be assigned to each forest condition in the forests of Arizona.

Secondary objectives were to test the applicability of suggested mensurational procedures for site curve construction (individual tree stem analyses, polymorphic curves, use of dominant trees only, age at breast height rather than total age), and effect of stand density upon height.

REVIEW OF LITERATURE

The term "site" or "site quality" is used in forestry to represent the sum total of environmental effects upon the quantity of wood grown upon an area by forest trees (Spurr 1952).[2] The one measure of growth found to be most independent of stand factors, and consequently most reliable for site evaluation, has been height of the dominant stand in relation to its age (Lynch 1958). As presently used, site index refers to the average height of dominant or codominant trees at a specific reference age, 100 years for most western species (Bruce and Schumacher 1950).

Site quality cannot be defined in an absolute sense. The same area may be capable of supporting different species, but their growth may be entirely different (Meyer 1953). A good site for pine may be a poor site for fir, even where both are found growing together.

The yield capacity of ponderosa pine has been studied in several other areas (Show 1925, Behre 1928, Dunning and Reineke 1933,

---

[1]*Director, Division of Forestry, Arizona Stage College, Flagstaff, Arizona. Publication of research reported here was a cooperative project of Arizona State College and the Rocky Mountain Forest and Range Experiment Station. Central headquarters of the station are maintained at Fort Collins, in cooperation with Colorado State University.*
[2]*Names and dates in parentheses refer to Literature Cited, page 7.*

Meyer 1938, Lynch 1958), but never in the Southwest. The major study of ponderosa pine yield and site index (Meyer 1938) included data from California, Oregon, Washington, Idaho, Montana, Wyoming, and South Dakota. The Southwest was not included in this study because the necessary conditions were considered unavailable.

Selection of the portion of the stand to be included in site-index determinations has been studied considerably in recent years. Several writers (Staebler 1948, Ker 1952, Spurr 1952, Hummel and Christie 1953) have shown that restricting the classes of trees used for site classification considerably reduces the number of measurements required for a given degree of accuracy. Use of only dominant trees reduces the variability in tree height and minimizes the subjective aspect of distinguishing both crown classes. Greater stability of the dominant stand is also advanced as an advantage of restricting sampling to dominant trees.[3] Guillebaud and Hummel (1949) found that 90 percent of the trees on permanent sample plots that were dominants at the beginning of the study were still dominants after 15 to 25 years.

A further aspect of site-index studies which has been revised with increased mensurational experience is the form and relationships of site-index curves. In the earlier yield studies in this country, height-age relations were defined as curves of the same form as the average site index, but differing therefrom by a constant ratio at all ages, in other words, anamorphic curves (Osborne and Schumacher 1935). Spurr (1952) has pointed out that this procedure involves some unsafe assumptions: (1) the sample must have included all ages and all sites, (2) the effect of site on height growth must be the same at all ages, and (3) the height-growth curves of trees on a good site must have the same shape as on a poor site.

Soundest procedure seems to be construction of polymorphic curves based upon stem

[3]*Turnbull, K. J. Stem analysis techniques and applications, and some studies of second-growth Douglas-fir in western Washington. 1958. (Unpublished master's thesis on file at College of Forestry, Univ. of Wash., Seattle.)*

analysis of individual trees (Bull 1931, Spurr 1952). The greatest weakness in this latter approach is that the curves developed represent height growth of individual trees rather than the stand. The more restricted the selection of trees for site determination, however, the less important this factor will be. Spurr (1952) advocated restricting site measurements to the tallest tree in the stand, claiming that the stem-analysis method was practically without error when this restriction was applied. A recent study of lodgepole pine, however, showed shifts in relative height of individual trees that introduced bias into height-age curves (Dahms 1963).

The effect of stand density on tree height growth, and correspondingly on determination of site index, has been a subject of considerable investigation and discussion in recent years. Variable and sometimes conflicting results have been reported for various species and locations. An excellent coverage of the subject of height and stand density is given by Lynch (1958). In a study of paired plots of ponderosa pine in the Inland Empire, he found a reduction in dominant heights on poorer sites (below 75) in overstocked stands.

COLLECTION OF DATA

Data were gathered from selected trees in uniform young-growth stands of ponderosa pine within a 100-mile radius of Flagstaff, Arizona. At most sample locations two trees were selected: (1) a dominant tree from a clump or group, and (2) an isolated dominant, at least 30 feet from the nearest tree, but of the same age and on the same apparent site as the group dominant. Sample trees were also required to be 100 to 150 years of age, be straight and sound with no apparent damage that would affect height growth, be free of insects and disease, and a core from breast height must show no evidence of fire scars or past mechanical damage.

No attempt was made to select the tallest tree from the stand or group, because analysis of repeated measurements of large sample plots at the Fort Valley Experimental Forest indicated considerable stability in the dominant crown class for local ponderosa pine. Of

50 randomly selected trees, tallied as dominant upon reaching 8 inches d.b.h. in 1930, 86 percent were still dominant as of February 1963. The remaining 14 percent were codominant or declining dominants.

The selected trees were felled (with stump height as low as possible, not to exceed 10 inches), total height was measured from ground to tip, and age was determined at the stump, at breast height, and at 10-foot intervals from stump to tip. In addition, basal area around the felled dominant tree (group dominant) was recorded by angle count, with a basal-area factor of 10 square feet per acre per tallied tree.

A total of 91 trees was measured; 43 paired samples plus 5 other trees chosen for certain characteristics for which no paired tree was available. Ages ranged from 85 to 158 years, site indices from 45 to 98 feet.

For each tree, ring counts on each section were converted to age from stump and age from breast height. Heights were then plotted over ages to permit exact determination of site index (total height at 100 years) on both total age and breast-height age bases. Distribution of sample trees according to site index (based on age at breast height), together with total number of sections counted, is shown in the following tabulation:

	Sample trees (No.)	Sections analyzed (No.)
Site index (ft.):		
45	2	12
50	5	29
55	10	63
60	9	63
65	16	119
70	12	94
75	9	71
80	6	51
85	9	82
90	8	77
95	4	39
100	1	9
Total	91	709

ANALYSIS OF DATA

Age Basis of Site Curves

Conventionally, site index is based upon total age of the dominant stand or tree. Methods of age determination normally involve count of annual rings on an increment core extracted at breast height (4.5 feet above ground) plus an arbitrary correction for number of years to reach breast height.

The time required for the 91 trees studied to reach breast height averaged 14.3 years, and ranged from 6 to 29 years.

	Trees (No.)	Years to breast height	
		(Average)	(Range)
Site index (ft.):			
50	12	16.2	9 - 27
60	22	14.9	8 - 29
70	28	14.6	6 - 24
80	12	12.5	9 - 17
90	15	12.7	9 - 25
100	2	13.5	12 - 15
All trees	91	14.3	6 - 29

Such variation makes an average correction seem very dubious, particularly at younger ages when an error of only 2 or 3 years may cause a 10-foot difference in estimated site index.

No definite relation was found between site index and age to breast height. Range within site classes was nearly as great as for all trees.

As described by Pearson (1950), ponderosa pine reproduction is subject to damage by drought, tipmoth, white grubs, gophers, porcupines, rabbits, small rodents, cattle, sheep, and deer. Early height growth can be expected to vary extremely because of these factors. Since all of the sample trees originated prior to the period of intensive livestock grazing in Arizona, variation in the sample is less than would be encountered in present-day regeneration.

DENSITY

In view of the reported instances where density has affected height of ponderosa pine (Weaver 1947, Krauch 1949, Baker 1953, Mowat 1953, Lynch 1958), an attempt was made in the present study to evaluate the effect of density by comparing growth of paired trees at the same age. The dominant tree from a group represented the small, even-aged, dense clumps typical of ponderosa pine in the Southwest, while the isolated tree at least 30 feet from the group was assumed to be free of extremes of competition.

In 21 of the 43 pairs studied, the group dominant was taller at age 100 at breast height, in 17 pairs the isolated tree was taller, and in 5 pairs heights were identical. Differences in height between paired trees averaged 4.9 feet, and ranged from 0 to 14 feet, at 100 years of age. When differences were plotted over site index, no trend could be discerned.

Heights of the paired trees at 50 years of age at breast height were analyzed similarly. In 24 pairs the group dominant was taller, in 13 the isolated tree was taller, and in 6 pairs the heights were identical. Differences in height averaged 3.9 feet, with a range from 0 to 13 feet. During the 50 years from age 50 to age 100, relative position changed in 21 of the 43 pairs.

Relation of basal areas to heights was also tested. No usable trends were found. Differences in heights of paired trees increased irregularly with increasing basal area up to 140 square feet, and decreased irregularly thereafter. This study showed no consistent effect of basal area on height.

Site-Index Curves

A first problem of the present study was to find a satisfactory form of equation for height in terms of age. The common transformation, found applicable to many species in the United States (Schumacher and Coile, 1960):

$$\log H = a + b \left(\frac{1}{A}\right)$$

in which H is dominant height in feet and A is age, did not prove satisfactory for the trees studied. Many transformations were attempted, until an equation of the form

$$H = a + b \sqrt{A}$$

was finally adopted. This equation corresponded quite well to the shape of the height-growth curves for all sites, and for breast height ages from 10 or 20 years up to 140 years. Accordingly, the data were computed to this range of ages.

In view of the possible polymorphism of site curves derived from stem analyses, separate equations were developed for each 5-foot site class. The data were sorted by site-index classes based upon actual tree height at 100 years of age at breast height.

The stem analyses provided ages, at 10-foot intervals, from breast height to the tip of the tree. Excluding sections at 4.5 feet, the 91 felled trees supplied a total of 709 ages at known height. Because conventional site curves express height in terms of age, a reversal of variables is involved. Spurr (1952) states that this is not usually a serious problem due to the high degree of correlation between the variables.

In this study, however, a separate regression analysis was made for each site class in the form

$$\sqrt{A} = c + bH$$

and the equation was then inverted to give a solution for dominant height (H) in terms of breast height at age (A):

$$H = \frac{1}{b}(\sqrt{A}) - \frac{a}{b}$$

From study of the equations of height in terms of age for each site class, it appeared that the inverted regression coefficients (1/b) were linearly related to site index. Accordingly an equation of the form

$$\frac{1}{b} = c + d(S)$$

was fitted. The resulting equation, based upon 12 observations, is:

$$\frac{1}{b} = -1.4003 + 0.1559 (S)$$

Appropriate analysis of variance showed both coefficients to be significant.

Substituting this relation, wherein site index (S) is an independent variable, gives for the original equation:

$$H = [c + d (S)] \sqrt{A} + [c + d (S)] (-a)$$

Introducing the reference age for site index (100 years) then gives:

$$H = S + [c + d (S)] [\sqrt{A} - \sqrt{100}]$$

or, for ease of computation,

$$H = S + c(\sqrt{A} - \sqrt{100}) + d(S)(\sqrt{A} - \sqrt{100})$$

With the substitution of the previously computed values of c and d, the final equation becomes:

$$H = S - 1.4003 (\sqrt{A} - 10) + 0.1559(S) (\sqrt{A} - 10)$$

RESULTS AND APPLICATIONS

Results of the study are summarized in table 1, and in the previous tabulations. Figure 1 presents the site-index curves derived from the final equation for height in terms of age and site index.

Field Application

To determine the site index of a given area, total height and age at breast height must be measured for selected dominant trees. From samples taken to test accuracy of site classification, it was found that, for a typical young-growth clump, a single dominant tree would give as good results as the average of several trees. In larger, uniform areas of young growth, however, a sample of five or more dominants is required for accurate site measurement.

The sample tree or trees must meet the following specifications:

1. must be young-growth ponderosa pine (blackjack or young intermediate);
2. must be a true dominant or an isolated tree with dominant characteristics;
3. must have no top damage; no crooks, scars, or forks due to squirrel, porcupine, snow or ice damage;
4. must be free of insects and disease;
5. a core at breast height should show no fire scars, mechanical injuries, nor any extended period of suppression followed by release.

Table 1.--Height of dominant trees, by age at breast height and site index (SI)

Age at breast height (years)	Height of dominant trees						
	SI 40	SI 50	SI 60	SI 70	SI 80	SI 90	SI 100
				Feet			
20	13	15	16	17	19	20	22
30	18	21	24	27	30	33	36
40	22	26	31	35	39	44	48
50	26	31	37	42	48	53	58
60	29	36	42	49	55	62	68
70	32	40	47	54	62	69	77
80	35	43	52	60	68	77	85
90	38	47	56	65	74	84	93
100	40	50	60	70	80	90	100
110	42	53	64	75	85	96	107
120	45	56	68	79	91	102	114
130	47	59	71	83	96	108	120
140	49	62	75	87	100	113	126

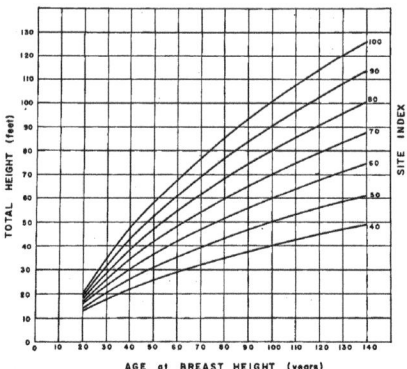

Figure 1.--Ponderosa pine site index.

Precautions in the actual measurement of age and height may seem superfluous. As pointed out by Coile and Schumacher (1953), however, mistakes in site classification can and do result from errors in measurement of both height and age.

For correct site evaluation, the height readings should be taken from a measured base line, not paced distance; corrections for slope must be made, though where possible the observer should measure out along the contour; repeated sights to tree base and tip are advised; increment cores for age should be extracted to the pith; and rings must be correctly identified and counted (use of a core slicer and hand lens is recommended).

If ages and/or heights of selected trees differ markedly, it is recommended that, instead of averaging the measurements, a separate site index be read for each to check for correspondence or for faulty sampling. This procedure will usually identify any abnormality or error in measurement of the sample tree.

Should it be desired to record site index closer than to the nearest 10-foot class, it is recommended that the following equation be solved, instead of attempting to interpolate from the table or graph:

Table 2.--Summary of field checks for site curves in Arizona and New Mexico

Area	Number of locations sampled	Range in age per location		Error in predicted site index per location	
		Average	Maximum	Average	Maximum
		Years		Feet	
ARIZONA:					
Coconino National Forest					
South	15	31	42	1.2	3
Lake Mary	5	64	109	5.0	9
Fort Valley	10	58	86	4.1	7
Prescott National Forest	12	35	52	6.4	17
Sitgreaves National Forest	8	64	94	2.9	6
North Kaibab National Forest	4	81	122	6.0	10
Apache National Forest	6	61	107	4.7	10
Fort Apache Indian Reservation	5	70	87	4.2	8
Tonto National Forest	5	38	60	9.6	16
NEW MEXICO:					
Carson National Forest	3	74	82	8.5	12
Cibola National Forest	2	46	53	7.7	8

Due to extreme variability in the time required (6 to 29 years in the sample trees) for local ponderosa pine to reach breast height, site curves were based upon ages at breast height rather than upon total ages.

Site curves are presented for site indices of 40 to 100 feet, ages 20 to 140 years. In the analysis of data, separate equations were calculated for each 5-foot site class. The regression coefficients were found to be linearly related to site index, however, and accordingly site was introduced as a variable in the final equations.

The curves were field checked on adjacent trees of varying age at 75 locations in Arizona and New Mexico. Errors in predicted site between young and old trees averaged less than feet per location.

LITERATURE CITED

Baker, F. S.
1953. Stand density and growth. Jour. Forestry 51: 95-97.

Behre, C. E.
1928. Preliminary normal yield tables for second-growth western yellow pine in northern Idaho and adjacent areas. Jour. Agr. Res. 37: 379-397.

Bruce, D. B., and Schumacher, F. X.
1950. Forest mensuration. Ed. 3, 483 pp., illus. New York: McGraw-Hill Book Co.

Bull, Henry.
1931. The use of polymorphic curves in determining site quality in young red pine plantations. Jour. Agr. Res. 43: 1-28.

Coile, T. S., and Schumacher, F. X.
1953. Relation of soil properties to site index of loblolly and shortleaf pines in the Piedmont region of the Carolinas, Georgia, and Alabama. Jour. Forestry 51: 739-744, illus.

Dahms, Walter G.
1963. Correction for a possible bias in developing site index curves from sectional tree data. Jour. Forestry 61: 25-27, illus.

Dunning, D., and Reineke, L. H.
    1933. Preliminary yield tables for second-growth stands in the California pine region. U. S. Dept. Agr. Tech. Bul. 354, 23 pp., illus.

Guillebaud, W. H., and Hummel, F. C.
    1949. A note on the movement of tree classes. Forestry 23: 1-14.

Hummel, F. C., and Christie, J.
    1953. Revised yield tables for conifers in Great Britain. Forestry Commission. Forest Record 24, 23 pp., illus.

Ker, J. W.
    1952. An evaluation of several methods of estimating site index of immature stands. Forestry Chron. 28: 63-74.

Krauch, Hermann.
    1949. Results of thinning experiment in ponderosa pine pole stands in central Arizona. Jour. Forestry 47: 466-469.

Lynch, D. W.
    1958. Effects of stocking on site measurement and yield of second-growth ponderosa pine in the Inland Empire.* U.S. Forest Serv. Intermountain Forest and Range Expt. Sta. Res. Paper 56, 36 pp., illus.

Meyer, H. A.
    1953. Forest mensuration. 357 pp., illus. State College, Pa.: Penns Valley Publishers, Inc.

Meyer, Walter H.
    1938. Yield of even-aged stands of ponderosa pine. U. S. Dept. Agr. Tech. Bul. 630, 59 pp., illus.

Mowat, E. L.
    1953. Thinning ponderosa pine in the Pacific Northwest--a summary of present information.* U. S. Forest Serv. Pacific Northwest Forest and Range Expt. Sta. Res. Paper 5, 24 pp., illus.

Osborne, J. G., and Schumacher, F. X.
    1935. The construction of normal-yield and stand tables for even-aged timber stands. Jour. Agr. Res. 51: 547-564.

Pearson, G. A.
    1950. Management of ponderosa pine in the southwest. U. S. Dept. Agr. Agr. Monog. 6, 218 pp., illus.

Schumacher, F. X., and Coile, T. S.
    1960. Growth and yield of natural stands of the southern pines. 115 pp., illus. Durham, N. C.: T. S. Coile, Inc.

Show, S. B.
    1925. Yield capacities of the pure yellow pine type on the east slope of the Sierra Nevada mountains in California. Jour. Agr. Res. 31: 1121-1135.

Spurr, S. H.
    1952. Forest inventory. 476 pp., illus. New York: Ronald Press Co.

Staebler, George R.
    1948. Use of dominant tree heights in determining site index of Douglas-fir. *U. S. Forest Serv. Pacific Northwest Forest and Range Expt. Sta. Res. Note 44, 3 pp.

Weaver, Harold.
    1947. Fire--nature's thinning agent in ponderosa pine stands. Jour. Forestry 45: 437-444, illus.

---

*Address requests for copies to the originating office.

rch 1965

U.S. FOREST SERVICE
RESEARCH NOTE RM-38

FOREST SERVICE
U.S. DEPARTMENT OF AGRICULTURE

Shrub Live Oak Control by Root Plowing

Floyd W. Pond,[1] D. T. Lillie,[2] and H. R. Holbo[1]

Successful seeding of adapted grasses in the Arizona chaparral depends on control of the competing shrubs. Since subsequent grass production is inversely proportional to shrub canopy (Pond 1961),[3] control methods that give high shrub kills are obviously preferred.

Root plowing is a relatively effective and moderately expensive method of controlling shrub live oak (Quercus turbinella Greene) on Arizona rangelands. Burning, railing, chaining, and single applications of most herbicides which are used at present may destroy the aboveground parts of plants, but sprouts from the massive root crowns quickly reoccupy the site (Pond and Cable 1960, Lillie 1962, Schmutz and Turner 1957). Some success has been achieved by repeated aerial applications of 2,4,5-T (Schmutz and Whitham 1962, Lillie 1963), basal application of a mixture of 2,4-D and 2,4,5-T in diesel oil (Cable 1957), and heavy applications of substituted urea compounds (Wagle and Schmutz 1963), but at the present stage these treatments are too expensive for widespread control programs.

[1]*Range Scientist and Associate Plant Physiologist, located at the Station's project headquarters at Tempe in cooperation with Arizona State University; central headquarters are maintained at Fort Collins in cooperation with Colorado State University.*
[2]*Formerly Research Agronomist, Crops Research Division, Agricultural Research Service, U. S. Dept. Agriculture, Tempe, Arizona.*
[3]*Names and dates in parentheses refer to Literature Cited, page 2.*

This paper evaluates the results of root plowing on one site near Prescott, Arizona, and makes recommendations for improving the effectiveness of the method.

Methods

To determine mortality of shrub live oak due to root plowing, 200 clumps, or clusters, of this species were selected on a 300-acre site of dense chaparral scheduled for plowing late in the summer of 1962. These clumps, 100 of them near each of two permanent points, were oriented to those points with a transit and stadia rod so they could be relocated after plowing. The clumps were thought to be individual plants, but excavation of several after plowing revealed that most were closely knit groups of as many as six separately rooted individuals (fig. 1). The canopy spread of each clump was estimated by averaging two cross diameters taken at right angles through the center of the crown.

Results

The clumps with one or more surviving individuals were counted in 1964, 2 years after the site was plowed. These survivors were examined to determine, if possible, why they were not killed.

Root plowing killed 81 of the 100 plants near each point. The stems and branches of most survivors had been cut below the soil surface, but the root crown of one or more of

Figure 1.--A clump of shrub live oak consisting of six individual plants; the root crowns were missed by shallow plowing 2 years before.

the individuals in the clump was not severed and had sprouted. All plants cut off below the root crown were killed. Successful root plowing depends on completely separating the root crown from the roots.

Many of the survivors were found to be from clumps large in diameter. Around one point, the average pretreatment diameter of the 100 clumps was 5.9 feet. The pretreatment diameter of the 19 clumps having one or more surviving members averaged 6.5 feet. Around the other point, average pretreatment diameter of all clumps was 5.4 feet, and that of the survivors was 5.9 feet. Clumps with large diameters probably contain more individuals than those with small diameters. This means more chance of missing at least one of the individuals with the plow.

The 81 percent kill of shrub live oak clumps could have been higher with more careful plowing. Plants survived root plowing for one of several possible reasons.

Improper plowing depth was one common reason for missed plants (fig. 1). Because shrub live oak root crowns are seldom more than 1 foot below the soil surface, the plow should operate at, or just below, this depth. Plowing at 2 or more feet should be avoided; small plants with shallow root systems can survive if they are not dragged completely out of the soil.

Some plants survived because the plow missed them. Apparently, the operator assumed that all loose or disturbed soil had already been plowed. Several survivors were found on the narrow unplowed strips, hidden beneath loose soil thrown up along each edge of a swath of plowed roots. Each plowing swath should include the entire width of the adjacent berm cast up by the preceding swath.

Several survivors were found in or near piles of dead brush. These piles were formed when the plow was lifted out of the ground to clear the accumulated debris. The plow evidently did not return to its effective depth for several feet after the debris was removed. These spots could be eliminated if the tractor operator would turn to one side to clear the debris, and then make sure the plow had returned to proper depth before continuing along the swath.

It is impractical to expect every plant to be killed. Some will be missed by the most conscientious tractor operators. If the above suggestions are followed, however, brush control on root-plowed sites should be considerably higher than 81 percent.

Literature Cited

Cable, Dwight R.
   1957. *Chemical control of chaparral shrubs in central Arizona. Jour. Forestry 55:899-903, illus.*

Lillie, D. T.
   1962. *Herbicide combinations for the control of shrub live oak. Res. Prog. Rpt., West. Weed Control Conf. Proc. 1962: 17-18.*

——— 1963. *Control of Arizona chaparral with 2,4,5-T and silvex. Jour. Range Mangt. 16: 195-199, illus.*

Pond, Floyd W.
   1961. *Basal cover and production of weeping lovegrass under varying amounts of shrub live oak crown cover. Jour. Range Mangt. 14: 335-337, illus.*

——— and Cable, Dwight R.
   1960. *Effect of heat treatment on sprout production of some shrubs of the chaparral in central Arizona. Jour. Range Mangt. 13: 313-317, illus.*

Schmutz, Erwin M., and Turner, Raymond M.
   1957. *Herbicide tests on fire sprouts of turbinella oak in the Arizona chaparral. Res. Prog. Rpt., West. Weed Control Conf. Proc. 1957: 44.*

——— and Whitham, David W.
   1962. *Shrub control studies in the oak-chaparral of Arizona. Jour. Range Mangt. 15: 61-67, illus.*

Wagle, Robert F., and Schmutz, Erwin M.
   1963. *The effect of fenuron on four southwestern shrubs. Weeds 11:149-156, illus.*

U.S. FOREST SERVICE
RESEARCH NOTE RM - 39

Some Sprouting Characteristics of Five-Stamen Tamarisk

Howard L. Gary and Jerome S. Horton [1]

Five-stamen tamarisk or saltcedar (<u>Tamarix pentandra</u> Pall.) now occupies many thousands of acres of flood plain and delta deposits in the Southwest. Water-user organizations and other agencies concerned with water resources believe that tamarisk consumes large quantities of water and that considerable water can be saved by controlling it.[2]

Control of tamarisk by use of mechanical equipment, various chemicals, and lowered water table have been tried with some degree of success. Poor results with some mechanical methods can often be traced to the vigorous sprouting ability of tamarisk stems. Knowledge of the physical sprouting characteristics of tamarisk can make it possible to design and time mechanical control programs for greater success.

Studies of the sprouting characteristics of tamarisk stems and roots were conducted under laboratory conditions during the period from March 1958 to December 1960. In pre-

[1] *Associate Range Scientist and Principal Plant Ecologist, located at Tempe, in cooperation with Arizona State University; central headquarters are maintained at Fort Collins, in cooperation with Colorado State University.*
[2] *Horton, J.S. The problem of phreatophytes. Symposium of Hannoversch-Munden, Internatl. Sci. Hydrol. Assoc. Pub. 48,1: 76-83. 1959.*

liminary studies in 1958, no difference was detected in sprout development from stem cuttings taken from various heights and locations within tamarisk shrubs. In a companion study, root cuttings taken at various distances away from the root crown failed to form new plants. No further studies with root cuttings were undertaken. Additional studies were undertaken to obtain information on relations of sprouting characteristics of stem sections to seasons and temperatures, moisture contents, and varying degrees of drying.

Season of Sprouting and Temperature Effects

The relation of sprouting ability to season was determined by planting stem sections at biweekly intervals from July 1959 through April 1960 in a heated and well-ventilated greenhouse. The cuttings were taken at random from several plants on a shallow-water table (0-2 feet) site near Granite Reef Diversion Dam on the Salt River, east of Phoenix, Arizona. Twenty cuttings, 0.5 to 1.0 inch in diameter and 6 inches in length, were planted singly in clay pots containing fine-textured alluvium soil. The potted cuttings were in normal vertical position with about 2 inches of the stem exposed above the soil surface. The soil medium was kept continuously moist. Similar planting procedures were followed for other portions of the study. All cuttings eventually produced sprouts. Length of time for 100 percent sprouting was greatly increased, however, during the cooler months (table 1).

To check temperature effects on sprouting rates, a duplicate set of 20 cuttings was placed in an unheated greenhouse on November 18, 1959. As shown below, sprouts appeared on cuttings planted in the heated greenhouse much sooner than in the cold greenhouse, but in the latter all cuttings eventually did produce sprouts in the warmth of spring:

Location and number of weeks after planting	Sprouting rates (Percent)	Average temperature (Degrees F.)
Heated greenhouse:		
4	20	75.0
8	80	70.8
12	85	76.0
16	100	79.5
Unheated greenhouse:		
4	10	54.7
8	10	47.6
12	40	50.8
16	80	55.3
20	100	67.4

Thus, ability to sprout is present in the stem tissue during the winter if temperatures are high enough to induce it.

Stem Moisture Content and Sprouting

The seasonal study was reoriented in 1960 to include cuttings taken from two diverse sites and to include a measurement of stem moisture content. All cuttings were collected along the Salt River--one-half were cut at the shallow water-table site near Granite Reef Diversion Dam, and the other half near Tempe with a water table deeper than 15 feet. From April to December 1960, 20 cuttings were collected at monthly intervals from each site, planted in a heated and ventilated greenhouse, and observed daily until the sprouts reached 0.4 inch in length.

One-year-old canes 0.5 to 1.0 inch in diameter and 2 feet long were cut from random portions of tamarisk plants. The canes collected in the field were placed in a watertight plastic bag. A wet burlap sack was then wrapped around the plastic bag to prevent excessive loss of moisture from the tamarisk canes. After immediate transport to the laboratory, each cane was cut into two 8-inch sections. One-inch sections were then cut from each end of the 8-inch sections and identified with the remaining 6-inch sections. The 1-inch sections were weighed immediately on a direct-reading balance, ovendried, reweighed, and percent moisture determined from ovendry weight:

Table 1.--Relation of sprouting of tamarisk to season in a heated and well-ventilated greenhouse, July 1959 to April 1960

Month	Number of cuttings	Number of weeks after planting					
		4	8	12	16	20	24
		Percent of cuttings with sprouts					
July	20	100					
August	40	75	100				
September	40	90	100				
October	40	75	95	100			
November	40	38	85	90	98	98	100
December	40	15	70	90	95	100	
January	40	58	100				
February	40	85	100				
March	40	95	100				
April	20	100					

$$M = \frac{G - D}{D} \times 100$$

where
M = percent moisture
G = green weight
D = dry weight

The percent moisture content of the 1-inch sections was used to approximate the moisture content of the planted 6-inch sections.

Sprout development was most rapid during the warmer months of the year and slowest in the colder months (fig. 1). Variance analysis did not show significant differences in rapidity of sprout development for cuttings collected from shallow and deep water-table sites.

The period of lowest moisture content of the cuttings was in March when tamarisk usually begins new growth (fig. 2). Moisture content was highest during the warmer months. The cuttings from the shallow water-table area show an increase in moisture content until June, and a downward trend for the remainder of the year. The cuttings from the deep water-table area usually had a higher average moisture content, but show the same general pattern of increasing moisture content during their active growing season. Monthly changes in stem moisture during the growing season, however, were more erratic for cuttings from the deep water-table area.

Stem Moisture Loss and Sprouting Ability

The effect of stem moisture loss on sprouting ability was followed from April through December 1960. Eighty tamarisk cuttings were taken monthly from plants growing on the shallow water-table site. The cuttings were weighed and dried for varying periods of time in the laboratory before planting in a heated and ventilated greenhouse. The study procedure was as follows:

1. Percent moisture content of 1-inch sections taken from each end of an 8-inch section was determined by the method discussed in the previous section.
2. After initial weighing of the remaining 6-inch sections, they were placed in horizontal position in a shallow tray and allowed to dry at room temperature (75° to 80° F). The room temperatures did not vary appreciably between summer and winter.
3. Random groups of 10 cuttings were then reweighed and planted after 8 drying periods that ranged from 15 to 116 hours.

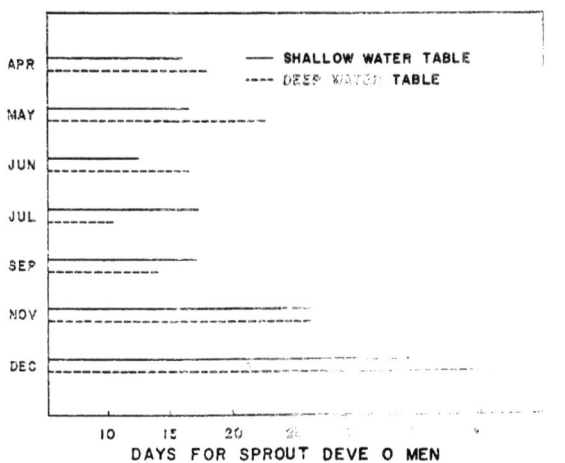

Figure 1.--Number of days for sprouts to reach 0.4 inch in length. Sprouting was 100 percent for all months. Twenty cuttings from each site were used in monthly tests.

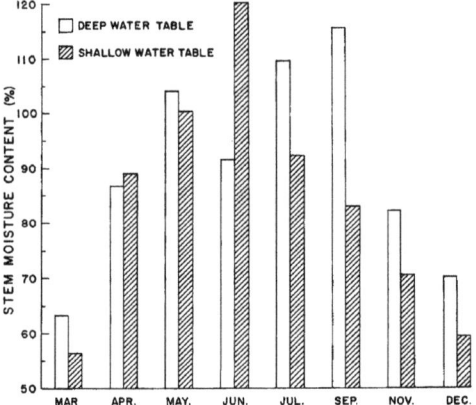

Figure 2.--Average stem moisture content (calculated from dry weights) for cuttings taken from tamarisk plants on shallow and deep water-table sites.

4. Percent water loss from cuttings dried for varying periods was approximated by the formulas shown below:

a. $CWS = \dfrac{IWC}{1 + M}$

where
CWS = calculated ovendry weight, 6-inch sections
IWC = initial weight, 6-inch cuttings
M = moisture percent, ovendry basis, of the two 1-inch end sections

b. $ML = \dfrac{WL}{CW} \times 100$

where
ML = percent moisture loss at planting
WL = water loss before planting
CW = calculated ovendry weight

5. Individual cuttings were observed until sprout growth reached 0.4 inch or for 4 months if no sprouting occurred.

A definite relationship of moisture loss (expressed as percent of ovendry weight) and sprouting ability was evident (fig. 3). Eighteen or more cuttings were represented in each moisture-loss class presented. A moisture loss of 2 to 5 percent did not affect the sprouting ability of the cuttings. Sprouting ability was only slightly affected up to 10 percent moisture loss, but dropped rapidly in each succeeding moisture-loss class. No sprouting ability was retained by any cutting after 45 percent moisture loss.

To better interpret the relation of drying to sprouting ability in regard to season, the June and November results were more closely analyzed (fig. 4). The green tamarisk cuttings collected in June dried rapidly and failed to sprout after they lost about 20 percent of their stem moisture (expressed in terms of ovendry weight). The hardened and less succulent stem cuttings collected in November dried at a much slower rate and, therefore, retained sprouting ability longer, but these cuttings lost their ability to sprout at about the same percentage of stem-moisture loss as the June cuttings. The more rapid drying rate of the June cuttings caused a more rapid loss of sprouting ability. Sprouting ability was 80 percent at 15 hours and dropped to 0 percent after 4 days of drying. The November cuttings retained 100 percent sprouting ability for 2 days, and sprouting ability was 50 percent after 4.5 days of drying. This rapid loss of sprouting ability in June when compared to

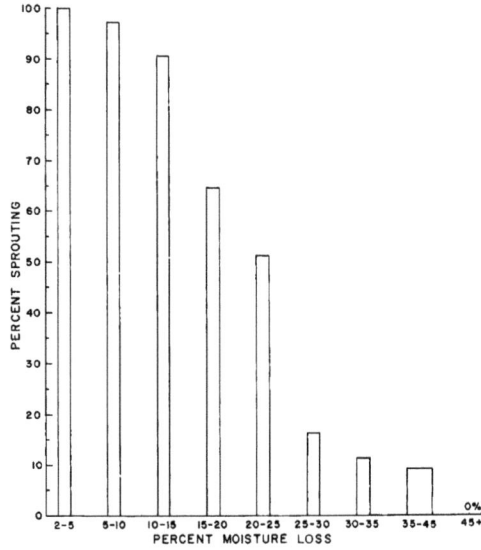

Figure 3.--Relationship between sprouting ability and percent moisture loss from tamarisk stem cuttings before planting, from a composite of seven tests (560 cuttings) conducted April to December.

the slower drying experienced in November is of significance in control of tamarisk. Clearing of tamarisk by mechanical means, such as bulldozing or root plowing[3] has often been unsuccessful because of vigorous sprouting of shoot material buried in the operation. Due both to slow drying of dormant tamarisk canes and to cold soil and weather conditions during the dormant season, chances of a successful clearing operation during winter are much reduced.

The effect of summer drying on sprouting ability was tested during a day in August. Ninety 6-inch stem cuttings were taken at random from several tamarisk plants and dried in the sun for 8 hours on a bare soil surface. The soil surface temperature averaged more than 120° F. during the drying period. At the end of the 8-hour period, the

[3]Horton, J. S. Use of a root plow in clearing tamarisk stands. U. S. Forest Serv., Rocky Mountain Forest and Range Expt. Sta., Res. Note 50, 6 pp., illus. 1960.

cuttings were planted in moist, alluvial soil and observed over a 3-month period. No sprouts or roots appeared on any of the cuttings. Thus, a few days of drying during the summer months in the Southwest may be sufficient to destroy most of the sprouting ability of tamarisk shrubs cut by mechanical equipment.

Discussion and Conclusions

Tamarisk stem tissue will sprout vigorously and form new plants if buried or partially buried in warm moist soil. In the active growing season, nearly all undried stem cuttings of all sizes and from any location in the crown of the original shrub produced roots and formed new plants under greenhouse conditions.

Sprouting was delayed during the winter period. In some instances, cuttings planted during the late fall and winter months did not sprout for 3 or 4 months. Undried tamarisk

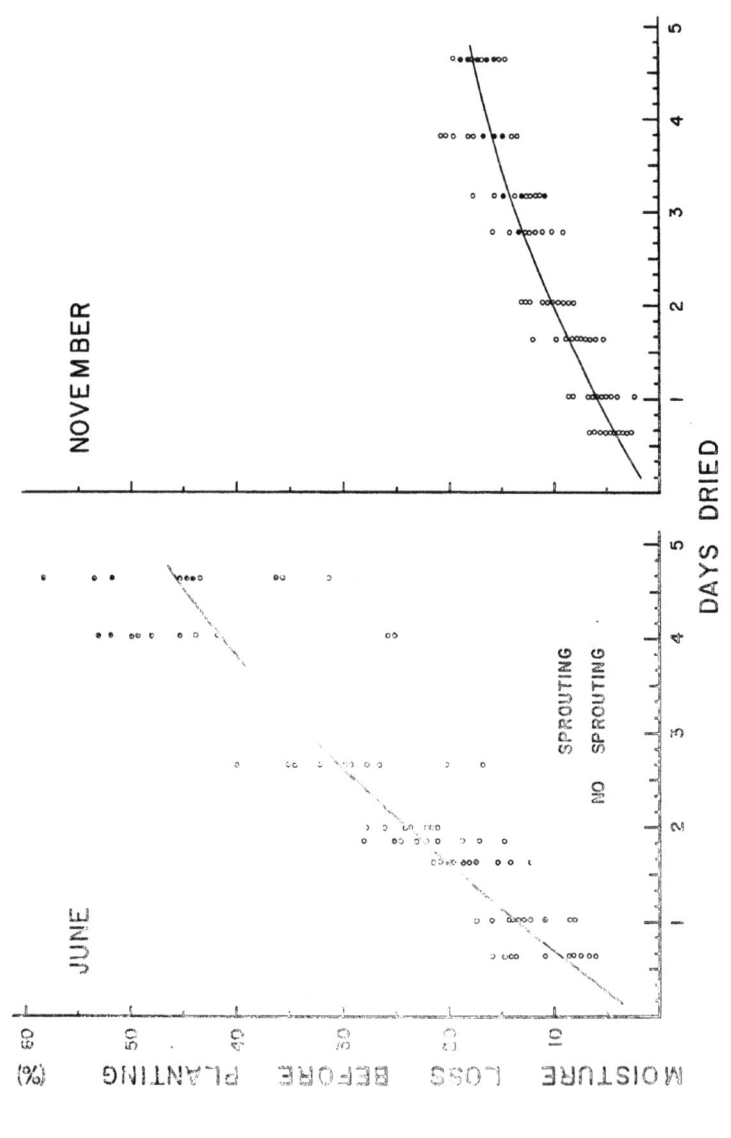

lent than cuttings made in the fall or winter, and lost moisture more rapidly. Summer cuttings also lost sprouting ability more rapidly.

The moisture level at which sprouting of tamarisk stem tissue ceases is quite variable and the rate of drying cannot be regulated for use in practical control measures. However, this study indicates that land managers can take advantage of the fact that any drying of stem tissue will reduce sprouting ability. Some management recommendations to prevent reestablishment of tamarisk by sprouting of severed stem portions are: (1) control operations should be done during the growing period when the soil is dry and weather warm; and (2) stems should be left on the surface of the ground and never be buried in moist soil.

Specific Gravity of Alligator Juniper in Arizona

Roland L. Barger and Peter F. Ffolliott[1]

Alligator juniper (Juniperus deppeana Steud.), largest of the western junipers, is found from southwestern Texas through New Mexico and Arizona. Commonly a medium-sized tree with short, heavy bole and broad, spreading crown, it may attain bole diameters exceeding 6 feet. The species characteristically occurs in mixture with other woodland and coniferous species from 4,500 to 8,000 feet elevation, seldom forming pure stands.[2] The small cones, commonly called "berries," are a valuable source of wildlife food.

Past utilization of the species has been limited largely to fenceposts and fuelwood; however, additional potential uses continue to create interest. The fragrant, deep reddish-brown heartwood of alligator juniper resembles eastern redcedar, which suggests potential uses in chests, cabinets, and novelty items. Recent interest has been shown in producing both charcoal and particleboard from the wood.

Appraising suitability for possible new uses requires some knowledge of the physical characteristics of the wood. Specific gravity provides the best single index to such properties as wood strength, stiffness, shock resistance, hardness or wear resistance, and charcoal or fiber recovery. The variability to be expected in these properties can similarly be inferred from specific gravity variation. Consequently, an adequate measure of specific gravity for the species is desirable.

Increment cores were collected from a random sample of alligator juniper trees on the Beaver Creek Watershed Evaluation Project,[3] as a part of other research studies underway. These cores were used to establish a measure of specific gravity, and variation in specific gravity, at breast height. Analytic procedures described by the U. S. Forest Products Laboratory were used to process the cores.[4] Specific gravity based on green volume and ovendry weight, and wood density in pounds per cubic foot, were computed for

---

[1] *Wood Technologist and Associate Silviculturist, respectively, located at Flagstaff, in cooperation with Arizona State College; central headquarters are maintained at Fort Collins, in cooperation with Colorado State University.*
[2] *Little, Elbert L., Jr. Southwestern trees. A guide to the native species of New Mexico and Arizona. U. S. Dept. Agr. Agr. Handb. 9, 109 pp., illus. 1950.*

[3] *A 275,000-acre watershed on the Coconino National Forest in northern Arizona where costs and benefits of intensive multiple-use land management are being evaluated as a part of the Arizona Watershed Program.*
[4] *U. S. Forest Products Laboratory. Methods of determining the specific gravity of wood. U. S. Forest Serv., Forest Prod. Lab. Tech. Note B-14, 6 pp., illus. 1956.*

Table 1. --Specific gravity and density, based on ovendry weight and green volume, of alligator juniper at breast height by the increment core method

Size or form class	Number of trees	Specific gravity			Density, 95 percent confidence interval for true mean
		Maximum	Minimum	95 percent confidence interval for true mean	
					Lbs./cu.ft.
By diameter class:					
0 - 10.9 inches	9	0.533	0.478	0.495 ± 0.013	30.9 ± 0.80
11 - 20.9 inches	8	.471	.372	.440 ± .027	27.5 ± 1.67
21 - 40.9 inches	20	.497	.398	.442 ± .012	27.6 ± .77
41 inches and over	9	.497	.399	.446 ± .023	27.8 ± 1.41
By stem form class:					
Single stem	23	.508	.372	.458 ± .015	28.6 ± .94
Fork between ground line and breast height	17	.497	.398	.442 ± .013	27.6 ± .84
Fork at ground line	6	.533	.426	.465 ± .040	29.0 ± 2.47
All classes:	46	.533	.372	.453 ± .010	28.3 ± .61

each tree (table 1). Since alligator juniper assumes several definite stem forms, both diameter and stem form classes were recognized.

Charcoal recovery can be estimated as one-third the weight and one-half the volume of the wood from which it is made.[5] Assuming an average solid wood content of 80 cubic feet per cord, charcoal recovery of approximately 750 pounds per cord could be expected. Because charcoal would have a density of approximately 19 pounds per cubic foot, it would probably require briquetting to facilitate marketing.

Other physical characteristics of the wood may be estimated from specific gravity. One of the more important properties of furniture and cabinet woods is hardness. Hardness represents resistance of the wood to wear and marring, and is commonly expressed as the load in pounds necessary to imbed a prescribed object in the wood. Hardness is directly related to specific gravity, and may be estimated by the equations:

End hardness = $3,740 \, G^{2.25}$

Side hardness = $3,420 \, G^{2.25}$

where G represents specific gravity based on ovendry weight and green volume.[4] Computed end and side hardness values for alligator juniper are approximately 630 pounds and 580 pounds, respectively. These values compare well with the hardness of eastern redcedar (760, 650), and are double the values for ponderosa pine (300, 310).[6] Alligator juniper then ranks among the harder softwoods, and is thus suitable for uses where moderate resistance to wear and marring is important.

[5] *U. S. Forest Products Laboratory. Charcoal production, marketing, and use. U. S. Forest Serv., Forest Prod. Lab. Rpt. 2213, 137 pp., illus. 1961.*

[6] *Markwardt, L. J., and Wilson, T. R. C. Strength and related properties of woods grown in the United States. U. S. Dept. Agr. Tech. Bul. 479, 99 pp., illus. 1935.*

A Survey of an Intentional Burn in Arizona Ponderosa Pine

James R. Davis[1]

As part of a program for learning how to use prescribed fire for land management purposes, 100 acres of Arizona ponderosa pine were intentionally burned on the Coconino National Forest at Buck Mountain, 40 miles south of Flagstaff, on November 24, 1959.

The results of the burning were surveyed in July 1960 [2] by the methods reported by Lindenmuth.[3] Sampling intensity was one plot for every 0.4 acre.

[1]*Associate Forest Fuels Specialist, located at the Station's project headquarters at Flagstaff, in cooperation with Arizona State College; central headquarters are maintained at Fort Collins in cooperation with Colorado State University.*
[2]*Measurements were made by forestry students from Arizona State College under the direction of Dr. M. B. Applequist.*
[3]*Lindenmuth, A. W., Jr. A survey of effects of intentional burning on fuels and timber stands of ponderosa pine in Arizona. U. S. Forest Serv., Rocky Mountain Forest and Range Expt. Sta., Sta. Paper 54, 22 pp. 1961.*

Burning Conditions

Forest flammability measurements were as follows: drought index[4] was moderate (70) and rate-of-spread index was low (10). Pine understory was dense. Twenty-three percent of the area had a potential for supporting crown fire during moderate drought index and low to moderate rate-of-spread index conditions.

The area was burned in one afternoon during relatively stable burning conditions. Ignition was by strips 20 feet apart.

Fire Intensity

Most of the area burned lightly or not at all. Percent distribution was as follows:

[4]*Lindenmuth, A. W., Jr. Development of the 2-index system of rating forest fire danger. Jour. Forestry 59: 504-509. 1961.*

	Burnable area	Burned area
	(Percent)	
Fire intensity class:		
Did not burn	37.8	0.0
Light surface fire	48.6	78.2
Hot surface fire	11.3	18.2
Crown fire	2.3	3.6
Total	100.0	100.0

Effects on Understory Trees

Because of the dense understory, many potential crop trees needed release. Only a small proportion of the area crowned or burned with a hot surface fire, however, so few were released.

Percent of total potential crop trees:	
Needing release	44.9
Released	4.3
Percent of those needing release that were released	9.7

Since overall fire intensity was low, few understory trees were killed or damaged. The proportion of plots stocked with understory trees was reduced by 5.5 percent. On an additional 5.1 percent of all plots the stocking was damaged. The best potential crop tree on the plot was either damaged or killed, which left the plot stocked by a less desirable tree.

Forest flammability conditions for the Buck Mountain burn were similar to those for the 27,000-acre burn reported by Lindenmuth.[3] Similar proportions of the two areas were found to have burned by light surface fire, hot surface fire, and crown fire. The similarity of the two burns suggests a pattern of fire intensity that can be expected in low-intensity or "cool" burns.

March 1965

U.S. FOREST SERVICE
RESEARCH NOTE RM - 42

U.S. DEPARTMENT OF AGRICULTURE

Rate and Spacing in Seeding Crested Wheatgrass in New Mexico

H. W. Springfield [1]

The general practice for seeding crested wheatgrass (Agropyron cristatum (L.) Gaertn.) on Southwestern ranges is to drill the seed in 12-inch rows at the rate of 6 pounds per acre. Questions have arisen as to what happens if the seeding rate is reduced to 4 pounds. The cost of seeding obviously becomes less, but how satisfactory is the stand of grass? Other questions have been asked about various drill row spacings. For example, what are the results of seeding in 6-inch rows, or 18-inch rows?

Information relating to these questions was obtained from an experiment conducted in northern New Mexico during the period 1951 through 1959.

Literature

Studies conducted by Hull [2] in Idaho showed no differences in yields of crested wheatgrass from drill row spacings of 6, 12, 18, and 24 inches. The 6- and 12-inch rows gave better protection against soil erosion and weed invasion, however, and produced a finer, more palatable forage. Other studies in Idaho[3] indicated that rate of seeding had no effect on the ultimate herbage production of crested wheatgrass. Rates of 2, 4, 8, 12, and 24 pounds per acre were tested. At the end of the third season herbage yield tended to be higher on plots seeded at the heavier rates, but by the end of the eighth season yields were as high for the 2- and 4-pound rates as for the 24-pound rate.

Tests at Fort Valley, Arizona,[4] indicated that the highest seeding rate (12 pounds per acre) produced the greatest yield during years of favorable moisture, but the lowest seeding rate (4 pounds per acre) gave the best yield during dry years. Likewise, the narrowest spacing (6 inches) produced the highest yield in wet years, whereas the widest spacing (18 inches) produced the highest in dry years.

---

[1] *Range Scientist, located at Albuquerque, in cooperation with the University of New Mexico; central headquarters are maintained at Fort Collins, in cooperation with Colorado State University.*
[2] *Hull, A. C., Jr. Depth, season, and row spacing for planting grasses on southern Idaho range lands. Amer. Soc. Agron. Jour. 40: 960-969, illus. 1948.*
[3] *Mueggler, Walter F. and Blaisdell, James P. Effect of seeding rate upon establishment and yield of crested wheatgrass. Jour. Range Mangt. 8: 74-76. 1955.*
[4] *Lavin, F. and Springfield, H. W. Seeding in the southwestern pine zone for forage improvement and soil protection. U. S. Dept. Agr. Agr. Handb. 98, 52 pp., illus. 1955.*

One study in Colorado[5] showed no differences in yield of crested wheatgrass due to rates of 5 and 10 pounds per acre or to row spacings of 6, 8, 12, and 16 inches. Another study by McGinnies[6] indicated that seeding rates of 2, 3, 6, and 9 pounds per acre had no influence on crested wheatgrass yields. Row spacings, however, did affect his yields. In 1956, a dry year, highest yields resulted from a 21-inch spacing and the lowest from a 7-inch spacing. Yields from a 14-inch spacing were significantly less than from a 21-inch spacing. Similar results were obtained in 1957, a year of average precipitation. Plants at the widest spacing were taller, coarser, and more robust. The trend was from highest yields with narrow row spacings during the first few years after seeding to highest yields with widest row spacings in later years.

Methods of Study

The San Antone experimental site, where this study was conducted, is 19 miles northwest of Tres Piedras, New Mexico, approximately 2 miles inside the Carson National Forest boundary. Before being seeded, the site was dominated by rabbitbrush (Chrysothamnus spp.), black sagebrush (Artemisia nova A. Nels.), and pingue (Hymenoxys richardsonii (Hook.) with scattered plants of slimstem muhly (Muhlenbergia filiculmis Vasey), blue grama (Bouteloua gracilis (H.B.K.) Lag.), bottlebrush squirreltail (Sitanion hystrix (Nutt.) J. G. Smith), and Arizona fescue (Festuca arizonica Vasey). The soil is medium textured, rocky, and shallow. Elevation is about 8,500 feet. Annual precipitation at the nearest U.S. Weather Bureau Station averages nearly 13 inches.

Competing vegetation was removed with a brushland plow in June 1951. Crested wheatgrass was drilled with a single disc grain drill July 10-12, 1951.

[5]Hervey, D. F. and Noll, F. E. Reseeding studies. Colo. Agr. Expt. Sta. Gen. Ser. Paper 632, Sect. 3, pp. 5-8. 1955.
[6]McGinnies, William J. Effects of planting dates, seeding rates, and row spacings on range seeding results in western Colorado. Jour. Range Mangt. 13: 37-39. 1960.

Test plots were arranged in a factorial design in two blocks. Three seeding rates, 2, 4, and 6 pounds per acre, were used in combination with three drill row spacings, 6, 12, and 18 inches.

No grazing was permitted until May 1953. Utilization by cattle was comparatively light each spring from May 1 to June 15 in 1953, 1954, and 1955. A fence was built around the experimental plots in April 1956, and no grazing was allowed from 1956 through 1959.

The plots were sampled in 1956, 1957, and 1959.

On July 2, 1956, the plots were sampled for herbage production by clipping 10 random 9.6-square-foot circular samples per plot. On August 16, 1957, the same procedures were used. In addition, 15 crested wheatgrass plants were selected at random on each plot, and basal diameter and compressed culm length were measured.

On June 26-28, 1959, herbage production was sampled on twenty 9.6-square-foot samples per plot. Approximately 175 individual plants in each plot were measured. Because culms had not formed, average maximum compressed leaf length together with basal diameter of each plant were measured. Basal cover of crested wheatgrass was computed from basal diameters and plant counts. Average basal diameter was converted to basal area per plant, then this figure was multiplied by average number of plants to give average basal cover per plot.

Precipitation

Precipitation at Skarda, an official U. S. Weather Bureau station 12 miles from the site, totaled 3.8 inches during August 1951, the month after seeding. Total precipitation in 1952 was 16.3 inches, 3 inches more than the long-term average (table 1). This period of favorable precipitation following seeding no doubt influenced plant establishment and early growth of the grass. But the years 1953 through 1956 were dry; annual precipitation for these 4 years was 33 percent less than average. The year 1956, when yields were

Table 1.--Precipitation recorded at Skarda, New Mexico, official U. S. Weather Bureau Station 12 miles southeast of the San Antone experimental site, at 8,500 feet elevation

Interval	Precipitation recorded								Long-term average, 1941-60
	1952	1953	1954	1955	1956	1957	1958	1959	
	- - - - - - - - - - - - - - - Inches - - - - - - - - - - - - - - -								
October through May	9.3	5.6	5.6	5.0	2.3	7.4	10.6	6.0	6.5
October through June	9.6	6.4	5.8	5.0	3.0	7.9	11.0	7.2	7.3
October through July	12.8	10.3	8.2	6.6	4.8	12.9	11.9	7.9	9.5
Total annual	16.3	10.8	7.5	10.2	6.3	20.2	17.8	14.7	13.1

measured for the first time, was especially dry; only 6.3 inches fell, which was less than half the long-term average. In 1957, the second year the plots were sampled, precipitation totaled 20 inches, nearly 60 percent more than average. Precipitation in 1959, the final year the plots were measured, was only 14 percent more than average.

Other studies have shown that, in the area of the study, crested wheatgrass growth is closely related to October-through-May precipitation. At Skarda, precipitation for these months was only about 33 percent of average in 1956, 10 percent more than average in 1957, and 10 percent less than average in 1959. Because the plots were sampled about July 1 in 2 years and in mid-August the other year, summer precipitation probably influenced measurements of the grass. Precipitation from October through June in 1956 was nearly 60 percent less than average, whereas in 1959 it equaled the average. In 1957, when samples were taken August 16, precipitation was 5.0 inches in July and totaled 12.9 inches for October through July. This abundance of moisture explains the exceptional growth and high moisture content of the grass in 1957. Precipitation was more nearly average in 1959 than in the other years of measurement, therefore yield and other plant data obtained that year may approach the average for the site.

Results

Herbage Production

Herbage production of crested wheatgrass varied widely from one year to the next (table 2). The greatest difference in production was from 1956 to 1957. Production figures reflect the extremely dry year (1956) and the unusually wet year (1957). In 1959, both precipitation and crested wheatgrass production were more or less intermediate (fig. 1).

Table 2.--Herbage production of crested wheatgrass for different rates of seeding and drill row spacings for dry year (1956), wet year (1957), and intermediate year (1959)

Drill-row spacings and year	Herbage production at a per-acre seeding rate of--			
	2 lbs.	4 lbs.	6 lbs.	Average
	- - - Pounds per acre - - -			
6-inch:				
1956	50	51	50	50
1957	1,097	1,144	1,035	1,092
1959	418	464	414	432
Average	522	553	500	525
12-inch:				
1956	55	54	55	55
1957	1,174	1,120	1,254	1,183
1959	470	450	446	455
Average	566	541	585	564
18-inch:				
1956	53	52	55	53
1957	1,180	1,216	1,241	1,212
1959	441	454	510	468
Average	558	574	602	578
Combined average:				
1956	53	52	53	53
1957	1,150	1,160	1,177	1,162
1959	443	456	457	452
Overall average	549	556	562	556

6-INCH SPACING

Figure 1.--Plots seeded at 2, 4, and 6 pounds per acre in 1951 and observed in 1959 showed:

2 LBS. PER ACRE — about the same except the drill rows were more distinct for the 18-inch spacing

4 LBS. PER ACRE — about the same except that drill rows were fairly distinct for both 12- and 18-inch spacing

6 LBS. PER ACRE — distinct drill rows and more exposed soil for both 12- and 18-inch spacing

12-INCH SPACING 18-INCH SPACING

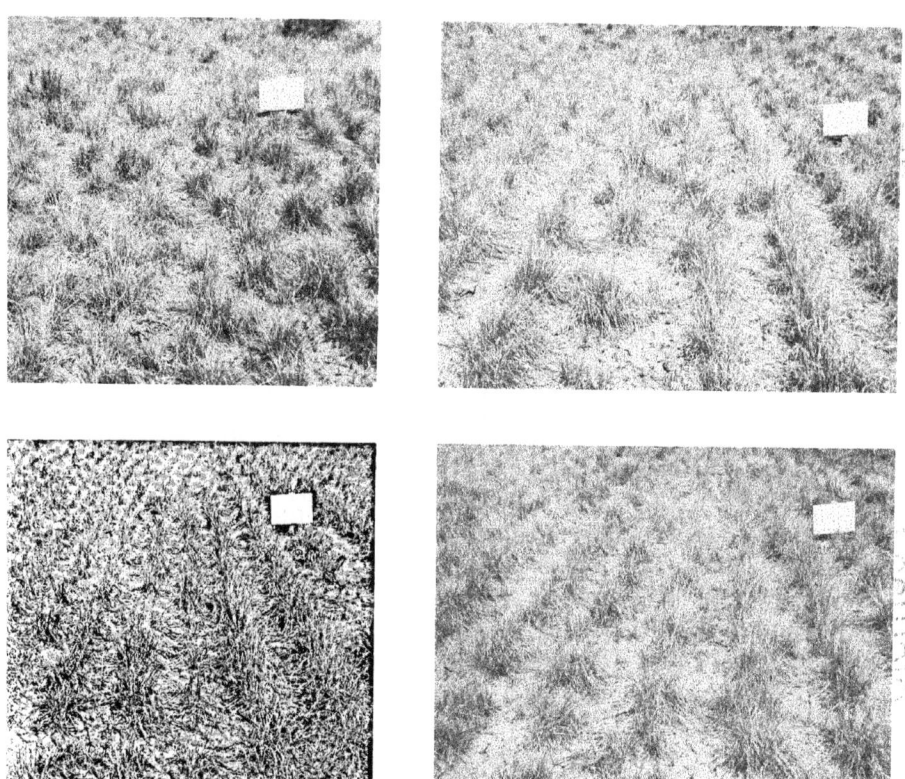

Table 3.--Moisture content of crested wheatgrass herbage from different drill row spacings, for dry year (1956), wet year (1957), and intermediate year (1959)

Drill-row spacings	Date of sampling and moisture content of herbage			
	July 2, 1956	August 16, 1957	June 27, 1959	Average
	- - - - - - - Percent - - - - - - - - - -			
6-inch	38.8	60.3	36.8	45.3
12-inch	34.7	61.6	36.9	44.4
18-inch	37.3	63.2	39.3	46.6
Average	36.9	61.7	37.7	45.4

The different drill row spacings had little or no influence on herbage production in the years of measurement. In 1956, when the seeded stands were 5 years old, production was uniformly low. No trend toward higher yield with wider spacing was apparent, although earlier results from Arizona and Colorado had indicated such a trend might be expected in a drought year. In 1957 and 1959, when the stands were in their sixth and eighth years, trends toward higher yields with wider spacings were evident. Because precipitation was above and near average in those years, such trends were not anticipated. These apparent differences in average yields between the 6-, 12-, and 18-inch spacings have little meaning, however, since the only statistically significant difference was between the 6- and 18-inch spacings in 1957.

Likewise, the different rates of seeding did not significantly affect crested wheatgrass production. By the time the stands were 5 years old, yields for the 2-, 4-, and 6-pound rates of seeding were practically the same.

Moisture Content of Herbage

Moisture content of the herbage varied considerably among years, but not among spacings (table 3). Moisture percentages at the time of sampling in 1957 exceeded 60 percent, mainly because precipitation during the previous 9 months was more than in any other year of record. In 1956 and 1959, moisture content for the various spacings averaged 35 to 39 percent.

Number of Plants

Number of plants per square foot in 1959, 8 years after seeding, showed no important differences regardless of seeding rate or spacing (table 4).

Number of plants per square foot showed an inverse relationship to yield of individual plants, as might be expected (fig. 2). Where the stand consisted of only 1.0 plant per square foot, individual plants weighed more than twice as much as where the stand contained 2.5 plants per foot.

Other attributes measured

No real differences were found in either 1957 or 1959 among culm and leaf lengths, basal diameters, or basal cover, regardless

Table 4. -- Number of crested wheatgrass plants per square foot for different rates of seeding and drill row spacings in 1959

Drill-row spacings	Plants per square foot at a per-acre seeding rate of--			
	2 lbs.	4 lbs.	6 lbs.	Average
	- - - - Number - - - -			
6-inch	1.8	2.1	1.8	1.9
12-inch	1.5	2.5	1.6	1.9
18-inch	1.8	1.7	1.4	1.6
Average	1.7	2.1	1.6	1.8

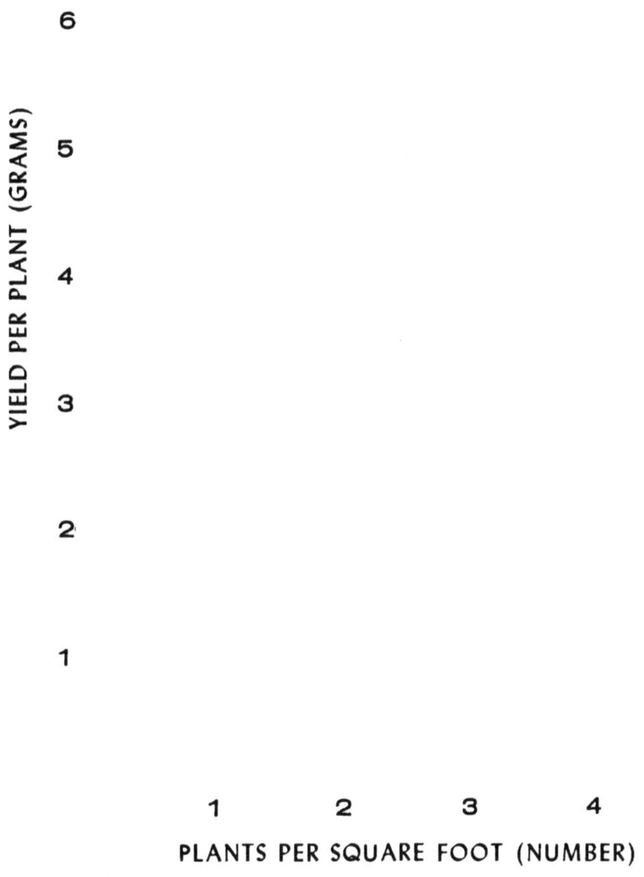

Figure 2.—Relationship between number of plants per square foot and air-dry herbage yield per plant in 1959.

of seeding rate or row spacing. Several differences in the numerical averages were indicated, but none of the differences were statistically significant.

Discussion and Conclusions

This experiment in New Mexico, in common with a number of experiments in other States, indicates that crested wheatgrass stands will reach an equilibrium with the environment within 5 to 8 years, regardless of rate of seeding or drill row spacing. Herbage yields were essentially the same for the 2-, 4-, and 6-pound per acre seeding rates and for the 6-, 12-, and 18-inch row spacing in the fifth, sixth, and eighth years after seeding. Contrary to findings from studies in Arizona and Colorado, no trend was found toward higher yield with wider spacing during a drought year.

Number of plants per square foot in the eighth year after seeding was about the same, regardless of spacing or seeding rate. Appar-

U.S. FOREST SERVICE
RESEARCH NOTE RM - 43

March 1965

FOREST SERVICE
U.S. DEPARTMENT OF AGRICULTURE

A Multiple BAF Angle Gage

Peter F. Ffolliott[1]

This Note describes the construction of an intercept angle gage[2] that allows a choice of different basal area factors (BAF's) in point-sampling, and automatically corrects for slope (fig. 1). It is simple to construct and inexpensive.

A sighting angle or critical angle is established, corresponding to a given basal area factor, by placing a crossarm of a known width on a rod of a known length. The angle gage described here has individual crossarms of different widths for different basal area factors. All crossarms are used with a rod of a constant length. Simply changing crossarms allows point sampling with any basal area factor desired. The crossarms, which swing freely when the rod is inclined, rotate around the line of sight by an amount equal to the slope, thereby automatically compensating for slope.[3]

---

[1]*Associate Silviculturist, located at Flagstaff, in cooperation with Arizona State College; central headquarters are maintained at Fort Collins, in cooperation with Colorado State University.*
[2]*Grosenbaugh, L. R. Point-sampling and line sampling: probability theory, geometric implications, synthesis. U. S. Forest Serv. South. Forest Expt. Sta. Occas. Paper 160, 34 pp. 1958.*
[3]*Bell, J. R., and Alexander, L. B. Applications of the variable plot method of sampling forest stands. Ore. State Bd. Forestry Res. Note 30, 22 pp. 1957.*

A straight-grained piece of hardwood (maple, ash, or other type) 3/4 inch by 1-1/4 inches by approximately 32 inches serves as the rod. A crossarm holder is attached to one end of the rod (fig. 2a). The distance from the notch in the crossarm holder to the opposite end of the rod is 30 inches. The crossarm holder is made from a piece of metal 3/8 inch by 1-1/4 inches by 3-1/2 inches (fig. 2b). A

Figure 1.--A multiple BAF angle gage.

slot 7/8 inch by 1-1/2 inches, cut in the center of the crossarm holder and in the rod beneath the crossarm holder, allows the crossarm to swing freely when in place (fig. 2c).

The material used in making the crossarms can be any heavy metal not exceeding 1/8 inch in thickness. Each crossarm has a

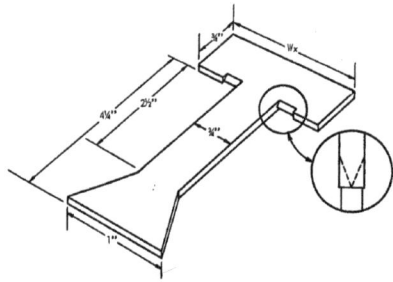

Figure 3.--*Crossarm design for multiple BAF angle gage. The width of sight blade will vary with basal area factor (dimensions in inches).*

sight blade and a base (fig. 3). The width of the sight blade, which determines the basal area factor, is obtained from the relationship:

width (inches) = crossarm length factor × × 30 (inches).

Common crossarm length factors can be determined for different basal area factors by the equation:

$$CLF = \sqrt{\frac{1}{\frac{43560}{4BAF} - 1}}$$

where
CLF = crossarm length factor
BAF = basal area factor

Grosenbaugh[4] gives crossarm length factors for commonly used basal area factors. The dimensions of the base of each crossarm are the same (fig. 3). The base acts as a pendulum, insuring free movement of the crossarm when the rod is inclined (fig. 2c).

Biltmore and hypsometer graduations can be stamped on the rod to provide an all-purpose cruising instrument.

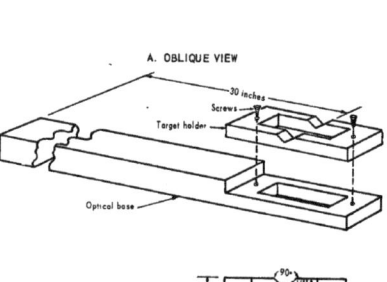
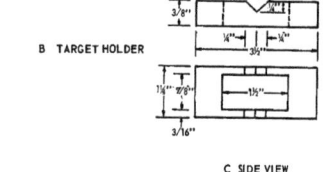
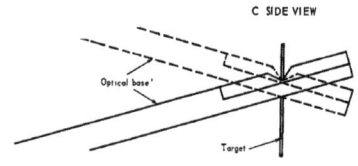

Figure 2.--*A. Crossarm holder is attached to the rod with notch of crossarm holder 30 inches from opposite end of rod (dimensions in inches). B. Crossarm holder design for multiple BAF angle gage (dimensions in inches). C. Crossarm swings freely when rod is inclined.*

[4] Grosenbaugh, L. R. *Better diagnosis and prescription in southern forest management.* U. S. Forest Serv. South. Forest Expt. Sta. Occas. Paper 145, 27 pp. 1955.

il 1965

U.S. FOREST SERVICE

RESEARCH NOTE RM - 44

REST SERVICE
. DEPARTMENT OF AGRICULTURE

Multiple Comparison Procedures

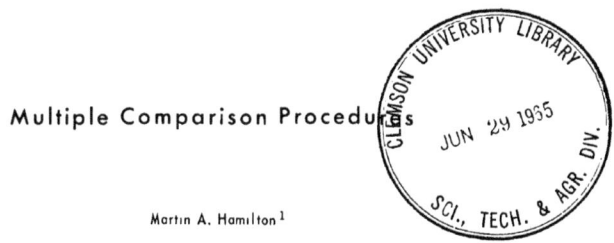

Martin A. Hamilton[1]

The standard method of comparing k experimental treatment means, $\overline{X}_i$, $i = 1, \ldots, k$, is to construct an analysis of variance table and conduct an F test. If the F test is significant, the experimenter can only state that all the means are not equal. But he usually wants to ask more specific questions about differences among treatment means than can be answered by this F test. In fact, the experimenter often wishes to decide which of the true treatments means, $\mu_i = E(\overline{X}_i)$, differ from each other.

Many methods are proposed in statistical literature for comparing experimental treatment means (Federer 1955; Hartley 1955; Scheffé 1959).[2] This paper is a review of that literature and an attempt at a unified presentation of multiple comparison methods for workers in the field.

The plan of this paper is to first provide a foundation on which different multiple comparison methods may be presented, and then to describe and compare some well-known procedures. The first section, therefore, discusses the types of α-error rates (levels of significance) provided by various multiple comparison tests, and defines terms that are used in subsequent sections. A general multiple comparison procedure is given in section 2. In section 3, five multiple comparison tests are individually described, and hints are given for selecting the appropriate test for a particular problem. Section 4 contains an example problem illustrating all five methods. The fifth and final section defines two methods of testing multiple contrasts among treatment means, discusses their applicability, and analyzes example data using both procedures. For most forestry problems, the field worker will find that sections 1.3, 1.5, 2, 3.3, 3.4, 3.6, 4.3, and 4.4 are of the greatest value.

1. α-ERROR RATES AND POWER

The experimenter must attach some nominal level of significance to his statements concerning differences between treatment means. If he has only two means to compare, the usual "t-test" at

---

[1]*Mathematical Technician during summer of 1964 at Rocky Mountain Forest and Range Experiment Station central headquarters at Fort Collins, in cooperation with Colorado State University; now a graduate student and candidate for Ph. D. degree, Statistics Department, Stanford University, Stanford, California.*

[2]*Names and dates in parentheses refer to Literature Cited, page 12.*

the α level of significance will yield a 100α percent chance of stating that the true means are different when they are actually equal. But if the experimenter has k experimental means to compare pairwise, he is simultaneously testing $_kC_2= k(k-1)/2$ null hypotheses of the form $H_0: \mu_i = \mu_j$ against the alternate hypotheses $H_1: \mu_i \neq \mu_j$ (e.g., if $k = 4$, the experimenter may want to make six inferences at the same time about the values of $\mu_4 - \mu_1$, $\mu_4 - \mu_2$, $\mu_4 - \mu_3$, $\mu_3 - \mu_1$, $\mu_3 - \mu_2$, and $\mu_2 - \mu_1$). An experiment yielding k means thus may require as many as $k(k-1)/2$ simultaneous "inferences." The α error (level of significance) for this case has been given more than one meaning (Hartley 1955). The following definitions of error will be encountered in this paper.[3]

1.1 Error Rate Per Comparison

α_c = error rate per comparison = (no. of erroneous inferences) / (no. of inferences attempted) = proportion of all comparisons expected to be erroneous when the null hypotheses are true. For example, with 100 experiments, each yielding 20 treatment means and 190 paired comparisons, the experimenter expects to wrongly reject 950 of the 19,000 null hypotheses if he uses an α_c error rate of .05.

This error rate is appropriate when:
 a. The specific comparison is the conceptual unit.
 b. The proportion of all erroneous inferences to all comparisons made is to be a constant.
 c. The experimental error variance is relatively stable from experiment to experiment (see section 1.5).
 d. A faulty inference does not affect the remaining inferences from the experiment (see section 1.5).

1.2 Error Rate Per Experiment

α_e = error rate per experiment = (no. of erroneous inferences) / (no. of experiments) = the expected number of erroneous inferences per experiment when the null hypotheses are true. For example, with 100 experiments, each yielding 20 treatment means and 190 paired comparisons, the experimenter expects to wrongly reject 9 or 10 of the 190 null hypotheses in <u>each</u> of the 100 experiments if he uses an α_e error rate of .05.

This error rate is appropriate when:
 a. The experiment is the conceptual unit.
 b. The average number of erroneous inferences per experiment is to be kept constant.
 c. The experimental error variance is relatively stable from experiment to experiment (see section 1.5).
 d. A faulty inference for one comparison does not affect the remaining comparisons (see section 1.5).

1.3 Experimentwise[4] Error Rate

α_w = experimentwise error rate = (no. of experiments with one or more erroneous inferences) / (no. of experiments) = expected proportion of experiments with one or more erroneous inferences when the null hypotheses are true. For example, with 100 experiments, each yielding 20 treatment means and 190 paired comparisons, the experimenter expects to wrongly reject one or more null hypotheses in <u>only</u> 5 of the 100 experiments if he uses an α_w error rate of .05.

This error rate is appropriate when:
 a. The experiment is the conceptual unit.
 b. The average proportion of experiments in which <u>one or more</u> faulty inferences are made is to be kept constant.
 c. The experimental error variance fluctuates from experiment to experiment (see section 1.5)
 d. The value of other inferences from the experiment is lowered as soon as <u>one</u> faulty inference is made (see section 1.5).

[3]*Federer, W. T. Error rates in experiments. (Lecture notes from Advanced Science Seminar in Mathematical Statistics, Dept. of Math. and Statis., Colo. State Univ., Ft. Collins, Colo., Aug. 7, 1964.)*

[4]*"Experimentwise" is the term suggested by J. W. Tukey in the early 1950's to identify this type of error rate.*

1.4 Duncan's Protection Level

D. B. Duncan (1955) defined the protection level concept for use in a particular type of multiple comparison test (see sections 3.5 and 4.5). This concept is difficult to explain in terms parallel to those used in sections 1.1, 1.2, and 1.3. For this reason, discussion of the protection level is limited to an interpretation of its use in Duncan's New Multiple Range Test.

An experiment is said to be of "type d," $d = 1, 2, \ldots, k$ if:
  i) It yields k experimental means, where $k \geq d$.
 ii) d of the k true treatment means are equal to μ.
iii) The remaining $k-d$ true treatment means are all different from μ and all different from each other.

In other words, an experiment is of "type d" if there is only one cluster of associated true treatment means, and this cluster is of size d.

Now let α_p = the level of significance the experimenter would choose for a test of the difference between any two means, assuming that the remaining means were not present. Then Duncan's protection level for an experiment of "type d" = $1 - (1 - \alpha_p)^{d-1}$ = (no. of experiments of type d with one or more erroneous inferences) / (no. of experiments of type d). For example, with 100 experiments, each yielding 20 treatment means and 190 paired comparisons, the experimenter expects to wrongly reject one or more null hypotheses in 62 of the experiments if he uses an α_p error rate of .05 and if each of the 100 experiments is of type 20. If each of the experiments is of type 2, the experimenter expects to wrongly reject one or more null hypotheses in 5 of the experiments when he uses an α_p error rate of .05.

This error rate is appropriate when:
a. The experiment is the conceptual unit.
b. The average proportion of experiments of type d in which one or more faulty inferences are made is to be kept constant.
c. The experimental error variance fluctuates from experiment to experiment (see section 1.5).
d. The value of other inferences from an experiment of type d is lowered as soon as one faulty inference is made, but the amount that the value is lowered is small if d is large (see section 1.5).

1.5 Discussion of α Error Rates

By comparing conditions c and d under sections 1.1, 1.2, 1.3, and 1.4, it seems reasonable to conclude that in most forestry experiments an experimentwise error rate, α_w, should be used (Hartley 1955). Errors of experimentation usually do affect the entire experiment. This is certainly true when the experimenter uses a multiple comparison procedure to help him choose some preferred treatments. If even one false inference is made, the experiment provides little information about the true relationships among treatment means. In forestry research, experimental error variance fluctuations from experiment to experiment are common. For example, varying climatic conditions affect the variance, but are impossible to control from experiment to experiment. For these reasons, this paper is slanted toward the use of experimentwise error rates. The experimenter must remember to consider all four definitions of error rate, however, and choose the one that is most appropriate for his situation.

1.6 The Terms "Conservative" and "Powerful"

The power of a test is defined as the probability of rejecting the null hypothesis when it is false. Power is a function of $\mu_i - \mu_{i'}$, the actual mean differences, of σ^2, the common variance, and of α, the level of significance. If two statistical tests are available for analyzing a set of data, the experimenter should use the test that guarantees the higher power for the error rate he has chosen.

Suppose the experimenter wishes to compare a test based on an error rate per comparison with a test based on an experimentwise error rate. It can be shown that if $\alpha_c = \alpha_w$, the test based on an error rate per comparison is more powerful. But this is not a true power comparison because the error rates, α_c and α_w, are not the same by definition. Although statisticians have compared them, the power functions of tests based on differently defined error rates should not be directly compared. For this reason, the term "conservative" is used in the following discussion. The statement "Fisher's test is more conservative than Tukey's test" indicates that Tukey's test is more powerful in the sense that the powers are compared at $\alpha_e = \alpha_w$.

A simple way to decide which of two tests is more conservative (more powerful if the tests are based on the same error rate) is to compare the lengths of the $1 - \alpha_o$, $1 - \alpha_e$, $1 - \alpha_w$, and $1 - \alpha_p$ confidence intervals derived from the tests, where $\alpha_o = \alpha_e = \alpha_w = \alpha_p$. The test producing the wider confidence intervals about differences between pairs of means is the more conservative.

2. GENERAL MULTIPLE COMPARISON TEST PROCEDURE

Let all k experimental means be based on n observations and have common unknown variance σ^2/n. The general multiple comparison procedure is to order the experimental means from smallest to largest, assigning consecutive indices so that $\overline{X}_1 < \overline{X}_2 < ... < \overline{X}_{k-1} < \overline{X}_k$. Then a table (see table 1) of differences of all possible pairs is formed. Each table entry is compared with an appropriate critical value $K(\alpha, \nu) s/\sqrt{n}$, where s^2 is an independent estimate of σ^2 based on ν degrees of freedom and $K(\alpha, \nu)$ is a tabular value. If $\overline{X}_i - \overline{X}_j$ is greater than $K(\alpha, \nu) s/\sqrt{n}$, the null hypothesis, $H_0: \mu_i = \mu_j$, is rejected and the alternate hypothesis, $H_1: \mu_i \neq \mu_j$, is accepted. The difference, $\overline{X}_i - \overline{X}_j$, is then said to be "significant." This is the same testing procedure as for the ordinary t-test, but with different tabled values.

Table 1--Differences between pairs of means

	$\overline{X}_1$	$\overline{X}_2$	...	$\overline{X}_{k-1}$	$\overline{X}_k$
$\overline{X}_k$	$\overline{X}_k - \overline{X}_1$	$\overline{X}_k - \overline{X}_2$	...	$\overline{X}_k - \overline{X}_{k-1}$	0
$\overline{X}_{k-1}$	$\overline{X}_{k-1} - \overline{X}_1$	$\overline{X}_{k-1} - \overline{X}_2$	...	0	
.	.				
.	.				
$\overline{X}_2$	$\overline{X}_2 - \overline{X}_1$	0			
$\overline{X}_1$	0				

Multiple comparisons based on an α_w error rate are sometimes better presented as simultaneous confidence intervals, where the probability is greater than or equal to $1-\alpha$ that simultaneously for all differences between pairs of treatment means,

$$\overline{X}_i - \overline{X}_j - K(\alpha, \nu) s/\sqrt{n} \leq \mu_i - \mu_j \leq \overline{X}_i - \overline{X}_j + K(\alpha, \nu) s/\sqrt{n}.$$

Simultaneous confidence intervals may, in turn, be regarded as tests of hypothesis if the null hypothesis $H_0: \mu_i = \mu_j$ is rejected when and only when the interval $\overline{X}_i - \overline{X}_j \pm K(\alpha, \nu) s/\sqrt{n}$ does not contain zero.

The experimenter should try to define his problem and choose an appropriate method of analysis before he looks at the data. If tests of differences between all pairs of experimental means are paramount, the multiple comparison procedure is to be applied directly--not after an F-test. Some experimenters use a multiple comparison procedure only if the F-test is significant. This is not an efficient approach. The F-test does not help solve the problem, but only succeeds in making the multiple comparison test more conservative.

The standard procedure is to calculate the experimental means, form an analysis of variance table, use the mean square error as an independent estimate of the variance, and apply the appropriate multiple comparison test.

3. SOME MULTIPLE COMPARISON TESTS

There are two types of multiple comparison tests. With one type, all differences, $\bar{X}_i - \bar{X}_j$, are compared with the same critical value. With the other type the differences, $\bar{X}_i - \bar{X}_j$, are compared with critical values that depend upon the number $i-j$. These procedures are called fixed range tests and multiple range tests, respectively.

The five tests discussed in this paper do not exhaust the literature on multiple comparison methods. These tests are, however, the best known and/or the most useful procedures.

3.1 L.S.D. or Multiple t-test; α_c Error Rate; Fixed Range

This test is conducted by letting $K(\alpha, \nu) = \sqrt{2}\, t(\alpha, \nu)$, where $t(\alpha, \nu)$ is the upper $100\alpha/2$ percent point of the t distribution based on ν degrees of freedom (Federer 1955). The differences $\bar{X}_i - \bar{X}_j$, are compared with the least significant difference (L.S.D.), $\sqrt{2}\, t(\alpha, \nu)\, s/\sqrt{n} = K(\alpha, \nu)\, s/\sqrt{n}$, as described in the general test procedure.

The α error associated with the L.S.D. test is error rate per comparison α_c. If the experimentwise error rate is important, this test can be misleading. The following tabulation shows that if 20 means are to be compared, the L.S.D. test based on $t(.05, \nu)$ actually allows an α_w error of 90 percent:

k = number of means	experimentwise error
2	.05
6	.34
12	.68
15	.72
20	.90

Needless to say, this is not a satisfactory procedure to use if we wish to control on experimentwise error rate.

The L.S.D. test was the first method suggested to solve the multiple comparison problem, but recently has found limited acceptance among experimenters.

3.2 Fisher's Test; α_e Error Rate; Fixed Range

Fisher's test is conducted exactly as the L.S.D. test, except that it is adjusted to insure an error rate per experiment, α_e (Harter 1957). This is accomplished by letting $K(\alpha, \nu) = \sqrt{2}\cdot t(\alpha/m, \nu)$ where m is the number of paired comparisons desired by the experimenter. Usually, $m = k(k-1)/2$, the total number of possible pairs of k experimental means. The general procedure is followed using the critical value $\sqrt{2}\, t(\alpha/m, \nu)\, s/\sqrt{n} = K(\alpha, \nu)\, s/\sqrt{n}$. Fisher's test is the most conservative procedure mentioned in this paper.[5] In fact, if $k = 6$, $n = 25$, and $\alpha_c = .067$, the corresponding experimentwise error rate is $\alpha_w = .05$ (Harter 1957).

3.3 Tukey's Test; α_w Error Rate; Fixed Range

Many textbooks (Federer 1955, pp. 22-23; Scheffé 1959, pp. 434-436) contain tables of the upper percentage points, $q(\alpha, k, \nu)$, of the Studentized range for various values of k, ν, and α. Tukey's test consists of finding $q(\alpha, k, \nu)$ in tables of the Studentized range, and comparing the differences $\bar{X}_i - \bar{X}_j$ with $q(\alpha, k, \nu)\, s/\sqrt{n} = K(\alpha, \nu)\, s/\sqrt{n}$ as in the general procedure. The experimentwise error, α_w, for this method is guaranteed to be less than or equal to the α in $q(\alpha, k, \nu)$. There are other fixed-range tests that control on experimentwise error rates (Scheffé 1959), but Tukey's test is the most powerful.

3.4 Newman-Keuls' Test; α_w Error Rate; Multiple Range

This test also depends upon the Studentized range but is less conservative than Tukey's test (Hartley 1955). The standard procedure is as follows:

[5] *Dunn (1961) has shown exceptions to this statement in certain well-defined situations.*

a. $\bar{X}_i - \bar{X}_j$ is said to significant if
   $\bar{X}_i - \bar{X}_j > q(\alpha, i-j+1, v) \, s/\sqrt{n}$, where $q(\alpha, i-j+1, v)$ is the upper 100α percent point of the studentized range for $i-j+1$ observed means and v degrees of freedom.
b. Construct the table of mean differences as illustrated in section 2.
c. Begin testing in the upper lefthand cell. If $\bar{X}_k - \bar{X}_1$ is not significant, state that all the means are equal and conclude the test. If $\bar{X}_k - \bar{X}_1$ is significant, test $\bar{X}_k - \bar{X}_2$ and $\bar{X}_{k-1} - \bar{X}_1$.
d. If $\bar{X}_k - \bar{X}_2$ is not significant, state that $\bar{X}_2 = \bar{X}_3 = \ldots = \bar{X}_k$ and test no further difference in the 2nd through kth columns. If $\bar{X}_k - \bar{X}_2$ is significant, test $\bar{X}_k - \bar{X}_3$.
e. Continue in this manner, testing a difference, $\bar{X}_i - \bar{X}_j$, only if significant differences have been found in all cells above and left of the cell containing $\bar{X}_i - \bar{X}_j$.

If there is only one "cluster" of true means, the experimentwise error is guaranteed to be less than or equal to α. But if there are m clusters of true means, α_w is only guaranteed to be less than or equal to $m\alpha$. A cluster is defined as two or more equal true means. For example, if the true relation among the means is $\mu_1 = \mu_2 < \mu_3 = \mu_4 < \ldots < \mu_{k-1} = \mu_k$ so that there are $k/2$ clusters of true means, the experimentwise error rate could be as high as $(k/2)\alpha$, which is certainly a limitation of this procedure.

3.5 Duncan's New Multiple Range Test; α_p Error Rate; Multiple Range

This test procedure is conducted exactly as the Newman-Keuls' test except that the tabled values, $q(\alpha, i-j+1, v)$, have been revised to provide a less conservative test (Duncan 1955). To use this method, the revised values, $q^*(\alpha, i-j+1, v)$, must be read from special tables, usually titled "Critical Values for Duncan's New Multiple Range Test" (Federer 1955; Harter 1960b). These values are slightly smaller than corresponding values in a standard Studentized range table. Duncan justifies this method by defining the protection level concept and argues that the experimentwise error rate is too strong a criterion. To illustrate the difference, if $k = 6$ and $n = 25$, Duncan's test must be run with tabled values of $q^*(.01, i-j+1, v)$ to insure an experimentwise error of .05 (Harter 1957).

Duncan's test is affected in a more complicated manner than the Newman-Keuls' test if there are $m>1$ clusters of the true means. This fact does not seem to be mentioned in the literature.

3.6 Selecting an Appropriate Test

In the preceding discussion, the term conservative was freely used. Power is a more meaningful concept to consider when selecting the better of two tests. To find a true comparison of the powers of these five multiple comparison tests, each method can be adjusted to yield the same experimentwise error rate. If this is done, computations indicate that all five tests have roughly the same power.

Since the powers are much the same, the choice of a test is actually governed by the choice of an appropriate α error rate. By considering the definitions and discussion of error rates given in section 1, the experimenter can avoid the confusion previously associated with the selection of a multiple comparison test. Note that if $k = 2$, all five methods are identical in both error rate and critical value.

Because the experimental error variance fluctuates from experiment to experiment in forestry work, the α_c and α_e error rates are not adequate in most cases. This fact generally eliminates the L.S.D. test and Fisher's test from consideration.

If it is assumed that the experimenter believes the true treatment means are not grouped in more than one cluster, how does he choose between Tukey's test, Newman-Keuls' test, and Duncan's test? An answer to this question depends upon the individual philosophy of the experimenter.

If he feels that the importance of a false inference diminishes as the number of true treatment means in the cluster increases, he will use the Duncan procedure. In using Duncan's test, he realizes that the probability of falsely rejecting one or more hypotheses is somewhere between α_p and $1-(1-\alpha_p)^{k-1}$. For the example in section 1.4 where $k = 20$, $\alpha_p = .05$, and $1-(1-\alpha_p)^{k-1} = .62$.

If the experimenter decides that one false inference decreases the value of the other inferences, regardless of the number of means in the cluster, he wants to control on an α_w error rate. This is usually the case in forestry research. Now either Newman-Keuls' test or Tukey's test can be chosen. The experimenter should realize that if he believes the Newman-Keuls' test at $\alpha_w = .05$ is too conservative, he can use a larger α_w error rather than adopting Duncan's procedure.

It is true that the experimenter can not know the relationship among the true treatment means. His guess as to the number of clusters of true treatment means is based on his experience and knowledge of the experimental situation. The statisticians can only state that if experimentwise error rate is important and the experimenter feels that the true means are not grouped in more than one cluster, the Newman-Keuls' test is appropriate. If the experimenter suspects that the true means are grouped in two or more clusters, he should use Tukey's test.

An experimenter can provide appropriate answers a large percent of the time if he routinely applies Tukey's test to every multiple comparison problem he encounters. This is true because generally experimentwise error is important, and because Tukey's test is valid no matter how the true means are grouped.

Sometimes the experimenter wishes to compare all treatments with a standard or a control. He may feel that only differences between treatment means and the control mean are of interest. The Newman-Keuls' test is appropriate for this situation. Dunnett (1955) proposes a fixed-range test for this case that requires a special set of tables.

3.7 Means Based on Unequal Numbers of Observations

One of the assumptions made in section 2 was that the experimental means are all based on the same number of observations. If this is not true, (i.e. $\bar{X}_i$ is based on n_i observations and has a variance of σ^2/n_i) the tests must be adjusted (Sarhan and Greenberg 1962).

To adjust the L.S.D. test and the Fisher's test, multiply the usual tabled value by $(1/n_i + 1/n_j)^{1/2}$ to test the difference $\bar{X}_i - \bar{X}_j$. The errors, α_c and α_e, are not affected.

To adjust Tukey's test, Newman-Keuls' test, and Duncan's test, multiply the usual tabled values by $\sqrt{s^2/2(1/n_i + 1/n_j)}$ to test the difference $\bar{X}_i - \bar{X}_j$. This is a conservative approximation for all three methods (Kramer 1956).

4. EXAMPLE

Hartley (1955) quotes data on the comparative yields of naphthalene dye stuff prepared from $k = 6$ different "treatments" of H-acid. Each treatment was replicated $n = 5$ times. The means, arranged in ascending order, are given below.

Treatment index, i	1	2	3	4	5	6
Treatment mean, $\bar{X}_i$	1,470	1,498	1,505	1,528	1,564	1,600

The analysis of variance shown below provides an estimate of the variance, $s^2 = 2,451$, with $v = 24$ degrees of freedom:

Due to:	Degrees of freedom	Sum of squares	Mean square
Between treatments	5	56,360	11,272
Within treatments	24	58,824	2,451
Total	29	115,184	

Next a table of mean differences is formed (table 2).

Table 2--Differences between experimental means

	$\bar{X}_1$	$\bar{X}_2$	$\bar{X}_3$	$\bar{X}_4$	$\bar{X}_5$	$\bar{X}_6$
$\bar{X}_6$	130	102	95	72	26	0
$\bar{X}_5$	94	66	59	36	0	
$\bar{X}_4$	58	30	23	0		
$\bar{X}_3$	35	7	0			
$\bar{X}_2$	28	0				
$\bar{X}_1$	0					

4.1 L.S.D. Method - $\alpha_c = .05$

$t(.05, 24) = 2.06$; $\sqrt{2}\, t(\alpha, v)\, s/\sqrt{n} = \sqrt{2}(2.06)(22.14) = 64.6$

The L.S.D., 64.6, is compared with the values in table 2 and the results are conveniently summarized by $\bar{X}_1\ \bar{X}_2\ \bar{X}_3\ \bar{X}_4\ \bar{X}_5\ \bar{X}_6$.

Any two means not underscored by the same line are significantly different.
Any two means underscored by the same line are not significantly different, as defined in section 2

4.2 Fisher's Test - $\alpha_e = .05$

$t(.05/15, 24) = t(.0033, 24) = 3.429$, $\sqrt{2}\, t(\alpha, v)\, s/\sqrt{n} = \sqrt{2}(3.429)(22.14) = 107.0$

The critical value, 107.0, is compared with the mean differences in table 2, and the results are summarized as in 4.1. $\bar{X}_1\ \bar{X}_2\ \bar{X}_3\ \bar{X}_4\ \bar{X}_5\ \bar{X}_6$

4.3 Tukey's Test - $\alpha_w = .05$

From tables of the Studentized range, $q(\alpha, k, v) = q(.05, 6, 24) = 4.37$.
$K(\alpha, v)\, s/\sqrt{n} = (4.37)(22.14) = 96.8$

The critical value, 96.8, is compared with the mean differences in table 2, and the results are summarized as in 4.1. $\bar{X}_1\ \bar{X}_2\ \bar{X}_3\ \bar{X}_4\ \bar{X}_5\ \bar{X}_6$

4.4 Newman-Keuls' Test - $\alpha_w = .05$

To find the critical value for the $\bar{X}_6 - \bar{X}_1$ cell, find $q(.05, 6-1+1, 24) = 4.37$ in the Studentized range table and multiply by $s/\sqrt{n} = 22.14$, so that $4.37(22.14) = 96.8$.

To find the critical value for the $\bar{X}_5 - \bar{X}_2$ cell, find $q(.05, 5-2+1, 24) = 3.90$ in tables of the Studentized range and multiply by $s/\sqrt{n}$, so that $3.90(22.14) = 86.3$.

The test was concluded when $\bar{X}_6 - \bar{X}_4$, $\bar{X}_5 - \bar{X}_2$, and $\bar{X}_4 - \bar{X}_1$ were all found nonsignificant. The results are summarized as in 4.1. $\bar{X}_1\ \bar{X}_2\ \bar{X}_3\ \bar{X}_4\ \bar{X}_5\ \bar{X}_6$

Table 3--Critical Values for Newman-Keuls' Method with α = .05, K = 6, n = 24

	$\bar{X}_1$	$\bar{X}_2$	$\bar{X}_3$	$\bar{X}_4$	$\bar{X}_5$	$\bar{X}_6$
$\bar{X}_6$	96.8*	92.3*	86.3*	78.2		
$\bar{X}_5$	92.3*	86.3				
$\bar{X}_4$	86.3					
$\bar{X}_3$						
$\bar{X}_2$						
$\bar{X}_1$						

*Indicates significance for data in table 2.

4.5 Duncan's New Multiple Range Test - α_p = .05

To find the critical value for the $\bar{X}_6 - \bar{X}_1$ cell, find $q*(.05, 6-1+1, 24)$ = 3.28 in a table of tical values for Duncan's new multiple range test and multiply by $s/\sqrt{n}$, so that 3.28(22.14) = 72.6.

To find the critical value for the $\bar{X}_4 - \bar{X}_1$ cell, find $q*(105, 4-1+1, 24)$ = 3.16 in the same le and multiply by $s/\sqrt{n}$ so that 3.16(22.14) = 70.0.

The test was concluded when $\bar{X}_6 - \bar{X}_5$, $\underline{\bar{X}_5 - \bar{X}_2}$, and $\underline{\bar{X}_4 - \bar{X}_1}$, were all found nonsignificant. The ults are again summarized as in 4.1. $\bar{X}_1$ $\bar{X}_2$ $\bar{X}_3$ $\bar{X}_4$ $\bar{X}_5$ $\bar{X}_6$

Table 4 --Critical Values for Duncan's Method with α = .05, K = 6, ν = 24

	$\bar{X}_1$	$\bar{X}_2$	$\bar{X}_3$	$\bar{X}_4$	$\bar{X}_5$	$\bar{X}_6$
$\bar{X}_6$	72.6*	71.5*	70.0*	68.0*	64.6	
$\bar{X}_5$	71.5*	70.0				
$\bar{X}_4$	70.0					
$\bar{X}_3$						
$\bar{X}_2$						
$\bar{X}_1$						

*Indicates significant cells for data in table 2.

5. TESTING MULTIPLE CONTRASTS AMONG TREATMENT MEANS

Many times an experimenter is interested in "multiple" contrasts, which are differences between groups of means. The data may suggest relationships among treatment means that previously were not apparent, or the experimenter may wish to test some multiple contrasts for which independent sums of squares cannot easily be partitioned in the analysis of variance table.

A linear contrast among k true treatment means is defined as

$$\psi = \sum_{m=1}^{k} C_m \mu_m = C_1\mu_1 + C_2\mu_2 + \ldots + C_k\mu_k,$$

where the C_m's are any constants subject to the condition:

$$\sum_{m=1}^{k} C_m = C_1 + C_2 + \ldots + C_k = 0.$$

One possible multiple linear contrast among six means is

$$\psi = (\mu_1 + \mu_5)/2 - (\mu_2 + \mu_4 + \mu_6)/3,$$

where the coefficients, $C_1 = 1/2$, $C_2 = -1/3$, $C_3 = 0$, $C_4 = -1/3$, $C_5 = 1/2$, $C_6 = -1/3$, sum to zero.

Differences between pairs of treatment means are actually simplified forms of multiple contrasts where each group of means contains only one member. In notation,

$$\mu_i - \mu_j = \sum_{m=1}^{k} C_m \mu_m, \text{ where } C_m = \begin{cases} 1, & \text{if } m = i \\ -1, & \text{if } m = j \\ 0, & \text{otherwise} \end{cases} \text{ and } \sum_{m=1}^{k} C_m = 1 + (-1) = 0$$

Methods for simultaneously testing such "simple" linear contrasts are described in sections 2, 3, and 4.

There are two general methods of placing simultaneous confidence intervals around multiple contrasts among treatment means (Scheffé 1959). Both provide an experimentwise error rate.

5.1 S-Method (Scheffé) - α_w Error Rate

Under the usual assumptions ($\bar{X}_1, \ldots, \bar{X}_k$ are independently, identically, normally distributed random variables), the probability is $1-\alpha$ that simultaneously for all possible independent linear contrasts,

$$\psi = \sum_{m=1}^{k} C_m \mu_m, \sum_{m=1}^{k} C_m \bar{X}_m - S(\sum_{m=1}^{k} C_m^2)^{1/2} s/\sqrt{n} \leq \psi \leq \sum_{m=1}^{k} C_m \bar{X}_m + S(\sum_{m=1}^{k} C_m^2)^{1/2} s/\sqrt{n},$$

where

$$S = \{(k-1)F\alpha, k-1, \nu\}^{1/2},$$

s is the estimate of σ based on ν degrees of freedom, and each experimental mean is based upon n observations.

5.2 T-Method (Tukey) - α_w Error Rate

Under the same assumptions as in 5.1, the probability is $1-\alpha$ that simultaneously for all contrasts,

$$\psi = \sum_{m=1}^{k} C_m \mu_m, \sum_{m=1}^{k} C_m \bar{X}_m - q(\alpha, k, \nu) s/\sqrt{n} \cdot 1/2 \sum_{m=1}^{k} |C_m| \leq \psi \leq \sum_{m=1}^{k} C_m \bar{X}_m + q(\alpha, k, \nu) s/\sqrt{n} \cdot 1/2 \sum_{m=1}^{k} |C_m|,$$

where $q(\alpha, k, \nu)$ is the upper 100α percent point of the Studentized range based on k means and ν degrees of freedom, s and n are as in 5.1, and $|C_m|$ is the absolute value of C_m.

Notice that, if the contrast is a simple linear contrast,

$$1/2 \sum_{m=1}^{k} |C_m| = 1/2 \{|1| + |-1|\} = 1$$

so that the interval above is precisely that given by Tukey's method of section 3.3.

5.3 Discussion

These confidence intervals may be used to provide a test of hypothesis. Reject the null hypothesis,

$$H_O: \psi = \sum_{m=1}^{k} c_m \mu_m = 0,$$

if the confidence interval does not contain 0, and accept the null hypothesis if the confidence interval does contain 0.

As pointed out in section 3.3, the T-method is more powerful for testing simple linear contrasts. It has been shown that the S-method is more powerful for testing multiple linear contrasts (Scheffé 1959). Thus a good suggestion is to use the T-method if only simple linear contrasts are to be tested or if a mixture of simple and multiple linear contrasts are to be tested. Use the S-method if only independent multiple linear contrasts are to be tested.

The S-method is valid for testing either simple or multiple contrasts among adjusted means from an analysis of covariance (Halperin and Greenhouse 1958).

Sometimes the assumption of independence among treatment means is not reasonable. But if the experimenter believes that all the covariances between means are equal, an extension of the T-method may be used to test linear contrasts among the means (Scheffé 1959).

5.4 Example

Consider the data presented in section 4. Suppose treatments 3, 5, 6 were administered in the presence of an impurity and treatments 1, 2, 4 were free of the impurity. The experimenter may feel that it is important to test the multiple contrast

$$\psi = \mu_1 + \mu_2 - \mu_3 + \mu_4 - \mu_5 - \mu_6.$$

S-method, $\alpha_w = .05$

$$\sum_{m=1}^{k} c_m \bar{x}_m = 1470 + 1498 - 1505 + 1528 - 1564 - 1600$$

$$= -173$$

$$\sum_{m=1}^{k} c_m^2 = 1^2 + 1^2 + (-1)^2 + 1^2 + (-1)^2 + (-1)^2 = 6$$

$F(.05, 5, 24) = 2.62$

$s/\sqrt{n} = 22.14$

$S = \{5(2.62)\}^{1/2} = 3.62$

Therefore,
$$Pr\{-173 - (3.62)(6)^{1/2}(22.14) \leq \psi \leq -173 + (3.62)(6)^{1/2}(22.14)\} = .95$$
or
$$Pr\{-369.4 \leq \psi \leq 23.4\} = .95$$

T-Method, $\alpha_w = .05$

$$\sum_{m=1}^{k} c_m \bar{x}_m = -173$$

$$\sum_{m=1}^{k} |c_m| = 1 + 1 + |-1| + 1 + |-1| + |-1| = 6$$

$q(.05, 6, 24) = 4.37$

$s/\sqrt{n} = 22.14$

Therefore,
$$Pr\{-173 - (4.37)(22.14)(6/2) \leq \psi \leq -173 + (4.37)(22.14)(6/2)\} = .95$$
or
$$Pr\{-463.3 \leq \psi \leq 117.3\} = .95$$

The results of both methods suggest that the average of means of treatments containing the impurity were not significantly different from the average of means of treatments not containing the impurity.

This example shows that confidence intervals about a multiple linear contrast can be much wider with the T-method than with the S-method.

LITERATURE CITED

Bose, R. C. and Roy, S. N.
   1953. Simultaneous confidence interval estimation. Ann. Math. Statis. 24: 513.

Duncan, D. B.
   1955. Multiple range and multiple F tests. Biometrics 11: 1.

Dunn, Olive J.
   1961. Multiple comparisons among means. Amer. Statis. Assoc. Jour. 56: 52.

Dunnett, C. W.
   1955. A multiple comparison procedure for comparing several treatments with a control. Amer. Statis. Assoc. Jour. 50: 1096.

Dwass, M.
   1959. Multiple confidence procedures. Ann. Inst. Statis. Math. 10: 277.

Federer, W. T.
   1955. Experimental design: Theory and application. 544 pp., New York: McMillan Co.

Halperin, M. and Greenhouse, S. W.
   1958. Note on multiple comparison for adjusted means in the analysis of covariance. Biometrik 45: 256.

Harter, H. L.
   1957. Error rates and sample sizes for range tests in multiple comparisons. Biometrics 13: 511; Correction, 1961, Biometrics 17: 321.

_____
   1960a. Tables of range and studentized range. Ann. Math. Statis. 31: 1122.

_____
   1960b. Critical values for Duncan's new multiple range test. Biometrics 16: 671.

Hartley, H. O.
   1955. Some recent developments in analysis of variance. Commun. on Pure and Applied Math. 8: 47.

Kramer, C. Y.
   1956. Extension of multiple range tests to group means with unequal number of replications. Biometrics 12: 307.

Roy, S. W.
   1954. Some further results in simultaneous confidence interval estimation. Ann. Math. Statis. 25: 752.

Sarhan, A. E. and Greenberg, B. G.
   1962. Contributions to order statistics. 482 pp., New York: Wiley and Sons, Inc.

Scheffé, H.
   1959. The analysis of variance. 477 pp., New York: Wiley and Sons, Inc.

May 1965

U.S. FOREST SERVICE
RESEARCH NOTE RM - 45

FOREST SERVICE
U.S. DEPARTMENT OF AGRICULTURE

Growth and Change in Structure of an Aspen Stand After a Harvest Cutting

E. C. Martin[1]

This report covers growth of quaking aspen (Populus tremuloides Michx.) on the Hart Prairie aspen plot for the 20 years, 1942-62. A previous report in 1949 covered the first 5 years of the study.[2] The small plot (0.12 acre), located 14 miles northwest of Flagstaff on the west slope of the San Francisco Peaks, contained 101 trees (857 per acre with a basal area of 69 square feet) when it was established in 1942 after a commercial cutting. Residual trees ranged from 2 to 8 inches in diameter (average 3.9) with half in the 2- and 3-inch classes (table 1), and averaged 50 years old. The residual merchantable volume[3] totaled 854 cubic feet, or 13.6 cords per acre in trees 4 to 8 inches in diameter.

---

[1]*Forest Research Technician, located at Flagstaff, in cooperation with Arizona State College; central headquarters are maintained at Fort Collins, in cooperation with Colorado State University.*
[2]*Herman, F. R. Growth of aspen following partial cutting. U. S. Forest Serv., Southwest. Forest and Range Expt. Sta. Res. Note 117, 3 pp. 1949.*
[3]*Partial volume--cubic contents of the peeled stem above a 1-foot stump to a 3-inch top diameter.*

Growth

Increment of the original merchantable trees in the plot is still good, although growth declined over the 20-year period. Periodic annual increment of these trees was 84.0 cubic feet[3] per acre for the 20 years, compared to 86.4 for the 10 years from 1942-52 and 88.0 cubic feet for the first 5 years from 1942-47. Trees reaching merchantable size during the 20 years accounted for an additional 11.8 cubic feet annually. Total annual net volume growth was 95.8 cubic feet, or 1.3 cords per acre (table 2). Average diameter of all trees, including those still of unmerchantable size, is 6.0 inches with a basal area of 142 square feet per acre (table 1). Basal area and volume more than doubled during the 20-year period.

Change Of Stand Structure

Trees 4 inches in diameter and larger made good diameter and volume growth. The larger trees maintained better vigor and made better growth than trees in the lower diameter classes, and none of them died between 1942 and 1962. On an acre basis, 136 trees in the 2-, 3-, and 4-inch diameter classes were killed by Cytospora canker or suppression during the 20 years. Cytospora canker is common in the San Francisco Peaks area. No restocking from sprouting took place (fig. 1).

Table 1.--Growth and change in structure by diameter class of aspen on the Hart Prairie plot, near Flagstaff, Arizona, 1942-62

Diameter class in inches	Trees			Basal area			Volume[1]			Annual increment	
	1942	1952	1962	1942	1952	1962	1942	1952	1962	1942-52	1942-62
	--Number--			Square feet			Cubic feet			Cubic feet	
1	0	0	0	0	0	0	0	0	0	0	0
2	32	12	3	.83	.34	.10	9.0	4.0	1.2	-.5	-.4
3	20	22	16	1.03	1.09	.87	14.0	14.5	12.2	.1	-.1
4	25	17	11	2.27	1.57	1.01	42.9	29.2	19.0	-1.4	-1.2
5	14	17	13	1.85	2.49	1.88	39.6	54.5	41.1	1.5	.1
6	7	16	14	1.33	3.16	2.85	30.6	72.8	66.1	4.2	1.7
7	2	8	12	.52	2.17	3.26	12.4	51.9	78.0	3.9	3.3
8	1	3	9	.34	1.08	3.14	8.3	26.2	76.5	1.8	3.4
9	0	2	4	0	.95	1.75	0	23.4	43.0	2.3	2.2
10	0	0	1	0	0	.58	0	0	14.0	0	.7
11	0	0	2	0	0	1.34	0	0	31.7	0	1.6
Total:											
Plot	101	97	85	8.17	12.85	16.78	156.8	276.5	382.8	12.1	11.4
Per acre	857	823	722	69.3	109.1	142.5	1331.0	2347.2	3250.0	102.7	96.7

[1] Entire unpeeled stem.

Table 2.--Periodic annual increment per acre of aspen on the Hart Prairie plot, near Flagstaff, Arizona, 1942-62

Aspen stand	1942-52		1942-62	
	Cu.ft.[1]	Cords	Cu.ft.[1]	Cords
Trees 3.6 in. and larger at time of plot establishment	86.4	1.2	84.0	1.1
Ingrowth: Trees growing into merchantable size (3.6 in. d.b.h.)	12.4	.2	11.8	.2
Total stand	98.8	1.4	95.8	1.3

[1] Merchantable.

Values

The scenery, recreation, watershed cover and wildlife food provided by aspen stands are immeasurable in terms of dollars. Aspen stands also act as a nurse crop for conifers. Scenic and recreational values (fig. 2), which are especially important, may outweigh other uses at this time.

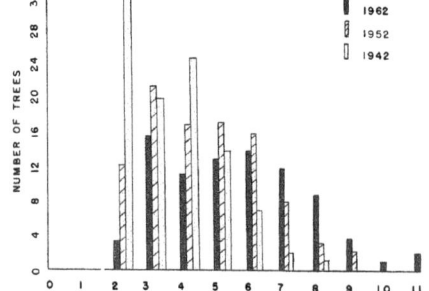

Figure 1.--Change in structure of Hart Prairie aspen plot over a 20-year period.

Figure 2.--An aspen stand on west slope of the San Francisco Peaks.

May 1965

U.S. FOREST SERVICE
RESEARCH NOTE RM - 46

FOREST SERVICE
U.S. DEPARTMENT OF AGRICULTURE

Snow Accumulation and Disappearance Influenced by Big Sagebrush

Boyd A. Hutchison [1]

The eradication of sagebrush on western grazing lands to increase forage produced by more palatable understory vegetation may also affect water yields from these lands.

Many of these grazing lands lie at elevations where a large portion of the annual precipitation occurs as snow. This snow is often redeposited in the lee of topographic and vegetative barriers by wind. Where sagebrush is the dominant overstory plant in these vegetative barriers, its eradication could affect snow accumulation and change the hydrology of these high-elevation grazing lands.

Studies are now underway to determine the effects of sagebrush eradication upon snow-accumulation patterns and water yields. To aid in evaluating these studies, more detailed studies of various hydrologic processes on these lands are being made. During the winter and spring of 1963, the influence of natural grassland and big sagebrush upon snow accumulation, snowpack profile characteristics, and snow disappearance was compared as a part of this program of work.

[1] Associate Hydrologist, located at Tempe, in cooperation with Arizona State University; central headquarters are maintained at Fort Collins, in cooperation with Colorado State University. Research reported was conducted in cooperation with the University of Wyoming, Laramie.

Past Work

Little work has been done in determining relationships between brush cover types and snow in the past. Connaughton,[2] in Idaho, found that snow accumulations in sagebrush were only slightly different from those on a denuded timber area.

Sonder and Alley[3] report that sagebrush control had no effect upon the snow-holding capacity in the Red Desert area in south-central Wyoming, where drifting of snow usually occurs. In the Big Horn Mountains, chemically controlled sagebrush areas appeared to retain snow longer than untreated areas.

Methods of Study

This study was conducted near Dubois, Wyoming, on sagebrush-covered rangeland on the southern flank of the Absaroka Mountain Range. The elevation of the study area is

[2] Connaughton, C. A. The accumulation and rate of melting of snow as influenced by vegetation. Jour. Forestry 33: 564-569. 1935.
[3] Sonder, Leslie W. and Alley, Harold P. Soil-moisture retention and snow-holding capacity as affected by the chemical control of big sagebrush (Artemisia tridentata Nutt.). Weeds 9(1): 27-35. 1961.

about 9,500 feet. Big sagebrush (<u>Artemisia tridentata</u> Nutt.) is the predominant species of sagebrush.

To determine how the big sagebrush canopy influences retention and disappearance of snow, these and related factors were measured on comparable natural sagebrush-covered and grass-covered plots. Sagebrush plots had a canopy cover density of about 50 percent.

These plots were 0.1 acre in area (1 chain square), and were situated on level ground within a broad stream-bottom site. Level sites were chosen to minimize snow trapping due to topographic configuration. Two replications of measurements were made. The plots in each replication were located 1 chain apart. The two replications were about 1-1/2 chains apart.

Measurements were made at monthly intervals throughout the winter. During the spring snowmelt period, the intensity was increased to two sampling dates per month. Data were compared by the analysis of variance technique.

A specially devised cylindrical sampler with a cross-sectional area of 3 square feet was used to obtain a measurement of snowpack water equivalent. This was done by converting the weight of snow contained in the sampler to inches of water. The average of five measurements per plot was taken as the amount of snow water accumulated on the plot.

This sampler was used to insure that representative measurements of the snowpack were obtained in the sagebrush cover type, where the snow-sagebrush crown intermixture made it difficult to obtain good samples with a Mount Rose snow tube. For purposes of comparison, this cylindrical sampler was used in both grass and sagebrush cover.

Snowpack profile characteristics were determined by excavating a trench on each plot on each sampling date. The characteristics of the profile were recorded by mapping and photographing. The densities of the strata within the profile were determined by means of a small density core sampler similar to SIPRE standard snow tube.[4]

The type and depth of soil frost was also determined on each plot. Distinction was made only between concrete and nonconcrete frost types. Frost depths were recorded in inches to a depth of 1 foot.

The rates of snowmelt were determined from periodic Mount Rose snow-tube measurements during a portion of the snowmelt period.

Snow Accumulation and Disappearance

Figure 1 shows the amounts of snow water accumulated on each sampling date. During January, the increase of snow water was greater in sagebrush than in grass. The sagebrush crowns were still exposed during this time.

In February, the crowns became completely covered and the rate of increase of water content became similar in both cover types. The sagebrush-covered plots continued to have greater water content through February and March, as a result of the initial greater efficiency of sagebrush crowns in inducing snow deposition. The differences in accumulated water on February and March sampling dates are significant at the 95 percent level of confidence.

After the March sampling date, snowmelt began and water losses were noted in both cover types. The metamorphism and subsequent melt of snow began earlier and proceeded at greater rates in and adjacent to sagebrush crowns. This is reflected in greater water losses from the sagebrush plots during the first month of melt. The unique radiative properties of snow are responsible for this difference.

[4]*Bader, Henri. The physics and mechanics of snow as a material. 79 pp. In Part II, Sect. B, Cold Regions Sci. and Engin. Phys. Sci. edited by F. J. Sanger. U. S. Army Materiel Command, Cold Regions Res. and Engin. Lab., Corps Engin., Hanover, N. H. 1962.*

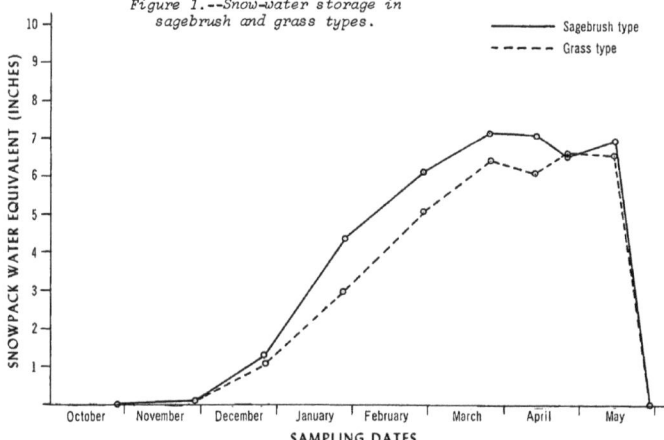

Figure 1.--Snow-water storage in sagebrush and grass types.

Solar (short-wave) radiation penetrates into a snowpack, but little is absorbed because of snow's high albedo for this type of radiation. Some of the incident radiation penetrates the snowpack, however, and intercepts sagebrush plant parts. The lower albedo of these materials allows absorption of the radiation, which results in a warming of the plant parts. Heat is then lost to snow by conductance or through long-wave radiation from the plants. For long-wave radiation, snow is nearly a perfect black body; that is, snow has great powers of absorption for long-wave radiant energy, and thus absorbs much of this energy form. The result of these two processes is a warming of the snow, which causes faster metamorphism and melt.

A characteristic melt pattern developed on the sagebrush plots as a result of the above processes. Depressions formed around individual sagebrush plants, while the snowpack between plants remained relatively unchanged. A hummock and depression topography resulted (fig. 2). Little melt occurred in the snowpack over grass during this time, and a

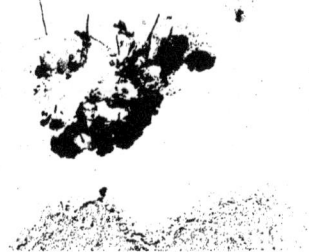

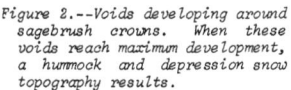

Figure 2.--Voids developing around sagebrush crowns. When these voids reach maximum development, a hummock and depression snow topography results.

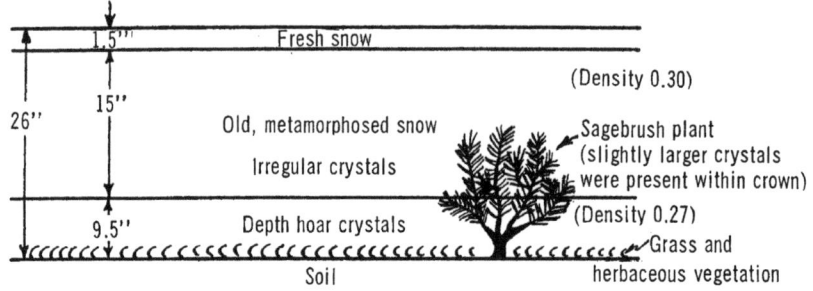

Figure 3.--Snowpack profile in sagebrush cover type (Feb. 26).

Figure 4.--Snowpack profile in grass cover type (Feb. 26).

net gain in water content was measured. With frequent spring snowfalls, there is a tendency for these depressions around sagebrush plants to fill with new snow. This may explain the slight rise in water content on sagebrush plots during the first half of May.

From May 6 to May 14, frequent Mount Rose snow tube samples were taken to determine the rates of snowmelt over the two cover types. The average rates of decrease were nearly the same in both types (0.38 inch per day in grass and 0.45 inch per day in sagebrush). The grass plots were completely free of snow by May 28, but some snow still persisted between sagebrush plants on the sagebrush plots.

Snowpack Characteristics

Examination of the snowpack profile yielded other information as to the influence of big sagebrush upon snowpack characteristics. Schematic representations of the winter snowpack on the sagebrush- and grass-covered plots (figs. 3, 4), show the only discernible differences in snowpack profile characteristics between cover types to be in the thickness of the various strata of the profile. Differences in the densities of the snow within these strata were slight throughout the winter (table 1).

The layer of depth hoar (figs 3, 4) was first observed in December, and persisted until the snow melted in the spring. The thickness of the layer decreased steadily throughout the course of the study, while the individual crystals grew larger with age.

The layer of old, metamorphosed snow increased in thickness throughout the winter as fresh snow aged and became incorporated into this strata. Throughout the winter, snow crystals in this layer found in and around sagebrush crowns were somewhat larger than those found elsewhere. The boundaries between the strata shown were sharply defined.

In both cover types, numerous small and discontinuous ice lenses were observed within the metamorphosed snow in March. Since these lenses were discontinuous and small, they appear to be of little hydrologic significance.

Table 1.--Densities of snow in strata of snow profile throughout period of study, winter and spring 1963

Date	Density of strata of snowpack by cover type							
	Grass				Sagebrush			
	Hoar above soil	Old snow	Hoar at surface	Fresh snow	Hoar above soil	Old snow	Hoar near surface	Fresh snow
January 29	0.27	0.23	([1])	([1])	0.26	0.21	([1])	([1])
February 26	.24	.30	([1])	([1])	.27	.30	([1])	([1])
March 26	.26	.33	([1])	([1])	.28	.35	([1])	([1])
April 10	.27	.34	0.28	0.22	.27	.32	0.29	0.24
April 25	.31	.34	.28	.23	.30	.34	.36	.24
May 14	.42	.44	([2])	.44	.38	.46	([2])	.39

[1] Not present.
[2] Strata had metamorphosed into old snow since preceding sampling date.

Figure 5.--
Sagebrush-covered
plot: snowpack as
of April 25, 1963.

In April, an important difference in the snowpacks between cover types was observed (figs. 5, 6). A continuous, thin ice sheet had developed in grass plots at the boundary between the depth hoar and metamorphosed snow above. In sagebrush, this feature was non-

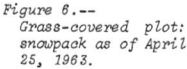

Figure 6.--
Grass-covered plot:
snowpack as of April
25, 1963.

the ice as surface flow. This type of flow would be faster than subsurface flow through saturated soils and, thus, the melt water could reach the stream channels more quickly. Earlier peak flows and incomplete soil moisture recharge could result. Continuous ice sheets within the snowpack could lead to similar results.

Since ice sheets were only observed on grass-covered plots, and since less snow accumulates on grass cover, the conversion of sagebrush areas to grass may understandably have profound effects upon the hydrology of these high-elevation grazing lands. Further study is needed to evaluate the effects of these features upon runoff, streamflow, and soil moisture on larger areas.

Conclusions

1. In areas where induced snow accumulation by topographic configuration is negligible, significantly more snow accumulates in sagebrush-covered areas than in comparable grass-covered areas because of the efficiency of sagebrush crowns in inducing deposition of drifting snow.

2. Continuous layers of ice observed during a considerable portion of the snowmelt period over soil and within the snowpack on grass-covered areas may change the hydrology of high-elevation grazing lands when sagebrush is eradicated.

3. The hydrologic importance of the characteristic melt pattern in sagebrush should be further investigated. The trapping of snow in the depressions after spring snow falls may be important in terms of water yields.

May 1965

U.S. FOREST SERVICE
RESEARCH NOTE RM - 47

FOREST SERVICE
U.S. DEPARTMENT OF AGRICULTURE

Phenology of Grasses of the Northern Arizona Pinyon — Juniper Type

Donald A. Jameson[1]

Phenology of forage plants can be used to predict time of range readiness, to predict amount of forage growth, as a guide to forage quality, and as an aid in designing grazing systems. To provide this information for the pinyon-juniper type in northern Arizona (fig. 1), height and stages of development of several important native grasses were recorded from 1957 to 1960. The five study areas, located 20 to 40 miles north, south, and west of Flagstaff, range in elevation from 5,800 to 6,500 feet, and average annual precipitation from 11 to 20 inches.

rainfall periods (fig. 2). One growth period is characterized by cool-season grasses; the other, by warm-season grasses, (table 1, fig. 3). During the spring growing season, which includes the period from about April 1 to about June 15, cool-season grasses are seasonally dominant. These include mutton bluegrass, prairie Junegrass, bottlebrush squirreltail, and western wheatgrass. These grasses utilize winter and spring precipitation. The summer growing season, which begins about the first week of July and ends

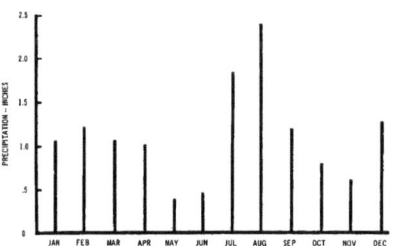

Figure 2.--*Mean monthly precipitation at Ashfork, Arizona, from 1909 to 1953. (from Smith 1956.)*

about September 15, is the time of best growth of blue grama, side-oats grama, spike muhly, and black dropseed. Black grama and galleta usually develop about 1 week earlier than blue grama. The summer growers utilize precipitation that falls from June through September. Periods of growth and maximum development of cool- and warm-season grasses are illustrated in figure 3 and table 1.

Cool-Season Grasses

Cool-season grasses maintained some overwinter greenness, but began active growth between March 10 and April 10 each year. These species are probably of northern origin (Bredemeier 1958, Hartley 1961)[2] and probably have developed in an environment where temperature was the principal factor limiting growth. Some year-to-year growth variation within species was noted during March and early April; less difference was noted from April 10 to May 10. In the following paragraphs the increase in height of each species after April 10 is described.

Mutton Bluegrass

Overwinter green height was about 5 inches. Maximum growth of this species occurred between early April and mid-May. On the average, plants grew 6.5 inches from April 10 to

[2]*Names and dates in parentheses refer to Literature Cited, page 7.*

Table 1.--Time of maximum height and period of green growth of cool- and warm-season grasses

Grasses		Inches	
COOL-SEASON:			
Mutton bluegrass *(Poa fendleriana* (Steud.) Vasey*)*	May 18	16	Yearlong
Prairie Junegrass *(Koeleria cristata* (L.) Pers.*)*	June 18	14	Yearlong
Bottlebrush squirreltail *(Sitanion hystrix* (Nutt.) J.G.Smith*)*	June 22	14	Yearlong
Western wheatgrass *(Agropyron smithii* Rydb.*)*	June 23	13	Mar. 30 - Dec. 1
Average	June 13		
WARM-SEASON:			
Galleta *(Hilaria jamesii* (Torr.) Benth.*)*	Sept. 11	15	Apr. 20 - Nov. 1
Blue grama *(Bouteloua gracilis* (H.B.K.) Lag.*)*	Sept. 12	10	May 20 - Oct. 1
Black grama *(Bouteloua eriopoda* Torr.*)*	Sept. 15	17	May 1 - Oct. 10
Spike muhly *(Muhlenbergia wrightii* Vasey*)*	Sept. 16	13	May 1 - Dec. 1
Black dropseed *(Sporobolus interruptus* Vasey*)*	Sept. 16	18	Apr. 1 - Nov. 10
Side-oats grama *(Bouteloua curtipendula* (Michx.) Torr.*)*	Sept. 21	22	Mar. 30 - Dec. 1
Average	Sept. 15		

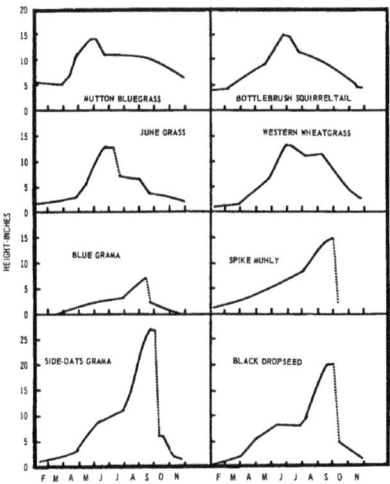

Figure 3.—Growth pattern of grasses 10 miles east of Ashfork, Arizona. Records are based on average maximum height of green leaves of 10 plants of each species measured for 3 to 4 years. Dashed lines indicate rapid drying of tops.

May 10 and another inch by May 20. Although growth of other cool-season grasses was not affected, relatively low temperatures during March 1958[3] evidently retarded development of mutton bluegrass near Ashfork, Arizona, as shown below.

Year	Average March temperature (F)	Average height April 10 (Inches)
1957	43.2	8.2
1958	36.6	5.9
1959	44.2	8.8
1960	46.3	8.0

[3]Temperature interpolated from U. S. Weather Bureau records for Williams and Ashfork, Arizona.

Bottlebrush Squirreltail

Overwinter green height was about 4 inches. This grass on the average grew 2 inches from April 10 to May 10, and another 4 inches by June 10. At some locations growth began in early March.

Prairie Junegrass

Overwinter green height was about 2 inches. Junegrass grew an average of 2 inches between April 10 and May 10. After May 10, growth was highly variable in different years.

Western Wheatgrass

Overwinter green height was about 1 inch. Spring growth of western wheatgrass began in late March. This grass grew an average of 2.5 inches from April 10 to May 10 and another 5 inches by June 10.

Height growth of the cool-season grasses between April 10 and May 10 is reasonably predictable. Squirreltail, western wheatgrass, and Junegrass grew about 1/2 inch a week during this period, and mutton bluegrass about 1-3/4 inches. By adding expected growth to existing growth, the time at which these species will reach a given height can be predicted. For example, if it were desired to begin grazing western wheatgrass when it is 4 inches high, and the height on April 10 was 2 inches, the predicted date of range readiness would be 4 weeks later, or May 8.

Warm-Season Grasses

Leaves and stems of warm-season grasses generally became entirely brown for at least a short period during winter. The apparently dormant period for blue grama, black grama, and galleta is from late November to early March. Black grama, however, will often retain some greenness at the stem nodes over winter, even though its internodes appear completely cured. Side-oats grama, spike muhly, and black dropseed are apparently dormant for about a month during December and January.

Height of warm-season grasses increased at a moderate rate in the spring; growth of most species then decreased and plant heights usually reached a plateau. Leaf height during this period of decreased growth is characteristic of the species:

Species	Height during early summer (Inches)
Blue grama	2-3
Side-oats grama	5-10
Black grama	2-4
Galleta	4-1/2-5-1/2
Black dropseed	7-8

The time at which the rate of growth began to diminish varied with elevation, apparently as a result of differences in temperature. For example, at the two low-elevation stations in this study (average elevation 5,900 feet), blue grama reached 2 inches in height on an average date of April 18. For the three high-elevation plots (average elevation 6,400 feet), the 2-inch level was reached on May 11. The other warm-season grasses began to decline in growth rate at about the same time as blue grama.

The general rate of growth of the warm-season grasses from spring through mid-July is low, particularly after growth rate begins to decrease in May. There will be little apparent difference in the growth stage of these grasses for a period of several weeks during early summer, and there will probably be little difference in the effect on the plan whether grazing begins early in this period semidormancy or late in the period.

In late July or early August, the warm season grasses begin to develop flower stalk and increase rapidly in height (fig. 3). In d) years, however, few flower stalks develop ar plant heights remain much the same as June.

Timing of plant growth corresponds, general, with timing of seasonal precipitatio Rains later than usual may delay growth, b there is good evidence that rains earlier tha usual do not result in earlier growth of warm season grasses. When blue grama seeds we) collected from several locations, planted to gether, and irrigated, the period of growth each collection was closely related to tl summer rainfall pattern at the place of see origin (table 2). This indicates that the peric of growth is at least partly controlled b physiological mechanisms peculiar to part cular grass strains. Strains that have deve oped under a particular rainfall regime hav mechanisms suited to that regime. The gram grasses probably originated in the Southwe: (Fults 1942), and local strains seem admirab suited to the normal Southwestern rainf pattern.

Some strains of grasses, especially sid oats grama, flower during seasons when t days reach a certain length (Olmstead 195

Table 2. --Relationship between growth of blue grama strains and distribution of seasonal precipitation at seed source

Location		Percentage of May-September total by August 1	
Seed source[1]	Weather station[2]	Growth[1]	Precipitation[2]
Great Plains	Scottsbluff, Nebraska	71	70
New Mexico-Texas	Roswell, New Mexico	52	52
Arizona	Natural Bridge, Arizona	40	45

[1] Data from Riegel, 1940. "Great Plains" includes seed from each State from Oklahoma to Montana, but these were averaged here because all showed the same pattern.
[2] Data from U. S. Dept. Agr., 1941. Weather stations were selected where 39- to 40-year records were available near the geographic midpoint of the region represented.

the flowering period is generally such that there are usually favorable moisture conditions in the source locality of the strain. Lavin[4] found that Arizona strains of blue grama were definitely short-day plants, and Olmstead (1952) reported similar findings for side-oats grama. In other words, these plants will not flower until the days get short in late summer.

Data presented by McGinnies and Arnold (939) show a definite periodicity of pounds of dry matter produced by grasses per pound of water consumed. The least efficient time of growth is, on the average, in May and June, and the most efficient time is in August and September.

The periodicity of flowering and water use demonstrates the principles of plant development outlined by Turesson (1931):

> Climate strongly influences the distribution of the biotypes within a species, and one climatic region therefore harbors a distinct biotype group, genotypically different from the biotype group of another region.

This points out the need for using local strains for reseeding.

AMOUNT OF GRASS GROWTH

Since the most variable condition in the environment of plants is amount of available

[4]*Lavin, Fred. Variations in the responses of different geographic strains of blue grama grass to photoperiod. 1953. (Unpublished Ph. D. dissertation on file at Univ. of Chicago.)*

soil moisture, one would expect that amount of grass growth is highly correlated with rainfall. Such is indeed the case, as has been shown several times. Some correlation coefficients between amount of rainfall and production are 0.94 in intermountain desert ranges (Hutchings and Stewart 1953), 0.93 for crested wheatgrass in New Mexico (Pingrey and Dortignac 1959), and 0.86 for a shortgrass range in Alberta (Smoliak 1956). Data reported by Nelson (1934) revealed a correlation coefficient of 0.96 between height growth of black grama and summer precipitation in southern New Mexico. Sneva and Hyder (1962) developed a formula for predicting production of range lands when the bulk of the precipitation falls in the winter, but most of the growth of the range plants occurs in the spring and early summer. Their equation is $Y = 1.11X - 10.6$, where Y is the percent of median forage production and X is the percent of median precipitation for the year. All that is needed to use this formula for a given area is to determine median precipitation and forage production for at least 1 year. The data of Pingrey and Dortignac (1959) apparently fall within the confidence limits of this equation, so it has been independently substantiated.

Relationships between height of cool-season grasses and precipitation in this study were not as clear as reported in the citations above. Heights of squirreltail and western wheatgrass were most closely related to January-March precipitation, while heights of mutton bluegrass and Junegrass were related to February-March precipitation (table 3). Precipitation before January and after April was also compared to height growth of cool-season

Table 3.--Maximum height growth of cool-season grasses and winter precipitation 10 miles east of Ashfork, Arizona

Year	Precipitation period and amounts[1]		Species and heights			
	January-March	February-March	Bottlebrush squirreltail	Western wheatgrass	Mutton bluegrass	Prairie Junegrass
	- - - - - - - - - - - - - - - - - Inches - - - - - - - - - - - - - - -					
1957	7.95	2.22	17.6	17.6	13.2	13.2
1958	6.69	6.28	16.8	15.0	23.0	17.8
1959	3.95	3.62	14.6	11.2	16.6	11.6
1960	4.18	2.44	14.5	10.2	15.4	12.8

[1] Interpolated from U. S. Weather Bureau records at Williams and Ashfork, Arizona.

grasses, but no relationship was apparent. That mutton bluegrass should have a later effective precipitation period than western wheatgrass and squirreltail seems paradoxical, since mutton bluegrass grows earlier than the other species. Arnold (1955) observed that mutton bluegrass made maximum growth when both precipitation and temperature were above normal for January, February, and March. His observation is generally supported by the data collected in this study.

In any event, it seems clear that precipitation before January and after April has little effect on height growth of the cool-season grasses. If the grazing season on these grasses is to be in the late spring and early summer, the amount of available feed is roughly predictable from the mid- to late-winter precipitation.

The growth of warm-season grasses is determined almost entirely from summer precipitation. Since these species are usually grazed during the time of effective precipitation, forage production cannot be predicted. The only help that the phenologic data collected in this study can be to a land manager in this regard is to provide guidelines to anticipate the probable growth a few weeks earlier than it actually occurs. For example, if a shortage of fall feed is apparent by late summer, a livestock operator may decide to advance the fall sale date to compensate for the expected feed shortage. Although summer precipitation-growth relationships could be developed, summer storms are usually very spotty and it would be unusual to have adequate rainfall data from which to predict growth on different parts of a range. For this reason, the approach used here is to predict plant height at the end of the season from growth made earlier in the season.

For blue grama, the earliest possible prediction date was August 15. Effects of dry periods up to August 1 can be offset by rainfall in early August, and, conversely, abundant rainfall in early summer may produce little growth if the late July-early August period is dry. By August 15, however, the growth pattern is fairly well set. Since maximum height of blue grama is attained about September 12, the land manager has about a 4-week lead in estimating total growth for the season. Maximum height at the end of the season will be about 1 inch plus 1-1/2 times the height on August 15 (fig. 4). Although there is some variation from this relationship, it is clear that if there is less than 4 inches of height growth by August 15 there will be less than 7 inches by the end of the season. If there is over 4 inches of height growth by August 15, the final height growth for the season can be 7 to 20 inches.

USE OF PHENOLOGIC DATA IN DESIGNING GRAZING SYSTEMS

In designing a sound grazing system, one should consider development of the important species of the range, particularly those species that are present in less than desired amounts. If warm-season grasses are to be favored, they should be protected from grazing from about July 15 to October 15. On most pinyon-juniper ranges, however, the cool-season grasses are much more in need of protection. The period from about April 10 to July 1 is probably most critical for them. The first parts of spring and summer growth periods are important for growth, and the last parts are important for seed maturation and dissemination. None of the grasses included in this study appear to be especially sensitive to grazing from October 15 to April 10, but repeated use during the winter might result in damage to associated shrubs.

SUMMARY

With a good mixture of grasses, a pinyon-juniper range should supply ample green forage from April 1 to September 30, and some green feed all winter. Phenology and height growth of several important grasses in the pinyon-juniper type near Flagstaff, Arizona, were observed from 1957 to 1960. Cool-season grasses reached peak height between May 18 and June 23, and remained partly green all year. Warm-season grasses were green only during spring, summer, and fall, and reached peak heights between September 11 and September 21.

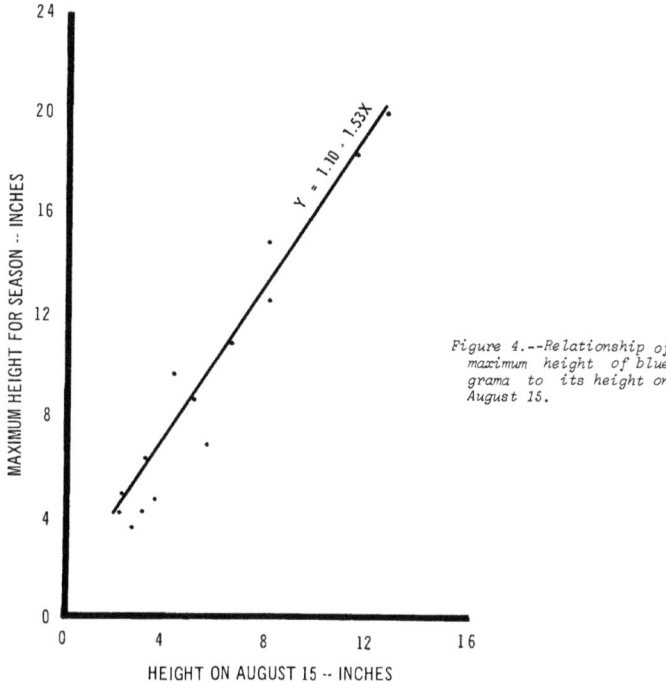

Figure 4.--*Relationship of maximum height of blue grama to its height on August 15.*

The amount of growth of each species is highly variable, and is determined mostly by the precipitation during or a month or two before the period of most active growth of each species. The dates at which certain growth periods occur, on the other hand, are orderly and fairly predictable. Cool-season grasses grow at a nearly uniform rate from April 10 to May 10. Maximum height of blue grama can be predicted 4 weeks before the maximum occurs.

Grazing systems should be designed to allow occasional rest for both cool- and warm-season grasses during their growth periods. Three periods should be recognized: "summer", July 10 to October 15; "winter", October 15 to April 10; and "spring", April 10 to July 10. Because of differences in time of peak development of important grasses, forage production measurements should be taken in June for cool-season species and in September for warm-season species. For most of the pinyon-juniper type, cool-season grasses need more protection than warm-season grasses.

LITERATURE CITED

Arnold, Joseph F.
    1955. Plant life-form classification and its use in evaluating range conditions and trend. Jour. Range Mangt. 8: 176-181, illus.

Bredemeier, Lorenz F.
    1958. Measurement of time and rate of growth of range plants with applications in range management. Jour. Range Mangt. 11: 119-122, illus.

Fults, J. L.
    1942. Somatic chromosome complements in Bouteloua. Amer. Jour. Bot. 29: 45-55.

Hartley, W.
    1961. Studies on the origin, evolution, and distribution of the Gramineae. IV. The genus Poa L. Austral. Jour. Bot. 9: 152-161. (Biol. Abst. 39: 12542.)

Hutchings, S. S., and Stewart, G.
    1953. Increasing forage yields and sheep production on intermountain winter ranges. U.S. Dept. Agr. Cir. 925, 63 pp.

McGinnies, W. G., and Arnold, Joseph F.
    1939. Relative water requirement of Arizona range plants. Ariz. Agr. Expt. Sta. Tech. Bul. 80: 167-246, illus.

Nelson, Enoch W.
    1934. The influence of precipitation and grazing upon black grama grass range. U.S. Dept. Agr. Tech. Bul. 409, 32 pp., illus.

Olmstead, C. E.
    1952. Photoperiodism in native range grasses. Sixth Internatl. Grassland Cong. Proc. 1952: 676-682.

Pingrey, H. B., and Dortignac, E. J.
    1959. Economic evaluation of seeding crested wheatgrass on northern New Mexico rangeland. N. Mex. Agr. Expt. Sta. Bul. 433, 80 pp., illus.

Smoliak, S.
    1956. Influence of climatic conditions on forage production of shortgrass rangeland. Jour. Range Mangt. 9: 89-91, illus.

Sneva, Forrest A., and Hyder, D. N.
    1962. Estimating herbage production on semiarid ranges in the Intermountain region. Jour. Range Mangt. 15: 88-93, illus.

Turesson, G.
    1931. The selective effect of climate upon the plant species. Hereditas 14: 99-152.

Acorn Yield of Gambel Oak in Northern Arizona

C. Y. McCulloch, O. C. Wallmo, and P. F. Ffolliott [1]

The acorns of Gambel oak (Quercus gambelii Nutt.) periodically provide quantities of food for deer, elk, squirrels, turkeys, and other wildlife in the forests of the Southwest. While the species currently has little commercial value for wood products, it is important for wildlife.

Acorn production by Gambel oak was studied cooperatively by the Arizona Game and Fish Department [2] and the Rocky Mountain Forest and Range Experiment Station on the Beaver Creek watersheds [3] in northern Arizona. The results suggest guides for acorn production in this area.

Methods

From 1958 to 1963, acorn production was sampled annually. The sampling areas were approximately 30 miles south-southeast of Flagstaff in the ponderosa pine type, on relatively uniform sites between 6,500 and 7,000 feet elevation. A total of 94 trees was selected within a radius of 3 miles, to represent the existing range of diameter classes (2 to 20 inches d.b.h.). Five vigor classes, based on ocular estimate of percent of live crown, were arbitrarily recognized in the field: A, 80-100; B, 60-79; C, 40-59; D, 20-39; and E, 0-19. When mean acorn yield for the 6-year period was analyzed, however, there were only three apparently different vigor classes among the original five crown-vigor categories: I, at least 80 percent of the crown alive; II, 40-79 percent live crown; and III, less than 40 percent live crown (tables 1).

Data taken on each tree included diameter, crown area (length times width), percent of live crown as an index of vigor, and occurrence of heart rot as determined from increment borings.

Prior to the acorn drop each year, one trap (a square 3.93 sq. ft. in area covered with 1-inch mesh wire) was placed under each of the 94 trees. The traps, supported with a permanent stake, were left in place until all acorns had fallen. The total number of acorns collected in each trap over the 6-year sampling period was considered representative of acorn yield from each tree.

Results

The 6-year sample included 3 years of heavy production (1958, 1961, and 1963), 2

---

[1] *Authors are, respectively, Research Biologist, Arizona Game and Fish Department, Phoenix, Arizona, and Wildlife Biologist and Associate Silviculturist, Rocky Mountain Forest and Range Experiment Station, Flagstaff. Station central headquarters are located at Fort Collins, in cooperation with Colorado State University.*
[2] *Under Federal Aid Project W-78-R; the study was initiated by Robert A. Jantzen who was formerly attached to Project W-78-R and whose efforts are gratefully acknowledged.*
[3] *A 275,000-acre watershed on the Coconino National Forest where costs and benefits of intensive multiple-use land management are being evaluated as a part of the Arizona Watershed Program.*

Table 1.—Distribution of Gambel oak acorn production sample, and derivation of recognized vigor classes from field data

Original (field) vigor class	Live crown	Trees	Mean[1] acorn yield	Final vigor class	Live crown	Distribution of trees by size class (inches d.b.h.)									
						2	4	6	8	10	12	14	16	18	20	Total
	Percent	Number	Number		Percent	Number
A	80-100	37	29.9	I	80-100	11	7	2	5	5	3	2	1	1	0	37
B	60- 79	11	19.5	II	40- 79	3	4	4	2	2	4	0	1	1	2	23
C	40- 59	12	19.2													
D	20- 39	12	8.0	III	0- 39	5	3	3	4	7	7	2	1	1	1	34
E	0- 20	22	8.3													
Total		94				19	14	9	11	14	14	4	3	3	3	94

[1] Mean of 6-year total catch of acorns per trap.

years of low production (1959 and 1962), and 1 year of no production (1960). Acorn yield was related to diameter classes within vigor classes to develop the curves shown in figure 1.

Healthy Gambel oak (vigor class I) attained maximum acorn yield in the range of 12 to 14 inches d.b.h., after which productivity fell rapidly. Maximum yield of trees with 40-70 percent live crown (vigor class II) occurred at 11 to 13 inches d.b.h., but was only equivalent to the yield of more vigorous trees at 6 to 7 inches d.b.h. Maximum yield of trees with less than 40 percent live crown (vigor class III) occurred at 8 to 10 inches d.b.h., but was only equal to the yield of vigor class I and II at 3 to 4 inches d.b.h.

While it might be expected that larger trees in vigor class I would be high producers of acorns, few trees live to large size in a vigorous condition in this area. Perhaps the larger trees in the sample were decadent, although it was not apparent in the condition of the crown.

Heart rot caused by *Polyporus dryophilus* is common in Gambel oak in the Southwest,[4] but no relationship between incidence of heart rot and acorn yield was found in the area where this study was conducted.

Conclusions

For wildlife benefits, forest management practices should aim at maximum acorn production, but in the interest of timber benefits, unproductive Gambel oak trees should be eliminated.

If removal of Gambel oak is necessary to meet other objectives of forest management, sacrifice trees with less than 80 percent of the crown alive (vigor classes II and III) and trees over 15 inches in diameter regardless of vigor. Save all Gambel oak trees with 80 percent or more of the crown alive (vigor class I) up to 15 inches d.b.h.; smaller diameter classes will provide growing stock to maintain acorn yield.

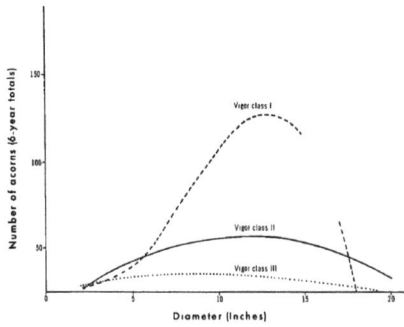

Figure 1.—*Gambel oak mast production by vigor class and diameter (based on the average number of acorns caught per trap for a diameter class).*

[4] Hedgcock, G. G., and Long, W. H. Heart-rot in oaks and poplars caused by Polyporus dryophilus. Jour. Agr. Res. 3: 65-77. 1914.

Reduction of Litter and Shrub Crowns by Planned Fall Burning of Oak-Mountainmahogany Chaparral

C. P. Pase and George E. Glendening [1]

Burning during periods of low-fire hazard appears to offer promise as a means of altering the density, stature and, to some extent, composition of chaparral stands in central Arizona. Fall burning in particular permits one winter and spring growing period to elapse before high-intensity summer rains occur. This greatly reduces risk of excessive soil movement.

A study on the Sierra Ancha Experimental Forest near Globe, Arizona, has provided some preliminary data on litter and crown reduction by such planned fall burning (fig. 1). The study area is in chaparral type composed of shrub live oak (Quercus turbinella Greene) and true mountainmahogany (Cercocarpus montanus Raf.) at an elevation of 5,300 feet. Annual rainfall at Sierra Ancha headquarters,

Figure 1.--This extensive topkill resulted when treated chaparral was burned during low-hazard conditions.

3/4 mile east and 200 feet below the study area, averages 24.98 inches. Summer rainfall for the 4-month period preceding burning was 7.87 inches in 1961 and 2.07 inches in 1962. This represents 92.6 and 24.4 percent of the long-time average, respectively.

Shrubs were dried prior to burning.--Shrubs were chemically desiccated to permit burning when fire would not ordinarily penetrate into untreated, high-moisture-content vegetation. Treatment was applied on 50-, 100-, and 200-foot wide strips, respectively, on three small drainages. The strips were run generally on the contour. Those designated for burning in September 1961 were sprayed by helicopter with 3 pounds of Dinoxol[2] in 10 gallons of diesel oil per acre, 6 weeks prior to burning.

On the 1962 strips, 4 weeks prior to the September burning, a mist blower was used to apply 1.5 pounds of Dinoxol in 10 gallons of diesel oil per acre. Little difference in final leaf-drying effects was noted as a result of the change in method of application and reduced dosage. Moisture content of heavily treated shrub live oak leaves on the sprayed strips dropped to 11.0 and 12.9 percent in 1961 and 1962, respectively, while the moisture content of untreated leaves was 90.5 and 93.8 percent.

Litter reduction varied with burning conditions.--Less than one-third of the litter was actually consumed by the September 1961 burn, while approximately half was burned in September 1962:

	1961	1962
Litter:		
Preburn tons per acre	6.8	4.6
Percent reduction	28.6	51.1
Shrub canopy:		
Percent preburn	60.8	67.1
Percent reduction	92.6	94.5

Nevertheless, in 1961 the fire was hot enough to topkill most of the shrubs (fig. 1). The greater litter and crown reduction in 1962 may have resulted from the higher burning conditions that year:

	1961	1962
Relative humidity, percent	41-62	28-42
Air temperature, degrees	65-73	77-93
Drought index	57 (low)	87 (high)
Rate of spread	5-10 (low)	10 (low)

[1] *Plant Ecologist and Research Forester, respectively, located at Tempe, in cooperation with Arizona State University; central headquarters are maintained at Fort Collins, in cooperation with Colorado State University. Glendening passed away December 30, 1963.*

[2] *"Dinoxol" is a mixture of 2 lbs. per gallon (acid equiv.) each, of the butoxy ethanol esters of 2,4-D and 2,4,5-T. It is produced by the Amchem Corporation of Ambler, Pa. Trade names and company names are used for the benefit of the reader and do not imply endorsement or preferential treatment by the U. S. Department of Agriculture.*

The Mechanism of Fenuron Injury to Plants[1]

Edwin A. Davis[2]

Fenuron (3-phenyl-1,1-dimethylurea), like other substituted phenylurea herbicides, is absorbed by plant roots and is transported upwards to the leaves where its major toxic action occurs (Minshall 1954, Muzik et al., 1954).[3] The substituted phenylurea herbicides are potent inhibitors of photosynthesis that block a reaction concerned with the production of oxygen (Bishop 1958, Cooke 1956, Spikes 1956, Wessels and van der Veen 1956). It has been proposed that the toxic symptoms produced by these chemicals are primarily a result of the lack of photosynthate brought about by the action of the chemicals (Gentner and Hilton 1960). It is true that in the absence of photosynthesis, starvation would result with the accompanying development of visible injury. But a blocked photosynthetic reaction might also be a direct rather than an indirect cause of injury.

The acorn of shrub live oak constitutes a sizable reservoir of foodstuff for the developing seedling. Consequently, if the hypothesis that visible leaf injury is the direct result of starvation is correct, young seedlings should not become visibly injured until the reserves in the acorns are exhausted. Bathing the acorns in glucose solution should then postpone starvation and further delay the onset of injury symptoms. Also, it would be expected that seedlings whose acorns had been excised would be injured soon after treatment, whereas seedlings with intact acorns would not develop injury symptoms until the acorn reserves were exhausted.

One objective of the experiments reported here was to evaluate the hypothesis that visible leaf injury from fenuron treatments is due directly to starvation. Additional objectives were to determine the influence of fenuron on root growth of shrub live oak seedlings, and to relate root growth to shoot injury.

Materials and Methods

Large acorns, collected from a single tree, were germinated on moist vermiculite. The acorns measured about 2.4 cm. long and 1.3 cm. wide. After germination started, acorns with radicles 2-4 cm. long were placed on squares of 1/4-inch mesh hardware cloth on top of wide-mouth quart jars capped with aluminum foil. The radicles projected through the hardware cloth and aluminum foil, and extended into Hoagland's nutrient solution with or without the addition of fenuron. The nutrient solutions were aerated continuously. The acorns were covered with a pad of absorbent packing paper kept moist with distilled water. The nutrient solutions contained 0, 5, and 25 p.p.m. fenuron.[4] There were seven seedlings for each treatment.

Root lengths were measured initially and then at intervals during the experiment. Root growth was calculated by difference. The initial heights of the shoots were recorded as zero, since the primary root grows to a considerable length before the shoot emerges.

Injury to the shoots was estimated as percent leaf injury. The development of new growth flushes was observed, and injury to each flush was recorded separately.

Results

Shoot growth was not inhibited for the first 71 days by 5 and 25 p.p.m. fenuron, whereas root growth was markedly inhibited by 25 p.p.m. fenuron. The 5 p.p.m. solution of fenuron affected root growth much less severely than the 25 p.p.m. solution during the first 50 days, after which root growth gradually ceased as leaf injury increased in severity. Root growth inhibition by 25 p.p.m. fenuron began before shoots emerged and, therefore, before the appearance of visible damage to the leaves. Although root growth was retarded by 25 p.p.m. fenuron, the roots continued to grow for 24 days after the appearance of leaf injury and while the injury increased in severity, which indicates that leaf injury occurred before the energy supply of the seedlings was exhausted. After 29 days, some of the plants treated with 25 p.p.m. fenuron developed moderate to severe leaf injury despite the fact that the food reserves of the acorns were not exhausted, as indicated by a positive starch iodine test. In an attempt to prevent injury to other seedlings, acorns of some uninjured seedlings were bathed in 5 percent glucose solution. The original sets of leaves of the glucose-fed plants and their controls were killed at about the same rate, however. Although feeding glucose through the acorns of fenuron-treated seedlings did not prevent the development of leaf injury, it prolonged the life of the seedlings by supplying energy for additional flushes of growth, all of which became injured and died.

Leaf-feeding of glucose also was attempted as a method of preventing visible injury by fenuron. Untreated leaves of both glucose leaf-fed and distilled water control plants were killed, and injury to both progressed at the same rate.

In another experiment, injury to young seedlings with and without acorns was compared. Excision of the acorns of control seedlings did not reduce root growth; the shoots were capable of supplying adequate nourishment for growth. But excision of the acorns of fenuron-treated seedlings reduced root growth drastically. Leaves of the initial flush of growth of fenuron-treated seedlings with or without acorns were killed. Acorns prolonged the life of fenuron-treated seedlings by providing foodstuff for new flushes of growth but did not prevent leaf injury, whereas fenuron-treated seedlings without acorns failed to produce new growth.

Discussion

The hypothesis on which this study was based is that visible leaf injury resulting from fenuron treatments is due directly to the depletion of the energy supply of the plant as a result of inhibited photosynthesis. This

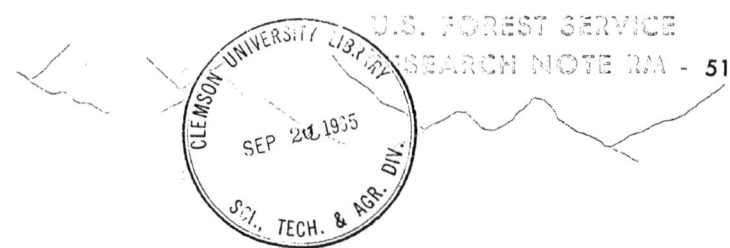

Explorations in the Germination of Sedges

W. M. Johnson,[1] J. O. Blankenship [2] and G. R. Brown [1]

There are 101 species of sedges (Carex spp.) known to occur in Wyoming. They grow on a wide variety of sites: some are found on the driest plains, while others grow in aquatic conditions. They can be found from the lowest to the highest elevations. Sedges as a group produce most of the palatable forage for game and domestic livestock on alpine and subalpine ranges in Wyoming.[3] In spite of their importance, very little is known about the ecology or physiology of the sedges. To manage rangelands wisely, especially at higher elevations, it is necessary to understand some of the basic factors involved in the reproduction and growth of the sedges. This paper reports the results of germination tests of several species of sedges as follows: under greenhouse conditions in petri dishes, from October 1962 to May 1963, with 27 species; a special test of C. raynoldsii, which was eliminated from analysis in the first test because of poor germination; and in the greenhouse in sand cultures, from February 22 to March 28, 1963, with 4 species.

---

[1] *Principal Plant Ecologist and Range Research Technician, respectively, located at Laramie, in cooperation with the University of Wyoming; central headquarters are maintained at Fort Collins, in cooperation with Colorado State University.*
[2] *Graduate Student at the University of Wyoming, Laramie, Wyoming.*
[3] *Johnson, W. M. 1962. Vegetation of high altitude ranges in Wyoming as related to use by game and domestic sheep. Wyo. Agr. Expt. Sta. Bul. 387, 31 pp.*

Literature

Literature dealing with the germination of sedges is rare. Bliss[4] reports 6.2 percent germination of arctic seed of C. bigelowii and 2.7 percent germination of C. aquatilis in light between moist filter papers. No germination was obtained in the dark. In another test of seed from alpine areas in Wyoming, no germination was obtained in either light or dark for C. aquatilis, C. drummondiana, or C. scopulorum, the only sedges tested. Of 99 species of flowering plants from Greenland tested by Sorensen in 1941,[5] seeds of 62 species germinated. Nearly half of those which did not germinate belonged to the sedge family. Comes[6] tested one lot of seed of C. aquatilis; he obtained no germination when blotters were moistened with distilled water, but 85 percent germination in 10 days when moistened with a 0.2 percent solution of potassium nitrate at 68°-85°F. Lee[7] germinated excised embryos of Carex lurida Wehl, C. stipata Muhl, and C. scoparia Schk. in culture mediums, and improved root and shoot growth

---

[4] *Bliss, L. C. 1958. Seed germination in arctic and alpine species. Jour. Arctic Inst. of N. Amer. 11: 180-188.*
[5] *Original article by Sorenson not available; quoted from Bliss (see footnote 4).*
[6] *Personal communication with Pichard Comes, 1962.*
[7] *Lee, Addison E. 1952. The growth of excised immature sedge embryos in culture. Torrey Bot. Club Bul. 79: 59-62.*

by adding sucrose to the medium. Rostrup[8] found that seeds of Carex paniculata planted in March, April, or May germinated the following spring. If they were planted as late as June, a second winter was needed for good germination.

The scanty literature available indicates that natural germination of Carex may be very low, and that inducing greater germination may be difficult. Sedges do germinate in nature, however, as evidenced by the prompt invasion of some species along road fills and other disturbed areas.

Methods

Germination was tested under greenhouse conditions in petri dishes. Four replications of 25 seeds were used for each species in each treatment:

1. Control: seed placed on germinating paper, moistened as needed with distilled water, and subjected to existing periods of natural light and darkness in a greenhouse.
2. Continuous darkness: same as control, except seeds placed between two sheets of heavy, blue germinating paper to exclude light.
3. 24-hour cold: seed stored in moist cold (refrigerator) at 34°-38°F., otherwise same as control.
4. 7-day cold: same as above except for length of storage period.
5. 30-day cold: same as treatment 3 except for length of storage period.
6. 90-day cold: same as treatment 3 except for length of storage period.
7. Sulfuric acid (H_2SO_4): seed soaked for 5 minutes in 95 percent sulfuric acid before being placed in petri dishes.
8. Potassium nitrate (KNO_3): same as control except moisture source was a 0.2 percent solution of potassium nitrate.
9. Hydrogen peroxide (H_2O_2): same as control except moisture source was a 1.0 percent solution of hydrogen peroxide.

[8]Rostrup, D. 1899-1900. Hvilken indflydelse har tidspunktit for spiringsforsøgets indledning paa spiringen forbob og spirvnens storrelse. Dansk frønkontrol. 1899-1900: 30-32.

10. Soil leachate: same as control except moisture source was a leachate obtained by soaking alpine soil in distilled water. A perforated 1-gallon can was three-quarters filled with top soil from the alpine zone of the Snowy Range. Distilled water was added and the percolate caught from the bottom of the can.
11. Sand scarification: seed placed in a bottle of coarse sand and shaken on a Burrell wrist-action shaker for 30 minutes before being placed in petri dishes.
12. Scarification plus leachate: a combination of treatments 10 and 11 (assumed to more nearly approach conditions of nature).
13. Leaching: seed washed for 24 hours in running tap water before being placed in petri dishes.

Greenhouse temperatures were controlled at 60°-70°F. at night and 70°-80°F. during the day. Trials were observed for a period of about 60 days.

All seeds used were collected during the summer of 1962 from alpine and subalpine zones in Wyoming. Seed was available for:
1. C. albo-nigra Mack.
2. C. aquatilis Wahl.
3. C. athrostachya Olney
4. C. atrata L.
5. C. chalciolepis Holm.
6. C. ebenea Rydb.
7. C. egglestonii Mack.
8. C. epapillosa Mack.
9. C. hoodii Boott
10. C. illota Bailey
11. C. kelloggii Boott
12. C. lanuginosa Michx.
13. C. limnophila Hermann
14. C. media R. Br.
15. C. microptera Mack.
16. C. nebraskensis Dewey
17. C. nelsonii Mack.
18. C. nova Bailey
19. C. petasata Dewey
20. C. phaeocephala Piper
21. C. physocarpa Presl.
22. C. praegracilis Boott
23. C. pseudoscirpoidea Rydb.
24. C. raynoldsii Dewey
25. C. rostrata Stokes
26. C. scopulorum Holm.
27. C. tolmiei Boott.

The germination trials began in October 1962 and terminated in May 1963. Not enough seed of all species was available for all treatments. For this reason, four separate studies were made involving different species and different treatments. A randomized complete block design was used for all trials.

Results

Two of the most notable results of these trials were the extreme variability in germination between the species, and the variability in the response of the species to different germination treatments. Some species failed to germinate, while others showed almost complete germination. Nine species either did not germinate at all or germination was so low regardless of the treatments applied that they were not included in the analyses. These were:

C. aquatilis   C. pseudoscirpoidea
C. lanuginosa   C. raynoldsii
C. media   C. rostrata
C. physocarpa   C. scopulorum
C. praegracilis

Treatment Effects

Some of the treatments proved to be ineffective, and in some cases actually reduced germination when compared with the distilled water control. Seed placed between heavy, blue germination paper (complete darkness) either failed to germinate at all or germination was drastically reduced. Seed stored in refrigerators for 90 days germinated less than the control, in most cases, and always less than seed similarly stored for shorter periods of time. The sulfuric acid and hydrogen peroxide treatments prevented or drastically reduced germination. These four treatments were later abandoned and results were not included in the analyses.

None of the eight treatments tested statistically were consistently successful in increasing germination. Some had both positive and negative effects, depending upon the species being tested. One treatment (sand scarification) had no effect on germination of any of the three species so treated (table 1).

Table 1.--A summary of treatment effects in relation to distilled water control on the germination of Carex seed

Treatment	Species tested	Germination-- Increased		Reduced		No effect	
	No.	No.	Pct.	No.	Pct.	No.	Pct.
24-hour cold	16	5	31	3	19	8	50
7-day cold	18	5	28	1	6	12	66
30-day cold	11	1	10	5	45	5	45
Potassium nitrate	13	3	23	2	15	8	62
Soil leachate	13	2	15	0	0	11	85
Sand scarification	3	0	00	0	0	3	100
Scarification plus leachate	3	2	67	0	0	1	33
Tap water leaching	16	1	6	2	13	13	81

The combination treatment of sand scarification with the soil leachate as a moisture source significantly increased the germination on two out of three species tested, however, but the germination of one of these species was increased a similar amount by the soil leachate treatment alone (table 2).

The cold treatments gave variable results (table 2). In comparison with the control, the 7-day cold treatment stimulated germination of 5 species, had 1 negative effect, and did not change the germination of 12 species. The 24-hour cold treatment stimulated germination of 5 species, retarded 3 species, and had no effect on 8 species. In contrast, the 30-day cold period produced only 1 positive effect, had a negative effect on 5 species, and had no effect on 5 other species. Reasons for this variability are not clear, but it would appear that long periods of cold (the 30-day period in the analysis and the 90-day period not analyzed because of its definite negative effect on germination) are not needed for germination of the sedges used in this study.

The use of potassium nitrate as a source of moisture in germination trials produced results similar to the shorter cold treatments: there were 3 positive effects, 2 negative effects, and 8 species were not affected.

The soil leachate treatment increased germination of 2 species of sedge. The leachate was not analyzed, however, so the causative factor or factors are unknown.

Table 2. --Average germination of 25 seeds of each Carex species as related to treatment

Species and test[1]	Treatments							
	Control	24-hour cold	7-day cold	30-day cold	Potassium nitrate	Soil leachate	Sand scarification	Tap water leaching
	Number							
TEST NO. 1:								
C. egglestonii	22.3	22.8	21.5	23.3	11.5	21.5	21.8	22.5
C. atrata	2.0	1.5	2.8	3.5	4.3	5.0	7.8	.5
C. ebenea	13.3	21.0	19.8	24.0	5.3	21.8	22.3	24.5
TEST NO. 2:								
C. nebraskensis	6.5	6.0	9.0	1.3	5.5	4.3		3.3
C. microptera	18.5	18.0	17.3	14.5	17.3	20.8		19.3
C. phaeocephala	16.3	21.5	20.8	16.5	20.5	19.0		18.8
C. chalciolepis	4.0	3.5	7.8	.8	6.5	5.0		2.8
C. epapillosa	5.0	6.8	5.5	0.0	5.5	6.0		4.8
C. hoodii	4.8	1.3	4.8	0.0	5.3	2.5		3.5
C. limnophila	20.8	25.0	22.0	0.0	21.5	23.3		22.3
C. nova	.5	0.0	0.0	.3	7.5	.8		.5
TEST NO. 3:								
C. illota	17.8	11.5	0.0					0.0
C. tolmiei	3.0	6.5	4.0					.3
C. kelloggii	.8	.8	1.8					0.0
C. petasata	1.8	5.3	4.0					.5
C. albo-nigra	2.0	0.0	.5					.5
TEST NO. 4:								
C. nelsonii	4.8		12.5		15.5	17.3		
C. athrostachya	.5		2.5		.3	.3		

[1] Least significant difference at .05 for each test No. 1 = 5.6, No. 2 = 3.4, No 3 = 2.0 No. 4 = 5.4.
[2] Underling indicates the species means that differed significantly from the control.

Leaching seed with running tap water was not an effective germination treatment.

Species Germination

Of the 27 species of sedge tested, only 5 can be considered to germinate well, either naturally or by one of the treatments tested (table 3). These are C. ebenea, C. egglestonii, C. limnophila, C. microptera and C. phaeocephala. All germinated between 80 and 100 percent. Both C. ebenea and C. egglestonii appear to germinate readily under almost any conditions. Three-year-old seed of these species has germinated as well as new seed. Seed collected from plants grown in the greenhouse, harvested at maturity, and tested immediately have consistently germinated between 90 and 100 percent. Two other species, C. illota and C. nelsonii, germinated fairly well, but for all others germination was less than 40 percent.

Special Tests of C. raynoldsii

Out of the group of nine species which were eliminated from the analysis because of very

Table 3. --Maximum germination of Carex seeds and treatment responsible

Species	Germination--	
C. aquatilis	0	--
C. albo-nigra	8	Control
C. athrostachya	10	7-day cold
C. atrata	31	Scarification plus leachate
C. chalciolepis	31	7-day cold
C. ebenea	98	Tap water leaching
C. egglestonii	93	30-day cold
C. epapillosa	27	24-hour cold
C. hoodii	21	Potassium nitrate
C. illota	71	Control
C. kelloggii	7	7-day cold
C. lanuginosa	0	--
C. limnophila	100	24-hour cold
C. media	5	24-hour cold
C. microptera	83	Soil leachate
C. nebraskensis	36	7-day cold
C. nelsonii	69	Soil leachate
C. nova	30	Potassium nitrate
C. petasata	21	24-hour cold
C. phaeocephala	86	24-hour cold
C. physocarpa	1	7-day cold
C. praegracilis	0	--
C. pseudoscirpoidea	0	--
C. raynoldsii	3	Cutting seed coat
C. rostrata	0	--
C. scopulorum	2	Control
C. tolmiei	26	24-hour cold

[1] Based on mean germination without regard to significance between treatments (see table 2).

oor germination, C. raynoldsii was selected or special supplementary testing. The same eneral conditions were involved, but the reatments applied to the seed were:
. Seed soaked in 95 percent solution of sulfuric acid for 30 minutes.
. Seed soaked in 95 percent solution of sulfuric acid for 45 minutes.
. Seed coat cut with razor blade.
. Seed scarified with sand for 3-1/2 hours.

ll of these treatments were designed to eaken the rather hard seed coat of this pecies. The 30-minute soaking in sulfuric cid dissolved the perigynia but left the seed oat hard. The 45-minute soaking softened the eed coat on most seeds but some were still rm. The 3-1/2-hour scarification appeared o do little except wear away the perigynia. utting the seed coat did reveal that the mbryo appeared to be alive and should be iable, but no viability tests were made.

No germination occurred in any treatment xcept where the seed coat was cut. In 45 ays, 3 percent of the seed germinated. This idicates that future treatments should be ased on destruction of the seed coat.

Rate of Germination

The rate of germination of sedge seed was as variable between species as was total germination. For example, seeds of C. microptera in the control treatment germinated very rapidly (fig. 1). Germination started on the 12th day and was finished by the 23rd day of the test. C. ebenea, on the other hand, began germinating on the 9th day and did not stop until the 31st day. C. egglestonii began rapid germination similar to C. microptera (but earlier, on the 9th day), slowed down during the middle of the test, then germinated very rapidly again between the 24th and 31st day. There was no further germination. C. epapillosa, at the low extreme, started germination late and continued to germinate very slowly until it stopped. Germination rates of other species were within the extremes illustrated.

Some treatments appeared to stimulate the rate of germination greatly, but again this varied between species. In some cases the treatments produced immediate and rapid germination, as was the case with the 30-day cold storage treatment in C. egglestonii (fig. 2).

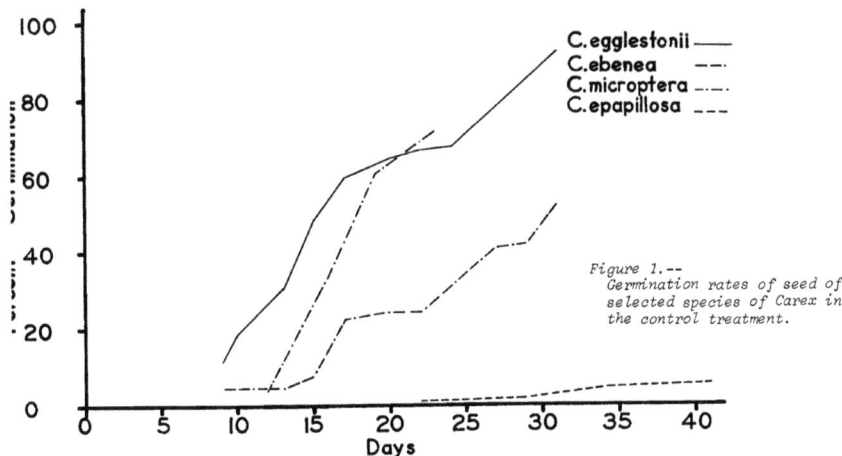

Figure 1.--
Germination rates of seed of selected species of Carex in the control treatment.

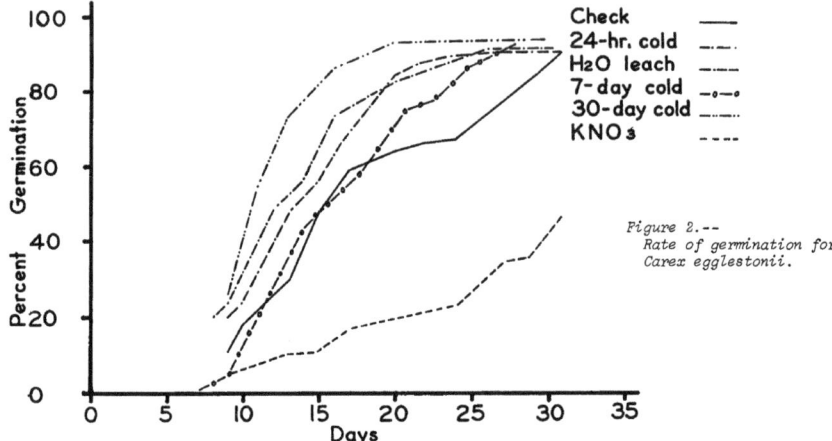

Figure 2.-- Rate of germination for Carex egglestonii.

With this treatment, germination was very rapid between the 9th and 20th days, and was complete at a much higher level than the control at that time. For this species, the tap-water leaching and 24-hour cold treatments had a similar effect. Although none of these treatments increased final germination of this species, they did affect the rate of germination.

Germination in Sand Culture

In still another germination trial, conducted February 22 to March 28, 1963, seeds of four sedge species were planted in sand (with the exception of the water-culture treatment) in waxed paper containers with perforated bottoms. The containers were placed in a tray to which tap water was supplied to maintain soil moisture. During this eight-treatment experiment (table 4), temperature in the greenhouse ranged from 70° to 80° F.; relative humidity and photoperiod were not controlled.

After germination began, containers were observed daily for a 25-day period. A seed was considered germinated when a shoot appeared above the surface of the sand. Except on cloudy days, the blocks of treatments were shaded with paper to reduce evaporation. The paper was elevated so light was not excluded.

First emergence was observed 10 days after planting. The number of plants germinating per day varied from 1 the first day of germination to 55 on the 16th day. C. ebenea and C. egglestonii germinated well, but less than in the previous experiment with petri dishes; C. hoodii and C. nova did not germinate or respond appreciably to any treatment (table 4).

Discussion and Summary

The problem of breaking dormancy in sedge seed is not simple. Each of the species studied seems to be an entity in itself. No single treatment can be listed as effective for all species. Nor can it be said that all species will germinate well or poorly. The study has indicated, however, that some treatments seem to be more generally effective than others. Some of the conclusions that might be drawn from the study are:

1. Light seems to be necessary for good germination. This is evidenced by the very

Table 4.--Percent germination of four species under eight treatments in a sand culture, and comparison of response of C. ebbenea and C. egglestonii[1]

Treatment	Percent germination of--				Comparison of response of C. ebenea and C. egglestonii[1]
	C. ebenea	C. egglestonii	C. hoodii	C. nova	
Control water only	25	23	0	1	No difference between species, but much lower than in the petri dish experiment
Wetting agents (chemical solutions in place of water for 10 days, then distilled water used):[2]					
Potassium nitrate (0.2% solution)	60	29	1	1	Appreciable increase in germination of C. ebenea but no effect on C. egglestonii
Hydrogen peroxide (1.0% solution)	43	62	1	0	Appreciable increase in germination of both species, in direct contrast to results in the petri dish experiment
Seed subjected to cold period (0°F.) prior to planting:					
24 hours	25	16	0	6	No effect on C. ebenea, decreased germination of C. egglestonii
7 days	31	12	0	0	Slight increase in germination of C. ebenea; decrease in C. egglestonii
Seed soaked in chemical solution for 1 hour prior to planting:					
Potassium nitrate (0.2% solution)	54	11	2	0	Germination doubled for C. ebenea, reduced by approximately 50 percent for C. egglestonii
Hydrogen peroxide (1.0% solution)	24	12	1	1	Germination not affected for C. ebenea, reduced 50 percent for C. egglestonii
Water culture (seed placed on blotter in container, no cover, this treatment most similar to petri dish experiment)	77	89	0	4	Germination increased for both species, reasonably comparable to results in petri dishes
Species mean	42.37	31.75	.62	1.62	

[1] C. hoodii and C. nova not compared, neither species germinated nor responded appreciably to any treatment.
[2] Containers placed in impermeable saucers to prevent chemicals contaminating the tap water in the tray.

low germination of seed placed between layers of heavy, blue germination paper, which can be considered complete absence of light. Also, the germination of seed covered by one-fourth inch of sand was much lower than that of seed of the same species in petri dishes exposed to diurnal light fluctuation. Subsequent studies of growth of C. ebenea and C. egglestonii in soil media have shown lower germination rates than were obtained in the petri dishes. Bliss[4] also observed the importance of light in germination of sedge seeds.

2. Chemical treatments to break dormancy gave highly variable and, in some instances, conflicting results. Sulfuric acid treatments cannot be recommended. Thin-walled achenes so treated were very rapidly consumed in many cases. For thick, hard walled achenes such as C. raynoldsii, the treatment was not effective.

3. Hydrogen peroxide as a moisture source decreased germination in petri dishes, but did appear to stimulate germination in sand cultures. Reasons for this are not obvious. As a scarifying agent (seed soaked for 1 hour before planting), hydrogen peroxide had no stimulating effect on germination.

4. Germination of seeds treated with potassium nitrate as a moisture source was highly variable, depending upon species. Exceptionally good results were obtained on some species in the petri dish experi-

ment. C. ebenea responded well in both the petri dish and sand culture studies; C. egglestonii did not respond in either study, and germination was actually inhibited in the petri dishes.

5. Surprisingly, the soil leachate appeared to stimulate germination in two cases. Just what factor from the soil is responsible for this stimulus is not known. It does indicate that sedge germination in natural habitats could be expected, and that nature provides her own stimuli.

6. Mechanical seedcoat scarification with sand did not increase germination, but the combination of sand scarification plus soil leachate as a moisture source was effective. This again indicates that natural conditions of the habitat provide some stimulation.

7. Cold treatments to break dormancy have variable effects on germination. Long periods (90 days) of cold storage have little effect on germination, and at least for some species may actually inhibit germination. Cold storage for intermediate or short periods does seem to be beneficial in most instances. The 7-day cold storage was especially beneficial.

The results of these preliminary studies indicate that the germination of sedge seed is not so difficult as earlier studies suggest, but it is highly variable. Although this study has provided some useful guidelines for future investigations of sedge species, additional methods or combinations of methods need to be tested. Among the most promising for future work would be the further testing of light and cold-storage techniques.

Determining Growth of Ponderosa Pine in Arizona by Stand Projection

Peter F. Ffolliott[1]

Growth of ponderosa pine in Arizona is normally determined by remeasuring permanently established plots. In many instances, however, it is desired to get growth rates without waiting. Growth rates can be determined from one sampling of a forest by applying the stand projection method described by Hasel.[2]

A permanent sampling system is established by locating strip cruise center lines and point samples, the suggested methods for developing stand tables required for stand projection. This system can then be converted to a permanent plot remeasurement method of growth determination. Mortality and ingrowth estimates will also become available with subsequent inventories.

How the Method Works

Hasel's stand projection method involves determining the gross change in numbers of trees per acre in each 2-inch diameter class for a projection period. This method is similar to other stand projection techniques in assuming the change in a future period will equal that of a past period. The change in a 2-inch d.b.h. class is the difference between the numbers of trees growing into and out of that class during the projection period. If mortality data are available, gross change can be converted to net change.

The change in numbers of trees per acre for each 2-inch d.b.h. class is multiplied by average individual tree volume for that class. By adding the volumes for all classes, growth is determined.

The method requires the following information:

1. A stand table of growing stock by 2-inch d.b.h. classes.
2. Average annual rate of diameter growth by 2-inch d.b.h. classes.
3. Height measurements corresponding to 2-inch d.b.h. classes to make local volume tables.

All of the information needed to apply the method can be obtained from a single "cruise" of an area.

---

[1] Associate Silviculturist, located at Flagstaff, in cooperation with Arizona State College; central headquarters are maintained at Fort Collins, in cooperation with Colorado State University.
[2] Hasel, A. A. A design for multi-purpose forest surveys of large area. 51 pp. 1961. (Unpublished manuscript)

Stand Tables

It is suggested that point sampling be used to develop stand tables describing growing stock distribution in the large pole and sawtimber size classes. The first step in initiating a permanent sampling system is completed by permanently locating the points and marking the trees measured.

A strip cruise should be used to develop a stand table describing growing stock distribution of sapling and small pole size classes. Point sampling should not be used to measure the smaller size classes because of the clumped pattern of distribution of these classes in southwestern ponderosa pine. Point sampling is similar to fixed-plot sampling for a given 2-inch d.b.h. class, and a small area will be sampled compared to the total area of the population. Too large or too small numbers are often obtained when numbers of trees of a clumped distribution are tallied from small sample areas and expanded to an acre basis.[3]

Which of the 2-inch d.b.h. size classes should be sampled by a strip cruise will depend on the basal area factor selected for point sampling. The smaller the factor, the smaller the 2-inch d.b.h. classes that can be sampled by a strip cruise.

For efficiency, locate the point samples at regular intervals along the strip cruise center line, and carry out the strip cruise and point sampling simultaneously.

Diameter Growth

Increment borings are needed to determine average annual diameter growth. These borings must describe accurately diameter growth within each 2-inch d.b.h. class in the population sampled. The first tree tallied on the point samples can be bored to meet this objective. Trees in the smaller size classes can be selected in a similar way.

Height Measurements

Height measurements corresponding to 2-inch d.b.h. classes must be taken to make local volume tables. The trees selected for diameter growth information can be used for these measurements. As these trees will have been bored, height and age data will be available.

Sample Design

Systematic sampling with multiple random starts[4,5] can be used to measure the variability between lines of strip cruise and point samples. This system will allow for computing measurements of variation in addition to insuring a representative sample of an area.

While there are unknown errors in the stand projection method, sampling errors should meet predetermined limits of precision. This means sampling intensities for different levels of precision and probable error must be computed, which requires knowing how much variability exists in the stands in terms of the data necessary to apply Hasel's method.

Measurements of variability become available from a systematic sampling design with multiple random starts. The number of point samples, and the area to be sampled by a strip cruise, necessary to develop stand tables at given limits of precision can be computed. Also, the number of increment borings and height measurements needed in each 2-inch d.b.h. class can be found. An efficient sampling system can be designed from these data.

Computations

Hasel's method is similar to the stand projection method described by Meyer.[6] The

---

[3]*Odum, E. P. Fundamentals of ecology. 546 pp., illus. Philadelphia-London: W. B. Saunders Co. 1959.*

[4]*Shiue, Cherng-Jiann. Systematic sampling with multiple random starts. Forest Sci. 6: 42-50. 1960.*
[5]*Freese, F. Elementary forest sampling. U.S.Dept. Agr. Agr. Handb. 232, 91 pp. 1962.*
[6]*Meyer, H. A. Forest mensuration. 357 pp., illus. State College, Pa.: Penn's Valley Pub., Inc. 1953.*

Table 1.—Hasel's stand projection method

(1)	(2)	(3)	(4)	(5)	(6)	(7)	(8)	(9)	(10)	(11)	(12)	(13)
D.b.h. class	Number trees per acre	N_i	Q_i	Log Q_i	b_i	g_i	$b_i g_i$	Antilog $b_i g_i$	r_i	$N_i r_i$	$(N_i r_i) - (N_{i+1} r_{i+1})$	V_i	G_i
2	612	798.20											
4	100	186.20	4.287	0.6322	0.3161	0.0913	0.0289	1.069	0.069	12.85	9.92	0.8	7.94
6	44.1	86.20	2.160	.3344	.1672	.0871	.0146	1.034	.034	2.93	1.67	2.3	3.84
8	16.8	42.10	2.048	.3113	.1556	.0833	.0130	1.030	.030	1.26	.75	4.8	3.60
10	9.48	25.30	1.664	.2212	.1106	.0798	.0088	1.020	.020	.51	.23	8.7	2.00
12	4.61	15.82	1.599	.2038	.1019	.0766	.0078	1.018	.018	.28	.13	14.2	1.85
14	2.24	11.21	1.411	.1495	.0748	.0736	.0055	1.013	.013	.15	.08	21.5	1.72
16	1.12	8.97	1.250	.0969	.0484	.0709	.0034	1.008	.008	.07	.03	30.5	.92
18	2.12	7.85	1.143	.0580	.0290	.0693	.0020	1.005	.005	.04	-.02	41.5	-.83
20	2.00	5.73	1.370	.1367	.0684	.0660	.0045	1.010	.010	.06	.01	54.5	.54
22	1.62	3.73	1.536	.1864	.0932	.0638	.0059	1.014	.014	.05	.01	67.6	.68
24	1.00	2.11	1.768	.2475	.1238	.0617	.0076	1.018	.018	.04	.02	84.5	1.69
26	.62	1.11	1.901	.2799	.1400	.0598	.0084	1.020	.020	.02	.01	100.	1.00
28	.37	.49	2.265	.3551	.1776	.0579	.0103	1.024	.024	.01	.01	121.	1.21
30	.12	.12	4.083	.6110	.3055	.0562	.0172	1.040	.040	.00	.00	138.	.00
Total													26.16

Step 1. Enter number of trees per acre by 2-inch d.b.h. classes in column 1.

Step 2. Compute cumulative total numbers of trees for each class, beginning with the largest 2-inch d.b.h. classes, and record in column 2 (N_i).

Step 3. Divide each total in column 2 (N_i) by the total in the next larger class, and record the quotients in column 3 (Q_i).

Step 4. Enter the logarithm of Q_i in column 4.

Step 5. Divide each logarithm of Q_i by 2 and record the quotients in column 5 (b_i).

Step 6. Enter average annual diameter growth (g_i) for each 2-inch d.b.h. class in column 6.

Step 7. Multiply each b_i in column 5 by the corresponding g_i in column 6, and record the products in column 7.

Step 8. Enter antilog of each product of b_i and g_i in column 8.

Step 9. Subtract 1 from each antilog in column 8 and enter in column 9. These r_i values are rates of ingrowth into each 2-inch d.b.h. class.

Step 10. Multiply the cumulative total numbers of trees for each 2-inch d.b.h. class (N_i) by the corresponding ingrowth rate (r_i) and record the products in column 10.

Step 11. Subtract outgrowth (ingrowth in next larger 2-inch d.b.h. class) from ingrowth for each 2-inch d.b.h. class ($N_i r_i$) - ($N_{i+1} r_{i+1}$), and enter the gross change in the number of trees in each 2-inch d.b.h. class in column 11. If mortality and cutting records are available, adjust gross change as follows: (Gross change) - (Mortality) - (Cut) = net change in each 2-inch d.b.h. class.

Step 12. Enter average volume of a tree (v_i) in each 2-inch d.b.h. class in column 12. V_i is volume of entire stem in cubic feet.

Step 13. Multiply the gross change in the number of trees in each 2-inch d.b.h. class in column 11 by the corresponding average volume of a tree (V_i) in column 12, and record products in column 13 (G_i).

Step 14. Add column 13. Summation is growth per acre per year.

ratio of cumulative numbers of trees in adjacent size classes was used to calculate Q by Hasel in place of q = the ratio of numbers of trees in adjacent d.b.h. classes used by Meyer. The procedure followed in applying Hasel's stand projection method is outlined in table 1. Data collected on a 450-acre watershed on the Beaver Creek Watershed Evaluation project in Arizona[7] are used to illustrate the procedure.

[7] A 275,000-acre watershed on the Coconino National Forest in northern Arizona where costs and benefits of intensive multiple-use land management are being evaluated as a part of the Arizona Watershed Program.

Test of Method

Hasel's stand projection method was used to determine ponderosa pine growth rates (gross) on a 450-acre watershed on the Beaver Creek Watershed Evaluation project. The results of this test illustrate how the method can be applied in Arizona.

Systematic sampling with four strata and four random starts (fig. 1) was the design placed on the test watershed. Each sample unit consisted of point samples at 3-chain intervals and a strip cruise 1/4 chain wide.

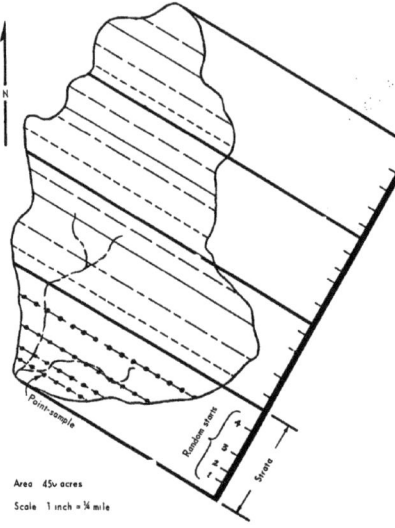

Figure 1.--Systematic sampling with four strata and four random starts.

Increment borings and height measurements were taken on the first tree tallied on the point samples. Point sampling with a basal area factor of 25 was used to develop stand tables for trees 8 inches d.b.h. and larger. Stand tables for trees less than 8 inches d.b.h. were constructed from the strip cruise.

Growth rates were determined for each sample unit, and an average was obtained for the watershed. The average growth rate was 34.5 ± 2.3 cubic feet [8] per acre per year. The coefficient of variation was 52 percent.

[8]Myers, C. A. Volume, taper, and related tables for southwestern ponderosa pine. U. S. Forest Serv. Res. Paper RM-2, 24 pp., illus. Rocky Mountain Forest and Range Expt. Sta., Fort Collins, Colo. 1963.

The number of point samples, using a basal area factor of 25, and the number of chains of strip cruise, 1/4 chain wide, needed to develop stand tables for different levels of precision for growth determination were determined from measurements of variability between sample units, as follows:

Level of precision	Chains of strip cruise	Number of point samples
P = 0.67:		
5 percent	2,279	540
10 percent	570	135
15 percent	254	60
20 percent	143	34
P = 0.95:		
10 percent	2,370	431
15 percent	1,054	193
20 percent	593	109

The average number of increment borings needed in each 2-inch d.b.h. class, based on 191 borings, was computed for different levels of precision:

Level of precision	P = 0.67	P = 0.95
5 percent	26	--
10 percent	7	34
15 percent	3	15
20 percent	2	9

The average number of height measurements needed in each 2-inch d.b.h. class, based on 187 measurements, was also calculated for different levels of precision:

Level of precision	P = 0.67	P = 0.95
5 percent	11	--
10 percent	3	14
15 percent	2	6
20 percent	1	4

Sampling intensities and number of increment borings and height measurements may be helpful in designing samples on areas similar to Beaver Creek.

August 1965

U.S. FOREST SERVICE
RESEARCH NOTE RM - 53

Snow in Natural Openings and Adjacent Ponderosa Pine Stands on the Beaver Creek Watersheds

Peter F. Ffolliott,[1] Edward A. Hansen,[1] and Almer D. Zander[2]

The Beaver Creek Watershed Project[3] was established to determine types of land treatments that would increase water yield in Arizona. Several pilot watersheds in the ponderosa pine (Pinus ponderosa Laws.) type are currently being calibrated. Annual precipitation on the watersheds is 24 inches, half of which comes during the period November 15-April 15. More than 99 percent of the annual runoff occurs during the same period, most of it originating from snowmelt. It is apparent from the role of snow in the runoff pattern that effects of overstory on snow accumulation and melt must be known to prescribe treatments to maximize water yield.

This exploratory study was designed to determine the relationship between snow accumulation and melt and overstory stocking conditions. There were no replications of the various stocking conditions. Factors such as slope and aspect were eliminated as much as possible to avoid confounding effects.

AREAS STUDIED

Snow accumulation and melt were studied in natural openings downwind from a timber edge, and in adjacent stands of ponderosa pine during the winter of 1963-64. The natural openings extended a minimum distance of 1,000 feet from the edge of the timber. The four areas selected for study represent existing levels of stocking and size-class distribution on the Beaver Creek Watersheds:

1. The ponderosa pine on this area was uneven aged with sapling, pole, and sawtimber size classes present. The basal area was 85 square feet per acre, and the average height of the dominant trees was 60 feet. This condition extended beyond 1,000 feet to the windward.

2. The timber here was a characteristic dense sapling and small pole stand common in southwestern ponderosa pine. The basal area was 65 square feet per acre, and the height of the stand was 20 feet. The stand was uniform 300 feet to the windward, beyond which was an uneven-aged pole and sawtimber stand.

---

[1] Associate Silviculturist and Associate Hydrologist, respectively, located at Flagstaff, in cooperation with Arizona State College; central headquarters are maintained at Fort Collins, in cooperation with Colorado State University.
[2] Range Conservationist with the Coconino National Forest, Flagstaff, Arizona.
[3] A 275,000-acre watershed on the Coconino National Forest in northern Arizona where costs and benefits of intensive multiple-use land management are being evaluated as a part of the Arizona Watershed Program.

3. The ponderosa pine on this area was even-aged, large sawtimber with a basal area of 115 square feet per acre. The height of the timber was 100 feet. This stand extended for 400 feet upwind, beyond which was an uneven-aged pole and sawtimber stand.

4. The size classes represented here were similar to those found on area 1. The stand was dense, however, averaging 135 square feet of basal area per acre. The height of the dominant trees was 40 feet. The stand was uniform for 1,000 feet to the windward.

All of the areas were located with a northeast aspect where slope was less than 10 percent to minimize slope and aspect as variables:

	Average slope	
	Openings	Timber
	(Percent)	
Area 1	1	6
2	3	4
3	2	3
4	1	6

METHODS

Water-equivalent measurements were made on snow courses the day following each storm. Total snow was measured at each point; then, the "new" snow was removed and the "old" snow measured at the point. The interface between the "new" powder snow and the "old" snow was easily distinguished due to crust formation during the long periods and warm temperatures between storms. Additional measurements were made at 3- to 4-day intervals during the spring melt period.

Because major winter storms generally come from the southwest, the snow courses were located along a southwest-northeast line perpendicular to the edge of the natural openings. Each course began at the edge of the timber and extended northeast into the opening (fig. 1). The length of each course depended on the height of the timber adjacent to the openings. Snow samples were collected at distances of "H" (average height of adjacent timber): 0, 1/4, 1/2, 3/4, 1, 1-1/2, and 2 out into the openings. Additional samples were

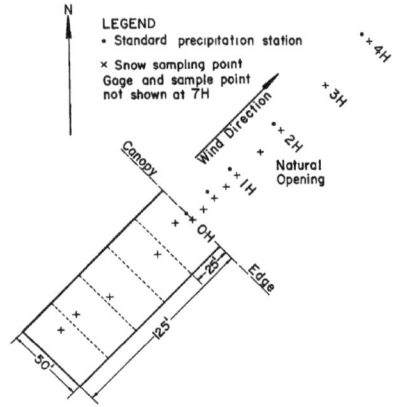

Figure 1.--Location of standard precipitation gages and snow sampling points in the natural opening and adjacent stand at area 4. Other areas were sampled similarly.

taken at 3, 4, and 7 H at area 4 to determine snow accumulation and melt at distances beyond 2 H.

Five sample points were selected in a plot 50 feet wide and 125 feet long in the timber adjacent to the opening to determine effect of overstory on snow accumulation and melt within the timber (fig. 1). Each plot was subdivided into five subplots of 50 by 25 feet, and one sample point was randomly located in each subplot. Basal area was determined at each sample point by point sampling with a basal area factor of 10.

RESULTS

Accumulation and Melt

Openings

Snow accumulation in the openings is shown in figure 2. In all cases the water equivalents at points out from the edge of the canopy were plotted in terms of tree height. The resulting accumulation profiles were quite similar regardless of stand condition, with the exception

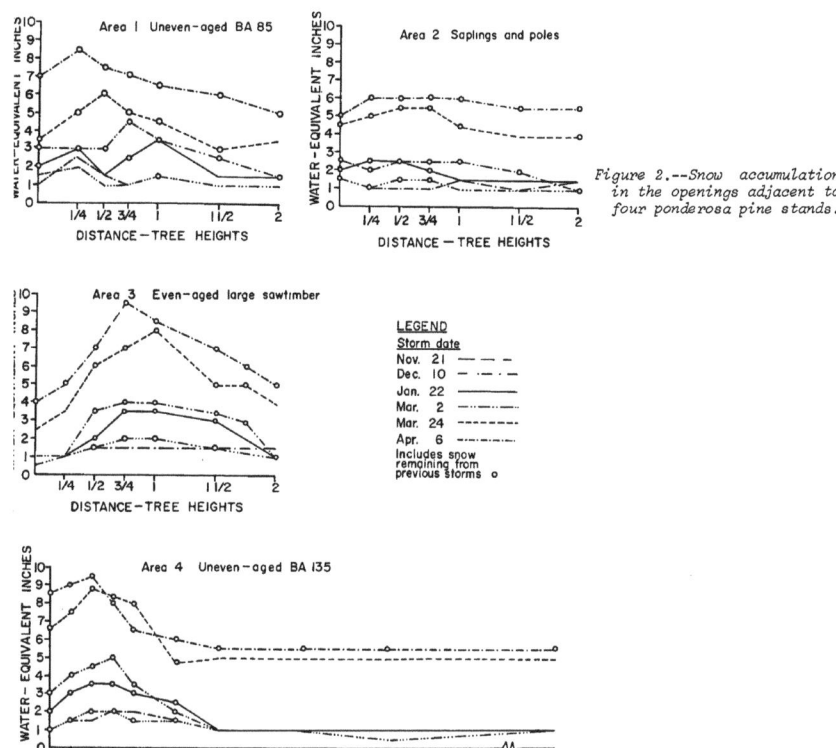

Figure 2.—Snow accumulation in the openings adjacent to four ponderosa pine stands.

f the opening adjacent to the sapling and pole tand, which accumulated somewhat less (fig. , area 2). The smaller catch in the sapling nd pole stand was possibly influenced by the earby taller stands.

Some snow was held through the winter in "zone of retention" extending from the edge f the natural openings to a distance of 1-1/2 to 2 H (see circled points in fig. 2). All snow eyond 2 H disappeared between successive torms without producing runoff, except for the last two storms when relatively large snowfalls occurred within a 2-week period. The "holding" of snow by the canopy resulted in an average of 2.0 inches of water in the snowpack on March 21 (6 days before start of runoff) at a point 1/2 H from the canopy. The average water equivalent of the snowpack from the canopy out to a distance of 1 H represented over 40 percent of the current winter precipitation. Lesser amounts remained out to 2 H with none remaining beyond 2 H. Although measurements were made beyond 2 H on only one area, it was observed that the other areas lost snow similarly.

Melt trends from April 7 to April 20 for the four areas are shown in figure 3. In general snow farthest from the canopy melted most rapidly. This resulted in the last snow lying in a narrow "zone of retention" directly adjacent to the canopy. An exception to this is the even-aged, large sawtimber stand (fig. 3, area 3). A "hole" in the canopy allowed the afternoon sun to shine on the snowpack adjacent to the canopy, thus depleting that portion of the snowpack more rapidly.

The melt data from the four areas were used to compute average daily melt rate at varying distances from the canopy. The resulting curve (fig. 4) shows that the canopy reduced melt rates out to 2 H. Directly adjacent to the canopy the melt rate was about half that of the unaffected areas.

In general, snow disappeared from the four openings at about the same time. An exception was the opening adjacent to the sapling and pole stand, where the snow left somewhat earlier due apparently to the smaller initial snowpack.

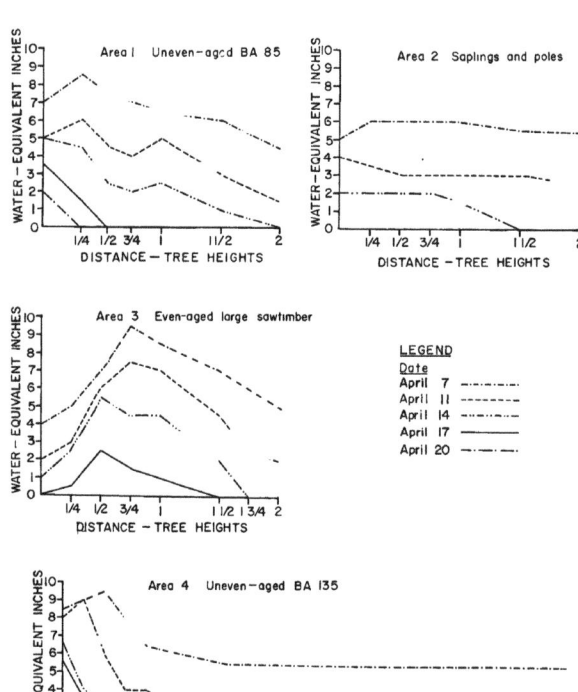

Figure 3.--Snowpack depletion in the openings adjacent to four ponderosa pine stands.

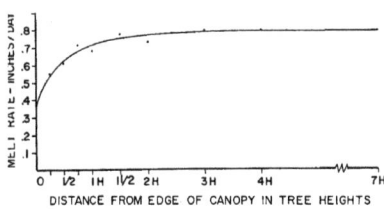

Figure 4.--*Average melt rate of snowpack from April 7 to April 20 (inches per day).*

Timber

The data obtained from four stands of timber are summarized in table 1. The water equivalent on March 21 shows the relative ability of the different stands to hold snow prior to spring runoff. March 21 was just prior to the last major snow storms of the season and start of spring runoff, so any snow remaining at that time contributed to runoff. Average water equivalent at the time of maximum accumulation, April 7, and subsequent melt in the timber are also shown. The amount of melt was computed for the period of major

Table 1. --Snow accumulation and melt in timber, and influence of various stand types

Size class and area number	Basal area	Water equivalent remaining March 21[1]	Accumulation, Apr. 7[2]	Melt, Apr. 7-14[3]	Influence of stand type on snow accumulation and melt
	Sq. ft.	- - Inches of water - -			
Saplings and poles (Area 2):	65	1.9	6.1	4.1	Held most water equivalent on Mar. 21, probably due to many small "holes" in canopy plus adequate shading provided by a canopy which was continuous down to the ground; maximum accumulation, greatest of all stands; melt measured during 7-day period similar to two other stands.
Uneven-aged (Area 1):	85	1.4	5.1	3.9	Canopy nearly continuous, water in snowpack on March 21 was 0.5 inch less than in sapling-pole stand, melt not significantly different from sapling-pole stand or uneven-aged stand of Area 4; maximum accumulation intermediate.
Uneven-aged (Area 4):	135	.6	5.6	3.3	Similar to Area 1 except stocking greater and canopy did not extend down to ground, water equivalent on March 21 was second smallest of areas studied; melt considerably less than other three areas, probably due in part to relatively high stocking level.
Even-aged, large sawtimber (Area 3):	115	.1	4.7	4.2	Characterized by large, scattered sawtimber, poorest in terms of water equivalent remaining March 21; smallest maximum accumulation, melt rate slightly higher, but probably not significantly different from Areas 1 and 2.

[1] Just prior to last major storms and start of spring runoff.
[2] Date of seasonal maximum accumulation.
[3] Period of major melt

melt, April 7 to April 14. The seasonal peak discharge on adjacent ponderosa pine watersheds on Beaver Creek occurred in the middle of this period (Apr. 11). The influence of the various stands on snow accumulation and melt is described in table 1.

PRECIPITATION DISTRIBUTION

In the opening at area 4, snowstorm precipitation was measured to the leeward of a forest edge by two methods: (1) with a snow tube and scales, and (2) with U.S. Weather Bureau standard precipitation gages (fig. 5). The standard precipitation gages were placed in a line perpendicular to the edge of the canopy and parallel to the prevailing southwest wind direction (see fig. 1). Distances

Figure 5.--*U. S. Weather Bureau precipitation gage at area 4.*

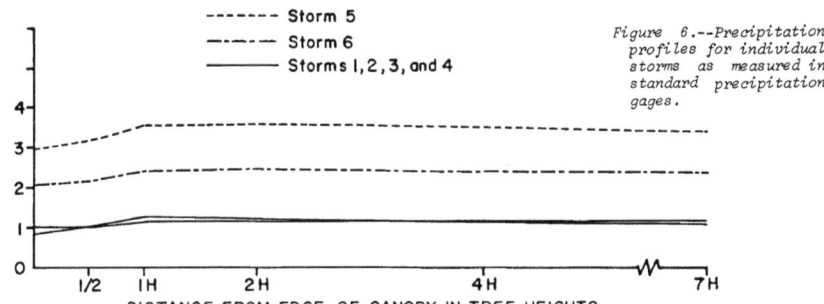

Figure 6.--Precipitation profiles for individual storms as measured in standard precipitation gages.

easured in the cans. The reason for this fference is not known, but it appears that it as not due to drifting of snow from farther it in the opening back toward the canopy. ich a situation would have resulted in snow-be measurements substantially less than the nount measured in the standard gages at me point in the opening. In addition, tem-:ratures during the storms were generally ild, and field observation showed little sign drifting in the area.

The amount of snow intercepted by the canopy varied from nothing to apparently considerable amounts. This interception appeared to have no effect on the distribution of snow out from the canopy. It is possible that the amount of snow on the ground as measured with the snow tube is close to the true amount deposited at that point, and that increased turbulence and eddy currents associated with a canopy edge reduced catches in the standard gages.

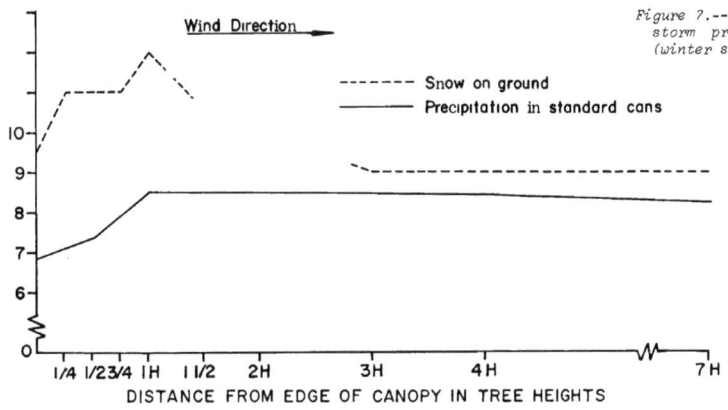

Figure 7.--Sum of snow storm precipitation (winter storms 1-5).

CONCLUSIONS

1. A sapling and pole stand held the most snow just prior to spring runoff, and had a relatively high melt rate in the spring. Such characteristics would be desirable for maximizing surface runoff in a short time period.

2. A small amount of snow held through the winter in an uneven-aged stand with basal area of 135 square feet melted slowly in the spring. This characteristic would be desirable for minimizing surface runoff and/or extending the timing of runoff.

3. An even-aged, large sawtimber stand held almost no snow throughout the winter, but had a fairly high spring melt rate.

4. An uneven-aged stand with a basal area of 85 square feet was intermediate in its influence on holding snow and melt rate.

5. Snow was held in a "zone of retention" in openings throughout the winter out to distances of 1-1/2 to 2 H, regardless of tree height or stocking conditions tested.

6. Forty percent of the winter precipitation that fell in a band 1 H wide adjacent to the canopy was held until just prior to the start of spring runoff.

7. All snow disappeared between successive winter storms at distances beyond 2 H with the exception of the last two storms, which occurred within a 2-week period and contained large amounts of snow.

8. There was more water equivalent in the snowpack from 0 to 3 H as measured by a snow tube than was caught in standard precipitation gages.

September 1965

U.S. FOREST SERVICE
RESEARCH NOTE RM - 54

FOREST SERVICE
U.S. DEPARTMENT OF AGRICULTURE

Gross Job Time Studies--

An Efficient Method for Analyzing Forestry Costs

David P. Worley,[1] Gerald L. Mundell,[2] and Robert M. Williamson[2]

Cost data from past forest operations are necessary for estimating the costs of future forestry jobs. If the job estimates appear excessive, cost data may indicate which operations could be modified to bring total costs down to an acceptable level. If costs are so high that an important forestry job cannot be done, cost data are needed to determine which operations need to be done in an entirely new way. When cost levels are not considered a problem, cost data are still needed to control total production for a given investment, and where investment outcome is considered in detail, for optimizing total returns.

Ordinarily three sources of cost data are exploited for these purposes:

1. Accounting data are often interpreted to determine the cost of doing forestry jobs. Such information is gathered for financial statements, however, and needs considerable adjustment to be used for costing a particular forestry job or operation. Often financial statements lack flexibility for estimating future jobs; frequently, necessary adjustments cannot be made at all.

2. Time-and-motion study results are available for many forestry jobs, but are not usually as useful in forestry as they are for industrial plant cost estimates because the variability in woods conditions is far greater than in industrial plants.

3. Special cost studies, if carefully conducted, can supply good data for local situations and a variety of uses.

A special cost study method is described here[3] in which cost data are collected for satisfying most cost objectives. It is a flexible, field-efficient, formal system of data collection to answer a number of pertinent cost questions. Described are the necessary

---

[1] *Principal Economist, located at Tempe, in cooperation with Arizona State University; central headquarters are maintained at Fort Collins, in cooperation with Colorado State University.*
[2] *District Rangers of the Beaver Creek and Long Valley Ranger Districts, respectively, Coconino National Forest, Arizona.*

[3] *Adapted from Barraclough, S. L., and Gould, E. M., Jr. Economic analysis of farm forest operating units. Harvard Forest Bul. 26, 145 pp. 1955; and Barraclough, S. L., and Pleasonton, A. Data for planning woodland opportunities on west Tennessee farms. Tenn. Agr. Expt. Sta. Bul. 276, 64 pp. 1957.*

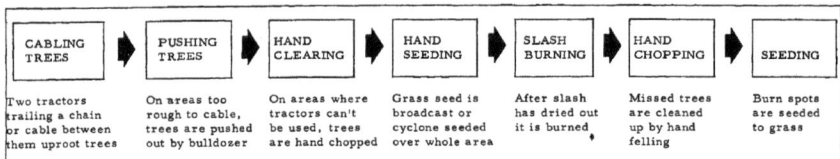

Figure 1.--This sample flow chart shows seven steps set up for the project of converting pinyon-juniper-covered areas to grass- and herb-covered areas on the Beaver Creek Pilot Watersheds in Arizona. The first three jobs could have been combined into a "juniper clearing" job. The two "hand-seeding" jobs could have been combined. Slash burning and hand chopping could have been lumped together as a "cleanup" job.

planning, data collection, and analysis methods to present a practical cost-determination system for field use.

General Method

Physical input-output data are collected rather than dollar costs and returns because it is easier to generalize from the former. Inputs collected include labor time, equipment time, direct supervision time, and materials. Other elements--travel time and machine inputs, for example--can be collected where these are to be analyzed. Outputs specify total production as acres treated, trees thinned, etc. Dollar costs of production are determined by multiplying inputs by appropriate wage rates, machine rates, and material costs. The sum of costs divided by the number of production units accomplished gives average unit costs.

Planning the Cost Study

Planning the cost study begins by breaking a treatment operation down into its component jobs. In this respect, it is similar to operational planning.

A flow chart (fig. 1) is a good means of breaking down a treatment operation, and sets the stage for the jobs to be costed. It is in this phase of planning that the cost analyst sets limits on what costs should be collected.

The flow chart tells us the general job objectives, but does not describe it.

The second planning step is to describe each job by listing the inputs to be recorded, the output unit to be recorded, and the job conduct as far as crew organization is concerned. The job descriptions need to set forth a clear understanding of how the jobs will be done, and to describe each job in detail. For example, to perform the cabling operation, we need to know: what size are the tractors? how are they equipped? is there a swamper for each or both? how long and what size is the cable or chain? need we collect machine inputs to determine a machine rate? what field servicing is done? what output units shall we use? Also, if we plan to tie to a time-and-motion study, its requirements need to be met. Since all these questions need to be resolved anyway for conducting the operation, the formal job description is not a big task, but it is important.

Collecting the Field Data

Data are collected on a specially imprinted 3- by 5-inch card (fig. 2), which provides for collecting basic input-output data. The back of the card is left blank, but additional supporting data could be incorporated there. For special situations the basic data format could be changed, but all elements shown in figure 2 need to be included. The job foreman records the data; the forester or

```
JOB  Slash burning              DATE  12/20/63
LOCATION  Watershed 1 (see map)
EQUIPMENT  5 real tite drip torches

MATERIALS  17 gals. fuel mixture 1/10 gasoline to fuel oil.

MEN   HRS.   MEN   HRS.    TOTAL PRODUCTION  (see map)
C.G.   7    ___   ___       72 acres (D.W.)
S.V.   7    ___   ___     TOTAL MAN HOURS   35
R.C.   7    ___   ___     SUPERVISOR  C.L. Working Foreman
W.D.   7    ___   ___     HOURS   7
```

JOB: Name of the job from the flow chart.

LOCATION: Designation of the treatment area.

EQUIPMENT: Kinds and numbers of equipment, and the hours or miles of use of each.

MATERIALS: Kinds and quantities of expended items. If machine rates are desired, items such as fuel, grease, oil filters, etc. can be included.

MEN AND HOURS: Initials of the men on the job and number of hours and fractions thereof that each was on this job. If, for example, two jobs are being conducted concurrently, a man might shift from one to the other. He would be dropped from one job card and would be picked up on the other job card. A case in point might be a thinning operation where one crew is felling and another is piling slash. If the felling crew got too far ahead of the piling crew, the foreman might drop some fallers off to pile for awhile. He would carry them on the slash-piling card while they were with that job.

TOTAL PRODUCTION: Number of production units. Some types of production units are difficult for a foreman to measure--acreage, for example. He can indicate the ground covered on a map or with a trace in the field, and the supervisor can planimeter the map or check the field. In this case the foreman would merely indicate "see map" to show where production units are to come from. The cards can be held for extended periods without posting daily production so as to get periodic production, or held until an area is completed.

SUPERVISOR AND HOURS: Initials and hours on the job. A foreman may divide his time between more than one job, as in the thinning case above. In this event, he would use his judgment to prorate his time.

APPROPRIATE REMARKS may be entered on the back of the card to help interpret the data: equipment breakdown, work slowdown due to weather, or unusual ground conditions.

Figure 2.--Job card for collecting field data, with detailed instructions on its use. Handwritten entries apply to the "slash burning" operation in the flow chart shown in figure 1.

supervisor in charge of the operation collects the cards daily and checks for accuracy or omissions.

The handwritten entries in figure 2 apply to the slash burning in the conversion operation shown in the flow chart (fig. 1). All entries except production are easily made by the foreman. In this case the day's production was shown on a map, which was later planimetered for acreage. Since the foreman both directed and worked on the slash-burning operation, his time was included in total man-hours. Additional input data can be obtained from this card. For example, the crew is paid for an 8-hour day. One hour then must have been used in some other way. Custom dictates that one-way travel be done on the worker's own time. The hour not recorded was probably travel on working time. Reference to a map shows the job location as 35 miles from the headquarters station; part of the travel is over rough, work trails. If the full 8 hours is to be accounted for, this rationalization could be documented on the back of the job card, or travel could be considered a special job subject for another card.

Summarizing the Data

To put the data into a form for analysis, a physical summary is made directly from the job cards. This chronological summary of the production can be converted easily to a cost summary. Job 2 from the flow chart (pushing trees) was used as an example (fig. 3). Given a machine rate of $12 per hour and a labor rate of $3 per hour, the physical summary was converted to a cost summary.

To compare results with those from an earlier study, data characterizing the independent variable of the earlier study are needed. For example, Cotner and Jameson[4] conducted an earlier time-and-motion study of pushing junipers, in which the independent

[4]*Cotner, M. L. and Jameson, D. A. Costs of juniper control: Bulldozing vs. burning individual trees. Rocky Mountain Forest and Range Expt. Sta., Sta. Paper 43. 14 pp., illus. 1959.*

variable was the number of trees per acre by height classes. To adapt data collected for the pushing job on Beaver Creek (fig. 3), we determined the number of trees per acre by height classes, entered that number in their time-and-motion study equation, and calculated the expected production to be 0.9 machine hour per acre. Cotner and Jameson suggest that the calculated rate should be within 10 percent of the actual rate. This requirement is met by the data for Beaver Creek, since the actual rate of 0.822 hour per acre is within 10 percent of the calculated rate.

As shown in the above juniper-pushing example, a time-and-motion study yields an equation that enables one to predict the cost of pushing stands of different density.

From the gross time study method, similar types of information can be developed by gathering data covering a number of conditions. A production-rate equation was thus developed for thinning precommercial ponderosa pine on Beaver Creek (fig. 4), in which 148 daily crew observations were included. Data were analyzed to show number of trees thinned per chainsaw hour for areas with thinning densities that varied from 100 to 1,500 trees per acre. Dollar costs then were computed, based on actual labor rates and published saw rates, to obtain the direct cost of $2.75 per chainsaw hour. From the additional

JUNIPER PUSHING							
PRODUCTION SUMMARY					COST SUMMARY		
Date	Direct operations			Production			
	Pushing	Service	Travel				
	- - - Hours - - -			Acres			
May 8	4	3	3/4	4	Average machine hours per acre	60/73	0.822
9	6		3/4	5	Average service hours per acre	7/73	.096
10	2		3/4	2			
20	6	1/2	3/4	9	Average travel hours per acre	8.25/73	.113
21	6	1/2	3/4	8	Average total hours per acre	75.25/73	1.03
22	6	1/2	3/4	8			
23	6	1/2	3/4	10			
24	6	1/2	3/4	7	Average machine cost per acre		
28	6	1/2	3/4	8	60 × $12 = $7.20/73		$ 9.86
29	6	1/2	3/4	6			
June 1	6	1/2	3/4	6	Average total labor cost per acre		
					75.25 × $3 = 225.75/73		3.10
Total	60	7	8-/14	73			
		75.25			Average total cost per acre		$12.96

Figure 3.--Production summary for juniper pushing, with computations for physical inputs and costs per unit production.

Figure 4.--Sample of job card with information tallied for 148 daily crew observations on a thinning operation in precommercial ponderosa pine on the Beaver Creek Project.

```
JOB  Thinning Jackson Sale           DATE  Aug. 28, 1963
LOCATION  Mule Park Area   Sec 19  R 9- T 16
EQUIPMENT  Carryall 25 miles   Chainsaws 5(6) = 30      hours
Other
MATERIALS

MEN    HRS.    MEN      HRS.    PRODUCTION  12,576 trees
H.O.    8     Petore     8                 on 10 acres.
S.P.    8                       FOREMAN   Julius Cal
N.M.    8                       HOURS   8 supervisor
Don     8                       REMARKS
```

labor and supervisor inputs shown on the job cards, total field cost was determined to be 1.5 times the direct chainsaw hour cost (fig. 5). The graph of production was developed by grouping the data according to 100-tree classes and drawing a freehand curve through the points. The table of production data was developed from the curve. Costs were then tabled and later graphed to show the cost curve. In this way a useful cost-prediction mechanism was produced for costing future thinning jobs.

Figure 5.--Production and cost curves and table computed from 148 job cards for a thinning operation in precommercial ponderosa pine on the Beaver Creek pilot watersheds.

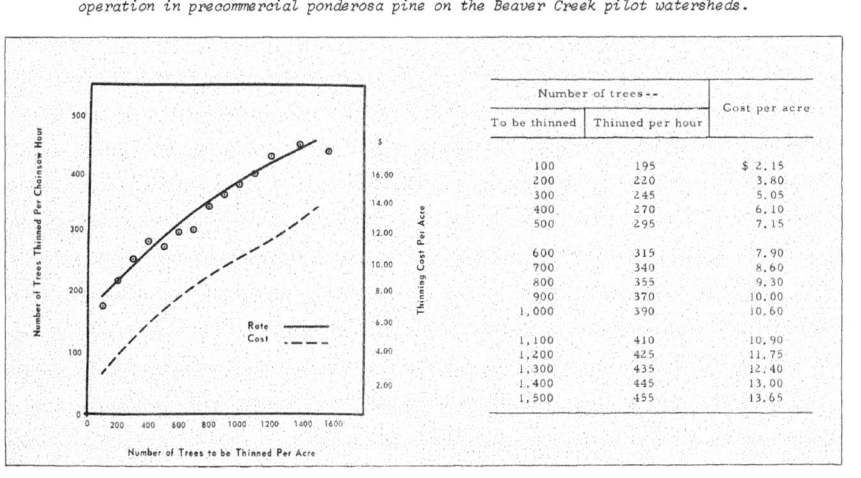

Number of trees		Cost per acre
To be thinned	Thinned per hour	
100	195	$ 2.15
200	220	3.80
300	245	5.05
400	270	6.10
500	295	7.15
600	315	7.90
700	340	8.60
800	355	9.30
900	370	10.00
1,000	390	10.60
1,100	410	10.90
1,200	425	11.75
1,300	435	12.40
1,400	445	13.00
1,500	455	13.65

This particular production-rate relation can be followed up in future jobs to determine its broad applicability as illustrated for the juniper pushing case.

Analyzing the costs

Operational Analysis

The whole operation is costed by adding up the costs for the different jobs. Of course, any of the inputs can be added to determine the machine and labor time required to complete an operation. A dollar-cost summation for the juniper-conversion operation on a 400-acre watershed on the Beaver Creek Project (fig. 6) was prepared so cost for each phase could be easily evaluated. It if were decided that $19.41 per acre was too high an investment for converting juniper to grass, the job breakdown and job descriptions could be examined to determine which jobs might be conducted differently to reduce total cost.

It is important to note that some jobs were not applied to all acres. This suggests that, in other cases, some jobs could be eliminated with a per-acre savings approximating the cost in the last column. In other situations, more area might need to be subjected to a particular job and that cost would rise. Each individual conversion, then, will be a unique operation, and the proportional acreage where each job is required should be determined. Thus, we cannot generalize from the total costs on this test area, but must restrict our attention to the unit costs and their expected variation to be applied to another operation.

Such generalization would be considerably easier if we could restrict our attention to specific jobs and/or job elements to which total costs are sensitive. By sensitive, we mean that the expected cost variation in individual jobs would make a big difference in total cost. A sensitivity analysis can be made from one, or at most half a dozen, properly documented case histories to indicate jobs needing improved methods or additional evaluation for prediction purposes.

Sensitivity Analysis

A sensitivity analysis is made to show which jobs in an operation or which elements

COST SUMMARY

Job	Number of acres covered	Cost per acre	
		Each job	Average on watershed
Cabling	304	$ 5.60	$ 4.25
Pushing	73	12.96	2.35
Hand clearing	16	49.00	1.96
Hand seeding	400	5.64	5.64
Burning	400	.61	.61
Hand chopping	300	2.94	2.22
Reseeding	100	4.72	1.18
Direct supervision	400	.55	.55
Travel (mileage)	400	.65	.65
Total cost per acre			$19.41

Figure 6.--*Dollar-cost summary to illustrate the operational cost analysis method. Data shown are for a juniper-conversion operation on a 400-acre watershed within the Beaver Creek Project.*

of a job can make the biggest difference in total cost. These are:

1. Job areas where greatest managerial care must be exercised to keep costs low, or
2. Job areas where more precise estimating is needed, or
3. Work areas where the manager should look for a new way to perform the element or job.

How much variation to expect in costs is a matter of judgment. If several case histories are available, or if the variation within a case history is available, we have a basis to help sharpen judgment. For example, 10 to 15 percent and no more than 20 percent variation in pushing costs would be expected from the internal analysis of the juniper-clearing case history presented earlier.

When the data were tabulated to make a sensitivity analysis for the 400-acre juniper conversion operation (fig. 7), results showed that the total cost could be expected to vary as much as 21 percent. Because one-third of the total variation can be expected from the conduct of the cabling job alone, it is the job where greatest cost savings are possible. Careful management will pay off here more

Figure 7.--*Example of a sensitivity analysis compiled from data collected for a juniper-conversion operation on a 400-acre watershed within the Beaver Creek Project (see fig. 6).*

SENSITIVITY ANALYSIS FOR JUNIPER-CONVERSION OPERATION ON A 400-ACRE WATERSHED

Job	Average cost per acre (1)	Likely deviation (2)	Acres to be applied (3)	Proportional average (4)	Effect of deviation on average per-acre cost on the watershed (5)	(6)
		Percent	Number	Percent		
Cabling	$ 5.60	30	304	76	$\frac{0.30\ (0.76)\ (5.60)}{\$19.41}$ (100) =	7%
Pushing	12.96	20	73	18	$\frac{0.20\ (0.18)\ (12.96)}{\$19.41}$ (100) =	2%
Hand clearing	49.00	30	16	4	etc.	3%
Hand seeding	5.64	10	400	100		3%
Burning	.61	30	400	100		1%
Hand chopping	2.94	30	300	75		3%
Burn seeding	4.72	30	100	25		2%
Direct supervision	.55		Indeterminate			
Travel mileage	.65		Indeterminate			
Watershed	$19.41					21%

Columns derived--
(1) From operations cost summary.
(2) Determined by judgment.
(3) From operations cost summary.
(4) Job acreage divided by total acreage.
(5) $\frac{(Col.\ 2)\ (Col.\ 4)\ (Col.\ 3)}{Total\ cost\ per\ acre}$ (100) equals Col. 6.
(6) Percentage of expected variation.

than elsewhere, and careful costing of this job may be warranted.

Within the cabling job, two independent variables exist--characteristics of the juniper stand and ground conditions. Estimates of cabling cost can be improved by conducting time-and-motion studies or a series of gross time studies on these two variables, which can then be subjected to a regression analysis like the juniper-pushing or thinning analysis discussed earlier. The results will feed back into total cost estimates to help define areas too expensive to convert, or conditions where a new approach should be tried.

Potential Applications

The data-collection and analysis system described in this paper is suitable for developing background cost data for a wide variety of forestry jobs and operations. By setting up field tests as described here on scheduled operations of various kinds, a background of costs will be developed to strengthen the forest manager's hand in planning future management. Rangers will be able to use these data as background locally for estimating similar operations, provided proportional acreage and unit costs are varied according to prospective operational conditions. Access to case-history cost data will sharpen the rangers' insight into ground and cover conditions that might affect costs, thus enabling them to design specific cost studies to help them account for these conditions.

By aggregating those data by Forests and Regions, superior cost data will be available for deciding program priorities, and for budgeting programs once the priority is established.

A Prefabricated Flume for Gaging Ephemeral Streams

Earl F. Aldon[1] and Fletcher J. Brown, Jr.[2]

The need for accurate water inventory data is particularly important as multiple use management of wildland resources intensifies. Designing devices to measure water yields from ephemeral streams presents particularly challenging problems for research to solve. Such devices should include, of course, the use of the most economical materials and methods. Fiberglass is one such low-cost material that warranted testing under field conditions. Its use in boats and for automobile body repairs is widely known--as is its durability. This Note outlines the steps taken to reduce costs by fiberglassing plywood panels and prefabricating other components of a trapezoidal flume (fig. 1).

A concrete version of the flume has been in operation for several years, and has worked satisfactorily. Based on the field experiences gained with the concrete flume, it was decided

---

[1] *Hydrologist, located at Albuquerque in cooperation with the University of New Mexico; central headquarters are maintained at Fort Collins, in cooperation with Colorado State University.*
[2] *Hydraulic Engineer, Division of Watershed Management, Region 3, Forest Service, U. S. Department of Agriculture, Albuquerque, New Mexico.*

to use this model for gaging five streams in New Mexico, but change construction details to reduce costs.

Construction Details for Fiberglassed Flume

Prefabricated Components

Three-quarter-inch exterior grade Douglas-fir plywood was cut and spliced to make the sidewall panels. A coating of polyester resin was applied, and strips of 44-inch-wide, 7-1/2 ounce, Volan chrome finish fiberglass [3] were laid over the wood with a 4-inch overlap (fig. 2). Resin was coated over the fiberglass and squeegeed to work out entrapped air and to insure a solid bond.

Catalyst was added to the resin just before it was applied, to speed the setting. Ideally, room or outdoor temperature should be 70°F. or higher. In lower temperatures, more catalyst should be added. A mixture of 12 cubic centimeters (cc.) of catalyst to 1 quart of resin did not harden before application was completed at shop temperatures around 65°F. (With experimentation, proper combinations can be worked out.) Unskilled men can easily apply the fiberglass and resin. If mistakes are made, the material can be sanded down and the process repeated.

Panels were fiberglassed on both sides and the edges were sealed with resin to prevent decay. When more than one coat of fiberglass was applied, the surface receiving the second coat was allowed to harden, then sanded lightly for the application of new material.

---

[3] *The mention of trade names or commercial enterprises is solely for necessary information; no endorsement by the U. S. Department of Agriculture is implied.*

Figure 2.--Fiberglass coating being applied to the plywood.

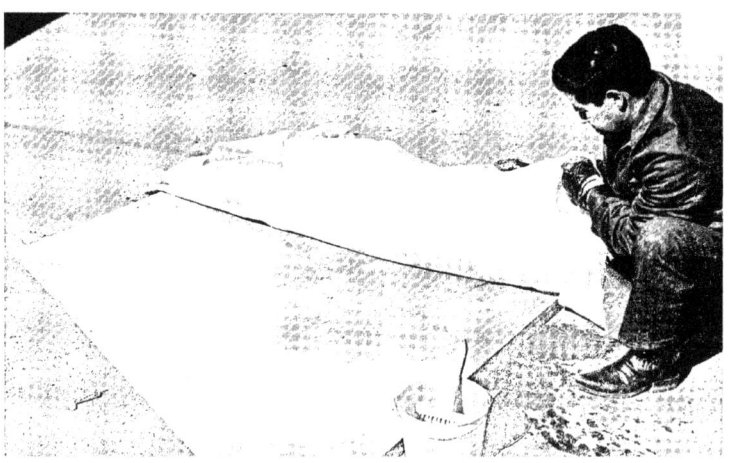

Figure 3.--Detail of steel angle support walls with the fiberglassed plywood panel in place.

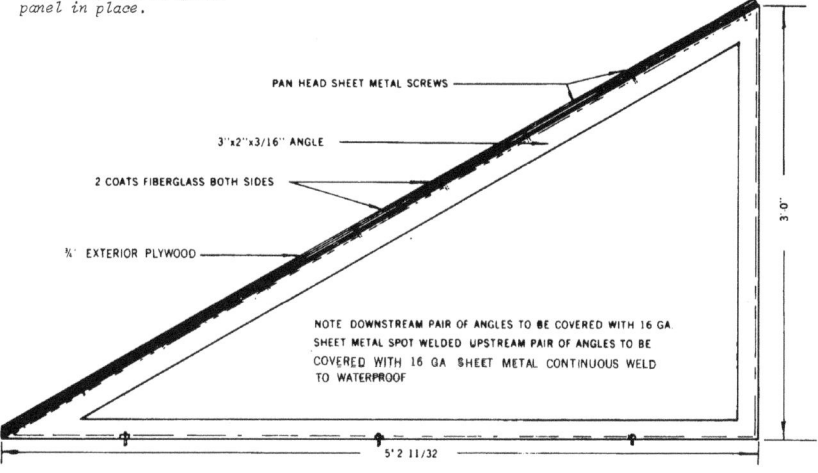

The angle iron used for the support walls was cut and welded to a 30° angle (fig. 3). Upstream steel support walls had a continuously welded cover plate of 16 gage steel to insure a watertight seal in the upstream face. The 16 gage steel cover plate on the downstream support walls was spot welded to hold the backfill.

The intake box was made from a steel box beam (fig. 4), 12 by 4 inches, by 3/16 inch thick. The front face, cut at 30° to fit to the flume sidewall, has a 1/4-inch slot running up its full length. The face plate is removable to facilitate cleaning out the inside. A 1-1/4 inch nipple was attached at the back of the box to connect, by pipe, the stilling well and the intake box. The flanges around the intake box which hold the sidewall panel were carefully placed, for it is important that the face of the intake box be set flush with the flume sidewalls. Protuberances or indentations could cause separation near the intake, which would result in miscalculation of water depth as shown in the stilling well.

Field Installation

Since scour and uplift pressures can be serious problems with this flume, field sites should be carefully chosen. If the flume is placed on bedrock, scour should not be troublesome. In several locations where such placement was impossible, a diverging section was constructed (fig. 5). Other methods might be employed to minimize scour, depending on field conditions.

A center line and cutoff walls were surveyed and staked after the site was chosen. The upstream cutoff wall was extended well into the streambanks to prevent water from flowing around the structure. All other walls were made just large enough to hold the steel support walls.

Footings were dug to 3 feet, and concrete was poured into the excavation. Cinder blocks were laid, reinforced, and filled with concrete to bring each wall about up to grade. Weep

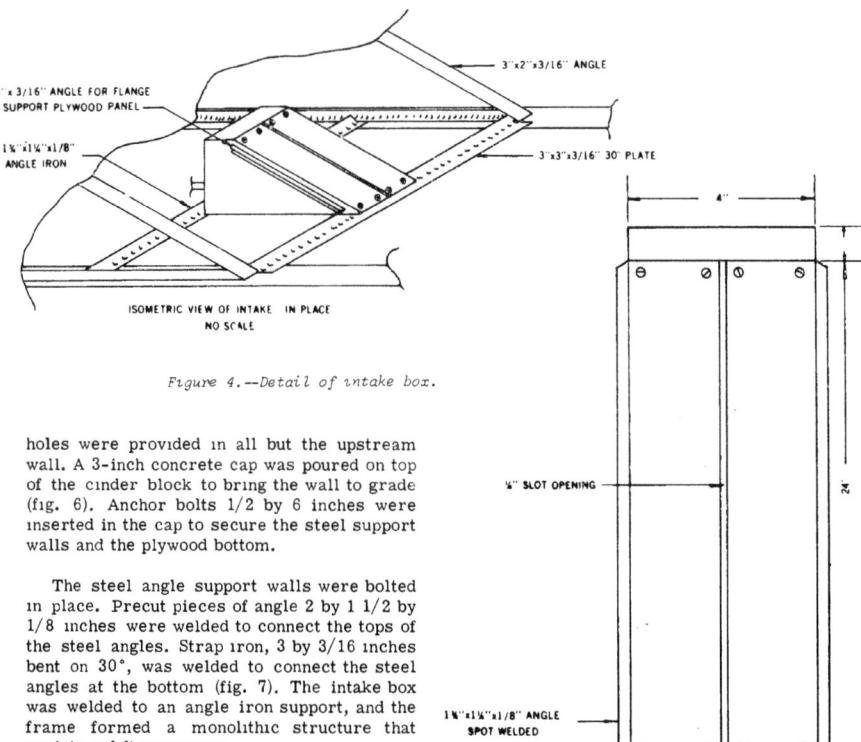

Figure 4.--Detail of intake box.

holes were provided in all but the upstream wall. A 3-inch concrete cap was poured on top of the cinder block to bring the wall to grade (fig. 6). Anchor bolts 1/2 by 6 inches were inserted in the cap to secure the steel support walls and the plywood bottom.

The steel angle support walls were bolted in place. Precut pieces of angle 2 by 1 1/2 by 1/8 inches were welded to connect the tops of the steel angles. Strap iron, 3 by 3/16 inches bent on 30°, was welded to connect the steel angles at the bottom (fig. 7). The intake box was welded to an angle iron support, and the frame formed a monolithic structure that resists uplift pressures.

The upstream cutoff wall was extended into the banks by means of a cinder-block wall. The blocks were reinforced and filled with concrete. Felt coated with roofing plastic on both sides was laid under the steel to insure a watertight seal, and the steel angles were bolted to the block wall. The upstream face of the wall was waterproofed with roofing plastic. The upstream excavation was backfilled with select material and tamped to prevent leakage under the flume.

The fiberglassed plywood panels were attached to the metal frames with 1/4 by 20 by 1-inch self-tapping sheet-metal screws; the joints and screw holes were covered with

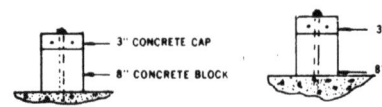

Figure 6.--Cross section of f and foundation walls.

Figure 5.--The flume with the diverging section attached to minimize the downstream scour.

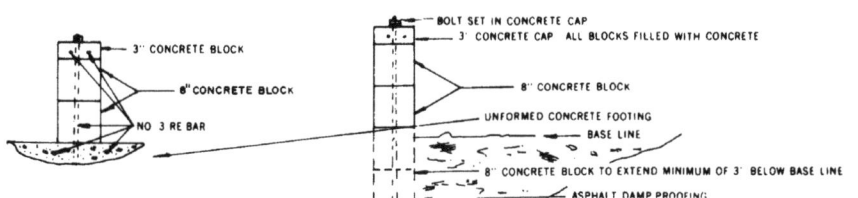

Figure 7.--Angle iron frame prior to attachment of prefabricated fiberglassed panels.

fiberglass in the field. The stilling well was set in concrete, provided with a drain, and connected to the intake box by a 1-1/4-inch pipe set level. The flume should be backfilled with small gravel or other pervious material that will allow any water which gets under the flume to pass through easily. A plywood instrument shelter was then placed on the culvert and the instrument installed.

Maintenance

Should the flume surface erode or should a panel be broken, it is a simple matter to replace the entire panel or to sand the damaged area and fill it with fiberglass. The flumes described here are operated only in summer. If the flume is operated in the winter, freezing problems can arise in the intake pipe, drain, and stilling well unless heat is provided.

Cost

A finished flume, constructed with a 4-man crew in 10 days, cost about $1,500--materials, about $500; labor $800; and the recording instrument, $200 (table 1). When a diverging section was included, material costs were slightly higher, but labor costs were virtually the same.

Table 1.--List of materials for a flume without a diverging section

Item	Quantity	Specifications	Item	Quantity	Specifications
ement	30 bags	Type I	Re-bars	220 feet	No. 3
				140 feet	No. 4
nd	8 yards	--	Fittings, pipe	--	Nipples, union, couplings--
ravel	12 yards	Small			1-1/4 inches
ofing plastic	5 gallons	--	Lumber for forms		
rames, angle iron	8	Prefabricated (15 feet)-- 3 by 2 by 3/16 inches each	Nails for building forms		
			Cinder blocks	150	8 by 8 by 16 inches
elt	30 feet by 3 inches	90 pound	Bolts, anchor	26	1/2 by 6 inches
ipe, culvert	1	18 inches by 8 feet, for stilling well	Screws, self tapping	300	1/4 by 1 inch
			Plywood	15 sheets	Exterior Douglas-fir, 4 by 8 feet
ipe, galvanized	8 feet	1-1/4 inches			
rap iron	32 feet	3 by 3/16-inch, bent on 30°	Fiberglass	90 yards	44 inches wide
			Resin, polyester	10 gallons	Volan chrome finish, or equivalent
ngle iron	32 feet	2 by 1-1/2 by 1/8 inch			
take box	1	Prefabricated -- 12- by 4- by 3/16-inch steel box beam	Catalyst	480 cc	--
			Acetone	--	Enough for cleanup

Field Experience to Date

Several flumes have received flow since construction. One particular event provided a quick evaluation of the sturdiness and ability of this prefabricated flume to withstand high sediment-carrying flows. The event took place on a 120-acre watershed with highly erosive granitic soils. A high-intensity summer convective storm released 1.57 inches of precipitation in about 20 minutes. The maximum flow was 1-1/2 feet in the flume, with a peak of 38 cubic feet per second (c.f.s.). This flow, and the resulting high sediment load it carried, sheared the downstream sediment basin wall with a resultant loss of some of the sediment in the trap (fig. 8). The 18 tons of sediment that remained, however, were cross sectioned in the basin after the flow. Boulders, small rock, and sand comprised the bulk of this sediment. No damage to the flume, except for minor scratching of the resin finish, was found. There were no dimensional changes in the flume. The scratched areas were easily re-covered.

Summary

An efficient, low-cost flume can be prefabricated and hauled to the field site for construction. The flume is of a modified trapezoidal design with a capacity of 222 c.f.s. It is accurate over a wide range of flow conditions. Fiberglassed plywood makes up the flume sidewall panels. Other prefabricated components include angle iron support walls and an intake box. Other low-cost materials bring the flume construction costs to about $1500. A four-man crew can construct the flume in about 10 days.

Maintenance costs are low, for the fiberglassed surface can be easily repaired--in much the same manner as automobile fenders and boats are repaired.

After Controlled Burning and Pringle Manzanita Chaparral[1]

P. Pase [2]

Figure 1.--A dense manzanita community in the Mazatzal Mountains before controlled burn. Dominant shrub is Pringle manzanita, with only minor amounts of shrub live oak and desert ceanothus. Yerba-santa was absent from the mature stand.

in October through May, 10.31 inches in June through September.

To improve flammability during the fall, the shrubs were sprayed by helicopter with 4 pounds per acre of the butoxyethanol ester of 2,4-D in a 1-to-5 diesel oil-water emulsion in

August 1962. One 30-acre area was sprayed and burned, one 10-acre area was sprayed but not burned, and a 30-acre area was unsprayed and unburned. Spraying alone killed an estimated 90 percent or more of the Pringle manzanita tops; as this species does not sprout, this represents a high degree of control. After burning was completed, all three areas were seeded to weeping lovegrass (Eragrostis curvula (Schrad.) Nees) and sand dropseed (Sporobolus cryptandrus (Torr.) A. Gray). Shrub seedling counts were made in early spring 1964, approximately 1 year after germination (table 1).

Number of shrub seedlings appeared highly correlated with intensity of burn, with virtually no seedlings of either shrubs or grasses on the "sprayed unburned" or "check" areas.

The dense stand of yerba-santa seedlings, over 100,000 per acre, deserves special mention. Careful examination of the area before burning revealed no living plants or identifiable dead remnants within the manzanita community. A few plants were noted along the cutbanks of a forest road penetrating the stand, but these had given no indication of spreading. The manzanita community was al-

Table 1. --Surviving 1-year-old shrub seedlings[a] on El Oso Block Burn, Tonto National Forest, Arizona, spring 1964

Botanical and common names of species		Burned in October 1962		Unburned	
		Intense burn[2]	Light burn[3]	Spray only	Check
		- - - - - Number per acre - - - - -			
Arctostaphylos pringlei Parry	Pringle manzanita	18,180	4,363	0	0
Ceanothus greggii A. Gray	Desert ceanothus	2,618	636	0	0
C. integerrimus Hook. & Arn.	Deerbrush	190	0	0	0
Cercocarpus montanus Raf.	True mountainmahogany	95	0	0	0
Eriodyctyon angustifolium Nutt.	Yerba-santa	101,293	16,453	0	0
Garrya flavescens S. Wats.	Yellowleaf silktassel	571	1,182	0	59
Quercus emoryi Torr.	Emory oak	143	364	0	11[a]
Q. turbinella Greene	Shrub live oak	48	91	0	0

[a] Oaks germinated in August 1963; all others, March-April 1963.
[2] Leaves and twigs mostly consumed.
[3] Shrubs dead but leaves and small twigs mostly intact, largely a "cool" or "ground" fire.

most literally "closed." As yerba-santa seeds are of moderately high density and not winged, one must conclude that they were stored in the soil, perhaps for many years. This conclusion is supported by the findings of Glendening and Pase.[3]

Increased germination of soil-stored shrub seeds has been reported by Gratkowski[4] and Horton and Kraebel.[5]

Occasional remnants of long-dead plants of desert ceanothus were found in the stand before it was burned, while deerbrush was apparently absent. Seedlings of these species

[3]Glendening, George E., and Pase, C. P. Effect of litter treatment on germination of species found under manzanita (Arctostaphylos). Jour. Range Mangt. 17: 265-266. 1964.
[4]Gratkowski, H. Brush seedlings after controlled burning of brushlands in southwestern Oregon. Jour. Forestry 59: 885-888. 1961.
[5]Horton, J. S., and Kraebel, C. J. Development of vegetation after fire in the chamise chaparral of southern California. Ecology 36: 244-262. 1955.

undoubtedly came from seed stored in the soil. The heavy acorns of Emory oak an shrub live oak were probably planted by pin yon jays or rodents on the burned areas. Th light, plumose seeds of true mountainmahogany could well have been windborn from adjacent unburned areas where it was abundant

Additional seedlings germinated the secon spring after the burn. In order of abundance these were Pringle manzanita, desert ceano thus, and yellowleaf silktassel. No new seed lings of yerba-santa were noted the secon spring; however, separation of seedlings an the abundant root sprouts of this species mad identification uncertain.

In conclusion, the use of fire to break u stands of mature Pringle manzanita may re sult in a great increase in seedlings of les desirable species, which may be in part offse by an increase in certain shrubs that ar highly desirable as game forage. Additiona control techniques to improve the composi tion of replacement vegetation are badly need ed before fire is widely used in such areas

f Forage Species Sites in New Mexico

Springfield[1]

12-foot rows, 1 foot apart. Two or more plots of every species were randomly selected at each site. Rows were made with hand tools, and the seeds were planted by hand during June and July. Rate of seeding usually was 20 to 30 seeds per foot of row. Seeds were covered with about 1/2 to 1 inch of soil. Wild plants were hoed from between the seeded rows during the first 2 years, after which the native vegetation was allowed to reestablish in the test plots.

The success of the seeding in each plot was rated at least twice a year from 1946 to 1952, once in 1954, and once in 1962. The following rating system, described by Hull[2] was used:

0	failure
1- 2	very poor
3- 4	poor
5- 6	fair
7- 8	good
9-10	excellent

The above numerical ratings were assigned in the field on the basis of number, distribution, and vigor of plants in the test rows. The rating represents the actual stand in relation to the best possible stand.

[2]*Hull, A. C., Jr. Rating seeded stands on experimental range plots. Jour. Range Mangt. 7: 122-124, illus. 1954.*

Table 1.--Description of study sites in pinyon-juniper type, New Mexico

Study site	Elevation	Precipitation		Length of growing season	Soil texture	Principal understory plants
		Annual	October through March			
	Feet	Inches	Percent	Days		
Glorieta Mesa	7,200	15	29	140	Sandy loam	Blue grama, western wheatgrass
Monica	7,500	12	29	123	Gravelly loam	Blue grama, ring muhly
Corona	6,300	15	30	175	Loam	Blue grama, western wheatgrass
Fort Bayard	6,300	14	33	194	Clay loam	Blue grama, side-oats grama
Taos Junction	7,200	13	37	146	Sandy loam	Big sagebrush, blue grama

Many seedings failed to produce satisfactory seedling stands. Species were judged to have been inadequately tested unless the stand rated fair or better within 1 year after seeding. Species likewise were not considered adequately tested when the stands were destroyed by rodents or rabbits.

Results

Species adaptability ratings are given in table 2, which lists all species adequately tested at one or more of the study sites. Species which persisted at the study sites for 14 to 16 years presumably met crucial tests of climatic adaptability. Winter temperatures in 1948 and 1949 were unusually low for the State as a whole, and precipitation in 1956 was the lowest on record.

The seeded species that rated fair or better in 1962 also had met other tests, including resistance to competition from other plants and to possible destruction by animals. At each of the sites the native plants gave increasingly greater competition through the years, especially at the Glorieta Mesa and Corona sites where western wheatgrass competed strongly with the seeded plants. Also, periodic observations at each site showed varying degrees of activities by ants, grasshoppers, gophers, rats, mice, cottontails, jackrabbits, and deer--all potential detriments to survival of the test seedings.

Introduced cool-season grasses, including Agropyron cristatum, A. desertorum, A. sibiricum, and Elymus junceus, grew well at the Taos Junction site. This site receives proportionately more winter precipitation than the other four, and is the only one of the sites where big sagebrush is a principal understory plant. The introduced cool-season grasses failed to persist at the Monica and Corona sites, which indicates lack of adaptability to environmental conditions there. They also failed to persist at the Glorieta Mesa site, where gophers destroyed the seeded stands before the species were adequately tested. The introduced wheatgrasses grew well for several years at the Fort Bayard site, but they gradually declined in vigor and failed to reproduce.

Seeded stands of Agropyron smithii, a native wheatgrass, survived at all five study sites and rated fair at four of the sites. The so-called "sand strain" showed no advantages over a regular commercial source.

Table 2.--Adaptability ratings for species tested at one or more pinyon-juniper study sites in New Mexico--
planted 1948-49, evaluated 1950, 1954, 1962

Species	Glorieta Mesa			Monica			Corona			Fort Bayard			Taos Junction		
	1950	1954	1962	1950	1954	1962	1950	1954	1962	1950	1954	1962	1950	1954	1962
ropyron cristatum	E	X		P	O		G	P	O	G	F	P	G	G	F
desertorum	G	X		F	O		F	P	O	G	F	P	G	E	G
elongatum	G	X		P	O		P	O		F	P	O	O		
inerme	F	X		F	O		F	O		--			G	F	P
intermedium	F	X		P	O		F	P	O	G	F	F	F	F	O
sibiricum	G	X		F	O		G	P	O	G	F	P	G	E	G
smithii															
Commercial	F	F	F	F	P	P	F	F	F	F	F	F	F	F	F
Sand	G	P	P	--			--			F	F	F	F	G	F
trachycaulum	O			P	O		F	O		--			F	O	
trichophorum	G	X		P	O		F	P	O	F	F	P	G	F	P
iropogon barbinodis	--			--			--			P	P	F			
caucasicus				--			--			P	P	F			
ischaemum				F	P	O	G	G	G	--					
~iplex canescens															
Las Cruces	--			G	E	E	E	G	F*	P*	P	P	G	P*	P
Taos	E	E	G	E	E	E	G	G	F*	G	G	G	G	G	G
uteloua curtipendula	--			P	O		F	P	F	--			--		
eriopoda				--			--						P	ᵥ	
gracilis															
Capulin				G	G	F	G	G	F	--			G	F	F
Commercial				F	P	P	F	P	P	--			F	G	F
Lovington				G	F	P	G	G	F	--			E	G	F
:hloe dactyloides	--			F	O		P	P	P	--			P	F	F
ymus glaucus	O			--			F	O					G	P	O
junceus	F	F	O	F	O		F	P	P	--			E	G	G
igrostis chloromelas	O			O			P	P	O	P	P	F	O		
curvula	--			O			F	P	O	G	P	F	O		
lehmanniana	O			O			O			G	P	O	O		
trichodes	--			F	O		G	F	P	--			--		
stuca ovina															
{aria jamesii	--														
curus phleoides	--			--			ι								
lilotus alba	F	O		P	O		--								
officinalis	G	O		F	O		F	O		--					
hlembergia wrightii	G	F	X	G	G	F	E	G	F	--					
ysopsis hymenoides	--			F	X		F	X		--					
nicum obtusum	--			F	O		F	G	F	--					
a ampla															
cale montanum	F	O		F	O		F	O		--					
tarıa macrostachya	--			P	P	O	P	P	P	F	F	P	--		
orobolus airoides	--			G	E	G	P	F	G	--			--		
contractus	--			G	F	P	--						--		
cryptandrus	F	P	P	G	F	F	G	G	G	--			G		
wrightii	--			P	F	G	F	G	G	--			--		
ipa columbiana	--			--									F	P	O
comata													F	F	P
viridula				--			--						F	F	P
idens albescens	--			F	O		F	F	P	--			--		
elongata	--			G	X		G	F	P	--			--		

KEY TO SYMBOLS:
O = Failure G = Good -- = Not adequately tested (stand did not rate fair
P = Poor E = Excellent or better within 1 year after seeding)
F = Fair X = Destroyed by rabbits or rodents * = Damaged by insects, rabbits, rodents, or deer

Andropogon ischaemum maintained good stands throughout the years at the Corona site. Two other species of Andropogon--A. barbinodis and A. caucasicus--survived as fair stands at the Fort Bayard site. These species were never adequately tested at the other sites.

Atriplex canescens survived and grew well at all five sites. Stands produced from seed collected near Taos generally rated higher than stands from seed collected near Las Cruces.

Three strains of Bouteloua gracilis persisted at the Monica, Corona, and Taos Junction sites. The commercial source (Kansas) generally was poorer than the Capulin and Lovington strains. B. curtipendula survived as a fair stand at the Corona site, but for unknown reasons was never successfully established by seeding at the Fort Bayard site, where it grows in abundance naturally.

Eragrostis chloromelas and E. curvula survived at the Fort Bayard site but failed at the other sites. A stand of E. trichodes at Corona that rated good in 1950 declined to a poor stand in 1962. E. lehmanniana failed to survive at any of the study sites; good stands of seedlings usually emerged soon after planting, but these consistently died the following winter except at Fort Bayard.

A number of the species tested appeared to be adapted to only one of the five study sites. Some of these species never were adequately tested at the other sites, whereas some species developed good stands that died out because of drought or cold weather. Examples are the Eragrostis species at Fort Bayard discussed above. Other examples are Hilaria jamesii and Panicum obtusum, species which rated fair at Corona, and Oryzopsis hymenoides, which rated fair at Taos Junction.

Melilotus officinalis produced fair to good stands at three sites but did not reseed itself. By 1962 no plants of this species were found at any of the study sites.

Muhlenbergia wrightii was the outstanding grass at the Glorieta Mesa, Monica, and Corona sites in 1950. Twelve years later, gophers had destroyed the test plots at the Glorieta Mesa site and only fair stands remained at the other two sites.

Secale montanum rated fair at four sites in 1950 but had completely disappeared by 1954. This grass produced a large volume of herbage for a few years, and may be useful for certain situations even though it is short lived.

Three species of Sporobolus rated high in 1962. Good stands of S. airoides and S. wrightii remained at the Monica and Corona sites. Stands of S. cryptandrus rated good at Corona and Taos Junction and fair at Monica.

Stipa species developed fair stands at the Taos Junction site. S. comata and S. viridula declined from fair to poor in adaptability ratings during the 8 years from 1954 to 1962, while S. columbiana disappeared.

Two species of Tridens were growing as fair stands at Corona in 1954 but declined to poor stands by 1962.

Conclusions

The following species seem to warrant special consideration for seeding pinyon-juniper ranges. These are species that in 1962 rated good at one or more, or fair at two or more, of the study sites:

Agropyron desertorum
A. sibiricum
A. smithii
Andropogon ischaemum
Atriplex canescens
Bouteloua gracilis
Elymus junceus
Muhlenbergia wrightii
Sporobolus airoides
S. cryptandrus
S. wrightii

The Agropyron species and Elymus junceus probably are primarily adapted to areas where big sagebrush grows or where winter precipitation is relatively abundant. The other species listed appear better adapted to other areas in the pinyon-juniper type.

under Tamarisk in Arizona

nd C. J. Campbell[1]

tics under *Tamarix pentandra* in central
ground-water wells within a circular area
ussed before and after vegetation removal.
nal fluctuations in selected wells were not
ined.

vegetation type containing mixed species of differing age, water withdrawal from the capillary fringe or water table is undoubtedly not uniform. Theis and Conover[4] proposed a system of actually measuring the amount of water involved in diurnal fluctuations of a water table. They suggested a line of observation wells be established and calibrated in a study plot; after calibration, the vegetation would be removed, and water-level measurements continued until sufficient data were collected for an analysis. Then, diurnal fluctuations prevailing before vegetation removal might be approximated by withdrawal of water by several small pumps. Discharged water would approximate water used by plants before their removal.

vegetation in lower Safford Valley, Arizona. U. S. Geol. Survey Water-Supply Paper 1103, 210 pp., illus. 1950.
[4]*Theis, C. V., and Conover, C. S. Factors for consideration in study of salvage of water used by phreatophytes. App. IV. Mimeographed report to the Salt Cedar Interagency Council by Salt Cedar Interagency Task Force. Albuquerque, N. Mex., Feb. 1959.*
[5]*Decker, J. P., Gaylor, W. G., Cole, F. D. Measuring transpiration of undisturbed tamarisk shrubs. Plant Physiol. 37: 393-397, illus. 1962.*

The primary objective of the study reported here was to evaluate the pumping technique for measuring ET losses from tamarisk. The following factors were determined: (1) degree of diurnal fluctuation of a shallow water table beneath a tamarisk stand, (2) effect of tamarisk removal on water-table fluctuations, and (3) whether diurnal fluctuations in a relatively small area could be simulated by pumping with sump pumps.

Study Area and Instrumentation

The study area was located east of Granite Reef Diversion Dam on a flood plain of the Salt River in central Arizona. Relatively constant river stage is maintained during spring and summer months, but by late fall the river is dry and ground-water levels drop 2 feet or more. All pumping tests and measurements of diurnal fluctuations were in a relatively mature tamarisk stand. The trees averaged 25 feet in height and contained 190 square feet (1 foot aboveground) of basal area per acre. Soil beneath the plot was mainly alluvial deposits of silty sand in the first 3 to 4 feet, grading into coarse sand and gravel to an unknown depth. Granite bedrock underlaid the entire flood plain.

Eight 8-inch wells were irregularly spaced around an FW-1 water-stage recorder-equipped well at distances ranging from 6 to 7 feet (fig. 1). Thirty 3-inch wells were asymmetrically located from 2.2 to 20 feet from the center FW-1 well. A control, recorder-equipped 8-inch well was located approximately 150 feet from the cluster of pumping wells. Vegetation on the site prevented uniform spacing of well casings. All wells except the recorder well were instrumented with a float and tape device [6] for measuring water-table fluctuations. Changes in water-table levels were detectable to the nearest 0.005 foot. Water levels during the study period were approximately 4 feet below the soil surface with water-table slope negligible. The entire length of all well casings was perforated.

[6]*Gary, Howard L. A simple device for measuring fluctuations in shallow ground-water wells. U. S. Forest Serv., Rocky Mountain Forest and Range Expt. Sta. Res. Note 68, 2 pp., illus. 1961.*

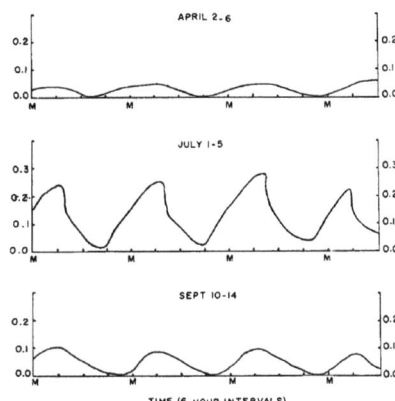

Figure 2.--Tracings from FW-1 recorder equipped well showing the water-table fluctuations in spring, summer, and fall months near Granite Reef Diversion Dam, central Arizona.

Table 1.--Water-level decline in 39 wells at 30-minute intervals and resulting sampling errors,[1] July 18, 1961

Time (Hours)	Water-table decline			Sampling error
	Maximum	Minimum	Mean	
	Ft.	Ft.	Ft.	Pct.
0700	--	--	--	--
0730	0.025	0.000	0.007	30.00
0800	.040	.000	.014	17.86
0830	.040	.010	.024	7.92
0900	.040	.015	.026	6.15
0930	.035	.005	.020	9.00
1000	.035	.005	.019	7.37
1030	.025	.010	.016	7.50
1100	.030	.010	.020	10.50
1130	.025	.005	.018	11.11
1200	.020	.005	.012	10.00
1230	.030	.010	.015	8.67
1300	.020	.005	.010	12.00
1330	.020	.005	.010	11.00
1400	.020	.005	.011	11.82
1430	.015	.005	.008	13.75
1500	.015	.000	.007	18.57
1530	.010	-.010	.002	55.00
1600	.005	-.005	.000	--
1630	.010	-.010	.000	--
1700	.000	-.015	-.004	--

[1] Indicate accuracy of 30-minute mean water-table change of 39 wells with probability of 95%, rate of water-table change in 8-inch wells similar to that of 3-inch wells.

of maximum plant growth and diurnal fluctuations. By first obtaining values from the float and tape devices in each well (readings required about 5 minutes) and by careful use of a transit, rod, and measuring tape, near simultaneous readings of water-table levels were possible. All tests showed about the same variability among wells, but no consistent relationship between any two wells. In one test on June 6, 1964, range of variation was 0.235 foot. Standard deviation(s) about the mean (0.109 ft.) from a common datum was 0.043 foot, which illustrates the variability in water-table elevation when the area was intensively sampled. Thus, the water table at any given time may be projected as an irregular surface when plants are actively transpiring.

Measurements of daily water-table depletion in the 39 wells also indicated nonuniform changes in water levels. A test conducted at 30-minute intervals (table 1) shows greatest variability between wells occurred during the first 3 hours following start of water-table depletion and again near the time of water-table rise.

Effect of Tamarisk Removal on Ground-Water Fluctuation

In the summer of 1961, tamarisk and arrowweed (Pluchea sericea (Nutt.) Coville) were removed from a nearby area in three stages.[7] Basal area of tamarisk and arrowweed stems averaged 120 square feet per acre. Areas cleared were:

	Radius (Ft.)	Area (Sq.ft.)
First treatment	12.5	491
Second treatment	17.7	984
Third treatment	30.5	2,922

[7]Gary, Howard L. Removal of tamarisk reduces water-table fluctuations in central Arizona. U. S. Forest Serv., Rocky Mountain Forest and Range Expt. Sta. Res. Note 81, 4 pp., illus. 1962.

After the initial treatment of 491 square feet, water-table fluctuation, measured by a centrally located recorder well, was significantly decreased in amplitude. No significant additional change resulted from second and third cutting treatments; however, combined treatments significantly reduced diurnal fluctuations.

On August 1, 1962, a similar clearing in tamarisk was made with a 12.5-foot radius (491 sq. ft.) around a recorder-equipped well (fig. 3). Approximately 2.0 square feet of basal area was removed. Contrary to results of the 1961 clearing, a change in diurnal fluctuation did not immediately occur. It was assumed, then, that lateral roots of mature tamarisk growing outside the cleared plot might be drawing water from within. A circular trench 1 foot wide and 4 feet deep, with a 15-foot radius was excavated, lined with polyethylene, and then refilled. Following the trenching, planimetered area of diurnal fluctuations as taken from recorder charts were reduced approximately 46 percent compared to the adjacent control well records. Since no roots were observed below 3 feet, the plants probably were using capillary water. Obervations of the excavated trench showed that capillary moisture extended to the ground surface.

Effect of Pumping on Water-Level Elevations

All pumping tests described were conducted on the site before vegetation removal to determine applicability of the sump pump technique and effects of pumping on water-level elevations. After vegetation removal on August 1, 1962, pumping tests were continued; however, the area soon flooded, and the wells filled with sediment and debris so pumping operations were discontinued.

Eight 8-inch wells surrounding the recorder-equipped well were used to determine possibility of influencing natural diurnal fluctuations before vegetation removal. Each 8-inch well was equipped with a small 1/70 h.p. electric sump pump that could be raised or lowered to desired depths and a float and tape device to obtain a measure of well drawdown (fig. 3). On some occasions the recorder-equipped well was similarly instrumented. In every pumping test, pumps were operated continuously at one predetermined elevation although flow rates of individual pumps varied with the hydraulic heads and transmissibility of flood plain deposits surrounding each well.

Many combinations of pumping tests were undertaken in wells P1-P9 at heads from 0.200 to 2.500 feet. During one pumping test conducted July 13, 1962, the water level in nine wells (P1-P9) was lowered as far as possible with the small pumps and maintained at approximately that level for 24 hours. Hydraulic gradients of more than 2 feet were maintained in each well being pumped. The steep gradients created by pumping did not appreciably influence water levels in the adjacent 3-inch observation wells, however, even after pump-

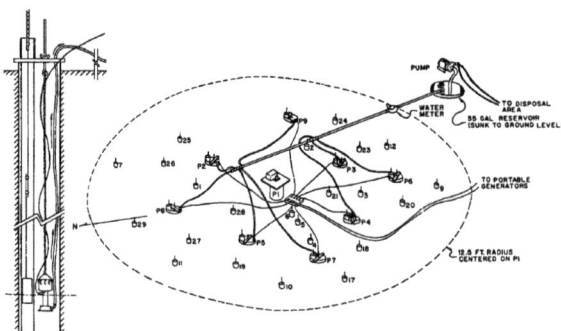

Figure 3. -- Isometric drawing of the pumping area and system used to remove the ground water. Dotted line shows the area cleared of vegetation. Enlarged section shows float and staff gage inside a 3-inch casing an sump pump mechanism in an 8-inch casing installed with pumps while the numbers 1-29 were the 3-inch observation wells.

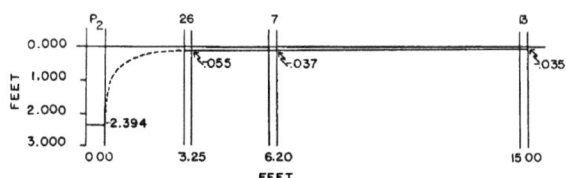

Figure 4.--Cross section through wells P2, 26, 7, and 13 showing water-table profile before and after 24 hours of pumping from P1-P9. Dotted line indicates probable slope of water table between P2 and number 26. Approximately 1,000 gallons of water were removed from nine wells. Pumping began at 0940 hours, July 13, 1965.

ing approximately 1,000 gallons of water from the nine wells. Water-table drawdown in one of the nine wells after 24 hours of pumping is shown in cross section in figure 4. Water level was apparently affected very little beyond a distance of 3 feet from any of the wells being pumped.

In another pumping test starting at 1700 hours and ending at 2305 hours June 22, 1962, eight pumps were used in wells P2-P9 to lower water table approximately 0.500 foot. Approximately 5 minutes elapsed before pumps lowered the water in well casings 0.500 foot below initial water-table level. Due to mechanical difficulties, water in well P9 was not lowered until 2030 hours. Water table level in well P2 and two nearby wells after the 6-hour period of night pumping is shown in figure 5. Well number 26 was a minus 0.006 foot below and well number 7 plus 0.090 foot above initial water level, which indicated normal rate of evening water table rise exceeded rate of water removal by pumping. Approximately 565 gallons of water were removed during this pumping run. Figure 6, which shows contour lines representing interpretations of water levels between well points at 2000 and 2300 hours, indicates transmissibility of flood plain deposits vary considerably in the relatively small area. Because obvious soil heterogeneity occurs in the pumping area, calculations of transmissibility were not attempted. In figure 6 the 2000 hours water level in P1 is shown as minus 0.041 foot as a result of pumping in wells P2-P9, but by 2300 hours water in P1 had raised to plus 0.012 foot. The minus 0.025-foot contour at 2300 hours indicates how night recharge affects the water table within the area being pumped.

None of the pumping tests influenced natural diurnal fluctuations. It was necessary to create a hydraulic gradient many times that of average diurnal fluctuations (0.250 foot) before the effects of water removal could be

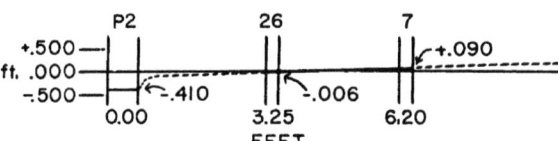

Figure 5.--Cross section through wells P2 - P7 showing the water-table profile before and after 6 hours of night pumping. Dotted line indicates the probable water-table profile. Approximately 565 gallons of water were removed from wells P2 - P9.

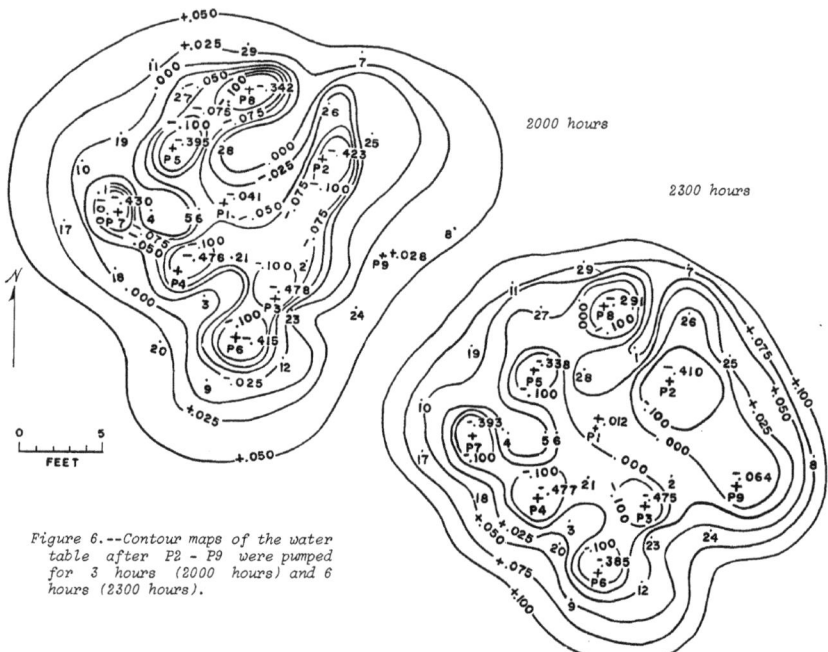

Figure 6.--Contour maps of the water table after P2 - P9 were pumped for 3 hours (2000 hours) and 6 hours (2300 hours).

detected in adjacent observation wells. Well casings were not clogged, because water could be seen pouring through perforations.

Discussion

Diurnal Fluctuations

Simultaneous measurements of water-table elevations in 39 wells within a 40-foot circular area showed considerable variation among wells. During one observation period, a maximum difference of 0.235 foot was indicated. Rates of water-table decline differed during all measurement periods. Greatest difference in daily rates of water-table depletion between wells was near start of decline and just before beginning of water-table rise.

Many factors influence the diurnal fluctuation of a shallow water table--age, structure, species or associations, temperature, atmospheric pressure, relative humidity, soil genesis, relative height of the water table an slope, and hydraulic conductivity of water bearing material. Also, the unequal distribu tion and physiologic activity of roots in th capillary fringe above a shallow water tabl result in variable water use by plants. Di urnal water-table fluctuations are reduce following the removal of flood plain vegeta tion. The amount of reduction depends o interaction of the above-mentioned factors Considerably more work is needed to full assess the effect of each variable.

Vegetation Removal

It has been recognized that, at points in an area, the amplitude of a diurnal fluctuation varies with the porosity (specific yield) of the material in which the fluctuation occurs--assuming ET losses occur uniformly over an area. If, however, withdrawal of water by plants does not occur uniformly over an area, the pumping technique is even more difficult to apply. Reference here is to the variation in ET--not in the variation measured in amplitude of the diurnal fluctuations. In any floodplain vegetation type, however, withdrawal from the capillary fringe is undoubtedly not uniform throughout a given area. The question arises: where should the wells be located to give an unbiased estimate of average rate and amount of ET losses for a plant or land area? The variability of diurnal fluctuations measured in a relatively small area with vegetation in place is evidence that results from such a well may be totally erroneous.

Pumping to simulate natural diurnal fluctuations was unsuccessful. The creation of small hydraulic heads in eight wells within an 8-foot radius did not appreciably lower the surrounding water table although a considerable amount of water was pumped from each well. Water movement in adjacent wells was never apparent except under hydraulic heads of more than 1 foot. It seems doubtful that pumps can be used successfully to simulate natural water-table depletions caused by ET from phreatophytes, even if well locations are unbiased and ET losses uniformly distributed. A basic difference between the pumping action on water-table drawdown and depletions caused by ET losses is that pumps remove free water from well casings stemming from the surrounding coarse gravel layers, while plant roots primarily draw water from the capillary fringe. As water is removed from the capillary fringe by vegetation, vertical recharge occurs from the water table beneath. It is only after ET losses decrease in the evening that excess recharge water can eliminate the moisture deficit created by vegetation each day.

Summary

Good estimates of ET losses from tamarisk on the site of the present study were not obtained with the pumping technique outlined by Theis and Conover.[4] Diurnal fluctuations of water tables were extremely variable between any two wells because of heterogeneous plant and soil conditions. Diurnal fluctuations were decreased by removal of vegetation on a small area and by elimination of roots from surrounding vegetation by trenching, but the amount of decrease was not predictable. Pumping removed ground water from well casings, but did not appreciably influence water levels in adjacent wells.

Height Growth Characteristics of Siberian Elm in Central Great Plains Windbreaks

Donald H. Sander [1]

Curves of tree height in relation to age have both practical and research value in Plains forestry:

1. Height-age curves are necessary to remove tree age as a variable in classification of soils for trees.
2. A knowledge of the shape of height-age curves can assist in classification and correlation of soil characteristics in terms of tree growth.
3. Curves are important to aid the forester in management decisions such as tree-row removal, thinning, and desirability of certain species combinations.
4. They are important for determining maximum effective windbreak heights, a factor used to determine the proper spacing intervals between windbreaks.

In 1959, a study was initiated to obtain height-age data for several species of Plains windbreak trees. Curves for Austrian and ponderosa pine have been reported.[2,3] This paper reports growth curves for Siberian elm, Ulmus pumila L., an introduced species used extensively in the Plains region. It is often called by the misnomer, Chinese elm.

Procedure

Ten dominant Siberian elm trees were measured in each of 15 field windbreaks planted by the Prairie States Forestry Project during the period 1937 to 1941. The windbreaks represented average tree-growing conditions for each area shown in fig. 1. A general description of the soils in each area is given in table 1. Water tables were beyond the reach of tree roots on all sites except in Morrill County, Nebraska, in the western Platte River Valley, and possibly in the sandy loams of Rice County, Kansas. The Morrill County windbreaks were also irrigated.

Height at different ages was determined by stem analysis on 10 dominant and codominant trees in each windbreak sampled. An attempt was made to select trees least influenced by adjacent rows of other tree species. The height and age data were smoothed by regression methods, and site index curves were constructed.

Results and Discussion

Growth Curves in Nebraska and Kansas

While height-age curves for ponderosa pine were similar on different soils or geographic areas in Nebraska,[2] the curves for Siberian

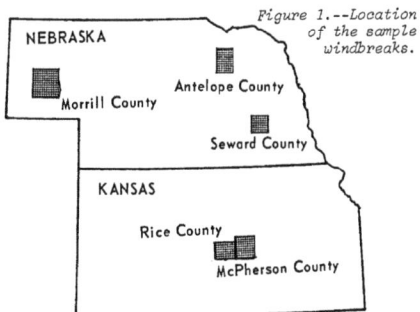

Figure 1.--Location of the sample windbreaks.

Table 1.--General description of the soils in sampling areas

State and County	Sample trees Number	Soil description
Nebraska:		
Antelope	30	Sandy loams, on level topography, developed from Peorian loess. Marshall-Monoma-Ida soil association.
Seward	50	Silty clay loams, on level topography with silty clay subsoil, developed on Peorian loess. Crete-Butler-Fillmore soil association.
Morrill	30	Fine sandy loams on level topography in Platte River Valley, developed from loess and alluvium. Tripp-Bridgeport-Bayard soil association.
Kansas:		
McPherson	20	Silty clay and silty clay loams on level topography with silty clay subsoil, developed on Peorian loess. Crete-Goessel soil association.
Rice	20	Sandy loams on level topography formed on outwash sands. Pratt-Abion-Derby soil association.

elm were different. Mean height-age curves for Siberian elms on the silty clay loam soils of Seward County were starting to flatten out at age 25, much earlier than the curves for trees on the sandy loam soils of Antelope and Morrill Counties (fig. 2). Although height growth was initially greater on the heavy-textured soils, this advantage was lost after 15 to 20 years. Rate of height growth on the heavy-textured soils exceeded growth on the sandy soils only for the first 10 years; thereafter growth rate was higher on sandy soils. This substantiates the observations of other investigators who have noted that tree height growth on light-textured (sandy) soils is generally greater than on heavy-textured soils.[4,5]

Height growth curves for the sandy loam soils of Antelope and Morrill Counties, Nebraska, were nearly alike. The soils in both areas are generally loam and sandy loam topsoils with loam, sandy loam, or silt loam subsoils. Although average annual precipitation in Morrill County is about 8 inches less than in Antelope County, irrigation of windbreaks in the western areas apparently equalizes growing conditions insofar as available moisture is concerned.

Height-age curves within the Seward County, Nebraska, sampling area were of two distinct forms (fig. 2). Soils in this area of the Loess Plains form a series association with tendency to develop claypans in depression areas. Growth of trees sampled on these claypan soils, known as Fillmore, had distinctly different curves than the trees on other loess soils. Although early height growth on these claypan soils was as rapid as on other loess-derived soils, the rate of height growth decreased rapidly after the first 5 years.

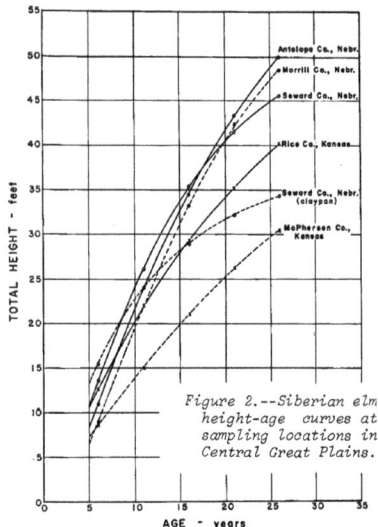

Figure 2.--Siberian elm height-age curves at sampling locations in Central Great Plains.

The rate of height growth at 20 to 25 years on the claypan soils was reduced to 0.5 foot per year (fig. 3), which indicates that the trees were approaching maximum heights on these soils. The heavy claypan undoubtedly limits root penetration and distribution, and this becomes more critical as the trees grow larger. Trees growing on the silty clay loam soils with no claypan averaged almost twice as tall at 20 to 25 years of age as those on the claypan soils. Height growth declined at about the same rate after 15 years of age on the non-claypan soils and the sandy loam soils in Antelope and Morrill Counties.

The downward slopes of periodic annual height growth in figure 3 are very similar for all Nebraska locations. This indicates that tree vigor as expressed by height growth is declining at about the same rate on all soils and locations sampled in Nebraska. Extrapolation of these height growth rates indicates that Siberian elm will essentially reach maximum height at 32 to 36 years of age on these sites in Nebraska. Although such extrapolation can be hazardous, the general performance of older Siberian elms reaching 35 years of age, seems to bear out this prediction.

Height growth of Siberian elm was much less in Kansas windbreaks than in Nebraska (fig. 2). On the sandy loam Pratt-like soils in Rice County, Kansas, total height was 8 to 10 feet less at age 25 than on the sandy loam soils in Nebraska. The rate of height growth for the first 5 years on these sandy soils was somewhat faster in Kansas, however.

Although the silty clay soils in Kansas were loess derived and similar to the silty clay loam soils in Nebraska, the rate of height growth for the first 20 years in Kansas was much less than in Nebraska. At 20 to 25 years of age, however, the growth rates on these heavy-textured soils in Kansas and Nebraska were identical (fig. 3). Possibly differences in climate or in the genetic constitution of Siberian elm influenced height growth more than the apparently similar soils.

While Siberian elm on the sandy loam soils in Rice County grew taller than on the heavy-textured silty clay soils in McPherson County, the curves for both soils were similar. In this case the similar climatic conditions of the geographic areas possibly influenced height growth more than did the differences in soil types.

Site Index

The height-age curves of Siberian elm vary according to soils and geographic location. Site index curves were therefore constructed for several combinations of location and soil (fig. 4). Since these windbreaks are relatively young, ranging from 20 to 25 years old, site index was determined on a base of 15 years.

The site index curves based on measurements in Seward County, Nebraska, (fig. 4A) should be reasonably applicable throughout the Nebraska Loess Plains area. Additional unpublished data indicate that most of the Loess Plains in Nebraska will have site indices for Siberian elm ranging from 24 to 30 feet at base age 15. In general, the Hastings soil series in the western Loess Plains have site indices from 22 to 27 feet. The Crete series of the eastern Loess Plains have site indices from 27 to 33 feet. Local areas where runoff water concentrates may have indices above 33 feet, whereas very eroded soils may have indices below 22 feet.

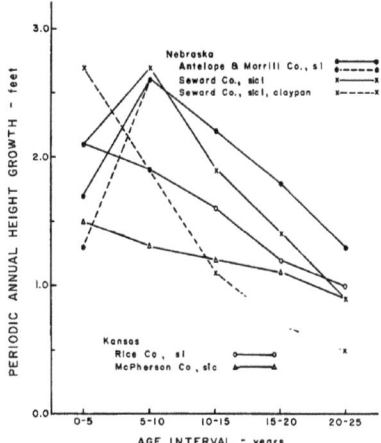

Figure 3.--Periodic annual height growth of Siberian elm at locations sampled in the Central Great Plains. (sl = sandy loam; sic - silty clay; sicl - silty clay loam).

Site index for Siberian elm on the Fillmore claypan series in the Loess Plains averages approximately 28 feet (fig. 4A), but indices may be lower or higher depending on local conditions. More information is needed for these soils to determine causes of slow height growth after trees reach 15 to 20 years of age. Root growth and distribution are very likely restricted by the shallow A horizon and physical characteristics of the claypan.

Since height-age curves for Siberian elms on the sandy loam soils of Antelope and Morrill Counties, Nebraska, were very similar, one set of site index curves can be used for both areas (fig. 4C). Although curve form is probably reliable enough for the locations sampled, other soils in these areas--for instance, soils without loess subsoil in the Antelope County area--may have slightly different curve shapes.

Although soils of the windbreaks sampled in Kansas were greatly different in texture, the height-age curves for Siberian elm were very similar in form. Therefore site index curves for Kansas include both the silty clay and sandy loam soils (fig. 4D).

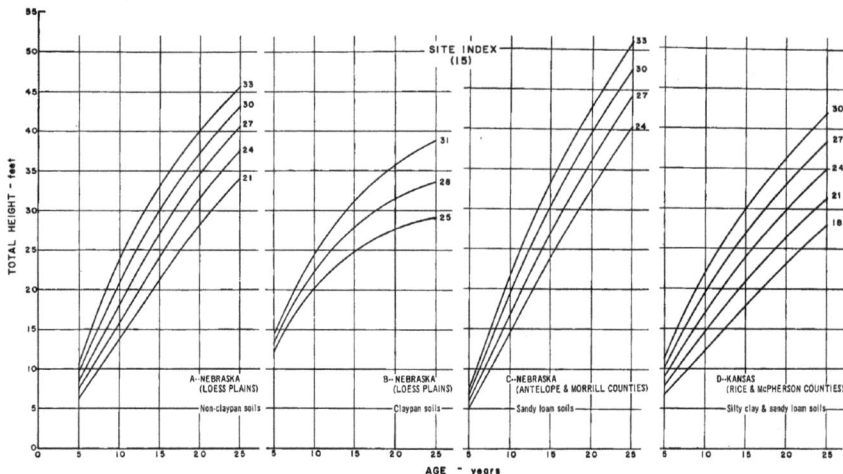

Figure 4.--Site index curves for Siberian elm in windbreaks sampled in Kansas and Nebraska, 1959.

Summary

Height-age data for Siberian elm were collected by stem analysis techniques from different general soil types and geographical areas of Nebraska and Kansas. Differences found in height-age curves depended on general soil characteristics and the geographic area sampled.

Siberian elm growing on silty clay loams derived from loess in Nebraska grew faster immediately after planting than trees growing on lighter textured soils, but after 10 to 15 years the rate of height growth on the sandy loam soils was superior. Siberian elm on heavy claypan soils grew rapidly at first, then slowed to only 0.5 foot per year by ages 20-25.

Height-age curves were similar in shape for trees on both heavy- and light-textured soils in Kansas, but the curves were different from those for trees in Nebraska on generally similar soils.

Extrapolation of height-growth rates indicates that Siberian elm may essentially stop growing in height at 32 to 36 years of age in Nebraska on all soils and at different locations. In Kansas, height growth will be maintained for a slightly longer period of years.

Site index curves are presented for the soils and geographic locations that have different height-age curves. Because of limited sampling, it is not known how well the curves represent the tree populations in each area, but additional data from the Loess Plains of Nebraska substantiate the site index curves for that area. Additional sampling will be necessary to determine how widely they can be applied.

[1] Soil Scientist, located at Rocky Mountain Forest and Range Experiment Station, Lincoln, in cooperation with Nebraska Agricultural Experiment Station, when research was conducted, now Assistant Professor of Soils, Kansas State University, Manhattan. The Rocky Mountain Station maintains central headquarters at Fort Collins, in cooperation with Colorado State University.
[2] Sander, D. H. Growth curves for ponderosa pine in Nebraska windbreaks. U. S. Forest Serv., Rocky Mountain Forest and Range Expt. Sta. Res. Note 82, 3 pp., illus. 1962.
[3] Sander, D. H. Height-age curves for Austrian pine in windbreaks on loess soils of Nebraska. U. S. Forest Serv., Rocky Mountain Forest and Range Expt. Sta. Res. Note RM-13, 2 pp., illus. 1963.
[4] Albertson, F. W., and Weaver, J. E. Injury and death or recovery of trees in prairie climate. Ecol. Monog. 15: 393-433 illus. 1945.
[5] Hayes, F. A., and Stoeckeler, J. H. Possibilities of shelterbelt planting in the plains region. Sect. 12. Soil and forest relationships of the shelterbelt zone. U. S. Forest Serv., Lake States Forest Expt. Sta. Special Pub., pp. 111-153, illus. 1935.

gement Areas and Topography

folliott,[1] and Almer D. Zander[2]

and Murray 1963), but determination of total soil depth is time consuming. Total soil depth did not provide appreciable additional information when Trimble (1964) measured slope position and slope percent to estimate oak site index. Furthermore, slope position and slope percent can be measured easier than total soil depth. Slope position has been shown to relate to herbage production on areas cleared of timber on Beaver Creek (Clary 1964) and to site index of ponderosa pine in the Black Hills (Myers and Van Deusen 1960). Concavity of the slope has been found to be important in estimating Douglas-fir site index (Tarrant 1950). The growth of ponderosa pine has been shown to be related to depth to clay or silty clay (Leven and Dregne 1963).

Soil survey information can be useful in predicting site productivity, particularly where topography is not too rough (Doolittle 1963). Stratification of paper birch productivity with the aid of soil and topographic maps reduces variation within management units and is an aid to silvicultural prescriptions (Cooley 1962).

Development of the Strata

The soils on the Beaver Creek watersheds have been described and grouped into soil management areas. [3] These areas consist of two or more soil types arranged in a pattern related to the shape of the land surface and the nature of the soil materials. The two major soil management areas in the ponderosa pine type on Beaver Creek area are (1) Siesta-Sponseller and (2) Stoneman. [3]

The Siesta-Sponseller soil management area is characterized by soils 20 to 60 inches deep derived from basalt and volcanic cinders. These soils occur on rolling uplands and cinder cones, and have exposed basalt outcrops and cobbles or stone on the surface. Slopes range from 2 to 40 percent. The soils often become clayey in the subsoil, though they are loamy on the surface. General productivity of this soil management area is considered "high." [3]

The Stoneman [4] soil management area is characterized by soils 12 to 36 inches

---

[3] Anderson, T.C., Jr., Williams, J.A., and Crezee, D.B. Soil management report for Beaver Creek watersheds of Coconino National Forest, Region 3. U.S. Forest Serv., 1960, 66 pp. (Mimeographed report on file at Region 3 Office, U.S. Forest Serv., Albuquerque, N. Mex.)

[4] The Stoneman soils and Stoneman soil management area is correlated as Brolliar in a USDA publication, "Soil Survey, Beaver Creek, Arizona," now in press.

Figure 1.--*Soil types and topographic positions of two soil management areas studied, Beaver Creek watershed, Arizona.*
   A. Siesta-Sponseller; swale
   B. Siesta-Sponseller; upland
   C. Stoneman; swale
   D. Stoneman; upland.

of up to 10-percent slope not dominated by stones and rock outcrops.
2. Upland
Rolling areas, including steep slopes and stone-littered areas.

Benefits of Stratification

The standard error of herbage production for the sample was reduced by 43 percent compared with simple random sampling. The actual amount of reduction depends upon the weights of each strata on a given area (Cochran 1963). In most situations on Beaver Creek, one or two strata will dominate, and the actual reduction in standard error will be less than that obtained in this sample.

A sample of herbage production on 54 areas supporting timber indicated no differences between the strata under existing timber stocking conditions (fig 2).

The reduction in the standard error of timber site index by subdividing the timber sample into the four strata was 30 percent. It should be reemphasized, however, that the actual reduction in standard error for an area depends on the distribution or weighting of the strata. The reduction usually obtained may be less than that found in this sample.

Summary

Land strata, useful for reducing the sampling variance for both herbage production on areas cleared of timber and site index on areas supporting timber, were designed for use on the Beaver Creek watersheds. Areas are divided into four strata based on soil management areas and topography. The different strata can be delineated by use of soil maps, aerial photographs or topographic maps, and limited ground checks. Guides are presented for identification of the strata in the field.

Literature Cited

Clary, Warren P.
1964. A method for predicting potential herbage yield on the Beaver Creek pilot watersheds. In Forage plant physiology and soil-range relationships. Amer. Soc. Agron. ASA Spec. Pub. 5: 244-250.

Cochran, William G.
1963. Sampling techniques. New York: John Wiley and Sons, New York; 413 pp.

Cooley, John H.
1962. Site requirements and yield of paper birch in northern Wisconsin.* U.S. Forest Serv., Lake States Forest Exp. Sta. Sta. Paper 105, 11 pp.

Doolittle, Warren T.
1963. Experience in site-evaluation methods for timber production. In Range research methods. U.S. Dep. Agr. Misc. Pub. 940: 64-68.

Klemmedson, James O., and Murray, Robert B.
1963. Use and measurement of site factors and soil properties in evaluation of range site potential. In Range research methods. U.S. Dep. Agr. Misc. Pub. 940: 68-77.

Leven, A.A., and Dregne, H.E.
1963. Productivity of Zuni Mountain forest soils. N. Mex. Agr. Exp. Sta. Bull. 469, 30 pp.

Meyer, Walter H.
1938. Yield of even-aged stands of ponderosa pine. U.S. Dep. Agr. Tech. Bull. 630, 59 pp.

Myers, Clifford A., and Van Deusen, James L.
1960. Site index of ponderosa pine in the Black Hills from soil and topography. J. Forest. 58: 548-555.

Tarrant, Robert F.
1950. A relation between topography and Douglas-fir site quality. J. Forest. 48: 723-724.

Trimble, G.R., Jr.
1964. An equation for predicting oak site index without measuring soil depth. J. Forest. 62: 325-327.

---

*Address requests for copies to the originating office.

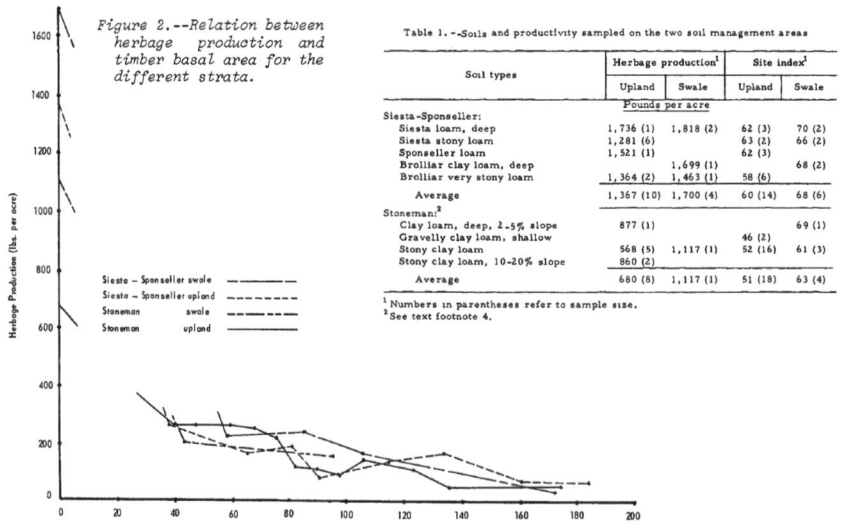

Figure 2.--Relation between herbage production and timber basal area for the different strata.

Table 1.--Soils and productivity sampled on the two soil management areas

Soil types	Herbage production[1]		Site index[2]	
	Upland	Swale	Upland	Swale
	Pounds per acre			
Siesta-Sponseller:				
Siesta loam, deep	1,736 (1)	1,818 (2)	62 (3)	70 (2)
Siesta stony loam	1,281 (6)		63 (2)	66 (2)
Sponseller loam	1,521 (1)		62 (3)	
Brolliar clay loam, deep		1,699 (1)		68 (2)
Brolliar very stony loam	1,364 (2)	1,463 (1)	58 (6)	
Average	1,367 (10)	1,700 (4)	60 (14)	68 (6)
Stoneman:[2]				
Clay loam, deep, 2-5% slope	877 (1)			69 (1)
Gravelly clay loam, shallow			46 (2)	
Stony clay loam	568 (5)	1,117 (1)	52 (16)	61 (3)
Stony clay loam, 10-20% slope	860 (2)			
Average	680 (8)	1,117 (1)	51 (18)	63 (4)

[1] Numbers in parentheses refer to sample size.
[2] See text footnote 4.

Accuracy of Soil Moisture Readings with Unsealed Access Tubes

Arnett C. Mace, Jr.[1]

Soil moisture measurements by the neutron-scattering technique are often made at depths above the zone of saturation, or water table, while other measurements must be taken where the water table is encountered. Sealing the bottoms of all access tubes during installation has been an accepted practice to prevent water from entering the tube, and thereby permitting readings from below the water table. It would be advantageous in some studies to utilize an access tube for both soil moisture and water table depths, provided condensation inside the tube does not significantly affect soil moisture readings, where loss of readings from the zone of saturation can be tolerated. The objectives of this study were to determine whether accurate soil moisture measurements could be made if access tubes were not sealed on the bottom, and also utilized as a water table well where desired.

Methods

Soil moisture was measured by the neutron-scattering technique during November, December, March, and April on four plots located in a north-facing grassland, a south-facing grassland, a mixed conifer and an aspen type on the Apache National Forest, Arizona. Slope gradient was low, ranging between 2 and 6 percent. Two aluminum access tubes, 2.000 inches, outside diameter (OD) and 1.900 inches inside diameter (ID), were placed 2.5 feet apart to a depth of 9.5 feet in each of eight plots, and 6.0 feet in the remaining eight plots. A portable drill used with air to flush out the soil left a hole of approximately 2.25 inches. One access tube in each plot was sealed with plastic roofing compound, No. 10-1/2 rubber stopper, and plastic electrical tape to prevent water from entering the tube. The other access tube was left unsealed and placed in the hole. The unsealed tubes were located downslope from the sealed tubes. Each tube was then backfilled with sand, tamped tightly, and capped with a rubber stopper and small tin can to prevent entry of moisture from above.

Results

Group comparison analysis of 978 measurements taken from both sealed and unsealed access tubes at all levels of the profile indicates no significant difference between tubes. Further analysis based on paired comparison and group comparison of data summarized by plots and depths indicated no significant difference at the 1 or 5 percent level. Average

---

[1]*Research Forester, located at Tempe, in cooperation with Arizona State University; central headquarters maintained at Fort Collins in cooperation with Colorado State University. Mace is now Instructor-Research Associate, Department of Watershed Management, University of Arizona, Tucson.*

water content in 6 inches of soil for each plot and access tube from depths 0 to 5.5 feet is shown below:

Plot No:	Sealed	Unsealed (inches of water)	Deviation
1	2.08	1.92	-0.16
2	1.99	2.08	.09
3	2.55	2.36	-.19
4	2.23	2.34	.11
5	2.22	2.46	.24
6	2.46	2.57	.11
7	2.46	2.85	.39
8	1.86	2.03	.17
9	2.14	2.17	.03
10	2.06	2.17	.11
11	2.30	2.15	-.15
12	2.18	2.12	-.06
13	2.29	2.21	-.08
14	1.99	1.90	-.09
15	2.19	1.91	-.28
16	2.13	2.28	.15
Total	35.13	35.52	.39
Mean	2.20	2.22	.02

The means of water content measured by the sealed and unsealed tubes are remarkably similar. Deviations between water content measurements on the individual plots may be due to lateral movement of water, especially under saturated conditions.

These results indicate it is not necessary to seal access tubes in areas where the water table is below the depth of installation. These conditions exist throughout the Southwest in the chaparral type, and in some areas of the ponderosa pine and mixed-conifer types.

In this particular study, the measurements taken above the zone of saturation were accurate since the presence of condensation inside the unsealed access tube had a negligible influence on measurements. In studies with water tables near the surface, it would be desirable to use sealed tubes, because entry of water could prevent accurate following of moisture-depletion rates by neutron readings and, also might cause short-circuiting and corrosion of the probe.

Agriculture --- CSU, Ft. Collins

Establishment of Lodgepole Pine Reproduction after Different Slash Disposal Treatments

Robert R. Alexander[1]

Prompt restocking with natural reproduction following clear cutting is one of the fundamental objectives of lodgepole pine (Pinus contorta Dougl.) management in the central Rocky Mountains. Because lodgepole pine here bears a high proportion of serotinous cones, most seed for regenerating clearcuts comes from cones left in the slash. How slash is treated largely determines the adequacy of reproduction.

How different slash disposal methods after clearcutting affect establishment of reproduction and reduce fire hazard was studied from 1958 through 1963 on the Medicine Bow National Forest in Wyoming. The effect of treatments on reproduction is reported here.

The Study

The study area was a single block, 12 chains long and 6 chains wide, where the mature overstory of lodgepole pine was cut in 1958. All trees left after logging were either felled or pushed over. Four plots of 1 acre each were treated; a fifth plot of about 3 acres was left untreated (fig. 1). Slash treatments applied in the fall of 1958 were:

[1]*Principal Silviculturist, Rocky Mountain Forest and Range Experiment Station, with central headquarters maintained at Fort Collins, in cooperation with Colorado State University.*

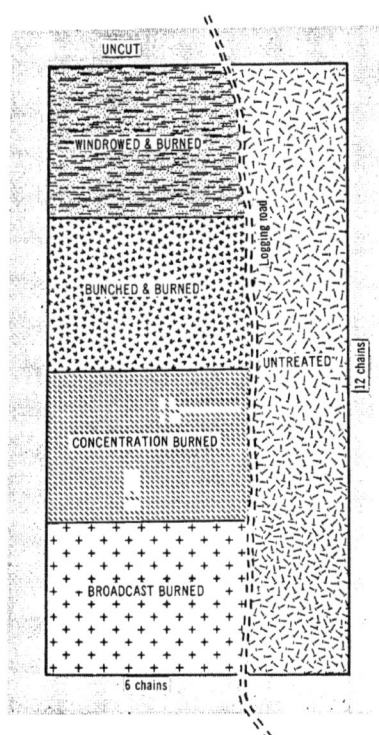

Figure 1.--*Diagrammatic sketch of study plots.*

1. Tractor windrowed and burned.
2. Tractor bunched and burned.
3. Concentrations burned.
4. Broadcast burned.
5. Untreated, as check.

Logging and slash disposal created the following nine seedbed-slash density classes:

1. Undisturbed seedbed--light slash.
2. Undisturbed seedbed--medium slash.
3. Undisturbed seedbed--heavy slash.
4. Disturbed mineral soil seedbed--no slash.
5. Disturbed mineral soil seedbed--light slash.
6. Disturbed mineral soil seedbed--medium slash.
7. Burned seedbed--no slash.
8. Burned seedbed--light slash.
9. Burned seedbed--medium slash.

There were no undisturbed seedbeds where slash was absent, nor any heavy slash on either disturbed mineral soil or burned seedbeds. Not all of the nine seedbed-slash density classes were represented on each slash disposal treatment.

Reproduction counts were made in 1959 and 1963. A random sample of 60 milacres was taken on each plot. Numbers and stocking of seedlings, seedbed condition, and slash density were recorded for each milacre sampled. Seedbeds were classified as (1) disturbed mineral soil, (2) undisturbed, or (3) burned on the basis of the condition containing the largest number of seedlings. If no reproduction was present, seedbeds were classified on the basis of the largest percentage of seedbed condition on the milacre. Slash density was rated on the percentage of ground actually covered on each milacre as follows:

1. None--less than 10 percent.
2. Light--10 to 39 percent.
3. Medium--40 to 69 percent.
4. Heavy--70 percent or more.

Results and Conclusions

Lodgepole pine seed in sufficient amounts to restock a clearcut area will not be dispersed more than 200 feet from standing trees.[2,3] Since all points on the study area were within 200 feet of uncut timber, seed for restocking came both from (1) cones attached to the slash or knocked from the slash and scattered on the ground, and (2) cones on standing trees.

Slash-borne cones release most of their seeds the first year after cutting. Since nearly all of those seeds will germinate the first year, slash-borne seeds were primarily responsible for restocking on disturbed mineral soil seedbeds and on undisturbed seedbeds with light slash (fig. 2). Most seedlings on burned seedbeds and on undisturbed seedbeds with medium and heavy slash originated after 1959 (fig. 2). Furthermore, about the same number of new seedlings became established each year. Seeds dispersed in more or less consistent quantities each year from trees standing around the perimeter of the study area were primarily responsible for restocking those seedbeds.

Numbers of new seedlings after 5 years differed with both seedbed condition and density of slash. Seedlings were most numerous on disturbed mineral soil seedbeds, and least on burned seedbeds (fig. 2). Numbers of new seedlings on disturbed mineral soil seedbeds decreased as slash density increased, but even where slash was heaviest seedlings were numerous. On undisturbed seedbeds, seedlings were most numerous where slash was light, less numerous where slash was heavier. The generally coarse residual slash on burned seedbeds had no apparent influence on reproduction (fig. 2).

Stocking after 5 years differed with seedbed condition, but density of slash apparently had little influence (fig. 3). Stocking was high

[2]*Dahms, Walter G. Dispersal of lodgepole pine seed into clear-cut patches. U. S. Forest Serv. Res. Note PNW-3, 7 pp. 1963. Pacific Northwest Forest and Range Exp. Sta., Portland, Ore.*

[3]*Tackle, David. Regenerating lodgepole pine in central Montana following clear cutting. U.S. Forest Serv. Res. Note INT-17, 7 pp. 1964. Intermountain Forest and Range Exp. Sta., Ogden, Utah.*

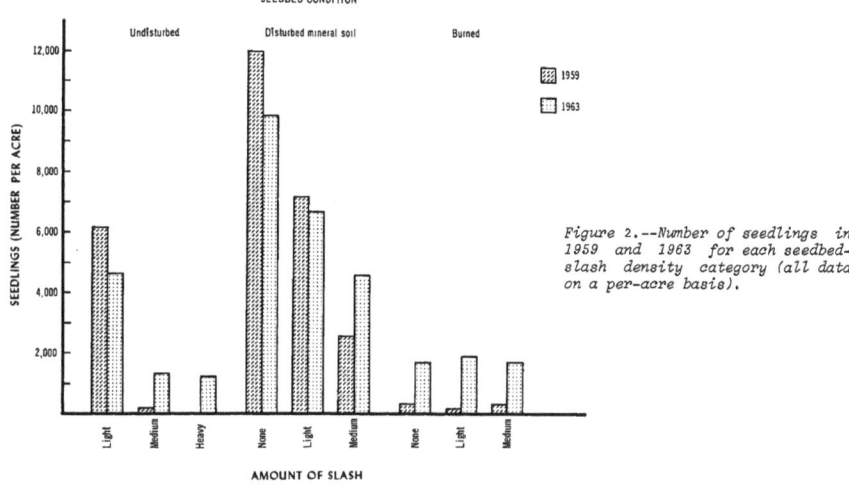

Figure 2.--*Number of seedlings in 1959 and 1963 for each seedbed-slash density category (all data on a per-acre basis).*

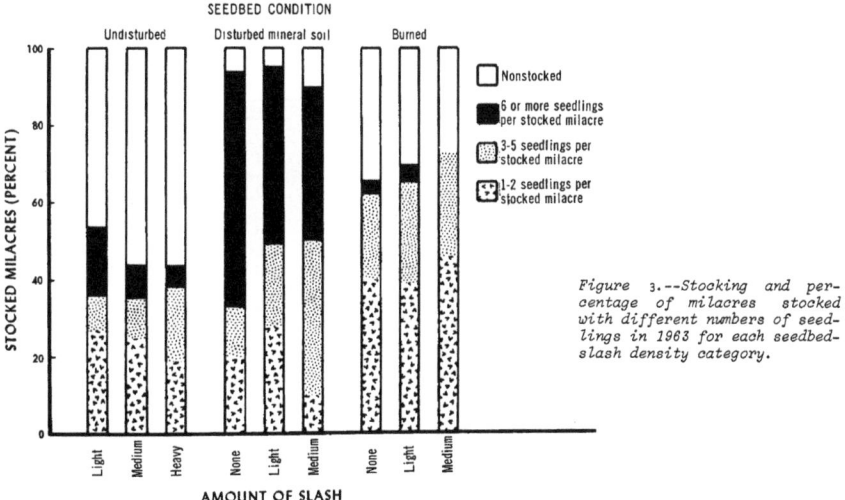

Figure 3.--*Stocking and percentage of milacres stocked with different numbers of seedlings in 1963 for each seedbed-slash density category.*

on disturbed mineral soil seedbeds, acceptable on burned seedbeds, and too low on undisturbed seedbeds. Because of uniform distribution of seedlings, however, burned seedbeds are considered to have the best stocking. All burned seedbeds had more milacres stocked with one and two seedlings, or one to five seedlings, than any other seedbed condition. Few milacres had more than five seedlings. Although total stocking was highest on disturbed mineral soil seedbeds, from 40 to 60 percent of the milacres sampled had six or more seedlings (fig. 3).

Stocking and number of seedlings in 1963 were related to the proportion of each plot in each seedbed condition (table 1). The concentrations burned plot, where most of the area was burned, had the most desirable stocking; it had a near-maximum proportion of milacres stocked with near-minimum total seedlings. More than 80 percent of the milacres were stocked with an average of only three seedlings. The broadcast burned plot, with comparable burned area, had the same number of seedlings on each stocked milacre, but fewer milacres were stocked. Stocking was high on the bunched and burned and windrowed and burned plots, but because more of the area had disturbed mineral soil, stocked milacres averaged five to eight seedlings. Lower stocking in relation to number of seedlings on the untreated plot resulted from the failure of seedlings to become established on undisturbed areas with medium and heavy slash (table 1).

Table 1.--Number and stocking of seedlings in 1963, and proportion of area in each seedbed category by slash disposal treatments (all data on a per-acre basis)

Slash disposal treatment	Seedbed condition			Seedlings	Stocking
	Undisturbed	Disturbed mineral soil	Burned		
	- - - Percent - - -			Number	Percent
Windrowed and burned	15	57	28	6,318	83
Bunched and burned	5	35	60	3,767	77
Concentrations burned	0	7	93	2,450	82
Broadcast burned	-	10	87	1,867	60
Untreated	75	25	0	2,650	53

Use of a Ponderosa Pine Forest in Arizona by Deer, Elk, and Cattle

Hudson G. Reynolds[1]

Ponderosa pine forests of Arizona provide important livestock range and game habitat during summer. They occupy about 8 percent of the area of the State, between elevations of 6,000 and 7,500 feet. In addition to their value for game and livestock, they are important for timber production, as watersheds, and as recreational areas.

Vegetation characteristics of ponderosa pine forests influence distribution of forage use by game and livestock. Maintenance and improvement of such ranges and habitats depends upon detailed knowledge of such use.

This study reports the use made of a ponderosa pine forest in Arizona as measured by accumulated dropping groups of deer, elk, and cattle. Use varied widely with presence or absence of woody plant overstory and kind and abundance of herbaceous vegetation. Findings suggest several possibilities for improving range conditions for cattle and habitat for deer and elk in similar forests.

---

[1]*Principal Wildlife Biologist, located at Tempe, in cooperation with Arizona State University; central headquarters are maintained at Fort Collins, in cooperation with Colorado State University.*

Study Area

Measurements were made in a logged-over ponderosa pine forest on the Apache National Forest in east-central Arizona. The area was bounded by the Black River on the south, West Fork of Black River on the east, the Buffalo Crossing-Maverick road on the north, and Centerfire Creek on the west (fig. 1). The total study area included about 7,500 acres. The terrain was generally uniform and about level.

The overstory was pure ponderosa pine (Pinus ponderosa Lawson). Herbaceous vegetation was dominated by Arizona fescue (Festuca arizonica Vasey) and mountain muhly (Muhlenbergia montana (Nutt.) Hitchc.). About 13 percent of the area was in natural forest openings characterized by spike muhly (Muhlenbergia wrightii Vasey). Numerous forbs grew in both openings and forest, especially in lighter stands of perennial grass.

The area was logged between 1951 and 1958 by the improvement-selection method for sustained yield. About 50 percent of the original volume of the forest was removed by logging.

The area is properly grazed by cattle from about June to October. Fairly high populations of both deer and elk use the area during summer. The importance of ponderosa pine habitat for deer is suggested by the estimate that in 1961 about 27 percent of the deer harvested in Arizona came from this kind of habitat.[2]

Methods

Since natural openings in ponderosa pine forests are believed to be key livestock range and game habitat areas,[3] 10 natural openings, of from 0.7 to 120 acres, were selected for

[2]McCulloch, Clay Y. *Watershed and game management.* In *The Arizona Watershed program in review.* Ariz. Watershed Symp. Proc. 6:25-27. 1962.

[3]Reynolds, Hudson G. *Use of natural openings in a ponderosa pine forest of Arizona by deer, elk, and cattle.* U. S. Forest Serv., Rocky Mountain Forest and Range Exp. Sta. Res. Note 78, 4 pp., illus. 1962.

the study. Four belt transects of equal length were started near the center of each opening, and extended an equal distance into adjacent forest.

Each belt transect was divided into contiguous sampling plots 2 by 50 feet. Deer, elk, and cattle dropping groups of unknown age were counted on each sampling plot. Overstory on the 1/10-acre around a sample plot was classified as to whether dominated by trees over 12 inches (mature), 11.5 inches or less (reproduction), or the plot was unstocked (fig. 2). Herbaceous vegetation on each sample plot was classified as perennial grasses or forbs.

Comparative Total Use of Forest and Openings

A comparison of accumulated dropping groups between forest and natural openings is

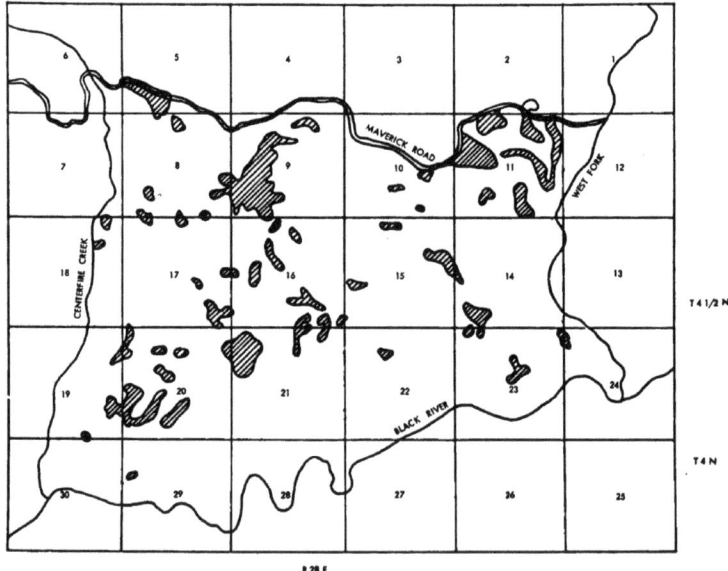

Figure 1.--Study area on the Apache National Forest about 10 miles west of Buffalo Crossing on the Black River. Shaded areas show distribution and size of natural openings in the ponderosa pine forest.

Figure 2.--*Above,* Ponderosa pine forest characteristics. The foreground is unstocked; mature trees in right background, reproduction in left background. *Below,* Natural openings were dominated by perennial grasses, mainly spike muhly, and numerous forbs.

assumed to indicate the relative use (foraging, resting, and bedding) of the two sites for deer, elk, and cattle. For deer, the average difference in number of dropping groups between openings and adjacent forest lands was negligible (fig. 3). For elk and cattle, however, dropping groups averaged more numerous in natural openings.

Elk dropping groups were consistently more numerous in individual openings than in the forest. With the exception of one opening, cattle droppings showed the same consistency. For deer, differences in dropping group densities between opening and adjacent forest were inconsistent.

Use In Relation To Forest Border

Average dropping-group densities for all animal classes varied greatly, but inconsistently, from one opening to another. This suggests that habitat factors, such as quantity and quality of forage, distance to water, and character of cover, influence the amount of use of any given opening. Since there was no consistent relation between dropping-group densities and size of openings, all openings were averaged together to establish the relation of animal use to forest border.

Density of dropping groups varied with distance from forest borders (fig. 4). Number

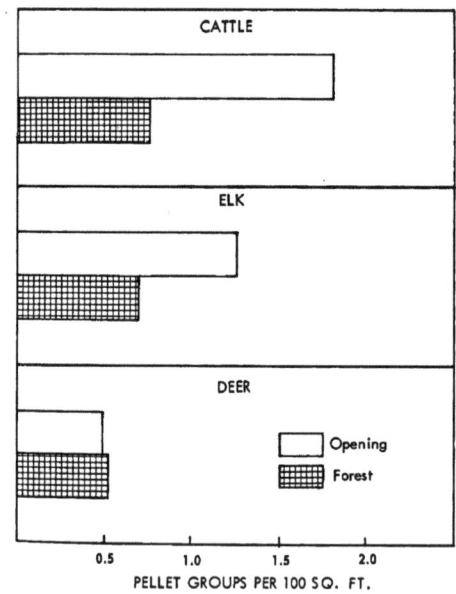

Figure 3.--Comparison of average dropping group densities for elk, deer, and cattle between all openings and adjacent forests.

of dropping groups for elk and cattle (within acceptable sampling variation) decreased with distance from border into forest, and became fairly constant at about 300 feet within the forest. Number of dropping groups of deer remained about the same with increasing distance into the forest from the border.

In openings, the relation of dropping-group densities to forest border depended on animal class. Cattle droppings were most numerous at distances of more than 1,200 feet from the forest border; densities were lowest between 600 and 1,200 feet, and intermediate at 500 feet or less from the forest border.

Elk droppings in openings were most abundant within 800 feet of the forest border, and decreased gradually thereafter (with slight sampling variation); no groups were found beyond 1,400 feet.

Deer dropping groups were slightly higher in openings than within the forest for about 600 feet from the forest border. Thereafter, densities decreased gradually until no droppings were found beyond 1,200 feet.

Opening Size In Relation To Use

Forest border relations suggest that distance across an opening influences use by deer and elk, but not cattle. Presumably, cattle use is not affected by shape and size of forest openings, because proximity of cover

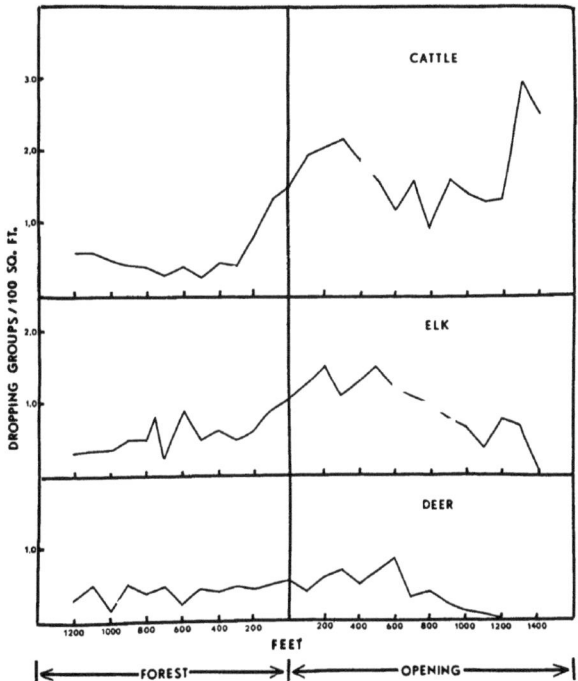

Figure 4.--*Abundance of dropping groups of deer, elk, and cattle in relation to distance from forest border.*

is relatively unimportant. In contrast, use of openings by deer and elk appears to depend strongly upon distance to cover.

Evidently, deer and elk do not use openings to any extent that are more than 2,200 or 2,600 feet across, respectively. For use of openings to be as high or higher than adjacent forest for both deer and elk, distance across an opening should not exceed 1,600 feet. A circular opening of this diameter would contain about 46 acres.

That border-opening relations vary with kind of habitat, species of animal, and population densities, is indicated by other findings. In the chaparral of California, black-tailed deer did not feed mcre than 300 feet from chaparral cover.[4] In the pinyon-juniper of Arizona, no statistically significant differences were measured between deer pellet groups in cover and up to one-half mile into clearings.[5]

Effect Of Herbaceous Plants On Use

Density of dropping groups varied with kind and abundance of herbaceous plant cover (fig. 5). The relations between plant cover and dropping groups were fairly consistent, however, for forest and openings.

For the vegetation conditions in this forest, greatest densities of dropping groups of elk and cattle were associated with perennial grass. Moreover, numbers of dropping groups were greater where there was more perennial grass. For deer, highest dropping-group densities were associated with forbs, also in keeping with their abundance.

Management Implications

Several management possibilities, at least of direction, are implied by these findings.

---

[4]*Taber, R. D., and Dasmann, R. F. The black-tailed deer of the chaparral. Calif. Dep. Fish & Game Bull. 8, 193 pp., 1958.*
[5]*Arizona Game and Fish Department. Wildlife news. Ann. Rep., 7 pp., 1961.*

Where trees are encroaching on natural openings, particularly on heavy clay, poorly aerated soils where the potential for forage production is higher than for tree growth, game habitat and livestock range could be improved by reduction or removal of the invading trees.

When trees are clear cut in strips, blocks, or natural-tree groups, openings less than 1,600 feet across (46 acres for a circular plot) would best coordinate timber management with deer and elk habitat improvement.

Large natural openings that are below potential for forage production could be more efficiently utilized if they were reseeded to perennial grasses preferred by elk and cattle.

After logging, skid trails, roads, and other disturbed areas could be seeded to forbs beneficial to deer, since deer seem to make better use of forested areas than cattle and elk.

Summary

Comparative use of timbered areas and natural openings within a cutover forest by elk, deer, and cattle was determined in a ponderosa pine forest of Arizona by counting accumulated dropping groups. The forest contained 13 percent natural openings, varying in size from 0.7 to 120 acres.

2. For deer, numbers of dropping groups in forest and openings averaged about the same, whereas dropping groups of elk and cattle were more numerous in openings than in forests.
3. With respect to distances into openings from forest borders -- cattle droppings were abundant beyond 1,400 feet, elk droppings were not found beyond 1,400 feet, and deer droppings were absent beyond 1,200 feet.
4. Greatest numbers of elk and cattle dropping groups were associated with perennial grasses; greatest deer dropping density was associated with forbs.
5. Cattle used all sizes of forest openings. Openings less than 1,600 feet across (46 acres for a circular opening) were used most effectively by deer and elk.
6. Several livestock range and game habitat management considerations are suggested by these findings. Among the practices that should be beneficial to deer, cattle, and elk are: (1) Reduce tree invasion into natural openings, particularly where heavy clay, poorly aerated soils exist. (2) When clear cutting in strips, blocks, or natural-tree groups, recognize that deer and elk use most effectively the zone within cleared areas up to 800 feet from the forest border. (3) When improving large natural openings, emphasize reseeding with perennial grasses acceptable to cattle and elk. (4) When seeding areas disturbed during logging, emphasize forbs palatable to deer.

Slash Cleanup in a Ponderosa Pine Forest Affects Use by Deer and Cattle

Hudson G. Reynolds[1]

Slash is commonly cleaned up after logging in many ponderosa pine forests. In general, slash is disposed of in areas of high fire danger, but left undisturbed in areas of little fire hazard.

Slash disposal can affect forest understory. In a ponderosa pine forest of northern Arizona, tree overstory reduction with slash cleanup produced greatest increases in herbaceous vegetation; greatest losses in herbaceous vegetation occurred on areas where there was heavy slash accumulation as well as on areas where tree canopy increased.[2]

To better coordinate timber management with wildlife habitat and livestock range use, further knowledge of the effects of slash disposal upon understory conditions and animal use is desirable. This report provides some additional information on these effects.

---

[1] *Principal Wildlife Biologist, located at Tempe, in cooperation with Arizona State University; central headquarters are maintained at Fort Collins, in cooperation with Colorado State University.*
[2] *Arnold, Joseph F. Effect of heavy selection logging on the herbaceous vegetation in a ponderosa pine forest in northern Arizona. J. Forest. 51: 101-105. 1953.*

Study Area

Measurements were made on an area logged in 1958 in the Big Springs working circle on the Kaibab National Forest. Timber overstory was dominated by ponderosa pine (Pinus ponderosa Lawson). Quaking aspen (Populus tremuloides Michx.) was present in widely dispersed patches.

About 40 percent of the net volume of merchantable trees was removed by selective logging. Tree selection was for: (1) high-risk trees (those that might die before the next cut in about 20 years), (2) mature trees that overtopped immature trees of good form and vigor, and (3) immature trees of poor form, quality, or vigor.

A fire-control access road passed through the sampling area. For fire-control purposes, slash was cleared and piled with a bulldozer for about 200 feet on either side of the road immediately after logging. Slash piles were burned in the fall of the following year.

Methods

Paired sample plots were established at 1/10-mile intervals through the sampling area. One sample plot was located midway in a slash-cleanup strip; the other plot was located on the same compass line, but about 200 feet beyond the cleanup strip.

The sample plot was oriented along a 50-foot tape. The halfway mark on the tape was taken as the center of a 1/10-acre plot for measuring basal area of tree overstory. Slash intercept was measured in hundreds of feet along the tape. Two 1- by 48-foot transects on either side of the tape were clipped at ground level to obtain green weight of herbaceous plants by species. Green weights were converted to dry weights by drying herbage samples for 24 hours at 70° C.

Accumulated deer and cow dropping groups, and aspen sprouts, were counted on transects of 2 by 50 feet on either side of the tape.

Overstory and Slash Comparisons

Tree overstory measured 164 square feet of basal area per acre over slash-cleanup areas, and 136 square feet over undisturbed slash areas. The difference can be accounted for by sampling variation. Hence, attributes that might vary with both overstory density and slash cover can be ascribed to slash alone.

Slash covered 6.8 percent of the ground where undisturbed (table 1), but only 3.2 percent of the ground where slash was cleared (statistically highly significant).

Most of the slash missed during bulldozer cleanup was in intercept classes of less than 4 inches. Undisturbed slash tended to be in larger intercept classes consisting of treetops, cull logs, and discarded butt cuts.

Effect of Slash on Understory Vegetation

Slash cleanup had no measurable effect upon total or class production of understory vegetation:

	Slash cleared	Slash undisturbed
	(No./200 sq. ft.)	
Aspen sprouts	3	3
	(Lbs./acre)	
Shrub herbage	2	1
Sedges	13	16
Perennial grasses	4	3
Forbs	7	7
Total herbaceous	26	27

Table 1.--Distribution of intercept measurements of slash by classes

Slash intercept class (Inches)	Slash cleared		Slash undisturbed	
	Percent of actual ground cover	Percent in size class	Percent of actual ground cover	Percent in size class
Less than 2.0	1.5	47	2.3	34
2.1 - 4.0	1.2	38	1.6	23
4.1 - 6.0	.3	8	1.1	17
More than 6.1	.2	7	1.8	26
Total	3.2	100	6.8	100

areas with lesser amounts of litter.³ Logs and treetops also probably present a greater access obstacle to cattle, while deer may feel more conspicuous in areas cleared of slash. Also, they are known to use rough areas as much as more accessible areas.⁴

Summary and Conclusions

1. An area of ponderosa pine on the Kaibab Plateau, logged in 1958, was measured for differences in tree overstory, slash, herbage production, and deer and cattle dropping groups in 1964. The findings may be unique to the specific conditions: a residual overstory of 136 to 164 square feet of basal area in ponderosa pine where understory herbage production is about 25 pounds per acre.
2. Basal area of tree overstory was the same on undisturbed and slash-cleared areas. There was about twice as much slash on the undisturbed area.
3. Slash clearing had no measurable effect upon total amount or composition of understory vegetation. Forage production was low, however, for ponderosa pine sites.
4. Cattle droppings were more numerous on areas cleared of slash; deer pellet groups were greater where slash was undisturbed.

[3] *Glendening, George E. Some factors affecting cattle use of northern Arizona pine-bunchgrass ranges. U. S. Forest Serv., Southwest. Forest and Range Exp. Sta. Res. Rep. 6, 9 pp. 1944. (Consolidated with Rocky Mountain Forest and Range Exp. Sta. in 1953.)*

[4] *Reynolds, Hudson G. Effect of logging on understory vegetation and deer use in a ponderosa pine forest of Arizona. U. S. Forest Serv., Rocky Mountain Forest and Range Exp. Sta. Res. Note 80, 7 pp. 1961.*

1966

U.S. FOREST SERVICE
RESEARCH NOTE RM - 65

FOREST SERVICE
U.S. DEPARTMENT OF AGRICULTURE

Effects of 3 Years' Grazing at Different Intensities on Crested Wheatgrass Lambing Range in Northern New Mexico

H. W. Springfield[1]

More than 80,000 acres of brush-infested rangeland in northern New Mexico have been plowed and seeded to crested wheatgrass (Agropyron desertorum (Fisch.) Schult.). These seeded ranges are a valuable resource. Not only is their grazing capacity higher than that of nearby unseeded ranges, but they also furnish much needed spring forage.

Crested wheatgrass stands at relatively low elevations now carry a substantial part of the grazing load during spring and early summer. Consequently, rangelands at higher elevations are grazed less heavily at that time, and the native vegetation is given a chance to become more productive.

Crested wheatgrass stands are proving especially valuable for sheep grazing and lambing in the spring. Thousands of sheep are herded onto the stands every year to utilize the succulent, nutritious forage. Little is known, however, about management of crested wheatgrass for lambing and spring grazing by sheep. The general belief is that lambing is a more severe use than grazing alone, but most of the information available has come from regions where environmental conditions are unlike those in New Mexico.

[1]*Range Scientist, located at Albuquerque, in cooperation with the University of New Mexico; central headquarters are maintained at Fort Collins, in cooperation with Colorado State University.*

Findings summarized in this paper are from a 3-year experiment in northern New Mexico in which crested wheatgrass was grazed at different intensities by sheep during the lambing season. Though not conclusive because of the short time involved, the results indicate that intensity of grazing for the short spring period where the grass was allowed to grow and mature after grazing was completed had little effect on crested wheatgrass production. However, the stands grazed most heavily were considered to be deteriorating after the 3 years of grazing.

Methods

Experimental Site

An area in Tank Canyon on the Laguna Seca Allotment of the Santa Fe National Forest, 12 miles north of Lindrith, New Mexico, was seeded to crested wheatgrass in 1950. Before the area was plowed and seeded, it produced mainly big and silver sagebrush (Artemisia tridentata Nutt. and A. cana Pursh), rubber and Douglas rabbitbrush (Chrysothamnus nauseosus (Pall.) Britt.) and (C. viscidiflorus (Hook.) Nutt.), and a sparse understory of herbaceous plants including western wheatgrass (Agropyron smithii Rydb.) and blue grama (Bouteloua gracilis (H.B.K.) Lag.). Pinyon pine (Pinus edulis Engelm.), Rocky Mountain and one-seed junipers (Juniperus scopulorum Sarg. and J. monosperma (Engelm.)

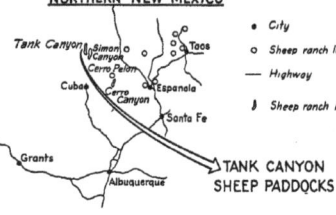

Figure 1.--The experimental site, seeded to crested wheatgrass in 1950, is surrounded by ponderosa pine and juniper.

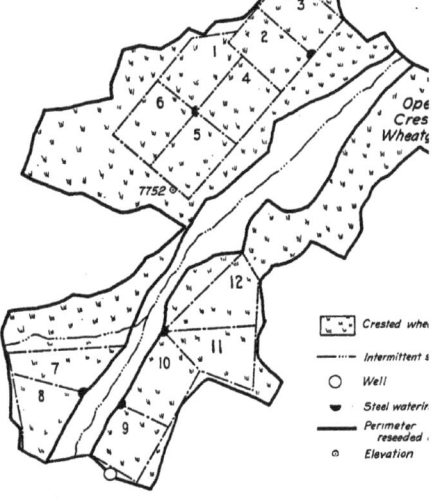

Sarg.), Gambel oak (Quercus gambelii (Nutt.), and ponderosa pine (Pinus ponderosa Lawson) surround the seeding (fig. 1).

Elevation of the experimental area ranges from 7,500 to 7,800 feet. Annual precipitation averages 16.5 inches. The soil, derived from sandstone and shale, is moderately deep and varies from a silt loam to a clay loam.

Twelve paddocks, 5.0 to 5.2 acres in size, were fenced sheeptight within the seeded area. Water and granulated salt were available to the sheep at all times.

Grazing Treatments

Four grazing intensities, replicated three times, were assigned at random to the paddocks. These intensities were intended to result in average utilization of 90, 75, 60, and 45 percent of crested wheatgrass herbage produced by the end of the grazing season. Rambouillet ewes grazed the paddocks during and after lambing as follows:

Year	Dates	Duration
1957	May 16 - July 2	(47 days)
1958	May 2 - June 24	(53 days)
1959	May 5 - June 10	(36 days)

Average stocking of the paddocks and resultant utilization of crested wheatgrass during the 3-year experiment are shown in table 1.

Vegetation Measurements

Production of crested wheatgrass was determined by harvesting herbage from four ungrazed plots in each paddock at the end of the grazing season. Protected from grazing by wire cages, the 38.4 square-foot plots were relocated at random each spring prior to

Table 1.--Production of crested wheatgrass on individual paddocks in 1957 and 1960, and changes in production under different grazing intensities

Relative use	Paddock number	Average stocking, 1957-59	Average utilization, 1957-59	Production		Change in production	
				1957	1960		
		Sheepdays/acre	Percent	Pounds/acre		Pounds	Percent
Lightest	7	76	41	1,555	747	-808	-52.0
	5	73	39	1,607	581	-1,026	-63.8
	6	75	37	1,589	609	-908	-61.7
	Average	75	39	1,584	646	-938	-59.2
Next to lightest	1	97	60	1,118	693	-425	-38.0
	10	100	50	1,975	761	-1,214	-61.5
	4	101	48	1,526	694	-832	-54.5
	Average	99	53	1,540	716	-824	-51.3
Next to heaviest	8	112	72	1,927	816	-1,111	-57.7
	11	115	72	1,311	909	-402	-30.7
	9	119	70	1,472	881	-591	-40.1
	Average	115	71	1,570	869	-701	-42.8
Heaviest	2	155	87	1,176	651	-525	-44.6
	3	153	86	1,821	670	-1,151	-63.2
	12	143	79	1,704	812	-892	-52.3
	Average	150	84	1,567	711	-856	-53.4

grazing. Current growth of herbage was clipped at ground level, air dried, and weighed. Yields were measured each year in late June or early July from 1957 through 1960.

Ground cover was measured by the loop method.[2] Records were obtained from two clusters of two transects each in every paddock in 1957 and 1960.

Forage utilization was determined by the ocular-estimate-by-plot method.[3] For this purpose, 100 9.6-square-foot circular plots were randomly located in each paddock 1 or 2 days after the sheep were removed at the end of the grazing period. Utilization of woody plants, as well as crested wheatgrass, was estimated.

To evaluate stand maintenance, 25 plots, 9.6 square feet in size, were randomly located in each paddock and exclosure in July 1960. Crested wheatgrass plants were classified and tallied on each plot according to age and percentage of dead crown.

To determine changes in basal diameter, leaf length, and culm length under the various grazing intensities, 100 crested wheatgrass plants were selected at random in each paddock and measured in July 1957 and 1960. All measurements were made with the foliage held upright and compressed.

Three exclosures adjacent to the paddocks revealed how the vegetation responded when not grazed by sheep.

[2] Parker, Kenneth W. A method for measuring trend in range condition on National Forest ranges. U.S. Forest Serv., Wash., D.C. (mimeo.), 22 pp., illus. 1951.
[3] Pechanec, J. F., and Pickford, G. D. A comparison of some methods used in determining percentage utilization of range grasses. J.Agr. Res. 54: 753-765. 1937.

Results

Crested Wheatgrass Production

Herbage yields of crested wheatgrass at Tank Canyon varied widely from year to year, mainly in response to winter-spring precipitation (fig. 2). The relationship between precipitation from January through May and herbage yield is indicated by a correlation coefficient of 0.996. Production in 1957, when winter-spring precipitation was high, was nearly four times that in 1959, when precipitation was low:

Year	Production (Pounds per acre)	Precipitation January through May (Inches)
1957	1,565	9.62
1958	1,206	7.64
1959	399	4.00
1960	735	5.18

Though declines in wheatgrass yield from 1957 to 1960 were not the same in all paddocks, there is no indication that grazing intensity influenced them. Yields in the most lightly grazed paddocks decreased 59 percent, whereas those in the most heavily grazed paddocks decreased 53 percent (table 1). These comparisons suggest that reductions in yield resulted from less moisture in 1960 than in 1957, not from grazing.

Stand Maintenance

In July 1960, the number of dead plants per 100 square feet averaged 3.2 in the most heavily grazed paddocks, 1.9 in the most lightly grazed paddocks, and 1.1 inside the exclosures (fig. 3). Except under heaviest grazing, all paddocks met the test of stand maintenance; that is, dead plants were being replaced by an equal or larger number of well-established young plants. Even in paddocks grazed most heavily, young plants almost equaled the number of dead plants.

Weakened plants (plants with more than three-fourths of their crown dead) were 5.4 times as numerous as young plants in the most heavily grazed paddocks. Comparable multiples for other grazing intensities were: 72 percent use--3.2; 53 percent use--1.9; and 39 percent use--1.4. Young plants were most abundant in paddocks that had been grazed the most lightly, and fewest in paddocks that had been grazed the most heavily. The relatively high ratio of dead or dying plants to young

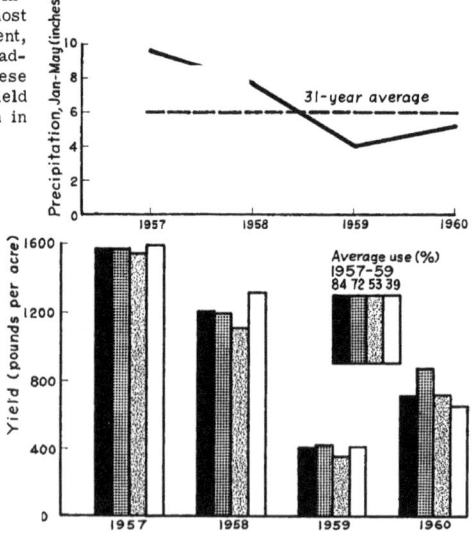

Figure 2.--*Crested wheatgrass yields at Tank Canyon from 1957 to 1960 under four intensities of grazing, and different amounts of January through May precipitation.*

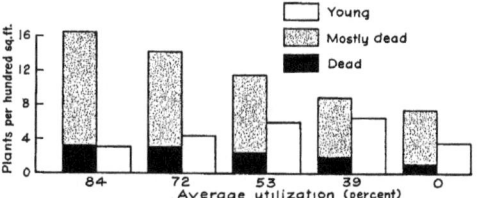

Figure 3.--*Number of dead plants, or plants with crown more than three-fourths dead, compared with number of well-established young plants of crested wheatgrass at Tank Canyon in July 1960.*

plants in the most heavily grazed paddocks indicates that those stands were deteriorating.

Of special interest is the relative scarcity of young wheatgrass plants inside the exclosures in 1960. Only 3.6 plants per 100 square feet were counted there, compared with 6.5 in the most lightly grazed paddocks, 6.0 and 4.4 in paddocks grazed at intermediate intensities, and 3.1 in paddocks grazed most heavily. Light or moderate grazing apparently favored establishment of young plants.

The unusually dry winter and spring in both 1959 and 1960 may have been partly responsible for the large number of dead or dying plants and the small number of young plants at Tank Canyon in 1960. Precipitation from January through May was only 4.00 inches in 1959 and 5.18 inches in 1960. The long-term average for that period is 5.95 inches.

Size of Crested Wheatgrass Plants

Plants were much smaller in 1960 than in 1957, irrespective of how closely they had been grazed (table 2). The smaller size probably resulted, first, from less spring moisture in 1960 than in 1957, and second, from fragmentation of plants under grazing.

Differences in size of plants among the different grazing treatments were not great, but the trend was toward smaller plants under heavier grazing (fig. 4). Although basal diameters were about the same in all paddocks

Table 2.--Average size of crested wheatgrass plants in Tank Canyon paddocks grazed at different intensities, 1957 and 1960

Average utilization (Percent)	Year	Basal diameter	Leaf length	Culm length
		- - -	Inches	- -
39	1957	3.30	14.28	20.42
	1960	2.23	7.41	10.93
53	1957	3.59	14.51	21.01
	1960	2.15	7.07	10.81
72	1957	3.44	13.26	20.02
	1960	1.88	6.96	11.08
84	1957	3.61	14.19	20.31
	1960	1.78	6.09	9.94

in 1957, a trend toward smaller diameters under heavier grazing was evident in 1960. Leaf length showed similar trends. Leaves were longest on the most lightly grazed paddocks and shortest on the most heavily grazed paddocks. Culm length in 1960 was nearly the same in all paddocks except those that had been grazed most heavily where the culms were about 1 inch shorter.

Changes in ground cover during the 3 years of observation were not statistically significant. Nevertheless, the following records indicate that ground cover was considerably less in 1960 where grazing had been heaviest:

Figure 4.--Crested wheatgrass plants in paddock 1 (above), where utilization averaged 60 percent over 3 years, were larger and more vigorous in 1960 than those in paddock 2 (below) where use averaged 88 percent.

	Crested wheatgrass	Litter	Bare soil
	- - (Hits per hundred) - -		
Grazing use:			
None	21.2	33.7	44.2
Lightest	17.3	28.7	52.5
Next to lightest	18.3	20.8	58.9
Next to heaviest	18.6	19.5	60.4
Heaviest	16.2	11.0	71.4

Crested wheatgrass plants occurred at about the same frequency in all grazed paddocks, but were somewhat more abundant inside the exclosures. Litter showed a definite decrease with increased grazing intensity. In paddocks grazed at the heaviest rate, litter was only about half as abundant as in paddocks grazed at intermediate rates and about one-third as abundant as inside the exclosures. Bare soil increased as litter decreased.

Although inconclusive, these findings further indicate that the crested wheatgrass stands were deteriorating under the heavier grazing intensities, particularly where use averaged 84 percent. Utilization of shrubs scattered throughout the crested wheatgrass stands (fig. 5) was proportional to intensity of use of wheatgrass.[4]

[4] *Springfield, H. W. Shrub use by sheep on seeded range. U.S. Forest Serv., Rocky Mountain Forest and Range Exp. Sta. Res. Note 49, 4 pp., illus. 1960.*

Summary

1. Crested wheatgrass stands in northern New Mexico were grazed at different intensities by sheep each spring from 1957 through 1959. Ewes were placed in twelve 5-acre paddocks in May just before lambing and kept there 36 to 53 days.

2. Utilization of crested wheatgrass under four stocking rates over the 3-year period averaged 39, 53, 72, and 84 percent, based on weight of herbage produced.

3. Crested wheatgrass can be effectively used as lambing range.

4. Production of wheatgrass apparently was unaffected by intensity of use during the lambing period. This finding must be considered inconclusive, however, because of the short duration of the study. Yields did vary with winter-spring precipitation, however, from about 400 pounds per acre in 1959, a dry year, to 1,565 pounds per acre in 1957 when growing conditions were favorable.

5. Deterioration of stands grazed most heavily was evident in 1960: Dead or dying wheatgrass plants were not being replaced as rapidly by young plants, old plants were smaller, and ground cover was sparse.

Figure 5.--
Appearance of big sagebrush plant in 1960 on paddock where the wheatgrass was utilized at an average of 88 percent from 1957 through 1959.

Use of Openings in Spruce-Fir Forests of Arizona by Elk, Deer, and Cattle

Hudson G. Reynolds[1]

Spruce-fir forests in Arizona and New Mexico provide important summer range for elk, deer, and cattle. Previous investigations in ponderosa pine forests of Arizona suggest that: (1) natural openings are important to both big game and livestock; (2) timber and range management practices can be modified for game habitat betterment; and (3) special measures can be taken to improve foraging conditions for grazing animals.[2,3]

This paper reports on the use of natural and created openings in spruce-fir forests by elk, deer, and cattle. Accumulated animal droppings were counted as an assumed index of use. From knowledge of wildlife habitat use, suggestions are made for integrating other land uses, such as timber, water, and recreation, with wildlife habitat improvement.

---

[1] *Principal Wildlife Biologist located at Tempe, in cooperation with Arizona State University; central headquarters are maintained at Fort Collins, in cooperation with Colorado State University.*
[2] *Reynolds, Hudson G. Use of natural openings in a ponderosa pine forest of Arizona by deer, elk, and cattle. U. S. Forest Serv. Rocky Mountain Forest and Range Exp. Sta. Res. Note 78, 4 pp. 1962. Fort Collins, Colo.*
[3] *Reynolds, Hudson G. Use of a ponderosa pine forest in Arizona by deer, elk, and cattle. U.S. Forest Serv. Res. Note RM-63, 8 pp., illus. 1966. Rocky Mountain Forest and Range Exp. Sta. Fort Collins, Colo.*

Study Areas

Three general areas of spruce-fir were studied: Burro Mountain and Haystack in the White Mountains of east-central Arizona, and the Kaibab Plateau of extreme north-central Arizona. Spruce-fir forests occupy the coldest, wettest, and highest lands (8,500 to 12,000 feet) in Arizona and New Mexico.[4,5,6] Two tree species, Engelmann spruce (Picea engelmannii Parry) and subalpine fir (Abies lasiocarpa (Hook.) Nutt.), dominate the forest composition. Other associated conifers include: blue spruce (Picea pungens Engelm.), and locally small amounts of white fir (Abies concolor (Gord. & Glend.) Lindl.) and Douglas-fir (Pseudotsuga menziesii (Mirb.) Franco). Forest composition varies from pure stands of spruce to a mixture of all of the above species. Herbaceous plants are scarce beneath dense forest stands.

Grasslands are interspersed throughout spruce-fir forests. These plant communities may exist as small openings or as fairly ex-

---

[4] *Nichol, A. A. The natural vegetation of Arizona. Ariz. Agr. Exp. Sta. Bull. 127: 187-230. 1952.*
[5] *Castetter, E. F. The vegetation of New Mexico. N. Mex. Quart. 26: 257-288. 1956.*
[6] *Rasmussen, D. I. Biotic communities of Kaibab Plateau, Arizona. Ecol. Monog. 3: 229-275. 1941.*

tensive areas. Among the important genera of dominant perennial grasses in dry situations are: Fescues (Festuca spp.), muhlys (Muhlenbergia spp.), bluegrasses (Poa spp.), and needlegrasses (Stipa spp.). The more abundant forbs include genera such as: Pussytoes (Antennaria spp.), buckwheat (Eriogonum spp.), fleabane (Erigeron spp.), phlox (Phlox spp.), cinquefoil (Potentilla spp.), and saxifrage (Saxifraga spp.).

In wet situations the flora is primarily several species of forbs or grasslike plants (Juncus spp. and Carex spp.). Prominent forbs include: Yarrow (Achillea spp.), agoseris (Agoseris spp.), fleabane, cinquefoil, buttercup (Ranunculus spp.), dandelion (Taraxacum spp.), and clover (Trifolium spp.). Although scarce, perennial grasses may include: Hairgrass (Deschampsia spp.), timothy (Phleum spp.), and bluegrass.

Methods

In all, 29 natural or clearcut openings were studied. Openings varied from one-half acre to nearly 100 acres in size. Measurements were initiated near the center of each opening. From here, four random transects were located across each opening; transects were continued into adjacent timber for a distance equal to the radius of the opening.

Transects were divided into contiguous sampling plots of 2 by 100 feet. Accumulated pellet groups of deer and elk, and droppings of cattle, were counted on each sampling plot. Herbaceous vegetation on each sample plot was classified as to whether dominated by sedges, perennial grasses, or forbs.

Comparative Use of Openings and Forest

Natural Openings

Average numbers of droppings computed for openings and adjacent timber for the three sampling sites were as follows:

	Dropping groups per 100 square feet		
	Cattle	Elk	Deer
North Kaibab:			
Opening	1.29	0	0.74
Forest	.40	0	2.00
Burro Mountain:			
Opening	.84	.29	.23
Forest	.19	.25	.76
Haystack:			
Opening	3.08	.41	.12
Forest	1.11	.48	.88

Droppings of cattle were about three to four-and-a-half times more abundant in openings than within adjacent forest. The opposite relation held for deer--their pellet groups were about three to seven times more abundant in adjacent forest than in openings. Numbers of elk pellet groups did not differ appreciably between adjacent forest and openings.

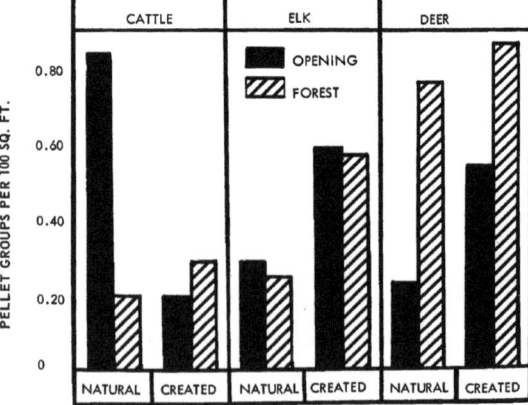

Figure 1.--Comparative numbers of elk, deer, and cattle dropping groups for natural and created openings and adjacent forests on Burro Mountain, Apache National Forest, Arizona.

Created Openings

Created openings in the study consisted of blocks of 10 to 30 acres that had been clear-cut about 6 years previously on Burro Mountain. Dropping group densities in these created openings were compared with those in natural openings on Burro Mountain that were used by the same game population.

For cattle, relative densities of dropping groups in created and natural openings differed strikingly (fig. 1). Natural openings had over four times as many dropping groups as adjacent forest, while the number of dropping groups in created openings and adjacent forests were about the same.

For elk and deer, created openings were preferred to natural; however, relative use between openings and adjacent forest was about the same for both situations. Elk droppings in openings and forests were about equal. Deer dropping groups were more abundant in forest than openings.

Differences in herbaceous plant composition may explain, in part, the situations preferred by elk, deer, and cattle. Perennial grasses made up 98 percent of the composition in natural openings, while in created openings, forbs comprised 68 percent of the composition. Since cattle are primarily grass eaters, they may have preferred natural to created openings because of the abundance of perennial grass. Physical obstacles of slash and debris in logged areas may also have reduced utilization by cattle.

Forest Border Relations

Forest borders adjacent to natural openings seem to have some special significance, especially for deer (fig. 2). Density of deer dropping groups increased sharply from the border into the forest. Number of groups declined gradually with distance out into openings. Within the forest, density of dropping groups exceeded the average for forest conditions at between 400 to 450 feet from the forest border.

Border use by elk was not as striking as by deer. There was, however, a tendency for dropping groups to be more numerous on both forest and opening sides of the border, with the number of groups decreasing at increasing distance from the border.

In general, density of cattle droppings decreased gradually with distance from the border into the forest, and increased with greater distance into openings.

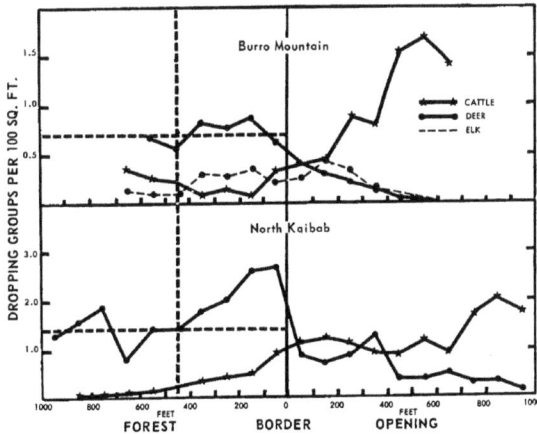

Figure 2.--Relation of abundance of dropping groups to forest borders for deer, elk, and cattle.

Effective Size of Opening

Since abundance of dropping groups of both deer and elk decreased with distance from forest border into openings, a maximum size of opening should exist for best use by deer and elk. To estimate best size of opening, abundance of dropping groups was related to size of openings. To adjust for density of animal populations associated with an area, dropping groups were expressed as a ratio between dropping groups of an opening and of adjacent forest.

Relative use by deer and elk declined sharply as size of opening increased. There was little use of areas larger than 20 acres. Conversely, as openings became smaller, relative use increased. Theoretically, circular openings larger than 20 acres would be little used, except next to forest borders.

Conclusions

1. Cattle, elk, and deer use natural grassland openings in spruce-fir forests of Arizona differently, as measured by accumulated dropping groups.
2. Cattle make greater relative use of grassland openings than adjacent forest, elk make about equal use of the two situations, while deer use adjacent forests more than openings.
3. For deer and elk, use of openings relative to adjacent forest is about the same for openings created by clearcutting as for natural grassland openings. Cattle do not use created openings relative to adjacent forest as intensively as natural openings. Possibly the sparsity of perennial grass and the presence of logging debris discourage more intensive use of created openings by cattle.
4. Deer and elk use is higher close to the border, on both forest and opening sides, than in areas more remote from borders. Cattle use increases from borders into openings, and decreases at greater distances from borders into the forest.
5. Openings smaller than 20 acres receive heaviest use by deer and elk. Circular openings larger than 20 acres (526 feet radius) are little used except around perimeters. Cattle preference for openings did not vary with size of opening.

Management Implications

Several management implications can be derived from the above conclusions with regard to coordinating wildlife habitat with timber and range management.
1. Small natural openings (at least up to 20 acres or less than 1/5 mile across) should be maintained in spruce-fir forests. Management practices for preserving natural openings for deer and elk could include:
   a. Removal of invading timber reproduction.
   b. Cleanup of logging slash and debris.
   c. Seeding any disturbed areas to forage plants palatable to deer and elk.
2. Creation of small openings in spruce-fir forests, by cutting in blocks or strips, should be beneficial to both elk and deer.
   a. Permanent block openings of less than 20 acres or strips less than 1/5 mile across should be most beneficial.
   b. For best habitat effects in connection with an even-aged system of timber management, clearcut areas should be widely dispersed, less than 20 acres in size if in patches, and less than 1/5 mile across if in strips.
3. Grazing capacity of spruce-fir forests for cattle should be based largely upon natural openings, since cattle make little use of dense timber or created openings.
4. In restoring, stabilizing, or improving natural openings in spruce-fir forests, seeding to perennial grasses should be given preference if cattle use is preferred; seeding to forbs should be emphasized if deer and elk use is to be encouraged.

Summary

Use of natural and created openings by deer, elk, and cattle was studied in spruce-fir forests of Arizona by measuring accumulated dropping groups. Cattle used openings more than adjacent forest, elk use was about the same in the two situations, while deer preferred adjacent forest areas. Cattle made more use of natural than created openings; elk and deer preferred created openings. Openings larger than 20 acres were used little by deer and elk, except near forest borders; all sizes of openings were grazed by cattle. Maintenance of natural openings and creation of small openings by cutting should improve deer and elk habitat.

1966

U.S. FOREST SERVICE
RESEARCH NOTE RM - 67

FOREST SERVICE
U.S. DEPARTMENT OF AGRICULTURE

Diurnal and Seasonal Fluctuations in Moisture Content of Pinyon and Juniper

Donald A. Jameson[1]

Fluctuations in moisture content of pinyon and juniper trees are important from the standpoints of fire and hydrology in the pinyon-juniper type. In the case of fire, both those interested in use of fire for juniper control and those interested in fire suppression are concerned with moisture content of fuels. In the case of hydrology, studies of moisture-content fluctuations may shed some light on moisture losses from the soil. This paper presents the results of a series of moisture determinations in the twigs and leaves of pinyon (Pinus edulis Engelm.), Utah juniper (Juniperus osteosperma (Torr.) Little), alligator juniper (J. deppeana Steud.), and one-seed juniper (J. monosperma (Engelm.) Sarg.).

Review of Literature

Diurnal Fluctuations

Moisture fluctuations have been published for many species of plants, but not pinyon or juniper. In all reported cases, moisture content is maximum at night and minimum in midafternoon. Diurnal fluctuations occur because water loss during the day is greater than water uptake, and water uptake at night exceeds water loss (Kramer and Kozlowski 1960).[2] Changes in the diurnal pattern usually follow meteorological conditions (Halevy 1960). In Bartlett pears, the general diurnal pattern held regardless of the season (Ackley 1954).

Seasonal Fluctuations

Because of cold or frozen soil and warm, dry air, conifers are often critically dry in winter (Boyce 1961). This condition is commonly called "winterkill."

Detailed investigations of moisture content of conifers have been reported less often than winterkill, but several species have been studied. Gibbs (1958) has analyzed moisture content records of many species, and has determined that species have their own characteristic water patterns. Pinus strobus at Montreal, Canada, for example, has a low point in early May and a high in mid-September (Gibbs 1958). P. ponderosa in Idaho, on the other hand, has a high moisture content in March (Parker 1954). P. rigida had a higher moisture content in summer than in winter (Meyer 1928).

The seasonal fluctuations are not as consistent nor as easily explained as diurnal fluctuations. Different seasonal patterns of

---

[1] Principal Plant Physiologist, located at Flagstaff, in cooperation with Northern Arizona University; central headquarters maintained at Fort Collins, in cooperation with Colorado State University.

[2] Names and dates in parentheses refer to Literature Cited, p. 7.

moisture apparently occur because of differential behavior of stomates. Although stomates usually close at night and open during the day (Kramer and Kozlowski 1960), not all species behave in this fashion. In mature conifer leaves, the stomatal action is incomplete (Parker 1956). Guard cells of southwestern junipers are partially lignified,[3] which would probably retard stomatal action. Stomates of some species may close during dry periods, which would retard transpiration and allow moisture content to increase (Kosikova 1956, other references reviewed by Kramer and Kozlowski 1960). Oppenheimer (1953), who has made an extensive study of such mechanisms, proposes the following nomenclature for various reactions:

Oligohydric--plants whose stomata close during drought, with lowered transpiration and increased moisture content.
Polyhydric--plants whose stomata remain open during drought, with increased transpiration and decreased moisture content.
Isohydric--plants with little seasonal fluctuation in moisture content ("homoiohydrous" according to Walter 1955).

Poikilohydric--plants with considerable seasonal fluctuation in moisture content ("poikilohydrous" according to Walter 1955).

Oppenheimer (1953) suggested that an oligohydric pattern is usual for conifers. Oligohydric patterns have been reported for P. strobus, Tsuga canadensis, and Larix europea (Gibbs 1958), but polyhydric patterns have been found in P. ponderosa (Parker 1954), Abies balsamea, and Picea rubens (Clark and Gibbs 1957).

Methods

Species and Locations

Mature pinyon and one-seed juniper trees were observed near Winona, Arizona, and Utah and alligator juniper trees were observed about midway between Williams and Ash Fork, Arizona. Rainfall at these locations generally comes in two distinct periods, one from December through April and another in July, August, and early September (fig. 1). At each location, a tree of each species was located so that one soil moisture sample would suffice for the two trees. Ten trees of each species were selected for study. Utah juniper trees growing on a dry hillside and adjacent to a flowing stream near Sedona, Arizona, were also observed.

Samples and Measurements

The sample of tree material consisted of 100 to 200 grams of twigs and attached leaves. The twigs were one-fourth inch or less in diameter. Wet- and dry-bulb temperatures were taken at a shaded location 48 inches above the ground at the time of sampling to determine temperature and vapor-pressure deficit. Light intensity readings with a photoelectric cell and translucent filter were also made when diurnal fluctuations were being studied.

[3] *Personal communication with T. N. Johnsen, Jr., U.S. Agr. Res. Serv., Flagstaff, Ariz. 1962.*

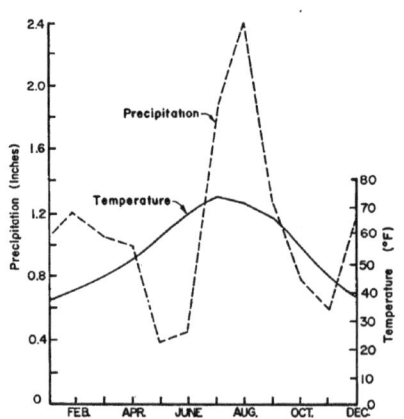

Figure 1.--*Seasonal trends in precipitation and temperature at Ashfork, Arizona (Smith 1956).*

Diurnal fluctuations were determined in early summer, late summer, winter, and spring by sampling 10 trees at 2-hour intervals from daylight to dark. A different set of 10 trees was selected for each sampling date.

Seasonal patterns were determined by collecting sample material at approximately 2-week intervals from February 1957 through January 1958, and in July and August 1958. The same trees were used throughout the study. Since the trees were quite large--about 15 feet in both height and crown diameter--and the sample size was about 100 grams, harvesting of sample material probably had little effect on the trees. Seasonal samples were collected at 4 hours after sunrise to help standardize conditions. This resulted in a nearly constant solar angle from March through October, but the solar angle from November through February was somewhat less.

One soil sample was collected for each tree location at each sampling date in the 3- to 12-inch zone. This sampling depth included virtually all of the C horizon of the soil at the Winona location, and the upper half of the C horizon at the Ash Fork location. Both tree and soil samples were weighed in the field, dried in the laboratory at $104°C$ for 48 hours, and weighed to determine moisture loss.

Results and Discussion

Diurnal Patterns

The different species of junipers uniformly showed a midday depression of moisture content during the summer months. This pattern is represented by the graph for alligator juniper in figure 2. This graph is similar to the graph of relative humidity, or graph of inverse of temperature or light intensity. Inverse moisture contents of junipers were, in fact, highly correlated with temperature and light intensity for the samples collected during the summer (table 1). Figure 2 is the classical curve presented in the literature, and can probably be adequately explained by the fact that absorption lags transpiration when potential transpiration rates are high. The correlations with temperature and light were probably as good as any such fit could be, since the correlation coefficients were about the same as the correlation coefficient between paired trees of Utah juniper and alligator juniper under identical situations ($r = 0.790$).

During the winter months, the significant relationship between juniper moisture content and meteorological conditions was lost. Samples collected in late March and early April had no clear pattern. Samples collected in January had an early-morning dip, followed by an increase through the rest of the day. This pattern is represented by the graph for Utah juniper in figure 2. The shape of this curve suggests that water uptake was limited by low soil temperature or low internal temperature of the trees. These temperatures would probably lag behind air temperature by

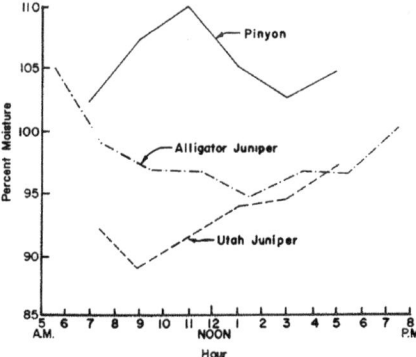

Figure 2.--Representative diurnal patterns of moisture content: pinyon during winter, alligator juniper during summer, Utah juniper during winter. Graphs of junipers are also representative of other species of junipers on these dates.

Table 1.--Diurnal patterns of moisture content of juniper and pinyon twigs and leaves and correlations with temperature and light

Species and date	Air temperature range, °F.	Type of pattern	Correlation coefficient of moisture content with--	
			Air temperature	Light intensity
One-seed juniper:				
Jan. 7, 1958	20-49	Early morning drop then increase	-0.116	-0.420
Mar. 28, 1957	25-62	None		
June 24, 1957	47-93	Inverse with temperature		
July 1, 1958	48-94	Inverse with temperature	-.673**	-.716**
Sept. 3, 1957	44-83	Inverse with temperature		
Utah juniper:				
Jan. 9, 1958	34-50	Early morning drop then increase	+.185	+.063
Apr. 4, 1957	30-53	None		
June 25, 1957	57-93	Inverse with temperature	-.886**	-.750**
Sept. 4, 1957	53-86	Inverse with temperature		
Alligator juniper:				
Jan. 9, 1958	34-50	Early morning drop then increase	-.275	-.266
Apr. 4, 1957	30-53	None		
June 25, 1957	57-93	Inverse with temperature	-.887**	-.736**
Sept. 4, 1957	53-86	Inverse with temperature		
Pinyon:				
Jan. 7, 1958	20-49	Morning rise, afternoon decrease	-.144	-.127
Mar. 28, 1957	25-62	Morning rise, afternoon decrease		
June 24, 1957	47-93	None		
July 1, 1958	48-94	None	-.078	+.063
Sept. 3, 1957	44-83	Decline throughout		

**Indicates significance at the .01 level. Correlation coefficients calculated within days.

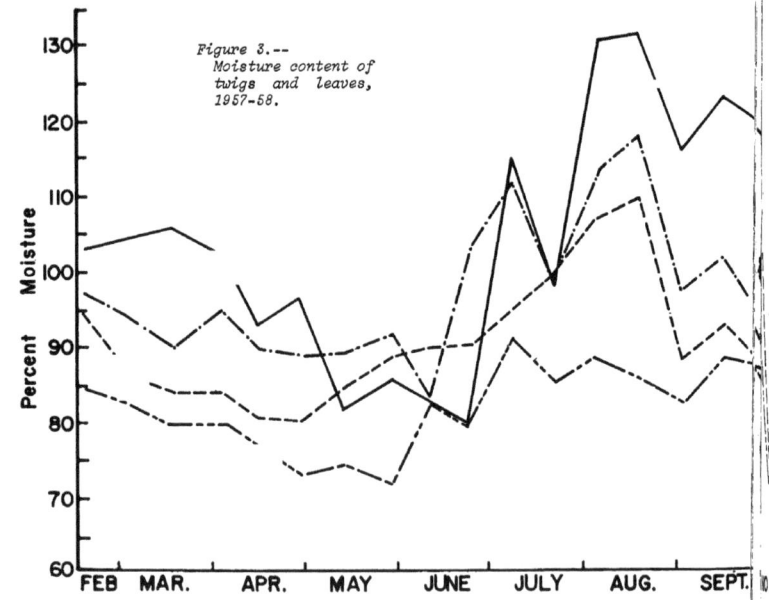

Figure 3.-- Moisture content of twigs and leaves, 1957-58.

- 4 -

an hour or two. During early morning in winter, temperatures were near or below freezing about 48 inches above the ground. Since soil temperature and internal stem temperature were not measured, a mathematical correlation was not possible.

Moisture content samples of pinyon were entirely unlike those of junipers. Early summer samples followed no distinct pattern. The samples collected in September gradually declined in moisture content through the day, but there was no upturn at the end of the day as for the junipers. There was no correlation of moisture content for pinyons with meteorological conditions. Apparently, pinyon leaves have some mechanism to retard the rate of moisture loss that would otherwise occur during summer days, while the mechanism in junipers is not fully adequate.

Pinyon did have a regular pattern for the January and March samples (fig. 2). Moisture content rose in the early morning, then dropped in the afternoon. This pattern is not clearly related to meteorological conditions.

Analysis of variance showed differences between moisture content of samples at times within days to be significant at the 1-percent level, except for the July 1 sample of pinyon and the January samples. For the January samples only, one-seed juniper showed significant differences between times, and that significance was at the 5-percent level. About 60 percent of the total sums of squares were associated with differences between trees; this shows the increase in sampling efficiency due to use of the same trees throughout the sampling day.

Seasonal Fluctuations

All species showed strong seasonal fluctuations of moisture content (fig. 3). These

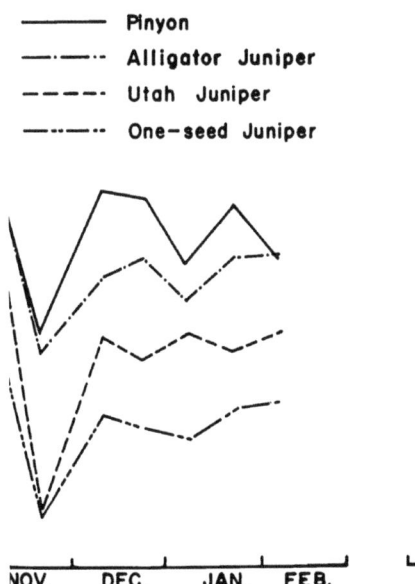
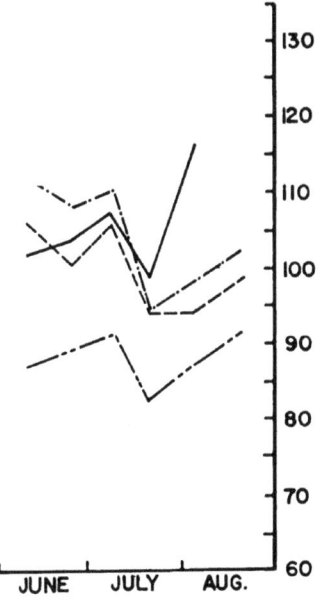

fluctuations were not clearly related to weather conditions as they were measured in this study. Multiple correlation and regression analyses with air temperature, vapor-pressure deficit, and soil moisture did yield significant correlation coefficients, but prediction equations from these analyses did not give accurate estimates of moisture content. Some of the coefficients were illogical or nonsignificant; for example, the soil-moisture coefficient was not consistent in sign and was in all cases nonsignificant. Vapor-pressure deficit and temperature were both positively related to moisture content at one site and negatively related at the other. The value of the constant terms in the regression equations was also quite different for the different species.

These results agree with those of Philpot (1963), who found no correlation between soil moisture and moisture content of P. ponderosa twigs. However, Namken (1964) and Philpot (1963) did find significant correlations with weather factors and cotton and Arctostaphylos viscida, respectively.

Because of these discrepancies, the data were also subjected to canonical analyses (table 2). These analyses resulted in more consistent equations than did the regression analyses. For the species with a significant correlation, the coefficients of vapor-pressure deficit were negative and the coefficients of soil moisture were positive, which are logical. The values of the constant terms were more consistent between species. Even though the equations were better, the correlation coefficients were still low, little of the total variation was accounted for by the equations, and estimated values of moisture content often did not follow the actual values.

Pinyon had a moisture-content pattern (see fig. 3) very similar to the long-term mean precipitation pattern for the study area (see fig. 1), but this fluctuation in moisture was not related to precipitation that actually fell during 1957. For example, pinyon twigs and leaves reached the lowest moisture content during May and June. Not even temporary upturns in moisture content were apparent, even with over 2 inches of rain in May and a June storm of 1 inch (interpolations from U.S. Weather Bureau records at Walnut Canyon, Arizona). In September, by way of contrast, there was no rainfall but moisture content was near the maximum for the study period.

Some of the changes in moisture content may have been related to growth of succulent young leaders. New and old growth were not separated in these samples, so the discrepancies introduced by new growth cannot be adequately evaluated. Supplemental samples

Table 2.--Correlation coefficients and equations (by canonical analysis) of the relationship of seasonal changes of moisture content of pinyon and junipers with vapor pressure deficit (VPD), temperature (T), T^2, and soil moisture (SM)

Species	Correlation coefficient	Equation
Utah juniper	0.560*	$Y = 74.26 - 1.28 \text{ VPD} + 0.03 \text{ SM} + 0.19 \text{ T} + 0.0013 \text{ T}^2$
Alligator juniper	.317	$Y = 97.33 + 10.33 \text{ VPD} - 0.09 \text{ SM} - 0.01 \text{ T} + 0.0001 \text{ T}^2$
One-seed juniper	.615*	$Y = 57.06 - 4.96 \text{ VPD} + 0.14 \text{ SM} + 0.18 \text{ T} + 0.0034 \text{ T}^2$
Pinyon	.499	$Y = 65.82 - 46.80 \text{ VPD} - 0.57 \text{ SM} + 0.57 \text{ T} + 0.0073 \text{ T}^2$

*Indicates significance at the .05 level.

Res. Counc. Israel Sect. D. Bot. 8D: 239-246. [Biol. Abstr. 35: 68068.]

Kosikova, P. G.
   1956. Water content in leaves and transpiration of perennial and annual cereals in relation to the growth of plants, and the effect of acid soil on them. Sbornik nauchno-Issled. Rabot Stud. Stavropolsk S.-Kh Inst. 1956 (4): 10-14. [Biol. Abstr. 35: 24784.]

Kramer, P. J., and Kozlowski, T. T.
   1960. Physiology of trees. 642 pp. New York: McGraw-Hill Book Co.

Meyer, B. S.
   1928. Seasonal variations in the physical and chemical properties of the leaves of the pitch pine, with especial reference to cold resistance. Amer. J. Bot. 15: 449-472.

Namken, L. N.
   1964. The influence of crop environment on the internal water balance of cotton. Soil Sci. Soc. Amer. Proc. 28: 12-15.

Oppenheimer, H. R.
   1953. An experimental study on ecological relationships and water expenses of Mediterranean forest vegetation. Palestine J. Bot. 8: 103-124.

Parker, J.
   1954. Available water in stems of some Rocky Mountain conifers. Bot. Gaz. 115: 380-385.

   1956. Drought resistance in woody plants. Bot. Rev. 22: 241-289.

Philpot, C. W.
   1963. The moisture content of ponderosa pine and whiteleaf manzanita foliage in the central Sierra Nevada.* U.S. Forest Serv. Res. Note PSW-39, 7 pp. Pacific Southwest Forest and Range Exp. Sta., Berkeley, Calif.

Smith, H. V.
   1956. Climate of Arizona. Ariz. Agr. Exp. Sta. Bull. 279, 99 pp.

Walter, H.
   1955. The water economy and the hydrature of plants. Ann. Rev. Plant Physiol. 6: 239-252.

*Address requests for copies to the originating office.

A Site Index Table for Aspen in the Southern and Central Rocky Mountains

John R. Jones[1]

The spectrum of aspen habitats was sampled and 177 mature trees were sectioned. Their individual height growth curves were used to construct nonharmonized, or natural, site index curves. The table represents height-age intercepts of the site index curves. Brief instructions are given for their use.

The following site index table was derived from natural site index curves based on 59 even-aged plots - - 48 in Colorado, 9 in New Mexico, and 2 in Arizona. Each natural site index curve was based on plots belonging in the site index class represented by that curve. The index age was 80 years.

To use the table, find the number of rings at breast height[2] and the total heights of three or more dominant trees. Enter the table with average height and ring count to obtain site index.

If the sample trees have fewer than 40 rings at breast height, site index estimates will be less reliable than if older trees are measured. With fewer than 30 rings, large errors may occur.

Aspen rings are often difficult to count accurately. A sharp increment borer makes them more distinct. The rings can usually be counted with a hand lens if the core is moistened and held toward the sky. If trees have been attacked by the Great Basin tent caterpillar, the resulting bands of very narrow rings are especially hard to count. Accuracy is possible, however, if the core is put into a clamp and one side smoothly shaved with a sharp razor blade. Rub the shaved surface with the side of a soft pencil lead. A strong hand lens then will usually show all the rings.

Aspen stands are composed of clones--patches of aspen within which each tree is genetically identical to every other tree. Different clones sometimes give considerably different site indexes.[3] When an aspen site is to be appraised, first look it over. Are there patches of the same age but with different heights on what appears to be a uniform habitat? If there are, take site index sample trees from more than one clone.

---

[1]*Associate Forest Ecologist, Rocky Mountain Forest and Range Experiment Station, with central headquarters maintained at Fort Collins, in cooperation with Colorado State University.*

[2]*Rocky Mountain aspen needed an average of 4 years to reach breast height. Because the actual time required was quite variable and poorly correlated with site quality, however, breast height age should be determined directly and not estimated from total age.*

[3]*Zahner, Robert, and Crawford, Ned A. The clonal concept in aspen site relations, pp. 229-243. In Forest-soil relationships in North America, edited by Chester T. Youngberg. Corvallis: Ore. State Univ. Press. 1965.*

Table 1.--Site index of aspen by height of dominant trees and age at breast height (4-1/2 feet)

Height of dominant trees (feet)	Breast height age (years)																												
	20	25	30	35	40	45	50	55	60	65	70	75	80	85	90	95	100	105	110	115	120	125	130	135	140	145	150	155	160
												- - Site index values - -																	
12	24	21																											
14	29	25	22	21																									
16	36	30	26	24	22	21	20																						
18	43	35	30	28	26	24	23	22	21	20																			
20	49	40	35	31	29	27	25	24	23	22	21	21	20																
22	55	45	39	35	32	30	28	27	26	25	23	23	22	21	21	20													
24	62	50	43	39	35	33	31	29	28	27	26	25	24	23	23	22	21	21	20										
26	69	55	47	42	38	36	34	32	30	29	28	27	26	25	25	24	24	24	22										
28	75	60	51	46	42	39	36	34	33	31	30	29	28	27	26	25	25	24	24										
30	82	65	55	50	45	41	39	37	35	34	32	31	30	29	28	27	27	26	25										
32	88	71	60	54	47	44	41	39	38	36	34	33	32	31	30	29	28	27	27										
34	94	76	64	57	50	47	44	42	40	38	36	35	34	33	32	31	30	29	28	31	30								
36		81	68	61	53	50	46	44	42	40	38	37	36	35	34	33	32	31	30	32	31	31							
38		86	72	64	56	52	49	47	44	42	41	39	38	37	36	34	33	32	31	33	32	32	31						
40		91	76	67	60	55	51	49	47	45	43	41	40	38	38	36	35	34	33	35	33	34	33	31					
42			80	70	63	58	54	51	49	47	45	44	42	41	39	38	37	36	35	34	33	32	31	31	31	31	30		30
44			84	74	66	61	57	54	51	49	47	46	44	42	41	40	39	38	37	36	35	34	33	32	32	32	32	31	32
46			89	77	69	63	59	56	53	51	49	48	46	44	43	42	41	39	38	37	36	35	35	34	34	34	33	32	32
48			93	80	72	66	62	59	56	53	51	50	48	46	45	44	42	41	40	39	38	37	36	35	35	35	34	34	33
50				84	75	69	64	61	58	56	53	52	50	48	47	46	44	43	42	41	40	39	38	37	36	35	34	34	33
52				87	78	72	67	63	60	58	56	54	52	50	49	47	46	45	43	42	41	40	39	38	37	37	36	35	35
54				91	81	74	69	66	63	60	58	56	54	52	51	49	48	47	45	44	43	42	40	40	39	38	37	37	36
56					84	77	72	68	65	62	60	58	56	54	53	51	50	48	47	46	45	43	42	41	40	39	39	38	37
58					87	80	74	70	67	64	62	60	58	56	55	53	51	50	49	47	46	45	44	43	42	41	40	39	39
60					90	83	77	73	69	67	64	62	60	58	57	55	53	52	50	49	48	47	45	44	43	43	42	41	40
62						85	80	75	72	69	66	64	62	60	58	57	55	54	52	51	49	48	47	46	45	44	43	42	42
64						88	82	78	74	71	68	66	64	62	60	59	57	55	54	52	51	50	49	48	47	45	45	44	43
66						91	85	80	76	73	71	68	66	64	62	60	59	57	56	54	53	52	50	49	48	47	46	45	44
68							87	83	79	75	73	70	68	66	64	62	61	59	57	56	55	53	52	51	50	48	47	46	46
70							90	85	81	77	75	72	70	68	66	64	62	61	59	58	56	55	54	52	51	50	49	48	47
74									85	82	79	76	74	72	70	68	66	64	63	61	60	59	57	56	55	53	52	51	50
78								90	90	86	83	80	78	76	74	72	70	68	66	65	63	62	61	59	58	57	56	54	53
82										91	87	85	82	80	78	76	73	72	70	68	67	65	64	63	61	60	59	58	57
86											92	89	86	84	81	79	77	75	73	72	70	69	67	66	65	64	63	61	60
90												93	90	87	85	83	81	79	77	75	74	72	71	70	68	67	66	65	64
94																		83	81	79	77	76	74	73	72	71	70	69	68
98														91	89	87	85	87	85	83	81	80	78	77	76	75	73	72	72
102															93	91	93	91	89	87	85	83	82	80	79	78	77	76	75
106																			93	91	89	87	86	85	83	82	81	80	79
110																					93	91	90	89	87	86	85	84	83
114																											89	88	87
118																								93	91	90	93	92	92

- 2 -

Height-Diameter Curves for Tree Species Subject to Stagnation

Clifford A. Myers[1]

Relationships between tree heights and diameters in even-aged stands of ponderosa and lodgepole pines can be expressed by the equation H = a + b log D.

Forest inventory instructions usually specify that only a sample of tree heights will be measured. Unmeasured heights are estimated from a graphical or mathematical relationship between height and diameter. Mathematical solutions are especially useful where a specific height-diameter relationship applies over a wide area. Standardized instructions can be included in computer programs, or used to guide least squares solutions on desk calculators. Workers who use graphical methods often find useful relationships represented on commercial graph paper. Linear and log-function graph papers make it easy to plot data for graphical solutions.

Comparison of several height-diameter relationships showed the following equation to be the most useful for even-aged stands of ponderosa (Pinus ponderosa Laws.) and lodgepole (P. contorta Dougl.) pines:

H = a + b log D

where

H = total height,
D = diameter at breast height,
a and b = regression constants.

Form of the relationship is not changed by variation in tree size or stand density. The model applies to stands so dense that height growth is reduced, as well as to those kept vigorous by repeated thinning. Relatively simple solutions of the height-diameter relationship are therefore possible, either by machine or on semilogarithmic paper.

Relationships recommended in American and European publications are tested to determine those most useful where stagnation of

---

[1] *Principal Mensurationist, Rocky Mountain Forest and Range Experiment Station, with central headquarters at Fort Collins, in cooperation with Colorado State University.*

growth is possible. Equations tested included the following:

$H = a + b \log D$

$H = a + b/D^2$

$H = a + b\ D^2$

$H = a + b_1 D - b_2 D^2$

plus multiple regressions involving two or more transformations of D.

Data from 91 ponderosa pine plots in the Black Hills of South Dakota and Wyoming were analyzed by least squares. Regressions with the lowest standard errors and best fit between measured and computed heights were identified for each plot. The ponderosa pine plots sampled wide ranges of stand characteristics:

Basal area--57 to 261 square feet.
Average stand diameter--2.0 to 17.5 inches.
Average stand height--13 to 85 feet.
Stand age--25 to 161 years.
Site index--36 to 76 feet (base 100 years).

Best solutions for the 91 ponderosa pine plots were distributed as follows:

Transform of diameter measure	Number of plots where transform was:	
	Best	Tied for best
log D	33	45
D - D^2	5	23
1/D^2	2	20
D^2	3	17

Log D was the best expression of diameter tested for 33 of the 91 sets of data. It was equal to or better than other forms of expression in 78 cases.

The frequently used relationship $H = a + b_1 D - b_2 D^2$ did not rank high. D and D^2 were both significant independent variables for only 37 of the 91 sets of data. Other multiple regressions tested did not produce valid relationships.

The 13 plots where log D was not as good as other transforms of diameter had no measured stand characteristics in common. Characteristics examined were: Average stand diameter, average height, dominant height, age, stand density, site index, and thinning history. In no case did a solution based on log D give results that were unacceptable for the usual purposes for which estimated heights are used. Standard errors were 0.7 to 3.1 feet.

Data from 47 lodgepole pine plots in Colorado and Wyoming were used to verify results of the ponderosa pine analysis. Stands varied much less in average diameter and other characteristics than did the ponderosa pine stands, but both dense and thinned stands were included. Height-diameter relationships of 45 of the 47 plots were closely represented by $H = a + b \log D$. On two plots, computed heights of the largest and smallest diameter classes differed from measured heights by 3 to 4 feet. There were only one or two trees in each of these classes, both on the two plots and in the sample.

1966

U.S. FOREST SERVICE
RESEARCH NOTE RM - 70

FOREST SERVICE
U.S. DEPARTMENT OF AGRICULTURE

Ten-Year Growth of Two Sources of
Large Grade Ponderosa Pine Transplants in Nebraska

Ralph A. Read[1]

In a 10-year-old plantation of ponderosa pine in north-central Nebraska, the large grade 2+1 stock from a Rosebud seed source grew faster than the same size and age class from a Niobrara seed source. Large grade stock of both seed sources survived better and grew faster than ungraded bedrun stock.

A small study involving two seed sources and three age classes of graded and ungraded ponderosa pine planting stock was established in Nebraska in spring 1954. First-year survival for the graded versus ungraded stock was reported earlier.[2]

One of the plantations in this study, which has developed normally on a sandy loam site in Holt County, (north-central) Nebraska, was measured for survival and height growth after 5 and 10 years. These data are reported in this Note, because of the particularly interesting results regarding growth of trees from the two seed sources.

The two sources of ponderosa pine seed are known as Rosebud and Niobrara. The Niobrara stands (from which these seed lots originated) are on the breaks of the Niobrara

---

[1] *Principal Silviculturist, located at Lincoln in cooperation with the Nebraska Agricultural Experiment Station; central headquarters maintained at Fort Collins, in cooperation with Colorado State University.*
[2] *Read, Ralph A. Grading of transplants may improve initial survival of ponderosa pine in Plains windbreaks. U. S. Forest Serv. Rocky Mountain Forest and Range Exp. Sta., Res. Note 16, 2 pp. 1955.*

River near Valentine, Nebraska, 90 miles due west of the study plantation. The Rosebud stands are in the breaks of the Little White River in Todd County, South Dakota, about 30 miles northwest of the Niobrara source stands. The two sources are not continuous; they are separated by 30 miles of treeless sandhills. Recent collections of ponderosa pine material from these two areas have revealed distinct differences in some taxonomic characteristics such as needle length, number of needles per fascicle, cone size, and color of seed wings and cone scales. Distinct genetic differences in the two stands are strongly suggested.

All planting stock was grown at Bessey Nursery, operated by the U. S. Forest Service near Halsey, Nebraska. The Rosebud source in this study was represented by 2+1 and 1+2 age classes, and the Niobrara source by 2+1 and 2+1+1. A large grade of stock was selected from the bedrun lots of each age class, and was approximately the largest one-third of transplants on the basis of stem caliper (8/32 to 15/32 inch), top size, and root size. Ungraded, bedrun material was represented only by 2+1 Niobrara stock. The field planting consisted of two rows with 25-tree linear plots of each class of stock randomly located within each of two blocks.

Typical specimens of the large grade of each age class and source are shown in figure 1. Although the 1+2 Rosebud transplants were largest, they were not the best. Well over half of this stock had damaged roots. Two consecutive years at 1-1/2-inch spacing in the transplant bed made it virtually impossible to separate these trees without stripping the roots. This alone probably accounted for the high first-year mortality of 1+2 Rosebud. Transplants of other age classes were separated easily without damage.

Survival and growth data are given in table 1. Significant differences between means in the following discussion were obtained by "t" tests.

There was no change in survival between the second and tenth years. All mortality occurred the first growing season. This emphasizes the importance of using high quality stock for attaining greatest survival and growth the first growing season. Differences in 10-year survival among the large grades of 2+1 and 2+1+1 stock were not significant. Survival of these large grade trees was far superior to that of ungraded, bedrun stock. The 66 percent survival of large grade 1+2 Rosebud stock was explained above; there were no losses of this material after the first year.

The only significant difference in height after 5 years was between the ungraded 2+1 Niobrara stock, which averaged 1.7 feet, and all large grades of the different age classes and sources, which averaged 3.0 feet. Thus the advantage gained in early height growth by using large grade stock is apparent.

Differences in total height among seed sources and classes of stock after 10 growing seasons are of special interest. In the large grade 2+1 category, the Rosebud source averaged 10.3 feet, while the Niobrara source averaged only 7.7 feet. Moreover, the survivors of the large grade 1+2 class of Rosebud outgrew the 2+1 Niobrara source (respectively, 9.4 feet and 7.7 feet). The 2+1 Rosebud trees, which were incidentally the smallest of the graded stock (fig. 1), averaged 1.42 feet height growth per year during the past 5 years.

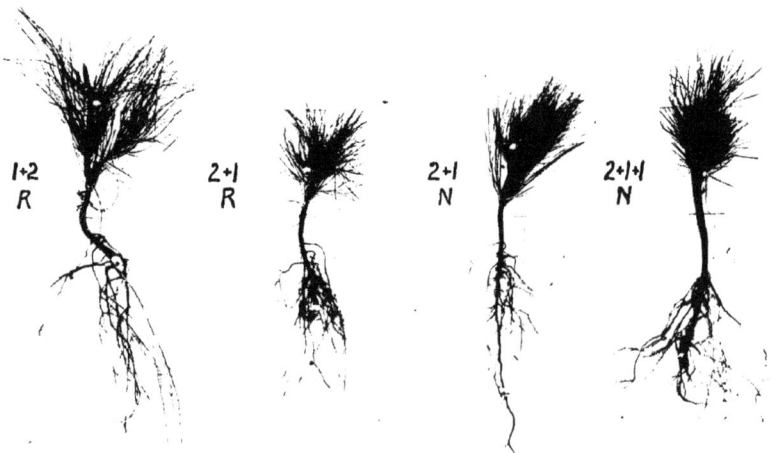

Figure 1.--Representative specimens of ponderosa pine planting stock used in the study. R = Rosebud source, N = Niobrara source.

Table 1.--Survival and height growth of two sources and three age classes of graded and ungraded ponderosa pine transplants in north-central Nebraska

Source, age class, and grade	Average height			Range in total height	Average annual height growth (last 5 years)	10-year survival	Basis: trees
	Planting stock	After 5 years	After 10 years				
	---------- Feet ----------					Percent	No.
NIOBRARA:							
2 + 1 Ungraded, bedrun	0.5	1.7	4.7	1- 9	0.60	51	54
2+1 Large grade	.7	2.9	7.7	5-10	.96	90	44
2+1+1 Large grade	.9	3.0	9.9	6-13	1.38	92	46
ROSEBUD:							
2 + 1 Large grade	.6	3.2	10.3	7-14	1.42	98	49
1 + 2 Large grade	1.0	3.0	9.4	3-12	1.28	66	33

Of the large grade Niobrara stock, the 2 + 1 + 1 transplants were significantly taller after 10 years than the 2 + 1 transplants (respectively, 9.9 feet and 7.7 feet). Although little difference in height was evident at 5 years' age, the trees developing from 2 + 1 + 1 stock are now growing almost 50 percent faster than trees from the 2 + 1 age class. They are, of course, 1 year older.

Average height of trees from large grade 2 + 1 Niobrara stock was significantly greater than that of trees from ungraded, bedrun 2 + 1 Niobrara stock (respectively, 7.7 feet and 4.7 feet). Although the maximum heights of graded and ungraded trees were about the same, the ungraded portion of the planting contains many shorter trees.

As a possible explanation for the differences in height growth rate of Rosebud and Niobrara sources, taxonomic data collected from 10 seed trees in each area in 1963 show:

	Niobrara	Rosebud
Number of trees predominately		
2-needle	7	3
3-needle	3	7
Average number of needles per fascicle	2.4	2.7
Length of needles (mm.)		
Average	179	209
Range	152-216	181-234

The greater vigor and height growth of the Rosebud source may thus be associated with a higher proportion of progeny having a greater photosynthetic area produced by 3-needle fascicles containing needles over an inch longer than the Niobrara trees.

Juniper Control by Individual Tree Burning

Donald A. Jameson[1]

For 100 percent kill of juniper trees with individual tree burning, 60 percent of the crown should be scorched. The time required to achieve enough scorch increased with wind and tree size, but decreased with temperature.

Because juniper trees have reduced the forage production on millions of acres of western rangelands, many ranchers and land management agencies are conducting juniper control programs. Burning individual trees is one suitable technique for killing junipers.

Where to Use Individual Tree Burning

Individual tree burning is best suited to open stands of small, nonsprouting trees such as one-seed juniper (Juniperus monosperma (Engelm.) Sarg.) and Utah juniper (J. osteosperma (Torr.) Little). Travel between widely scattered trees is fairly rapid[2] (fig. 1) and small trees are quickly burned[2] (fig. 2). Large trees, however, require so much time to burn that the expense becomes prohibitive. Individual tree burning is not appropriate for trees over 10 feet tall, nor should it be used for sprouting species such as alligator juniper (J. deppeana Steud.) and redberry juniper (J. pinchotii Sudw.).

---

[1] *Principal Plant Physiologist, located at Flagstaff, in cooperation with Northern Arizona University; central headquarters maintained at Fort Collins, in cooperation with Colorado State University.*

[2] *Data for figures 1 and 2 from-- Cotner, Melvin L., and Jameson, Donald A. Costs of juniper control: Bulldozing vs. burning individual trees. U. S. Forest Serv. Rocky Mountain Forest and Range Exp. Sta., Sta. Paper 43, 14 pp., illus. 1959.*

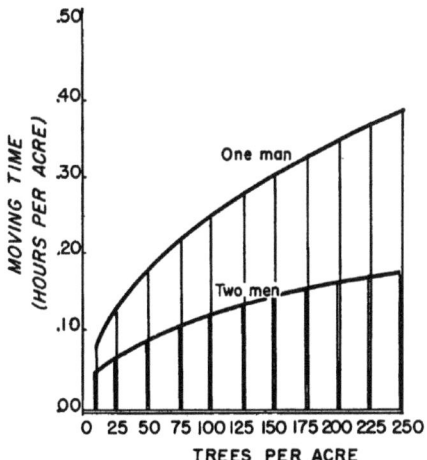

Figure 1.--Moving time per acre for burning trees individually with one- and two-man crews.

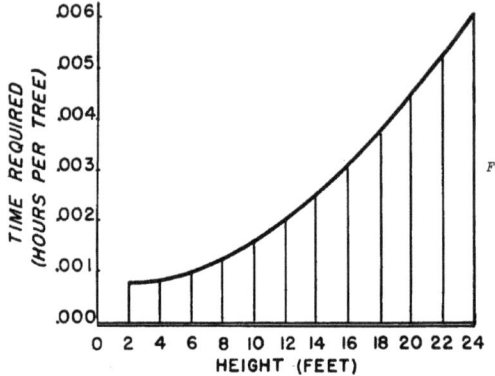

Figure 2.--Time required for burning individual juniper trees of various heights with a propane torch.

Equipment

Many types of torches can be used. A torch that produces a large flame will reduce the time required--an important factor when labor costs are high. Propane torches have been satisfactory in our studies. The oil-burning torches many ranchers have on hand are also suitable.

Precautions

Junipers should be burned only when it is certain that the fire will not escape from the planned area. If there is fuel on the ground, firebreaks should be built before the burning begins. Ordinarily, however, if the range has been at least moderately grazed, there is insufficient fuel for the fire to spread.

Weather Conditions

The main consideration on weather conditions is flexibility of operations. The best days for individual tree burning are hot and dry with little or no wind. Winds 12 miles per hour or greater blow the torch flame away from the tree without igniting the tree tops. If a particular day turns out to be too cold, wet, or windy, the burning should be postponed until the job can be done more cheaply.

How to Burn

Perhaps the most troublesome question in individual tree burning is: How much burning time is required? To answer this question, a study was conducted to relate the appearance of the trees immediately after burning to the survival of the trees 1 year later. Leaf scorch is easy to identify on a newly burned tree, and was the most useful indicator of mortality we found. Plant kill was satisfactory when 60 percent or more of the tree crown was scorched (fig. 3). The emphasis in procedure should be to get enough crown scorch without spending excessive time on the trees.

We also inspected the apparent amount of stem burning. It is very difficult to girdle a tree with flame, and we have found that amount of stem burning is poorly related to plant kill.

Figure 4 shows an ideal burn. The operator has scorched about two-thirds of the tree and stopped the flame. Figure 5 shows two wrong techniques. The operator is taking too much time with the small tree in the foreground, while the tree just behind him has been inadequately burned and will survive.

In spite of the apparent difficulties, most torch operators soon develop a "feel" for the proper amount of burning and naturally accomplish the job in nearly optimum time.

Figure 3.--Top kill and plant kill of trees, based on percent of leaf scorch apparent just after burning. Each point represents five trees.

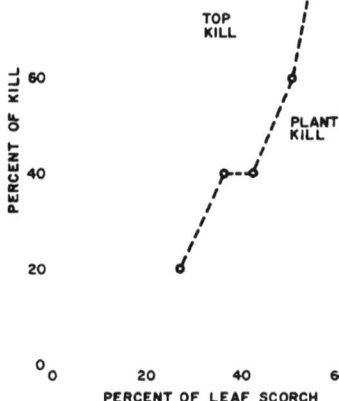

Figure 4.--Ideal burning technique. About two-thirds of the crown has been scorched.

Figure 5.--Improper burning techniques. Excessive time is being taken with the tree in the foreground. The tree behind the operator has been inadequately burned and will live.

Expected Costs and Contract Specifications

Expected time required for individual tree burning can be calculated by adding the travel time per acre (fig. 1) to the time required to burn all the trees per acre (fig. 2). For example, a stand of 100 trees 10 feet tall would take two men 0.113 hour for travel and $0.0047 \times 100 = 0.47$ hour for burning, for a total of 0.583 hour. Fuel costs are calculated for burning time only. The torches we have studied use 20.5 gallons of propane per hour. For 0.47 hour of burning, fuel consumption would be $20.5 \times 0.47 = 9.6$ gallons.

For contract jobs, acceptable work can be evaluated by using figure 3. Sixty percent or more crown scorch should give nearly 100 percent tree mortality. Scorch can be evaluated as soon as the trees have cooled.

1966

U.S. FOREST SERVICE
RESEARCH NOTE RM - 72

FOREST SERVICE
U.S. DEPARTMENT OF AGRICULTURE

Stocking of Reproduction on Spruce-Fir Clearcuttings in Colorado

Robert R. Alexander[1]

Stocking on 200- to 400-foot-wide clearcut strips was determined on 99 cutting units on 8 National Forests. Stocking to reproduction and residual understory trees of good quality will insure an adequate replacement stand on all cutting units examined. Stocking to new reproduction was related to seedbed condition, aspect, slope, amount of slash, vegetative abundance, soil texture, width and direction of cut strip, and the number of years since cutting.

One of the most difficult problems in the management of Engelmann spruce (Picea engelmanni Parry) subalpine fir (Abies lasiocarpa (Hook.) Nutt.) forests in Colorado is the apparent inconsistency of natural regeneration after clearcutting. Seedlings become established on many clearcut areas in a reasonable period of time if seed is available in sufficient quantities. There are other clearcut areas, however, that fail to restock even though conditions appear to have been favorable for regeneration.

In 1959, recently clearcut spruce-fir stands were surveyed to determine the relative importance of several environmental factors and cutting-unit characteristics influencing seedling establishment. This paper summarizes the effect on stocking of the factors and characteristics considered.

---

[1] *Principal Silviculturist, Rocky Mountain Forest and Range Experiment Station, with central headquarters maintained at Fort Collins, in cooperation with Colorado State University.*

Study Areas

Observations were made on 99 cutting units on the following 8 sale areas in Colorado:

Drainage	National Forest
Supply Creek	Arapaho
Trap Creek	Roosevelt
East Fork Willow Creek	Routt
South Fork Slater Creek	Routt
Beaver Creek	San Isabel
North Fork Mancos River	San Juan
Silver Creek	White River
Red Sandstone Creek	White River

The cutting units sample a wide range of conditions. Slopes vary from 10 to about 60 percent, and aspect embraces all compass directions. Soils are mostly light-textured, gravelly and sandy loams, derived mainly from granitic and coarse sedimentary rocks. Ground vegetation, principally grouse whortleberry (Vaccinium scoparium Leiberg), was little altered by cutting.

All cutting units were logged between 1952 and 1956. Timber was harvested by commercial clearcutting in either alternate strips 200 feet wide at right angles to the contour, or alternate strips 200 to 400 feet wide parallel to the contour. The clearcut strips differed in length, but all points on the units sampled were within 200 feet of a seed source. Logging slash and unmerchantable residual understory trees were left untreated. Seedbed preparation was limited to that created by logging. Logs were skidded with horses on most areas, but tractors and jammers were used on some.

Field Examination

Approximately 1 to 1-1/2 percent of the area cut on each unit was systematically sampled with 1/300-acre plots. The following information was recorded on 1,748 plots:

Stocking: Growing stock was classed as (1) subsequent reproduction, (2) advanced reproduction, and (3) residual understory (trees 3.6 inches d.b.h. and larger). Spruce and fir were tallied separately. Only advanced growth of good quality and subsequent reproduction 1 inch tall or taller were considered to be growing stock.

Seedbed: Classified as (1) undisturbed, (2) disturbed, and (3) skidroad, on the basis of the condition containing the oldest subsequent reproduction. If no subsequent reproduction was present, seedbeds were classified on the basis of the largest percentage of seedbed condition on the plot. Condition was determined in 1959 on the basis of the probable condition immediately after logging.

Aspect: Recorded to the nearest cardinal point.

Slope: Measured in percent.

Slash cover: Rated on the percentage of ground actually covered on each plot as (1) none--less than 10 percent, (2) light--10 to 39 percent, (3) medium--40 to 69 percent, and (4) heavy--70 percent or more.

Abundance of vegetation: Rated on the basis of the percentage of ground actually occupied by vegetation as (1) light--scattered cover with bare soil between plants, (2) medium--moderate cover, and (3) heavy--dense cover.

In addition, time since cutting, width, direction with respect to the contour, direction with respect to the prevailing winds, parent soil material, and general soil texture were recorded for each unit.

Analysis of Data

Total stocking on areas sampled was rated on the proportion of sample plots stocked by all species and classes of reproduction as:

Fully stocked--100 percent,
Well stocked--70 to 99 percent,
Moderately stocked--40 to 69 percent,
Poorly stocked--10 to 39 percent,
Nonstocked--less than 10 percent.

Stocking to subsequent reproduction only was used in evaluating the effects of environmental factors and cutting-unit characteristics. Apparent relationships were tested by "Chi Square" and regression analyses.

Results

Stocking: Average stocking to all classes of growing stock was 83 percent (fig. 1). About two-thirds of the sample plots were stocked to fir, and more than half were stocked to spruce. Advanced reproduction stocked 61 percent of the plots sampled, and subsequent reproduction stocked 54 percent. Stocking to advanced reproduction was predominantly fir, but stocking to subsequent reproduction was evenly distributed between spruce and fir (fig. 1).

Seedbed condition: Spruce and fir reacted differently to seedbed condition. Spruce stocking was significantly better on disturbed and skidroad seedbeds than on undisturbed seedbeds. Stocking to fir was significantly better on undisturbed seedbeds than on skidroad seedbeds, but did not differ significantly between disturbed and undisturbed seedbeds (fig. 2).

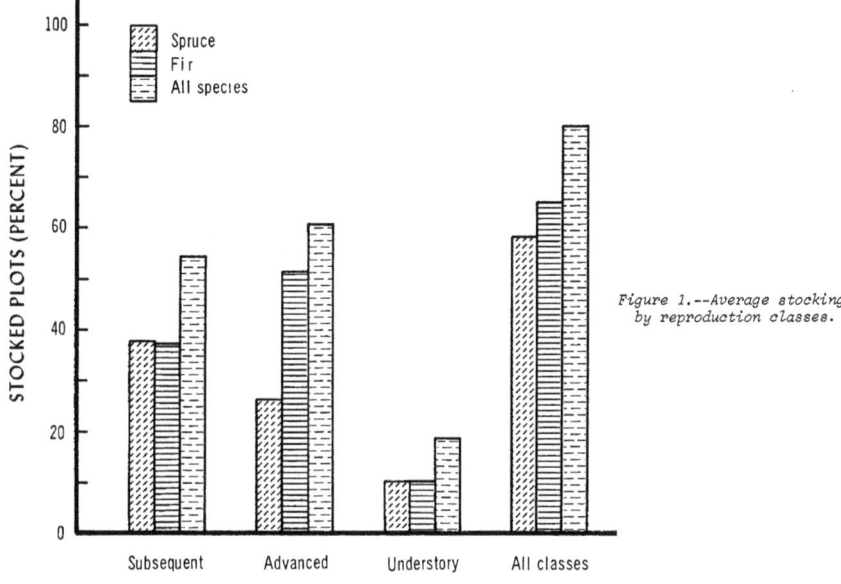

Figure 1.--Average stocking by reproduction classes.

Aspect:[2] Stocking to both spruce and fir differed substantially among aspects. In general, stocking was higher on northerly and westerly aspects and lower on southerly aspects (S and SW in particular). Stocking on east aspects represented about average conditions for exposure (fig. 3).

It seems reasonable that slope should influence stocking differently among different aspects. Reason dictates that there is likely to be little difference in stocking between northerly and southerly aspects as slope gradient approaches zero, but as slope steepness increases, difference in stocking between those aspects should increase. Minimum stocking on southerly aspects should be on slopes that face at right angles to the sun in midsummer, but there is no reason to believe that slopes of 20 to 30 percent on northerly aspects should be less favorable to reproduction than level ground. However, our sample was too small to establish dependable averages of stocking for combinations of aspect and slope.

Slope:[2] Stocking to both spruce and fir was related to slope gradient. Stocking was lowest on plots with the least slope (10 percent), and remained relatively unchanged as slope steepness increased to about 20 percent. Stocking then increased rapidly as slopes became steeper and was maximum on the steepest slopes encountered (fig. 4).

Slash cover: The proportion of ground covered by residual slash influenced stocking to both spruce and fir. Stocking was above average on areas where slash covered less than 40 percent of the plot area, and below average where slash cover was 40 percent and greater (fig. 5).

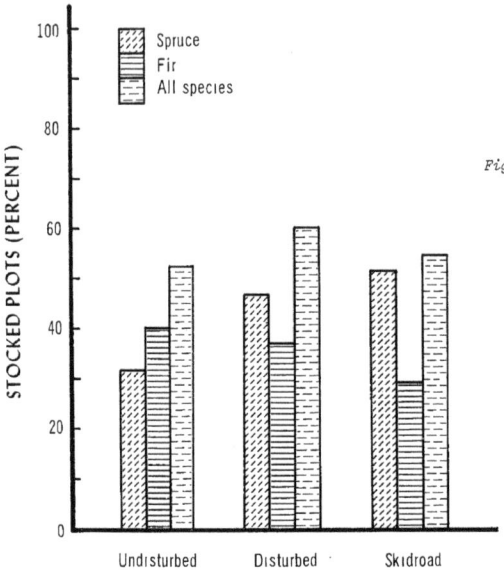

Figure 2.--Average stocking to subsequent reproduction, by seedbed condition.

Abundance of vegetation: Ground vegetation was beneficial to both spruce and fir stocking. Stocking to spruce was significantly better where vegetation was medium or heavy than where it was light (fig. 6). Where vegetation was heavy, competition appears to have offset any additional beneficial effects. Stocking to fir was highest where vegetation density was heaviest (fig. 6). The increase in stocking associated with an increase in vegetation density may have been due to an improvement in microenvironment caused by shading and mulching.

Cutting-unit characteristics: Stocking to spruce decreased as size of opening increased, but stocking to fir increased. Stocking to spruce averaged 39 percent on units 200 feet wide compared to 32 percent on units 400 feet wide. Stocking to fir averaged 32 percent on units 200 feet wide, and 65 percent on units 400 feet wide.

Cutting units at right angles to the contour were better stocked to spruce (43 percent) than units with boundaries parallel to the contour (29 percent). Stocking to fir averaged 45 percent on units parallel to the contour compared to 33 percent on units at right angles to the contour.

Average stocking to both spruce and fir was little influenced by the direction of cutting-unit boundaries with respect to prevailing winds. Spruce was stocked on 40 percent of the units with cutting boundaries parallel to the direction of the prevailing westerly and southwesterly winds, compared to 35 percent on units with cutting boundaries at right angles to the prevailing wind. Average stocking to fir was 37 to 38 percent, respectively.

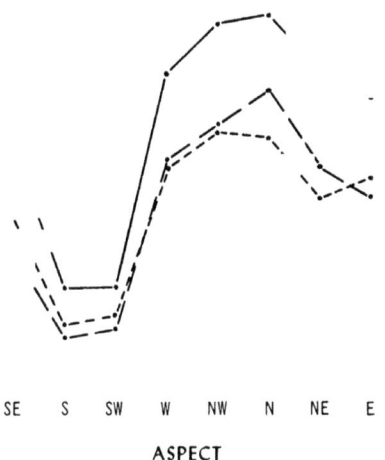

Figure. --Average stocking of subsequent reproduction, by aspect.

Parent soil material influenced stocking more than soil texture. Stocking to both spruce and fir was better on light-textured soils derived from coarse sandstone than on light-textured soils derived from granitic rock. Stocking was also below average on medium-textured soils derived from a variety of parent materials (table 1).

Stocking to both spruce and fir increased with time since logging, but fir established more quickly than spruce. Stocking to spruce was above average 6 or more years after cutting, and was highest after 7 years. Stocking to fir was above average after 4 or more years, but did not increase with additional time beyond 4 years (table 1).

Conclusions and Summary

Present stocking to reproduction and residual understory trees of good quality will insure an adequate replacement stand on all cutting units examined. The North Fork Mancos River and Beaver Creek were rated as moderately stocked; all other areas were rated as well stocked.

Advanced reproduction contributed substantially to total stocking on all areas examined. Although the composition was largely fir, advanced reproduction is established growing stock, and care should be taken to minimize logging damage to this valuable resource.

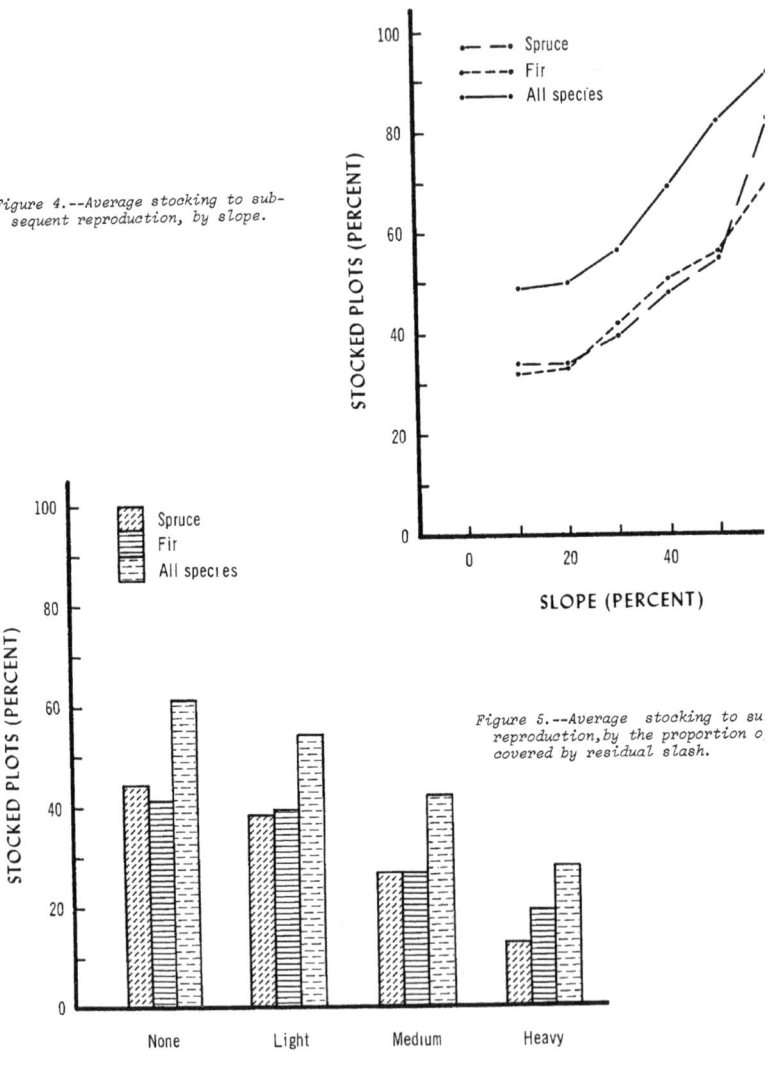

Figure 4.--*Average stocking to subsequent reproduction, by slope.*

Figure 5.--*Average stocking to su reproduction, by the proportion o covered by residual slash.*

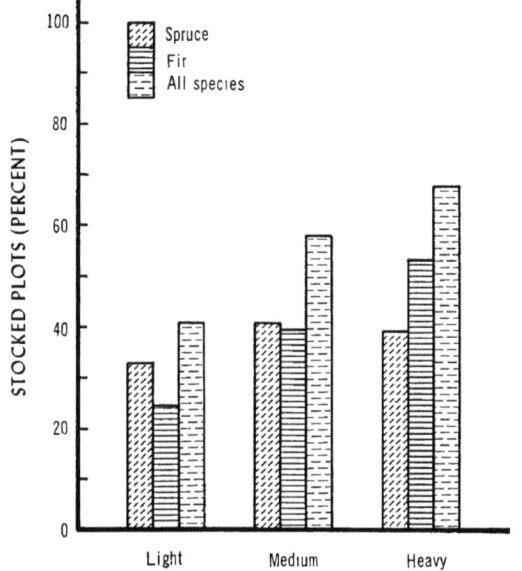

Figure 6.--Average stocking to subsequent reproduction, by abundance of vegetation.

Table 1.--Relation of average stocking to subsequent spruce and fir by soil type and length of time since timber harvest

Characteristics of area	Percent of total sample	Percent of species stocked		
		Spruce	Fir	All
Parent soil material and texture:				
Sandstone (Light)	41	47	51	69
Granitic (Light)	38	34	27	46
Other (Medium)	21	27	30	42
All	100	38	38	54
Length of time since timber harvest:				
3 years	20	17	7	19
4 years	38	34	46	60
6 years	18	43	46	62
7 years	24	56	42	69
All	100	38	38	54

Average stocking to subsequent reproduction was nearly as good as stocking to advanced reproduction. Furthermore, subsequent spruce was stocked on as many sample plots as subsequent fir, and stocking to spruce has continued to improve with time.

Composition and stocking of subsequent reproduction was related to the several environmental factors and cutting-unit characteristics observed. Conditions where stocking to subsequent spruce and fir was above and below average are shown in table 2. Stocking to spruce and fir each averaged 38 percent.

Table 2. --Stocking of subsequent reproduction and its relation to environmental factors and cutting-unit characteristics

Characteristics of area	Engelmann spruce		Subalpine fir	
	Average or above	Below average	Average or above	Below average
Seedbed	Disturbed and skidroad	Undisturbed	Undisturbed and disturbed	Skidroad
Ground covered with slash	Less than 40 percent	40 percent or more	Less than 40 percent	40 percent or more
Aspect	N, NE, E, W, NW	SE, S, SW	N, NE, E, W, NW	SE, S, SW
Average density of ground vegetation	Medium to heavy	Light	Medium to heavy	Light
Slope	Above 25 percent	25 percent or less	Above 25 percent	25 percent or less
Length of time since areas cut	6-7 years	3-4 years	4-7 years	3 years
Relation of cutting unit to contour	At right angles	Parallel	Parallel	At right angles
Width of cutting unit	200 feet	400 feet	400 feet	200 feet
Soil texture and derivation	Light textured, derived from sandstone	Light textured, derived from granitic rock; and medium textured, derived from various parent materials	Light textured, derived from sandstone	Light textured, derived from granitic rock; and medium textured, derived from various parent materials

Racial Variation in Ponderosa Pine at Fort Valley, Arizona

M. M. Larson[1]

Ponderosa pines from eastern and southeastern seed sources of the species range survived at Fort Valley, whereas trees of northern and western sources failed. In general, sources closest to Fort Valley grew best. Black Hills sources grew well in some instances.

A ponderosa pine seed source plantation was established at the Fort Valley Experimental Forest near Flagstaff, Arizona, during 1913-17. Results of this provenance study have never been published except for brief mention by Pearson (1950),[2] Roeser (1926), Schreiner (1937), and Squillace and Silen (1962). Also, a typewritten progress report was prepared by Pearson.[3]

The Fort Valley plantation is one of several ponderosa pine seed source studies established at various locations throughout the West from 1909 to 1926. Squillace and Silen (1962) reviewed the literature pertaining to these studies, and presented results of plantations in Idaho, Washington, and Oregon, based on data collected after the 1955 growing season.

Detailed analysis of the Fort Valley plantation data is limited by poor survival of trees and lack of an experimental design to adequately test source differences. The results, however, do provide additional information to that obtained from the other ponderosa pine seed source tests.

The Study

Ponderosa pine seed was obtained from 19 National Forests over the range of the species (fig. 1). Collection data are missing except for the local Coconino seed lots, which were all collected near Fort Valley. All the planting stock was grown at Fort Valley, with the exception of two lots of San Isabel stock which were grown at the Monument, Colorado,

---

[1] *Forest Physiologist, Rocky Mountain Forest and Range Experiment Station, located at Flagstaff in cooperation with Northern Arizona University; central headquarters are maintained at Fort Collins in cooperation with Colorado State University.*

[2] *Names and dates in parentheses refer to Literature Cited, p. 7.*

[3] *Pearson, G. A. Source of seed--western yellow pine. 14 pp., Jan. 20, 1920. (Unpublished progress report on file at Rocky Mountain Forest and Range Exp. Sta., Flagstaff, Arizona.)*

Figure 1.--The geographic location of ponderosa pine seed sources tested at the Fort Valley Experimental Forest, Arizona.

nursery and one lot of Coconino stock which was grown at the Fort Bayard, New Mexico, nursery. Stock was grown to 2-1 transplants and outplanted in 1913, 1914, 1916, and 1917. The main planting site, designated area A-1, was located one-fourth mile west of the Experimental Forest headquarters at an elevation of 7,300 feet. The soil was gravelly clay loam derived from basalt. All stock was hand planted in east-west rows with a 6-foot spacing between trees and rows. Rows, each a single seed source, varied in length up to 10 chains. Survivors were counted every year until 1919, and then in 1928, 1961, and 1964.

Heights were taken in 1928, and both heights and diameters were measured in 1964, 47 to 51 years after planting.

Untagged trees in the north one-half of area A-1 are excluded from this report. Also excluded are the remnants of three sources decimated by sheep grazing on area D-1, 3 miles northeast of the Experimental Forest headquarters on the San Francisco Peaks.

Comparisons of diameter and height growth between sources are based upon the largest one-third of the trees in each source, as recommended by Munger (1947) and Squillace and Silen (1962).

Results and Discussion

Ponderosa pines from 11 of 19 National Forests survived at Fort Valley (fig. 1). Survival, however, was poor--no source exceeded 40 percent (table 1). The survival pattern clearly reveals that sources from the eastern and southeastern part of the species

Table 1.--Growth, survival, and planting year of localities of seed origin

Year stock[1] planted	Locality of seed origin by National Forest	Total planted	Alive (1964)	Survival	Average diameter of 1/3 largest (1964)	Average height of 1/3 tallest (1964)
		Number		Percent	Inches	Feet
1913	San Isabel[2]	288	98	34	6.57	23.3
	Coconino	1,056	241	23	7.22	25.2
1914	Black Hills	273	49	18	7.83	27.6
	San Isabel[2]	319	53	17	6.86	22.1
	Coconino[3]	372	146	39	7.12	25.8
	Coconino	242	44	18	8.46	27.9
1916	Payette	65	1	2	--	--
	Black Hills (Harney)	100	20	20	7.69	25.1
	Roosevelt	200	14	7	5.64	19.8
	San Isabel	100	6	6	6.45	19.0
	Coconino	200	19	10	9.42	28.3
1917	Black Hills (Harney)	52	3	6	6.30	17.0
	Ashley	65	6	9	4.00	21.0
	San Isabel	84	10	12	7.73	27.3
	Manti-La Sal	84	18	21	9.60	28.7
	Santa Fe	84	20	24	8.33	24.6
	Gila	87	5	6	4.90	21.5
	Coconino	914	81	9	8.16	25.3
	Bitterroot	78	0	0		
	Boise	26	0	0		
	Salmon	43	0	0		
	Fishlake	14	0	0		
	Siskiyou	22	0	0		
	Tahoe	12	0	0		
	Klamath	(4)				
	Angeles	(4)				

[1] All stock grown to 2-1 transplants.
[2] Stock grown at Monument Nursery, Colorado.
[3] Stock grown at Fort Bayard Nursery, New Mexico.
[4] All seedlings killed in nursery, November 2, 1916, by freezing (temperature -3°F.).

range survived, whereas northern and western sources were failures. Payette is listed as a surviving source, but only a single tree remained.

Insects and unfavorable weather were the major causes of mortality during the early years.[3] Weather was favorable in 1913 and 1914, but the May beetle larvae killed many seedlings of all sources. The spring of 1916 was unusually dry, and early, hard freezes the following fall killed all the Angeles and Klamath seedlings and nearly all the Tahoe seedlings while still in the nursery. In 1917, a severe fall drought eliminated 6 of the 14 sources planted on the study area the preceding spring.

At the Fort Valley nursery, Pearson[3] observed that seeds of the central and southern Rocky Mountain sources were smaller and germinated faster without stratification than seeds of northern and western sources. Seedlings of these latter sources, he noted, were greener, taller, formed a more compact crown, and developed "a splendid root system for planting." Yet these northern and western source seedlings, Pearson reported, did not withstand planting well and were sensitive to frost and drought.

Seedling losses between 1928 and 1964 were small and about evenly divided among the sources. The effect of nurseries on survival and growth was usually confounded by the effects of site, stocking, and year of planting. However, Coconino trees from the Fort Valley nursery planted in 1914 grew better than Coconino trees from the Fort Bayard nursery (fig. 2).

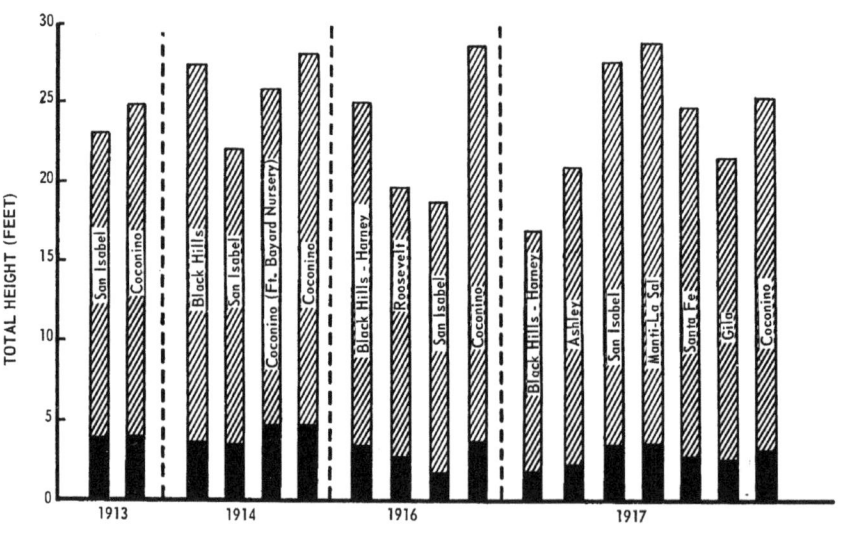

Figure 2.--Total average height of the tallest one-third of the trees from each source in 1928 (solid bar) and in 1964 (diagonal lines) for each planting year.

The local Coconino source trees grew larger in diameter and height than other sources planted in 1913, 1914, and 1916 (table 1, fig. 2). In the 1917 planting, Manti-La Sal source trees from southeastern Utah grew tallest (28.7 feet) with San Isabel second tallest (27.3 feet) and Coconino third (25.3 feet). However, some of the Coconino rows planted in 1917 were located in the lowest and poorest part of the planting area. The tallest trees were usually largest in diameter (table 1).

Roosevelt and San Juan trees were also planted in 1917, but the stock was accidentally mixed together. Growth of these trees was slightly less than that of Coconino trees. Since data for these two sources cannot be separated, none are shown in table 1 or figure 2. The one remaining Payette tree grew only 16.0 feet tall; its measurements are excluded from figure 2.

These data indicate that local Coconino trees and Manti-La Sal trees, the next closest source, grew best at Fort Valley. In contrast, Squillace and Silen (1962) found that trees of southern Rocky Mountain sources, and especially the Coconino source, grew poorly in the northern Idaho and Washington-Oregon tests. They noted, however, that height growth generally decreased with increasing distance of the seed source from the experimental site. A similar trend, with Black Hills source an exception, is suggested in the data reported here.

Sources ranked by height for each planting year remained virtually unchanged between 1928 and 1964 (fig. 2). A test of correlation between 1928 and 1964 average heights of the 1916-17 plantings revealed a correlation coefficient of +0.87, highly significant. Average heights of Coconino trees in 1964 varied little between the 4 planting years. Average heights of other sources varied more, but these averages were usually based on fewer trees. Also, the records indicate that different seed lots were used when a source was planted in more than 1 year, which may have contributed to variation in height between planting years.

Needle characteristics of sources at Fort Valley completely confirm the findings of Weidman (1939) and Squillace and Silen (1962). Trees from the central Rocky Mountains-- Black Hills, Roosevelt, and San Isabel--were typically two-needled rather than three-needled. Also, needles of these sources appeared thicker and averaged 1/2 to 1-1/2 inches shorter than needles of trees from the southern Rocky Mountains.

In 1928, leader growth of San Isabel and Black Hills trees was far in advance of Coconino trees on May 28. Apparently, no other notes of growth periodicity were taken. Squillace and Silen (1962) reported delayed bud bursting of Coconino trees in the Oregon-Washington study, however, and cite data of Daubenmire (1950) which revealed that Coconino trees in the Idaho study started cambial growth 2 weeks later than local sources. Thus, phenological traits seem very reliable indicators of racial differences.

Coconino trees had the straightest stems in 1964 (fig. 3). Other sources appeared somewhat more crooked, and Santa Fe trees were exceptionally gnarled (fig. 4). Except for Santa Fe trees, stem taper appeared to be influenced more by stand density than seed source, although no measurements were taken.

Summary

Ponderosa pines from eastern and southeastern seed sources of the species range survived at Fort Valley, whereas trees of northern and western sources failed. At the Fort Valley nursery, seedlings of northern and western origin appeared larger and healthier than other sources, but were unable to withstand the frost and drought periods of the Southwest.

In general, sources closest to Fort Valley grew best. Coconino and Manti-La Sal trees were largest of the 11 surviving sources. Black Hills sources grew well in some instances.

Trees from the Black Hills and central Rocky Mountains were typically two-needled; trees from the southern Rocky Mountains grew longer needles, usually in fascicles of three.

Figure 3.--Coconino source trees (center rows) survived well and formed straight stems in this part of the study area. The two large older trees in the foreground are outside the study area.

Figure 4.--An example of two Santa Fe trees (foreground) that formed crooked, multiple stems. Not all Santa Fe seed sources would necessarily express this trait.

Coconino source trees formed straighter stems and began leader growth later in the spring than trees from the central Rocky Mountains and Black Hills.

Literature Cited

Daubenmire, R. F.
1950. The comparison of season of cambial growth in different geographical races of Pinus ponderosa. Bot. Gaz. 112: 182-188.

Munger, T. T.
1947. Growth of ten regional races of ponderosa pine in six plantations. U.S. Forest Serv. Pacific Northwest Forest and Range Exp. Sta., Res. Note 39, 4 pp.

Pearson, G. A.
1950. Management of ponderosa pine in the Southwest. U.S. Dep. Agr. Agr. Monog. 6, 218 pp.

Roeser, J. Jr.
1926. The importance of seed source and the possibilities of forest tree breeding. J. Forest. 24: 38-51.

Schreiner, E. J.
1937. Improvement of forest trees. U.S. Dep. Agr. Yearbook 1937: 1242-1279.

Squillace, A. E. and Silen, R. R.
1962. Racial variation in ponderosa pine. Forest Sci. Monog. 2, 27 pp.

Weidman, R. H.
1939. Evidences of racial influence in a 25-year test of ponderosa pine. J. Agr. Res. 59: 855-887.

1966

U.S. FOREST SERVICE
RESEARCH NOTE RM - 74

FOREST SERVICE
U.S. DEPARTMENT OF AGRICULTURE

Differences in Herbage-Timber Relationships Between Thinned and Unthinned Ponderosa Pine Stands

Warren P. Clary and Peter F. Ffolliott[1]

Herbage production under a thinned and an adjacent unthinned ponderosa pine stand was compared. Herbage production under the thinned stands was significantly greater than under the unthinned stands for given timber basal areas of less than 70 square feet per acre.

Many herbage-timber relationships have been described for forested areas. Herbage or forage production has been related to crown cover, basal area, or tree litter (Gaines et al. 1954, Pase 1958, Pearson 1964, Halls and Schuster 1965).[2] Such relationships may provide a basis for estimating the amount of herbage to be produced if the timber stocking is reduced (Ffolliott and Worley 1965, Halls and Schuster 1965).

A study was conducted on the Beaver Creek watershed (Worley 1965) in Arizona to determine whether differences existed between herbage-timber relationships on a thinned area and on an adjacent unthinned area.

Study Area

This study was conducted in the ponderosa pine (Pinus ponderosa Lawson) type. Principal grasses and grasslike plants included blue grama (Bouteloua gracilis (H.B.K.) Lag.), sedge (Carex spp.), spike muhly (Muhlenbergia wrightii Vasey), muttongrass (Poa fendleriana (Steud.) Vasey), bottlebrush squirreltail (Sitanion hystrix (Nutt.) J. G. Smith), and black dropseed (Sporobolus interruptus Vasey). The principal forbs and half-shrubs were western ragweed (Ambrosia psilostachya DC.) showy aster (Aster commutatus (Torr & Gray) A. Gray), and broom snakeweed (Gutierrezia sarothrae (Pursh) Britt. & Rusby).

The soils, derived from volcanics (mostly basalt with some cinders), are classified into the Siesta-Sponseller and the Stoneman soil management areas.[3] The distribution of soils

---

[1] *Associate Range Scientist and Associate Silviculturist, located at Flagstaff, in cooperation with Northern Arizona University; central headquarters are maintained at Fort Collins, in cooperation with Colorado State University.*

[2] *Names and dates in parentheses refer to Literature Cited, p. 4.*

[3] *Anderson, T. C., Jr., Williams, J. A., and Crezee, D. B. Soil management report for Beaver Creek watersheds of Coconino National Forest, Region 3. U.S. Forest Serv., 1960, 66 pp. (Mimeographed report on file at Region 3 Office, U.S. Forest Serv., Albuquerque, N. Mex.)*

is similar across the entire study area. There is no measurable difference in herbage production between the soil management areas under similar timber basal areas (Clary et al. 1966).

An area of approximately 2,000 acres was thinned in 1958. This thinning consisted of a commercial timber sale of all mature sawtimber and dwarfmistletoe-infected immature sawtimber, a commercial timber sale of trees 6 to 12 inches d.b.h., and a precommercial thinning of trees less than 6 inches d.b.h. Gambel oak (Quercus gambelii Nutt) was poisoned and alligator juniper (Juniperus deppeana Steud.) was girdled.

The adjacent area for comparison had not been logged for 20 years.

Methods

Six years after thinning, the study areas were sampled to determine possible differences in herbage-timber relationships.

Ninety plots were located in the thinned area and 334 plots in the unthinned area. Herbage production was determined by weight estimate (Pechanec and Pickford 1937) on a 9.6-square-foot plot, and timber basal area was determined by point sampling with a basal area factor of 10 (Grosenbaugh 1952) at each plot.

Timber basal area of the plots on the thinned area ranged from 20 to 150 square feet per acre. Therefore, to develop herbage-timber relationships of equivalent situations, only plots within the same range of basal areas were used from the unthinned area. Ninety plots were used to calculate the herbage-timber relationship on the thinned area, and 279 plots were used from the unthinned area.

Results and Discussion

Herbage production on the thinned area was significantly higher than on the unthinned area at basal areas of less than 70 square feet per acre (table 1). The difference between the slopes of the two regression lines was highly significant (fig. 1). A standard error of the difference between the two curves was calculated following Meyer (1942) except that $\sqrt{2F}$ was used as the confidence coefficient.

Table 1.--Differences in herbage production on thinned and unthinned areas of ponderosa pine under different tree basal areas

Basal area (Sq. ft. per acre)	Herbage production		Difference	$S \sqrt{2F}$ difference	Significance (d = 0.10)
	Thinned	Unthinned			
	Pounds per acre				
20	566.6	376.8	189.8	117.6	
30	459.9	318.5	141.4	85.1	
40	384.2	277.1	107.1	64.1	*
60	277.5	218.8	58.7	43.2	
70	236.9	196.6	40.3	41.3	NS
80	201.8	177.4	24.4	43.0	NS
100	143.0	145.2	-2.2	52.2	NS
120	95.1	119.0	-23.9	63.3	NS
140	54.5	96.8	-42.3	74.1	NS
150	36.3	86.9	-50.6	79.2	NS

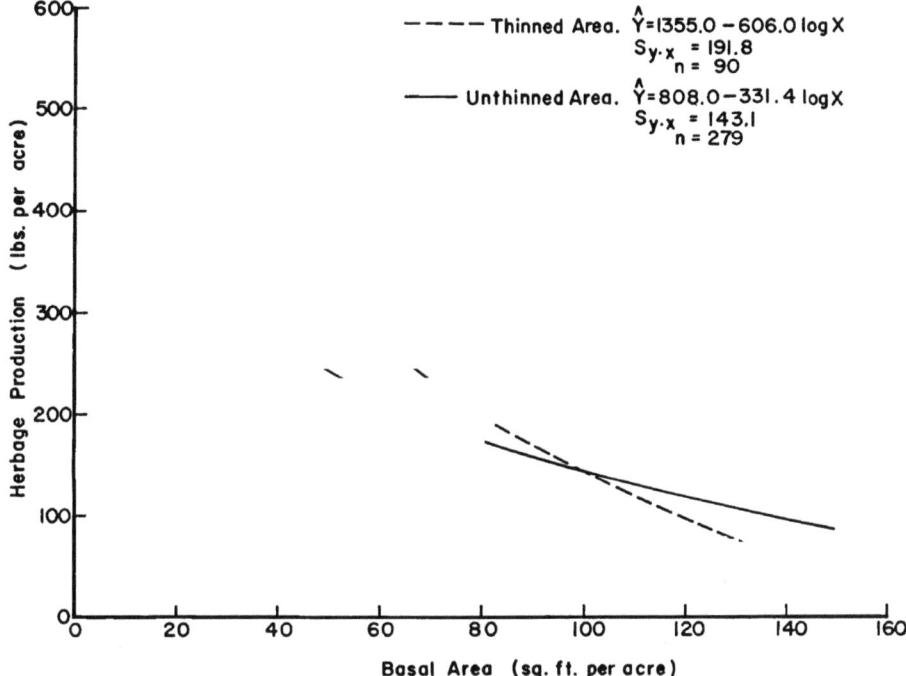

Figure 1.--Relationship between herbage production and timber overstory basal area on thinned and unthinned areas.

The significant differences found indicate that relationships developed on unthinned areas may give low predictions of herbage production on areas thinned to less than 70 square feet basal area.

It is not known whether the difference in the herbage-timber relationships between thinned and unthinned areas is of short duration. If it is a function of stocking arrangement and size class distribution, it may be of a semipermanent nature.

Average production on the thinned area was 257 pounds per acre, while the production on the unthinned area was 157 pounds per acre, a highly significant difference. Herbage composition on the two areas was similar. Timber basal area on the thinned area averaged 72 square feet per acre, while the unthinned area averaged 106.

Conclusions

The thinned area differed from the adjacent unthinned area as follows:

1. The slope of the herbage-timber relationship was significantly steeper.
2. Herbage production for a given basal area was significantly greater for basal areas less than 70 square feet per acre.
3. Average herbage production was significantly higher.

Because relationships from unthinned areas are of questionable value in predicting herbage production to be obtained by thinning, it can be concluded that, when residual timber overstory is reduced, the herbage-timber relationship should be redetermined.

Literature Cited

Clary, Warren P., Ffolliott, Peter F., and Zander, Almer D.
    1966. Grouping sites by soil management areas and topography.* U.S. Forest Serv. Res. Note RM-60, 4 pp., illus. Rocky Mountain Forest and Range Exp. Sta., Ft. Collins, Colo.

Ffolliott, Peter F., and Worley, David P.
    1965. An inventory system for multiple use evaluation.* U.S. Forest Serv. Res. Paper RM-17, 15 pp., illus. Rocky Mountain Forest and Range Exp. Sta., Ft. Collins, Colo.

Gaines, E. M., Campbell, Robert S., and Brasington, J. J.
    1954. Forage production on longleaf pine lands of southern Alabama. Ecology 35: 59-62.

*Address requests for copies to the originating office.

Grosenbaugh, L. R.
    1952. Plotless timber estimates--new, fast, easy. J. Forest. 50: 32-37.

Halls, Lowell K., and Schuster, Joseph L.
    1965. Tree-herbage relations in pine-hardwood forests of Texas. J. Forest. 63: 282-283.

Meyer, H. Arthur.
    1942. Methods of forest growth determinations. Penn. Agr. Exp. Sta. Bull. 435, 93 pp.

Pase, Charles P.
    1958. Herbage production and composition under immature ponderosa pine stands in the Black Hills. J. Range Manage. 11: 238-243, illus.

Pearson, Henry A.
    1964. Studies of forage digestibility under ponderosa pine stands. Soc. Amer. Forest. Proc. 1964: 71-73, illus.

Pechanec, Joseph F., and Pickford, G. D.
    1937. A weight estimate method for determination of range or pasture production. J. Amer. Soc. Agron. 29: 894-904.

Worley, David P.
    1965. The Beaver Creek pilot watershed for evaluating multiple-use effects of watershed treatments.* U.S. Forest Serv. Res. Paper RM-13, 12 pp. Rocky Mountain Forest and Range Exp. Sta., Ft. Collins, Colo.

1966

U.S. FOREST SERVICE
RESEARCH NOTE RM - 75

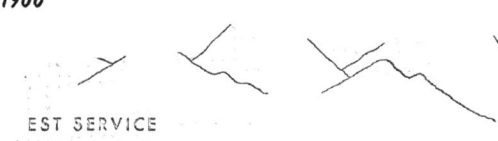

EST SERVICE
S. DEP RTMENT OF AGRICULTURE

Pot Tests of Productivity and Nutritive Status of Three Alpine Soils in Wyoming

W. M. Johnson and Dixie R. Smith[1]

Greenhouse tests showed alpine soils developed on glacial till to be more fertile than those developed on volcanic ash or breccia. Phosphorus was limiting growth on till soils, and nitrogen was the limiting nutrient in ash and breccia soils.

Management of high-altitude sheep ranges in Wyoming might be improved if we had more knowledge of the relative production and nutritive status of the soils. At the present time very little is known about the alpine and subalpine soils of these ranges. In the present study the surface soils from three distinct parent materials were subjected to laboratory analysis and greenhouse tests of productivity. Only the surface 6-8 inches of soil were studied. The results are presented here to help fill the gap in present knowledge.

The Soils

Soil from glacial till was obtained from the Libby Flats area of the Snowy Range west of Laramie, Wyoming, at an elevation of approximately 10,500 feet. The soil was derived from glacial till containing a large amount of quartzite. It was a very strongly acid, sandy clay loam with relatively high organic content (table 1). Such soils support a good cover of native vegetation typical of the Carex-Deschampsia community described by Johnson.[2]

Soil from volcanic ash was obtained from Carter Mountain, in the Absaroka Range west of Meeteetse, Wyoming, at an elevation of approximately 11,000 feet. These ash outcrops are very common throughout the Absaroka Range. Occasional native plants may be found, but in general the soils are devoid of vegetation.

The soil was a loam with some interesting characteristics. For instance, it was almost impossible to extract leachates in the laboratory. In the field, these soils become very boggy when wet from spring snowmelt, but later become very hard when dry.

Soil from volcanic breccia was obtained from the same general area as soil from vol-

---

[1] *Principal Plant Ecologist and Plant Ecologist, respectively, located at Laramie, in cooperation with the University of Wyoming; central headquarters are maintained at Fort Collins, in cooperation with Colorado State University.*

[2] *Johnson, W. M. Vegetation of high altitude ranges in Wyoming as related to use by game and domestic sheep. Univ. of Wyo., Agr. Exp. Sta. Bull. 387, 31 pp. 1962.*

Table 1.--Properties of three high-altitude soils from Wyoming

Item	Unit of measure	Glacial till	Volcanic ash	Volcanic breccia
Mechanical properties				
Sand	percent	58	41	59
Silt	percent	16	36	15
Clay	percent	26	23	26
Texture		Sandy clay loam	Loam	Sandy clay loam
Saturation	percent	56	56	39
Electrical conductance	mmho/cm.	0.8	0.2	0.2
pH (paste)		4.8	6.8	6.6
Organic matter	percent	6.5	0.0	2.9
Chemical analysis (extractable cations)				
Calcium	meq./100 g.	1.8	12.7	9.0
Potassium	meq./100 g.	.6	.9	.4
Sodium	meq./100 g.	.1	.4	.1
Magnesium	meq./100 g.	.3	11.6	7.6
Available phosphorus	p.p.m.	37.7	28.8	24.9
Nitrates[1]	p.p.m. of N	.7	.04	.04

[1] Values questionable because of delay between collection and analysis.

canic ash. The soil texture was very similar to that of the glacial till soil. The saturation percentage was lower, it was less acid, and it had a lower organic content. This soil also supports a good cover of native vegetation typical of the Carex-Deschampsia community.

Methods

Two tests of the productivity of these soils were made, both by the same general procedures. Each soil was thoroughly mixed and sifted through a 1/4-inch-mesh screen. Nine hundred grams of air-dry soil were placed in 6-inch plastic pots. Seeds of the test species were planted in shallow depressions and lightly covered. After germination, each pot was thinned to five vigorous seedlings.

Distilled water was added to keep the soil at or about field capacity. Temperature in the greenhouse was maintained at 70° ± 5° F. Humidity and photoperiod were not controlled. The studies were made from October through May in 1962-63 and 1963-64.

Analysis of variance was used as a statistical tool, and a probability level of 0.05 was accepted as adequate protection for the interpretation of results.

The first greenhouse test compared the productivity of the three "natural soils." It was a randomized complete block design consisting of three replications. Two cultivated plants, oats (Avena sativa L.) and beans (Phaseolus vulgaris L.), and three native plants, Eggleston sedge (Carex egglestonii Mack.), ebony sedge (Carex ebenea Rydb.), and alpine avens (Geum rossii Ser.) were used as test species. It was hoped that one of the fast-growing cultivated species would respond in the same manner as native species so that it could be used in future tests to evaluate the response of native plants.

Numerous criteria were measured to evaluate the response of different species to the three soils. These criteria were: (1) percent germination, (2) average leaf height, (3) ovendry weight of shoots, (4) ovendry weight of roots, (5) total ovendry weight of plants, and (6) shoot-to-root ratios.

The nutrient status of the three soils was compared in the second greenhouse test, with oats as the test species. The experimental design was a randomized complete block with three replications. Treatments were a factorial arrangement of the following series:

Soils (3)
Glacial till
Volcanic breccia
Volcanic ash

Nitrogen (2)
N_0 (Check)
N_1 (80 pounds per acre)

Phosphorus (2)
P_0 (Check)
P_1 (200 pounds per acre)

Potassium (2)
K_0 (Check)
K_1 (200 pounds per acre)

Minor Elements (2)
M_0 (Check)
M_1 (Present)

Nitrogen was added as ammonium nitrate, phosphorus as calcium phosphate, and potassium as potassium chloride.

Minor elements were added at the following rates:

Element	Chemical	Pounds of element per acre
Boron	H_3BO_3	22.4
Manganese	$MnCl_2 \cdot 4H_2O$	24.7
Zinc	$ZnSO_4 \cdot 7H_2O$	2.5
Copper	$CuSO_4 \cdot 5H_2O$	2.8
Molybdenum	$H_2MoO_4 \cdot 4H_2O$	1.8
Magnesium	$MgSO_4$	2.2
Iron	$FeSO_4 \cdot 7H_2O$	0.4
Calcium	$CaSO_4 \cdot 2H_2O$	5.0
Sulfur	(from above)	11.4

The elements required for each pot were dissolved in 100 ml. of distilled water. This solution was then added to the soil and thoroughly mixed.

Shoot and root production were used as measurement criteria.

Results

Productivity Tests

Germination of the various species was not significantly affected by kind of soil (table 2), but there was some indication that germination of oats and alpine avens was lower in the ash soil.

Production varied among the three soils; the nature of this variation depended upon the species. Glacial till, however, produced more oats, Eggleston sedge, and ebony sedge than did breccia and ash, which were equally productive (fig. 1). Means for alpine avens, though not significantly different, followed this same pattern. In every case, beans responded differently from the other species. Oats followed the same pattern of response as the native species, although the magnitude of the response was different.

The shoot/root ratio followed no consistent pattern. Each species reacted differently to the various soils.

Leaf lengths (fig. 1), root weight, and total weight of plants showed the same responses on the three soils as shoot production. In every case beans failed to respond in the same manner as other species. Oats followed the same pattern of response as the native species, although the magnitude of the response was different.

Nutrient Status Tests

In the second greenhouse test, addition of the minor element solution depressed shoot production of oats on all soils. The effect was observed even before harvesting when the tips of the leaves turned brown and died. Evidently, one or more elements (perhaps boron) was added in toxic quantities. The magnitude of reduction in yield varied among the three soils. Micronutrients reduced production, when averaged over all other treatments, by 0.31 grams per pot on glacial till soils, 0.20

Table 2.--Summary of plant response to three mountain soils

Response by soil type	Unit of measure	Oats	Beans	Eggleston sedge	Ebony sedge	Alpine avens
Germination	Percent					
Glacial till		100	90	83	79	40
Volcanic ash		87	90	93	78	27
Volcanic breccia		100	90	97	76	53
Average leaf height	cm.					
Glacial till		30.0	22.5	17.6	18.2	6.3
Volcanic ash		15.7	26.1	4.6	3.4	2.3
Volcanic breccia		20.7	23.5	5.8	9.2	3.3
Ovendry weight, shoots	g./pot					
Glacial till		1.31	2.06	1.77	1.84	0.31
Volcanic ash		.27	2.54	.14	.04	.05
Volcanic breccia		.45	2.02	.55	.12	.08
Ovendry weight, roots	g./pot					
Glacial till		3.37	1.87	3.31	1.98	.23
Volcanic ash		.53	.88	.24	.12	.06
Volcanic breccia		.81	.86	.49	.19	.08
Total weight, plants	g./pot					
Glacial till		4.68	3.93	5.08	3.82	.54
Volcanic ash		.80	3.42	.38	.16	.11
Volcanic breccia		1.26	2.88	1.04	.31	.16
Shoot-to-root ratio						
Glacial till		1: 2.55	1: 0.91	1: 1.87	1: 1.08	1: 0.74
Volcanic ash		1: 1.96	1: 0.35	1: 1.71	1: 3.00	1: 1.20
Volcanic breccia		1: 1.80	1: 0.43	1: 0.89	1: 1.58	1: 1.00
Duration of tests, all soils	Days	68	29	117	118	118
Stage of growth at harvest		Early bloom	Full bloom	Vegetative	Vegetative	Vegetative

grams per pot on ash soils, and 0.10 grams per pot on breccia soils. In this case the soil × micronutrient interaction was significant, and each soil responded differently.

The depressive effect of minor elements was increased by the addition of nitrogen. The toxic interaction of these two treatments was of the same magnitude on all soils. On the average soil, without nitrogen, yield was reduced by 0.9 gram per pot, but with nitrogen yields were reduced 0.33 gram per pot. Reasons for this response are not clear. In this case the soil × micronutrient × nitrogen interaction was not significant, and therefore all soils responded similarly.

The addition of potassium increased shoot production on the glacial till soils by 0.11 gram per pot, but decreased production on soils from volcanic ash by 0.07 gram per pot. Shoot production on soils from volcanic breccia showed a slight but not significant decrease.

The effects of phosphorus, nitrogen, and soils represent a complex interaction (fig. 2). Phosphorus alone increased shoot yield only

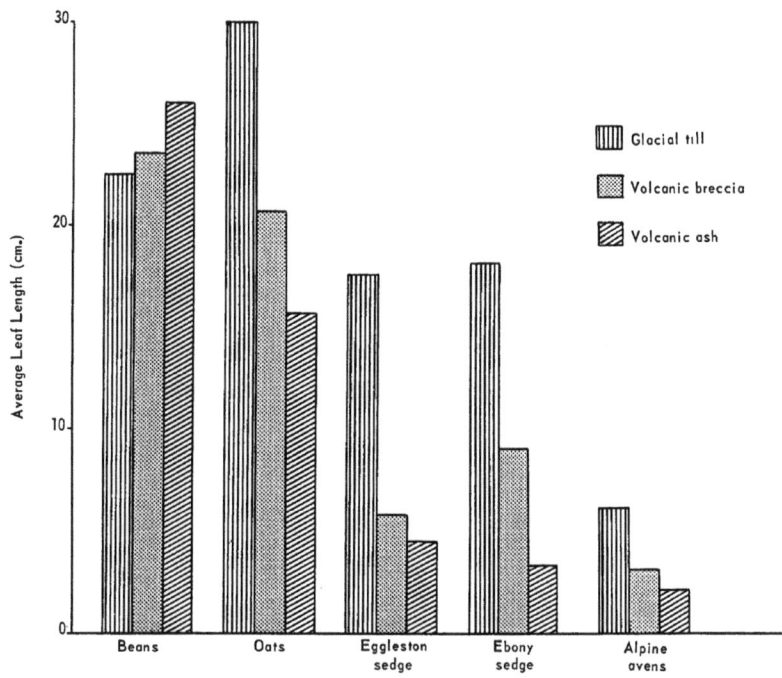

Figure 1.--Average leaf length of test species as related to soil origin.

on soil derived from glacial till. The increase amounted to 0.52 gram per pot.

Nitrogen alone increased shoot growth on all soils. The increase was similar on soils from ash and glacial till -- 0.21 and 0.16 gram per pot, respectively. The response on breccia was much greater -- 0.46 gram per pot.

The effect of nitrogen was complemented by phosphorus on ash and breccia, where phosphorus alone failed to increase yield. The complementary effect of phosphorus amounted to 0.51 and 0.50 gram per pot, respectively.

On soils developed from till, the effects of nitrogen and phosphorus were statistically independent.

Phosphorus increased the weight of roots on soil from glacial till by about 75 percent. The minor elements significantly retarded the development of roots in all soils. No other root responses were statistically significant.

Discussion and Summary

These greenhouse tests suggest that the soils derived from glacial till are naturally

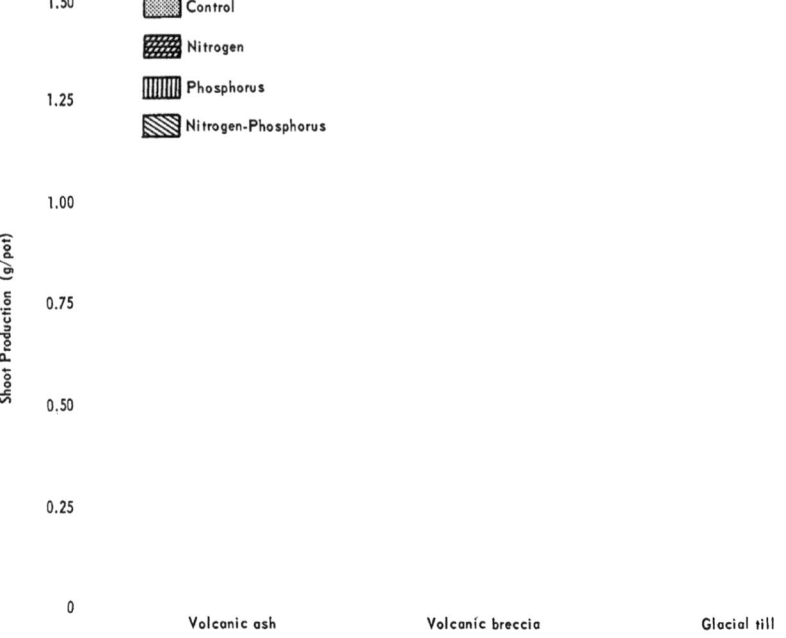

Figure 2.--Effect of nitrogen and phosphorus amendments on shoot production of oats on three soils.

more fertile than soils derived from either breccia or ash. They do support good stands of native vegetation. Phosphorus was the most limiting nutrient in this soil, although potassium and nitrogen fertilization also increased shoot production slightly.

Soils derived from volcanic breccia ranked next to the soils from glacial till in natural fertility. Nitrogen was the most limiting nutrient, but with nitrogen fertilization phosphorus became limiting. Maximum yields were obtained when both nitrogen and phosphorus were added to the soil.

Soils from volcanic ash were primarily deficient in nitrogen, and once nitrogen was supplied phosphorus became limiting. Although these soils did not grow any appreciable amount of vegetation in the field, they did produce vegetation, without fertilization, in the greenhouse where soil moisture was maintained at a favorable level. Other evidence, such as the extreme difficulty in obtaining extracts, the quicksandlike properties in the field when saturated, and the rocklike hardness that develops upon drying, also suggest that the natural sterility of these soils is related primarily to the moisture regime.

Greenhouse trials are not always indicative of field responses, but these studies do indicate that herbage production on soils from till and breccia may be increased through fertilization. Ultimate answers as to the practicality of such fertilization will depend upon field trials and economic evaluation.

Unless the soil moisture characteristics of ash soils are improved, there is little possibility of greater production through fertilization. Therefore, these soils should be accepted as being naturally unproductive and management plans made on this basis.

Lightning Source UK Ltd.
Milton Keynes UK
UKHW012231110219
337137UK00006B/1178/P